Jan-Peter Voß, Nora Rigamonti, Marcela Suárez, Jacob Watson (eds.)
Sensing Collectives

Sociology

Jan-Peter Voß (Prof. Dr.), born 1973, heads the chair of Sociology of Politics and Governance at Technische Universität Berlin. He did his doctorate at the department of science, technology and policy studies of the University of Twente. His research is located at the intersection of sociology, political science, and science and technology studies (STS), focusing on the intertwining of epistemic, political, and aesthetic practices in late modern process of innovation and governance.

Nora Rigamonti is a research associate in the project "Taste! Qualitative-sensoric 'citizen science' on the practice and aesthetics of eating" at the chair of Sociology of Politics and Governance at Berlin University of Technology. In her PhD, she focused on different entanglements of political and aesthetic practices and related in(ter)ventive democratic practices at the interdisciplinary DFG Graduate School "Innovation Society Today", where she was a research associate from 2015 to 2018 and is now an associate member.

Marcela Suárez (Dr.) received her PhD in political science from Freie Universität Berlin (FU) and is an associate researcher and lecturer at the Lateinamerika-Institut at FU. She investigates the socio-political dynamics of governance, asymmetries of knowledge, techno-scientific feminisms and digital culture. Since 2018 she has been part of the research group DiGiTal Transformation where she is working on the project "Feminist politics and the fight against violence in the era of digitalization".

Jacob Watson is a freelance translator and editor for sociology, philosophy, law and history. He co-runs the agency/network "Translabor" for text related tasks.

Jan-Peter Voß, Nora Rigamonti, Marcela Suárez, Jacob Watson (eds.)
Sensing Collectives
Aesthetic and Political Practices Intertwined

[transcript]

We acknowledge support by the Open Access Publication Fund of Technische Universität Berlin.

Bibliographic information published by the Deutsche Nationalbibliothek
The Deutsche Nationalbibliothek lists this publication in the Deutsche Nationalbibliografie; detailed bibliographic data are available in the Internet at http://dnb.d-nb.de

This work is licensed under the Creative Commons Attribution 4.0 (BY) license, which means that the text may be remixed, transformed and built upon and be copied and redistributed in any medium or format even commercially, provided credit is given to the author.
Creative Commons license terms for re-use do not apply to any content (such as graphs, figures, photos, excerpts, etc.) not original to the Open Access publication and further permission may be required from the rights holder. The obligation to research and clear permission lies solely with the party re-using the material.

First published in 2023 by transcript Verlag, Bielefeld
© Jan-Peter Voß, Nora Rigamonti, Marcela Suárez, Jacob Watson (eds.)

Cover layout: Kordula Röckenhaus, Bielefeld
Translation, proofreading, copy editing & typesetting: Jacob Watson, Berlin
Printed by: Majuskel Medienproduktion GmbH, Wetzlar
https://doi.org/10.14361/9783839457450
Print-ISBN 978-3-8376-5745-6
PDF-ISBN 978-3-8394-5745-0
ISSN of series: 2703-1691
eISSN of series: 2747-3007

Printed on permanent acid-free text paper.

Contents

Preface
Jan-Peter Voß, Nora Rigamonti, Marcela Suárez, Jacob Watson 7

Sensing Collectives, an Introduction
Jan-Peter Voß, Nora Rigamonti, Marcela Suarez, Jacob Watson 11

Aesthetic governance – and reflexive engagements with it

Re-designing the Sensory Order
Forms, Practices, and Perception
Sophia Prinz 51

Escape, Erase, Entangle
Three Aesthetic Regimes Re-composing the Californian Ideology
Jonathan Luke Austin, Anna Leander 73

Sensory Governance
Managing the Public Sense of Light and Water
Nona Schulte-Römer 95

Packaging Pleasures
Design, Play, and Consumer Change
Susan C. Stewart 123

Hegemonic Sensory Practices of the Smart City
And a Collective Remaking of Data-based Urban Commons
Miguel Paredes Maldonado 145

We Thought It Was Fog, We Thought It Was Just Some Weather
Sensing, Datafication, and Governance of Urban Air Pollution
Hanna Husberg, Agata Marzecová 165

Aesthetic innovation – and collective re-ordering

How to Better Sense What is Happening?
A Political Lesson from Taste and Tasting
Antoine Hennion 185

Provoking Taste
Experimenting with New Ways of Sensing
Jan-Peter Voß, Michael Guggenheim, Nora Rigamonti, Aline Haulsen, Max Söding 199

The Beauty of Feeling
On the Affective Politics of Sensing Collectives
Friederike Landau-Donnelly 219

"Wir sind das Volk!"
How the PEGIDA-demonstrations aesthetically practice
an exclusive collective identity
Sebastian Sommer 239

Digital Violence as Affective Disciplining after Feminist Protests
The Case of #NotLikeThatLadies
Marcela Suárez and Mirjana Mitrović 255

Performing Disruptions
A Bodily Encounter with Misogyny in Lifestyle Television
Rose Beermann 277

Sensing Collectives as Sensing Selves
Two Artistic Interventions and Two Theories of the Self
Jacob Watson, Vanessa Farfán, Markus Binner 291

Authors in Order of Chapters 309

Preface

Jan-Peter Voß, Nora Rigamonti, Marcela Suárez, Jacob Watson

The journey to this book started when we, now the four editors of this volume, met in conferences and seminars driven by our interest in "artivism." Artistic activism appeared to be a practice of engaging with collective orders in a mode of creativity, sensation, and affect—rather than rational argumentation and interest bargaining. What interested us was how, in artivism, art, and politics come together and what effects this generates.

Starting to read our way into and around the subject, and discussing possible ways to conceptualize and study artivism as a combined practice of art and politics, we soon recognized that we would have to frame the topic more broadly. In particular, we quickly found aesthetic modes of engaging with collective orders also in protest and alternative lifestyle initiatives featuring sensory and affective strategies. There are, for example, the songs of political protest, special choreographies of street protest, the design of posters, agitative speeches… Furthermore, we found that sensory and affective modes are not limited to attempts at disrupting and renewing collective orders—but are also widespread in strategies to build, stabilize, protect, and expand already dominant orders. Here we come across governmental public relations, party campaigns and sensorily oriented strategies of steering human behavior. Also, private corporations work with the senses and affects to generate acceptance and support for products, technologies, brands, policies, and broader visions of collective life and progress.

We found that aesthetic practices are obviously as much a means of stabilization, control, and governance as they are of disruption, emancipation, and innovation. At this point, artivism seemed to reflect a broader issue: a hitherto not much studied aesthetic dimension of governance and innovation. Thus, we became interested in all the different ways collective ways of living are shaped in the dimension of sensory experience and affect—and with how this relates to politics, that is with how we usually think of the shaping of collective orders: through the articulation of interests, collective strategies, norms, and rules.

This is what led us to publish a call for such studies and organize a workshop to bring them together. Wary of the limits of translating sensory experience into words, we invited not only academic contributions but also artistic performances and activist demonstrations to offer cases for reflections and discussion. We held the workshop "Sensing Collectives—Aesthetic and Political Practices Intertwined" on 14–16 November 2018 at Institute for Cultural Inquiry (ICI) and Hybrid Lab of the Berlin Universities of the Arts and of Technology. We asked all contributors to extract from their cases how aesthetics is practiced: How is it that patterns of sensory attention, experience, affect, and appreciation are engaged with and become shaped? Symmetrically, we asked them to extract how politics is practiced: How is it that patterns of collective subjectivity, identity, will, interest, and agency are engaged with and become shaped?

The workshop began with public keynotes and a reception at the ICI. Sophia Prinz (Zurich University of the Arts, ZHdK) and Antoine Hennion (Centre for the Sociology of Innovation, Paris) opened the discussion with two complementary perspectives, one focusing on hegemonic political and sensory orders and the potential of art to bring them into motion, the other focusing on the continuous emergence of new ways of tasting by letting objects and subjectivities co-emerge in experimental practices. Their two lectures, brought into view two complementary orientations in current studies of aesthetics and politics. One starts from examining the sensory dimensions of dominant orders ("aesthetic governance"), the other starts from attempts to work with the senses for opening up and renewing collective orders ("aesthetic innovation"). For this book we have arranged revised versions of workshop contributions accordingly.

The cases range from governmental public relations to insurgent artistic interventions, from feminism to the design of infrastructures, from moving and eating to listening and seeing, from corporeal fervor to digital data, from Dresden to Beijing and the Silicon Valley, from undermining and disrupting collective orders to building and stabilizing them. The chapters are authored by scholars of various branches of social research and by activists working artistically. Some chapters are more analytical, others more poetic or agitating. What they all do is to show how the making and unmaking of sensory experiences and affects is deeply intertwined with the making and unmaking of collective subjectivity, will, and agency. Together with the conceptual framework outlined in the introduction, these case studies can start us off at differentiating specific patterns in which political and aesthetic practices intertwine in constituting sensing collectives.

The workshop and publication were made possible with support from the research training group Innovation Society Today and the Chair of Sociology of Politics and Governance at the Department of Sociology at the Berlin University of Technology (TU) and from the Institute for Latin American Studies at Free University of Berlin. The open access publication is supported by the TU Berlin publication fund. We thank Jacob Horstmann and Annika Linnemann at transcript Verlag for their support on the side of the publishing company. Most importantly, however, we wish to thank all the contributors for their openness and engagement in embarking on this long process of collective inquiry and bringing it to publication in the form of this book.

Berlin, February 2022
Jan-Peter Voß, Nora Rigamonti, Marcela Suarez, Jacob Watson

Sensing Collectives, an Introduction

Jan-Peter Voß, Nora Rigamonti, Marcela Suarez, Jacob Watson

1. ENTANGLEMENTS OF AESTHETICS AND POLITICS

It may seem obvious today that aesthetics and politics touch or even intermingle, but to look for how they intertwine is no easy task. Trace them carefully and entanglements abound: They are relevant both for building, upholding, policing, and stabilizing orders of collective life, that is for governance, as well as for undermining, disrupting, renewing, and transforming established orders, that is innovation. To really get a feel for how this is weaved together, let us go through a few examples.

Artistic activism is a clear case for the latter. Aesthetic practices of modulating sensations and affects here call into question established norms and knowledges. Artivism mobilizes collective subjects who identify with an artistically expressed discontent with dominant political orders and discourses (Groys, 2014; Weibel, 2015; Nossel, 2016; see also chapters in this volume by Prinz, Paredes, Husberg & Marcecova, Beermann, Watson). In Germany, the Center for Political Beauty has gained some ambiguous fame in recent years for their radical interventions into the public discourse on the refugee crisis, which included throwing refugees to the tigers and digging graves in front of the German parliament (Stange et al., 2018; Rigamonti, 2022 see also chapter by Landau-Donnelly in this volume). But also, less spectacular and more classical forms of political protest, like public assemblies, rallies, sit-ins, camps, festivals, songs, and performances clearly work with sensation and affect to express and mobilize subjectivities that are felt not to be adequately represented in institutionalized politics (Stoehrel, 2017; see also chapters in this volume by Sommer and Suarez & Mitrovic). The Occupy Movement can be considered an example of performing experiences of precarity through vulnerably and living in solidarity in camps on urban plazas (Butler, 2015; Bassett, 2014). The white supremacist movement in the USA, too, is well versed in aesthetics and politics, as shown in a coordinated gathering of Tiki-torch-bearing, "acceptable, well-dressed college students" as a recruitment tactic in the lead up to the deadly "Unite the Right" rally in Charleston, USA (Davey & Ebner, 2017). In different modalities of sensing, the slow food movement combines aesthetics and politics by mobilizing a social movement via collective tasting experiences and "visceral identification" with more attentive ways of eating (Hayes-Conroy & Martin, 2010; Bentia, 2014; see also chapter by Voß et al. in this volume).

These cases may count as examples of aesthetics and politics becoming entangled in processes of innovating collective orders, but there are also cases where they combine in the governing of collective orders. Take, for a start, when in 2015 then US president Barack Obama sang "Amazing Grace," a song written by a rueful slave trader, and was openly moved to tears at a public obsequy for victims of a massacre at a Black church, thus performing a caring and responsible state in connection with racism (Mondada et al., 2016; Kloppers, 2020). There are many more examples of aesthetics involved in governmental strategies if we look at the campaigning of political parties, the staging of summits, conventions, negotiations, and at governmental public relations (Edelman, 1988; Marcus et al., 2000; Hitzler, 2002; Hajer, 2010; Aronczyk et al., 2017). Even in the everyday work of legislative debate and decision-making there is a sensory and affective dimension (Manow, 2010; Dányi, 2015), and in the practice of partaking in elections (Nicholson, 2015). A more mundane attempt at governing with the senses is the display of grotesque images of disease and death on tobacco packages as a strategy to push non-smoking norms (Argo & Main, 2004; Keane, 2014; Burton et al., 2021). Finally, states are not the only ones engaging in aesthetic governance. Individual businesses and whole industries use multi-sensorial design and marketing strategies to shape appreciation for their projects, create attachment and desire for their products, and grow brand communities of people who affectively identify with their commercial strategies (Hennion et al., 1989; Spence & Gallace, 2011; Lindstrom, 2005; see also chapters in this volume by Austin & Leander, Schulte-Römer, Stewart, Voß et al.).

These examples give a taste of what we are after when stating that aesthetics and politics are in fact entangled in many instances where collective orders of life get engaged with in an effort to shape or shift them. We claim that we may indeed look at any process of what is nowadays studied under the broad rubrics of governance or innovation and we will find that this process entails both a dimension of actively engaging with ways of sensing and feeling as well as articulations of collective will and interest. And that both are very closely intertwined. With this book, we take up the challenge of analyzing this apparently very widespread and influential means of shaping collective orders.

The entanglement of aesthetics and politics comes as no surprise when we consider that both reflexively engage with ways of living together, constituted as they are in ways of sensing and feeling and in ways of commonly identifying with values and interests that mobilize collective agency and legitimize norms. If collective orders always comprise an amalgam of sensory and political orders, however, then obviously attempts at shaping such orders also must engage with established ways of sensing and collective identity.

What we set out to investigate is how—specifically—aesthetics and politics intertwine in the shaping of collective orders. First, this entails some conceptual consideration of what aesthetics and politics are in practice, how concretely they are done, and how they work. It requires us to sharpen our analytical tools for dissecting the aesthetic and political dimensions of innovation and governance processes. Second, it demands a closer look at a diverse range of empirical cases for reconstructing the patterns in which aesthetic and political practices intertwine and how they jointly constitute and transform collective ways of living.

A considerable part of this introductory chapter thus is devoted to laying out and honing our analytical tools against a review of relevant debates on the relation between aesthetics and politics. The other part gives an overview of the broad set of empirical cases handled in the subsequent chapters for how they describe the intertwining of aesthetics and politics—according to our overall conception.

Turning to the challenge of devising an analytical framework, we need a conception of aesthetics and politics that allows us to follow each thread through rather complex and contingent entanglements in practice, also beyond their traditional conception as institutionalized forms of the professional art world and policy-making by the state. But a close up view also brings the two to the brink of collapsing into one another, as we shall see. So, at the same time, we must keep the two apart in order to recognize each empirically.

A look into the vast literature on relations of aesthetics and politics suggests that the conceptual tools for such a balancing act are not readily at hand. Essentially, there are two extremes: On the one hand, there is the modernist conception of aesthetics and politics as two functionally differentiated systems with two autonomous and mutually incompatible logics of operation (e.g., Bourdieu, 1996 [1992]; Bourdieu, 2001; Luhmann, 1996, 2000; or, more tentatively, for art also Becker, 1982; and for politics Easton, 1979 [1967]). On the other, a post-modernist conception completely abandons the distinction between aesthetics and politics as a mere discursive construction, while indeed all doing is conceptualized as equally aesthetic and political (e.g., Foucault, 2020 [1984]; Lyotard, 1994 [1979]; or, more explicitly, Rancière, 2015). If we want to know more specifically how aesthetics and politics are done practically and how they intertwine, however, these two extreme positions cannot do the job.

Yet, beyond the two extremes which strike the eye when first entering the field, there are also some other, more recent attempts at conceptualizing aesthetics and politics—not as two distinct social systems or spheres, but as specific types of practices (for a general overview of practice-oriented study approaches see Theodore R. Schatzki et al., 2001; Reckwitz, 2002; Shove et al., 2012; Nicolini, 2012). Rather than starting from abstract principles and functions, these studies trace the activities that *do* certain things, that produce specific effects. For aesthetics, the relevant effects are sensorial experiences and affects. Aesthetic practices then are the concrete doings that produce these (Hennion, 2004; Schwarz, 2013; Reckwitz, 2016). For politics, the relevant effects are collective subjectivities and the mobilization of collective agency and the legitimation of norms by way of referring to we-identities, collective will, values, and interests (Latour, 2003; Saward, 2006; Disch, 2011). Pursuing such a *practice turn* in studying aesthetics and politics allows us to empirically trace various patterns of entanglement and study how they are jointly involved in shaping collective orders or, more pointedly, how they together fabricate *sensing collectives*.

The remainder of this introductory chapter reviews established ways of studying aesthetics and politics and the gap they leave (Section 2), it traces more recent developments and what they offer us (Section 3), and then it moves on to sketch a praxeological analytics of aesthetics and politics (Section 4). This provides us with a conceptual framework for presenting an overview of the following chapters and for situating the different cases and their findings within the overall project (Section 5). We conclude with an analytical reflection on the specific forms of aesthetic and political practices that can be found across the chapters and on how they intertwine in stabilizing and renewing collective orders (Section 6).

2. PURIFIED SYSTEMS OR ALL DISTINCTIONS COLLAPSED?

For a long time, the relation between aesthetics and politics had been framed as an interaction, often interference, between two distinct, if not opposing, values, logics, spheres, or systems (Rebentisch, 2012; Hoggett & Thompson, 2012; Reckwitz, 2015). Aesthetic philosophy and theories of art had emphasized that creative expression should not be constrained by rules and must not be suffocated by moral, ethical or normative concerns, or commitments to certain programs of social change. It must stay aloof of struggles for the power to rule. In order to stay alive, aesthetics must celebrate the free play with sensation and affect, irrespective of political considerations. Likewise for politics, the main tenets of occidental philosophy and modern culture had been that it should remain above sensitivities and feelings. It ought to pursue sober analysis, rational argumentation and deal primarily with serious controversy for the collective good. Power was a matter of public responsibility, not capricious play. Politics required an intrepid, objective, calculating, regulative approach to the world, rather than a sensitive, subjective, empathetic, affective approach.

This idea of differentiating, demarcating, functionally purifying, and distinctly rationalizing aesthetics and politics had led to analytical frameworks which indeed took their separation for granted. Guided by normative considerations based on constructions of unique functions fulfilled by each separately for society as a whole, both aesthetics and politics were then observed, analyzed, and evaluated as independent spheres, and became institutionally shaped thusly: Politics was the public questioning and shaping of collective orders through discursive means and a struggle for power within the institutions of the nation state (Easton, 1979 [1967]; Bourdieu, 2001; Luhmann, 2000). Aesthetics, on the other hand, was either a private affair, as *"de gustibus non est disputandum,"* or, in its public role as "the arts," a form of amusing stimulation and well-contained play with conventions (Becker, 1982; Bourdieu, 1996 [1992]; Luhmann, 1996).

Distinct concepts of purpose and corresponding functional theories had given politicians and artists alike a shared professional orientation. Each could maintain their own legitimation for requiring autonomy and immunizing against interference by non-professionals. Each could argue a rationale in support of their demands for broader public authority, recognition, and institutional and monetary support. This modern functionalist perspective viewed the intermingling of aesthetics and politics with skepticism. Either aesthetic freedom ran the risk of being strangled by instrumental reason and order-bent politics (Adorno, 1973; Debord, 1995 [1967]) or the serious business of politics was under threat from reckless and irresponsible stoking of sensations (Lerner & Lasswell, 1951; Habermas, 1981).

These were the rules of the long-running game that art and politics played by, at least on the surface. Beneath that though, official accounts and declarations art, of course, could never stay detached from interests and power, often taking issue with and engaged in the struggle over rules and orders. And politics, of course, could never stay detached from sensations and affect, and often consciously worked with feelings. The line of separation was less clear-cut than often claimed (Rieff, 1953; Eagleton, 1990; Rockhill, 2014). It was eventually squinted away depending on the angle of observation, once institutionalized modern ideals of autonomous art and democratic politics were given a hard look, or the actual practices of doing aesthetics and politics taken into view.

Consequently, in the 1970s a counter-reaction to this modernist separation arose. The new social movements and their intellectuals sought to erase categorical differences for their discretionary constructed-ness and for the power and control they exerted (Foucault, 1972; Deleuze & Guattari, 1988 [1980]; Lyotard, 1994 [1979]; Ryan, 1989; Harvey, 1989). In the course of broader philosophical debates and re-oriented empirical studies and practical orientations, the dominant position of essentializing categorical distinctions and functional differentiation began to erode (P. M. Rosenau, 1991). Gradually, it became acknowledged that art had always been constitutively linked to collective orders and the struggle for power to shape them (Lewis, 2013 [1990]; Groys, 2008; Sartwell, 2011). New concepts of engaged art emphasized participatory experiments, social sculpturing, aesthetic happenings as part of the ongoing collective ordering (Beuys, 2007 [1986]; Roberts, 1990; Plant, 2002; Heinich, 2014). Likewise, it became acknowledged that politics had always worked with sensations and affects, and that it must do so in order to be effective (Ankersmit, 1996; Nussbaum, 2013; Ahmed, 2013). Newer concepts of politics downright included the sensory and affective dimensions (Lefebvre, 1991 [1974]; Marcuse, 1979; De Certeau, 1980; Laclau & Mouffe, 2001 [1985]; Thrift & Amin, 2013).

A pronounced version of this reaction to the modern separation of aesthetics and politics is articulated by Jacques Rancière. His conception collapses aesthetics and politics into one integrated concern with the expression and perception of subjectivities (Rancière et al., 2001; Rancière, 2010). The relevant tension, for him, is between politics and the political—and both are defined in aesthetic terms. While politics is administrative, objectifying, regulatory, and repressionist, the political is creative, subjectifying, enabling, and expressionist. Politics establishes the "police order" and an "illusory democracy." The political, however, is liberating and truly democratic. Both politics and the political have their own ways of sensing, their own aesthetics. Politics administers a specific "distribution of the senses," an order that defines the sensory as that which is perceptible—i.e. that which is permissible to be seen and expressed in a society, and who is entitled to do so. The political in contrast is to bring subjectivities freely into expression, to make formerly imperceptible and excluded social actors sensed and felt in the common space of social life, and thereby break through and open up the dominating sensory order, and trigger a re-distribution of the senses. In this perspective, there is no politics nor anything political that is not sensory and aesthetical, too, as it is all about different styles of expression and perception. Political order and change are simply identical with sensory order and change. The political is aesthetic and the aesthetic is political. All is one, but in different temperatures and aggregate states, one could say.

Such post-modern reactions against the modern presumptions of progressive functional differentiation are influential in political theory, especially radical democracy (Little, 2019), and in aesthetic theory and in the history of art (Hinderliter et al., 2009). For our purpose, however, they seem to throw the baby out with the bathwater. Seeking to overcome the rigid foundational conception of aesthetics and politics as two opposing logics and their institutional containment in modern institutions of autonomous art and the liberal-democratic state, they give up on any conceptual differentiation altogether and forfeit any analytical purchase on studying varying patterns of intertwinement. Completely deconstructing aesthetics and politics as analytical categories means that both vanish as anything that can be studied for where and how it occurs and with what specific effects. Even if we endorse that foundationalist modern functionalism inadequately defines aesthetics and politics, we still require some conception of what they are in order to study them.

We have hinted at our approach of conceptualizing them generically as two different types of practices by starting from their effects, from what they do, and then empirically trace back to how this is done: How are specific aesthetic and political effects fabricated? For aesthetics we take sensory experiences and affects as the relevant effects, for politics collective subjectivity as a lever for mobilizing collective agency and legitimizing norms. We will elaborate this a bit further into a conceptual frame, which we then use to discuss the contributions to this volume for what they show in terms of patterns in which aesthetic and political practices intertwine in governance and innovation. Before we do that, however, we briefly review three more recent strands of research that can give us some inspiration and conceptual background for articulating such analytics of intertwining aesthetic and political practices.

3. EMERGING ALTERNATIVES

Over the last decades, three strands of research have emerged that we can draw on. The first are developments in the social studies of the senses that offer a broader conception of aesthetic practices embedded in everyday life, not limited to the arts. The second are shifts towards social studies of governance that include culture, materiality, and bodies for conceiving the shaping of collective orders beyond words and rules. And the third strand emerges from an original interest in laboratory work in science and technology studies (STS) which was then extended to other forms of experimental practices.

3.1 Sensory studies

For developing a praxeological understanding of aesthetics, we can draw on the emerging field of the social studies of the senses (Howes, 2005; Bull et al., 2006; Vannini et al., 2012; Göbel & Prinz, 2015). Initially opened-up by conceptual and methodological work in anthropology (Stoller, 1989; Howes, 1991; Classen, 1997; Pink, 2009) and a broader re-entry of materiality, the body, practices, and affects in social research (Merleau-Ponty, 2013 [1945]; Synnott, 1993), the field re-discovered early precursors of a sociology the senses (James, 1983 [1890]; Dewey, 1896; Simmel, 1992 [1908/1907]).

It focuses on how the ways in which human bodies sense are recursively related to the ways in which people socially organize through shared signs, symbols and meanings, values, norms and rules, technology and infrastructure. This includes, for one, how the ways we live together actually shape the ways in which we sense ourselves and the world. But also vice versa, how sensing shapes the ways we socially relate and bond, and how we interpret and discursively reflect and regulate social life.

An example is that the predominance of seeing over other modes of sensing (like hearing, touching, smelling, tasting) and of particular ways of control-oriented seeing appear to have been shaped in the course of the development of modern cultures (McLuhan & Fiore, 1967; Prinz, 2014). Seeing appears to have co-evolved with a specifically modern outlook on the world, a basic interest in and orientation towards objective knowing, functional analysis and instrumental control, and a specifically modern subjectivity of the thinking individual that exists autonomously and detached from its surroundings, especially from material objects and nature. Vice versa, this particular way of seeing which objectifies, plans out, and measures the world appears to be constitutive and shape-giving to modern forms of life, identities, epistemologies, institutions, and other forms of social order (Cosgrove, 2003).

A key notion here is the "sensory order" (Vannini et al., 2012, pp. 126–147; Howes & Classen, 2014, pp. 65–92; Reckwitz, 2016). The term depicts specific patterns of social life in which knowledge, values, and rules intertwine with particular ways of sensing. It is used to point out the conditioning and structuring effects of such socially ordered ways of sensing. They are analyzed for constituting specific forms of power that work through the configuring of sensory experiences, perceptions, and affects. As such they can also be exposed to incorporate the senses into systems of dominance and hegemony. Such analyses link up with earlier structural accounts of taste, as exemplified by Bourdieu's concept of habitus (Bourdieu, 1987), but they move beyond the symbolic dimensions of cultural consumption and turn to the training of corporeal capacities for actually sensing and being affected in certain ways (Hennion, 2004).

Also, more micro-oriented approaches are developed within this broader sensory turn in social research. They focus not so much on broader patterns and their structuring effects, but rather on the situational contingency and the dynamics of social sensing, and on the agency and reflexive capacities of humans to depart from, play with, subvert, and disrupt culturally dominant patterns of sensing, and on our creative capacities to re-invent and shape our own ways of sensing. Such reflexive engagements with sensory orders and with one's own habitualized ways of sensing are studied as aesthetic practices or techniques that actively seek to provoke and modulate sensorial perceptions and affects (Becker, 1953; Gomart & Hennion, 1999; Hennion, 2004; Schwarz, 2013; Reckwitz, 2015, 2016).

Recent sociology and anthropology of the senses thus offer a much more mundane and distributed account of aesthetics—not a logic, sphere, or system, but rather an integral dimension of social life. Against the background of sensing being something practiced in culturally specific ways, both formed in social relations and shaping them, the aesthetic here appears as any kind of reflexive engagement with culturally established ways of sensing, either evoking and actualizing them or modulating and changing them. This is done professionally in art, design, advertisement, etc. but is also practiced more widely throughout society, as well as in everyday private settings, and as part of other professionalized activities, for example, political campaigning and science communication. This offers us a generic conception of aesthetics specific enough to identify particular doings as aesthetic practices and yet open enough to let us empirically reconstruct how concretely they are configured.

3.2 Cultural governance

A, for our purposes, complementary development to the social studies of the senses has also unfolded with regard to conceptions of politics, power, and governance over the last decades. For a long time, social order and control was primarily understood in terms of norms and rules. Governance was analyzed as the making and implementation of rules through the institutions of the state, most importantly law-making undergirded by a territorially bounded monopoly on violence. Most of classical modern social science thus defined politics, in one way or another, as the processes of capturing and deploying the ordering power of the state (e.g., Weber, 1992 [1919]; Easton, 1979 [1967]; Neuman, 2005; and, critically, Nash, 2010).

This has changed dramatically over the last decades. Across the social sciences, conceptions of governance have been widened beyond a focus on rules and the state's monopoly on violence. A first extension included informally negotiated norms and rules outside the state (J. N. Rosenau & Czempiel, 1992; Kooiman, 1993; Rhodes, 1996; Mayntz, 1998; Pierre & Peters, 2000). This is a key topic of neo-institutional political science and economics. In most parts of political science, it led to analyzing politics and governance with a view to actors, processes, and modes of rule-making and compliance well past the democratic and the bureaucratic institutions of the state.

A second and deeper extension of the notion of governance can be understood as the result of a broader "cultural turn" in the social sciences (Mitchell, 1991; Steinmetz, 1999; Nash, 2001; Bevir & Rhodes, 2010). In the course of this turn, and its several components, like the linguistic, the practice, the material turns (Bachmann-Medick, 2016), several layers and dimensions of formerly naturalized orders came to be appreciated as social products, conventions, and habits. Language, social knowledge, gendered bodies, scientific facts, technology, and infrastructure were first de-constructed as necessary results of a functional process of natural evolution, and then re-constructed for their always power-laden and power-wielding social histories. Accordingly, they are now analyzed for how they contribute to establishing and stabilizing collective orders, or how subverting or disrupting them entails consequences for other dimensions of social life as well, and may imply an unravelling of the social fabric.

Foucault's studies of orders of language and discourse and how they constitute rationalities and subjectivities marked a starting signal for interrogating various other dimensions of culture for their ordering effects and for how they are shaped, how they have been shaped historically and are imbued with power relations, and how they are continuously reproduced, or could also be resisted and done otherwise (Foucault, 1972, 1980; Burchell et al., 1991). Butler's work is most prominent for interrogating gender orders and the cultural constitution of the body in this regard (Butler, 1990). Latour is the most famous name for interrogating what is regarded as objective reality, scientific facts, and technological functionalities with a view to their practical making and reproduction (Latour, 1987).

With regard to our interest in relations of aesthetics and politics, the sensory studies come in here by also making sensory orders analytically accessible as a dimension of governance (Vannini et al., 2012, pp. 126–147; Howes & Classen, 2014, pp. 65–92), as part of a broadened and deepened understanding of collective orders and how they are shaped. Turning attention to these various modes of cultural ordering of collective life, and the power inscribed in and exerted by them, it becomes clear that their active shaping, and their public problematization and controversial negotiation, is in fact an extended realm of material-cultural politics. These politics are focused not on rule-making by the state but on the configuration of collective life in dimensions of language, presumed ontologies, morals, science, technology, architecture, gendered bodies, lifestyles—and ways of sensing. Against this background, sensing and affects start to draw attention as a dimension of collective ordering (Reckwitz, 2012, 2017) and open a view on "sensory governance" (Schulte-Römer et al., 2017), "aesthetic governance" (Voß & Guggenheim, 2019), "governing affects" (Penz & Sauer, 2019) and "affective politics" (Bargetz, 2015).

3.3 Practices of world-making

Alongside emerging social studies of the senses and culturally extended conceptions of governance, we find inspiration in the field of science and technology studies (STS). STS originally started with a similar move for science as the one we pursue here for aesthetics and politics: turning from functionally rationalized norms and institutions to practices (Pickering, 1992). This move yielded methodological and conceptual inventions that are useful for studying aesthetic and political practices as well.

Initially, STS simply focused on what was actually done in laboratories and scholarly communities for articulating and establishing facts and developing technologies (Latour & Woolgar, 1979; Knorr Cetina, 1981; Shapin, 1984; Lynch, 1985; Bijker, 1987). They side-stepped existing normative philosophies and idealistic methodologies that portrayed science as selecting its theories and hypotheses by neutrally testing them against objective, universal, eternal, passive nature; and the same with theories of technology development as evolutionary progress towards some objective functional optimum. Studying the practices of science, STS scholars reconstructed technoscience as a specific mode of shaping collective orders that works via the laboratory, where new, theoretically ordered realities are experimentally constructed in "secluded research," within the confines of an artificially simplified microcosm and among a select group of trained experts (Hacking, 1992;

Callon et al., 2009). Scientific claims gain authority by being publicly presented as discoveries of independently and universally given objective orders, as *representations of nature* rather than specific manmade constructions of reality. These claims are then more readily accepted as facts and undergird projects to use constructed effects technologically by replicating laboratory-realities elsewhere. Science is therefore performative in the sense that it contributes to creating the realities it represents (Latour, 1987; Pickering, 1994; Callon, 2007, 2010). Scientific accounts become true, also beyond the laboratory, when they are taken up for the definition of social problems and action strategies, and when they provide blueprints for technologically reconfiguring the world. So, more and more actors may become enrolled for replicating and expanding the artificial reality of the laboratory (Latour, 1983). Rather vague and speculative initial conceptions of order thus are gradually materialized, built up and expanded into a kind of ordered reality. The STS turn to practices has thus shown that instead of selecting theories against nature, the sciences experimentally work towards ordering nature and thereby realizing theories.

From within STS, the approach of reconstructing functionally rationalized and purified accounts of science by looking into practices has over the last decades been extended to other key institutions of modern societies, like politics and art. Political practices, for example, have been reconstructed as performatively representing collective subjects and their interests in processes of "group-making" (Latour, 2003; 2013, pp. 134–136 and 327–356; Disch, 2008, 2010, 2011). Rather than neutrally mirroring a given reality of collective subjectivities and interests, "representative claims" are studied for how they creatively invoke and shape the groups, constituencies, and broader polities that they claim to represent (Saward, 2006). This view has inspired a new constructivist theory of political representation (Disch et al., 2019).

In the same vein, artistic practices have been reconstructed with concepts from STS as a specific way of experimentally constructing prototypes, visions or scenarios of alternative realities that are performative with respect to sensory experiences and affective relations (Thévenot, 2014; Surmann, 2015; Kanngieser, 2016; Rigamonti, 2022). Artistic practices draw people's attention to their works by implicitly claiming to represent an intensity of experience that is valuable also to their audiences and generally relevant as a way to become humanly alive (Dewey, 2005 [1934]; Becker, 1982, pp. 352–365; Gisler & Shehu, 2017). If audiences then attend to and participate in works of art, and open up themselves to be affected, what they are actually participating in is the co-creation of intense sensory experiences and receiving a feeling of being alive (Berleant, 1970; Joy & Sherry, 2003). Like this, artistic practices engage with and shape collective orders by planting desires and aesthetic predilections into human bodies.

Beginning with science, STS thus has opened a broader agenda of exploring various practices of experimentation for their performativity, that is for bringing about the world that they investigate, probe, and describe (Marres et al., 2018; Lezaun et al., 2016). Politics and art, like science, generate a specific power and authority by performatively representing some "source beyond or above" (Arendt, 1958, 83). In science and technology, it is objective reality and functionality. In politics, it is collective subjectivity, will, and interest. In art, it is intense experience and the feeling of being humanly alive. Invoking these transcendental unities empowers these practices to draw attention and draw agents into following, who then, by aligning their orientation and activities, contribute to realizing that unity and make its representation true, if only *ex post*.

In the following section, we outline an approach that brings together the three strands of research as reviewed here. We combine elements from them for articulating a praxeological analytics of aesthetics and politics in which they feature as specific practices of world-making, one engaging with orders of sensing and feeling, the other with culturally established group identities.

4. A PRAXEOLOGICAL ANALYTICS

The core challenge in articulating a praxeological approach to study how aesthetics and politics intertwine is to conceptualize such practices broadly enough to capture a wide variety of empirical patterns, on the one hand, also those beyond the historically specific modern institutions of autonomous art and liberal-democratic nation states. On the other, however, aesthetic and political practices equally need to be conceptualized narrowly enough to discern them empirically and analyze the specific patterns in which they intertwine and co-produce collective orders. Our approach for articulating such a generic but at the same time incisive conception is to start from the specific effects that each of these practices produces. From there we can empirically trace what is actually being done, and how, in order to produce said effects. This is where we can study in detail the various different ways in which empirically specific aesthetic and political practices are configured, how they are embedded in broader material-cultural contexts, and how specifically they work together in the shaping of collective orders.

It is the evocation and shaping of sensory experiences and affects that we take to be specific effect of aesthetic practices, and the evocation and shaping of collective subjectivities and agencies that we take to be the specific effect of political practices. Analyzing aesthetic and political practices then is a matter of reconstructing the doings that produce such effects.

We should note, however, that our interest lies in studying how aesthetics and politics intertwine in the shaping of collective orders. It is not the habitualized doing of certain sensory experiences and collective subjectivities that we are after, but rather specifically those practices that reflexively engage with and shape collective sensing and willing. We are after the ways by which sensing and willing are actively evoked and modulated. We set out to find and reconstruct the doings that reflexively engage with sensory experiences and collective subjectivities to modify and shape the ways we sensorily relate to each other and to the world and to the ways we understand ourselves collectively and, the recursive level, individually, too.

4.1 Practices

But what are such doings, activities, or practices that shape sensory experiences and collective subjectivities? In order to empirically reconstruct and analyze them, we turn to generic theorizations of such practices as sensitizing concepts (Bowen, 2006; Hillebrandt, 2014).

Practice theory is helpful in our endeavor because it suggests that how we sense, experience, and think is not a property of an individual human being, nor of encompassing social structures, but that it is in fact a property belonging to specific practices in which humans participate. We then train our minded bodies and our embodied minds in specific ways, and thereby develop sensory capabilities and subjectivities in relation to discourses and materialities.

Practice theory takes practices to be the basic constituting units of social life (Theodore R. Schatzki et al., 2001). Practices can generally be conceptualized as patterned ways of doing something, consisting in relations of human bodies (with certain incorporated experiences, skills, and predilections), meanings (discursively constructed knowledge, definitions, framings, norms, and values), and materialities (both designed artefacts and architecture as well as 'natural' materiality) (Reckwitz, 2010, pp. 190–192; Shove et al., 2012).

Compared to alternative accounts of social life, such as action theory and phenomenology, practice studies decenter the intentional individual as a source of patterned social activities. Instead, they presume that practices are relationally constituted by heterogeneous elements. Recursive relations between human bodies, meanings, and materialities grant practices a life of their own. This generates patterns of doing with a certain continuity, but no determination (Schäfer, 2016).

As dynamic compounds in themselves, the practices are the ones recruiting individual human bodies into their processual logic and shape human sensitivities and subjectivities as well as our capacities for reflexive action (Foucault, 1982; Butler, 1988; Reckwitz, 2004; Alkemeyer & Buschmann, 2016, 2017). Sensing and thinking are then features of practices more than of individual human beings, they emerge only in relation with discourses and materialities.

In contrast to biological and psychological theories, and the methodologically individualist social sciences that build on them, practice theory does not assume the senses to work as fixed transmitters of information from the environment to the body (Reckwitz, 2016; for an early critique of the psychological model see Dewey, 1896). Rather, specific ways of sensing are part of specific practices.

The same goes for consciousness and subjectivity. Departing from Descartes, the *"cogito"* is not assumed to be a given core of human existence, but it is studied as a result of bodies participating in practices: Subjectivity is continuously being shaped in relation to discursively constructed meaning and interaction with material settings and artefacts, and with other bodies enacting culturally established conceptions of the human self.

This praxeological conception of sensing and willing allows us understand and study them not as internal, proper, and private to individual human beings but indeed as a feature of heterogeneous relations, or specific patterns of those relations that constitute specific kinds of sensing collectives.

Wider patterns of collective life, or what in other accounts is referred to as social formations or structures, is in the praxeological approach conceptualized as networks or webs of practices (Theodore R Schatzki, 2015; Hui et al., 2016; Everts, 2016). Linkages between practices exist in the dimension of people, discourses, and materialities, i.e., human bodies circulating between various different practices, symbols, and concepts being used and worked at in the context of different practices, as well as material devices and infrastructures supporting several practices at once (Shove et al., 2012). Such broader complexes of connected practices make up specific kinds of cultures performing their own realities (also in terms of ontological worldviews). They are variously conceptualized as specifically patterned material-semiotic relations and actor-networks (Mol, 2002; Law, 2009), as practice-discourse formations (Reckwitz, 2008) or, in the tradition of Foucault and Deleuze as heterogeneous assemblages, agencements, dispositives or apparatuses (Collier & Ong, 2005; DeLanda, 2006; Venn, 2006; Phillips, 2006; Barad, 2007; Legg, 2011; Nail, 2017; Scheffer, 2021).

Against this background for a basic conception of practices, we can now move to conceptualize aesthetic and political practices as specific kinds that are marked by the effects they produce.

4.2 Aesthetic practices

We suggest conceptualizing aesthetic practices as those that induce and shape sensory experiences and affects. They modulate collective ways of sensing and feeling. While specific ways of sensing are part of any practice (such as seeing and listening are part of the practice of crossing the street), we refer to those that reflexively attend to sensing and are oriented towards evoking and creatively shaping sensory experiences as specifically aesthetic, namely "sense perceptions not embodied in instrumental or normative practice, but rather performed for the sake of their affective effects on the subject" (Reckwitz, 2016, p. 64; 2015, pp. 21–31; Dewey, 2005 [1934]; Teil & Hennion, 2004; Hennion, 2015).

This still comprises a broad range of activities, such as going for a walk through the woods, creating and exhibiting a painting, designing a website, or choreographing a street rally. In this broad and generic sense, aesthetic practices are not limited to art; they are part of everyday life and may occur in a variety of professional contexts. The dedicated evocation and shaping of sensory experiences and affects are furthermore part of home furnishing, celebratory rituals, corporate design and marketing, political speeches and campaigns, science communication, etc. Taken together then, we look for instances where sensory experiences and affects are reflexively and creatively being engaged with. From there we trace and reconstruct the specific ways in which this is done.

4.3 Political practices

Political practices, symmetrically, can be understood as those that induce and shape collective subjectivities and agency. They modulate collective identity, will, values, and interests that mobilize collective agency and legitimate norms. Often, the notion of politics is used more broadly to mark any activity of shaping collective orders (Mannheim, 1995 [1929]; Nash, 2001) or wherever programs to do so come in conflict with each other (Barry, 2012; Brown, 2015) or whenever distributional issues are at stake (Lasswell, 1936). A much narrower conception of politics, on the other hand, concentrates on making collectively binding decisions through the institutions of the state (Weber, 1992 [1919]; Easton, 1979 [1967]). We suggest a middle way between broadening out to include almost everything as politics and narrowing down to only very specific forms of institutional state politics.

At the core of our conception to study political practices here is the reflexive engagement with the ways people bond into groups to construct a collective identity as part of a 'we' with a common will, values, and interests (Alkemeyer & Bröckling, 2018; Delitz, 2018). Speaking and acting with reference to or on behalf of such a collective subjectivity can generate political authority. This specific form of power legitimates demanding actions and allows them to be aligned to realize collective goals or behavior to be regulated by collective norms (Bourdieu, 1985). The formation of such collective subjectivities is not naturally given, however (Brubaker & Cooper, 2000); there could as well be heterogeneous and diverging, singular, and idiosyncratic subjectivities that would never act jointly or approve of a common good. Such a 'we' thus needs to be performed, appearing rather as a fascinating and continuously ongoing cultural achievement (Latour, 2003). We therefore propose to take the evocation and modulation of collective subjectivities—the construction of a common will—to be the root of political action and the specific fulcrum for how political practices leverage processes of collective ordering.

As such, however, political practices are not merely tools for state governance but are, indeed, also available to companies, professional teams, scientific communities, neighborhoods, families, collectives—and just among friends going out and quarrelling over questions of what *we* want (to do, to eat, to see, to demand, etc.). Looking out for political practices may focus on the articulation of "representative claims" on behalf of some collective identity, will, value or interest (Saward, 2006), and how they are used to mobilize agency and legitimize norms (Disch, 2011).

4.4 The intertwining of aesthetic and political practices

With a more precise understanding of aesthetic and political practices, we may have a fine-grained look at the various ways in which they intertwine. We are particularly interested in how their interplay, be it convergent or conflicting, becomes effective in ongoing processes of collective ordering.

What the specific kinds of collective orders are that they jointly contribute to uphold or renew may vary from case to case. The chapters of this book discuss how they intertwine in governing and innovating colonial relations of power, techno-capitalism, technological infrastructures, consumer culture, urban living, relations with the environment, taste and ways of eating, political culture, populist discourse, gender relations, protest culture, and even scholarly conferencing.

Analyzing the intertwining of practices goes beyond viewing the relation of aesthetics and politics as an interaction through an exchange of their ready-made products, for example, when governments use works of art for public relations or when art thrives on state protection and funding. The praxeological approach instead reveals the entanglement of aesthetic and political practices in the making. This may be connections within the medium of people, symbols, or materialities themselves being part of both aesthetic and political practices. Or aesthetics and politics may integrate each other's effects for their very constitution and productivity. Political mobilization, for example, may work with the creation of sensory attention and affects (e.g., protest songs or national anthems). And aesthetic projects may work with the creation of collective will and agency (e.g., public interventions, flash mobs, large-scale artworks, theater, film, architecture). The practice turn allows us to zoom in on various specific ways in which aesthetics and politics are constitutively intertwined—not only how they interact, but also how they imply and co-constitute each other.

5. OVERVIEW OF THE CHAPTERS

The book explores how fruitful a practice-oriented approach can be. We hope to learn from case studies that trace specific forms of aesthetic and political practices and how they jointly contribute to the shaping of collective orders. This, we expect, can contribute a novel approach to studies of governance and innovation, one that goes beyond the usual focus on institutional, discursive, and cognitive dimensions of collective ordering. What results should be sensitive to the fabrication of sensation, feeling, will, and agency.

Contributions to this volume provide detailed accounts of how dedicated engagement with collective ways of sensing is intertwined and co-productive with the reflexive work at collective ways of self-understanding, willing, and acting. The authors take up the challenge to explicate aesthetic and political practices in how they are related and work together on specific forms of collective orders. In the remainder of this introduction, we first give an overview of each chapter and then tabulate the aesthetic and political practices that jointly contribute to either governance, that is, stabilize a dominant order, or those that jointly contribute to innovation, that is, nurture new alternatives.

We have sorted the chapters by this rough classification in terms of whether they focus their analysis on the aesthetic and political dimensions of some dominant order (governance) or of some disrupting and renewing engagement with a dominant order (innovation). Interestingly, though, all chapters also include accounts of the respective other side: Analyses of dominant orders also point out how they are contested and renewed. And analyses of disrupting and renewing engagements also take a look at the background of established orders against which that happens or at the building and stabilization of new orders as part of a struggle against the old ones. The clusters in which we present them, one on governance, the other on innovation, therefore fold into each other. Every chapter also contains a part that belongs to the other grouping. We start each part with a chapter opening-up a broader conceptual orientation, either focused on dominant collective orders (to be reflexively broken by creative interventions) or focused on the reflexive renewal of orders (by way of experimentally nurturing alternatives into being).

5.1 Aesthetic governance – and reflexive engagements with it

Sophia Prinz in her chapter *Re-designing the Sensory Order: Forms, Practices, and Perception* provides a conception of sensory orders as "topologies of form" based on the Foucauldian concept of orders of discourse developed by Merleau Ponty. She uses this conception to reconstruct the case of Italian architect Lina Bo Bardi taking up the task to design a museum of modern art in Salvador de Bahia by making it a museum of Afro-Brazilian popular culture, thereby critically engaging with hegemonic Western cultures of modernity and exposing creative work of the local population as form of modern art in its own right. Aesthetic practices here appear as Bo Bardi's reflexive dialogue both with Western sensory orders and with the self-developed topology of forms of the local people, by sensorily engaging with it, learning it, and interactively nurturing its development in the museum. They are closely entangled with political practices of articulating and empowering an autonomous collective subjectivity of the Afro-Brazilian people with its own aesthetics, not subordinate but equivalent to allegedly global standards of Western culture. Prinz shows how aesthetic practices of reflexively engaging with sensory orders and political practices of engaging with collective subjectivities are closely entangled in such ventures of "critical design" or "design from below."

Jonathan Luke Austin and *Anna Leander* in their chapter *Escape, Erase, Entangle: Three Aesthetic Regimes Re-composing the Californian Ideology* engage with how corporations from the Silicon Valley seek to govern the affective qualities of their new digital technologies. They study how Google, Tesla, and co. "ignite our senses," "make us feel" and create "resonance" for their products. They distinguish three "aesthetic regimes" appealing to specific subjectivities: "Escape" offers an aesthetics of salvation beyond mundane human life on Earth. "Erase" scrubs new technological developments from visibility by making them disappear or appear to be natural and traditional. "Entangle" aesthetically links into accustomed styles, fashions, and practices of the everyday, strategically suggesting intractability. For engaging with the aesthetic politics of techno-capitalism, they propose that "the fissures and frictions generated by this overlaying of aesthetic regimes are also helpful" as they "become indicators of possible openings for political agency and change. Driving a wedge into the cracks might widen these openings and so pave the way for responsible and reflective re-workings the of contemporary technological aesthetics and their politics."

Nona Schulte-Römer in her chapter *Sensory Governance: Managing the Public Sense of Light and Water* investigates how the sensing of technical infrastructures is managed by experts. They seek to "make public infrastructures as unobtrusive as possible, up to the point where they get literally removed from the public eye." By nature of their being below surface, the aesthetics of infrastructures entail "inattentional blindness" also strategically furthered by their managers. But, in the wake of changes to address sustainability, the aesthetics of new functions are bringing these structures to the surface (e.g., warmth LED vs. old fashioned gas lighting). Engaging in sensory politics activists pursue tactics of nurturing alternative ways of seeing or smelling infrastructural systems (Marcel de Certeau). Unanticipated publics then arise around—literally—"sensitive issues" opening up "sensory controversies." Often, the new publics stand in the way of progress in terms of sustainability. "Sensory governance" is the term and concept that Schulte-Römer gives to the expert's challenge. Beyond the visual and olfactory qualities, they must manage the affects that infrastructures give rise to and do so by exerting control over the perception of the objects under their care, trying to make innovations palatable. The chapter cautions, however, against objectifying "average perceptions" and instead calls for reflexivity towards the situatedness of sensory experience.

Susan C. Stewart in her chapter *Packaging Pleasures: Design, Play, and Consumer Change* explores the sensory and affective qualities of ecologically harmful packaging and discusses the difficulties society faces in stepping out of this trajectory. She investigates how bodily habit and sensory reward reinforce the hegemonic dominance of single-use plastics. It is the playful affect they induce in consumers that makes them seemingly indispensable, beyond keeping crisps crisp. The chapter conceptualizes wrappers as affect generators (Andreas Reckwitz) and problematizes that "[o]ur interactions with disposable packaging trigger deep-seated pleasures that inhere within the sensing collectives of our fast-paced consumer worlds." The analysis works with widely circulated "unboxing" videos as evidence of human's fascination with packaging and with a typology of different forms of play (Roger Caillois). Stewart calls for designers of reusable packaging to harness dynamics of play to leverage aesthetic practices to break the hold that plastics have and shift practices of consumption by "redirect[ing] such euphoria to the powerful exercise of restraint."

Miguel Paredes Maldonado in his chapter *Hegemonic Sensory Practices of the Smart City and a Collective Remaking of Data-based Urban Commons* analyzes how the collective sensing of city dwellers is governed through smart city projects and presents an experiment to 'hack' the standardizing aesthetics of computational measurements. His starting point is that "bodily embedded sensory practices in the city—and the sensory orders they give rise to—are gradually being displaced by digitally mediated forms of 'sensing' which are, in turn, predicated on our interactions with a range of dynamic data ... These digitally mediated practices of sensing follow a particular set of computational logics that change the sensory orders that regulate collective life in the city. ... [B]y changing the ways in which people move about in the city, smart cities and platform labor applications also affect how people performatively represent the 'polis' as a collective subject." He points out that the problem of cybernetics is its emphasis on stasis, and the hegemonic order that prevails in such systems today is heavily weighted towards maximizing commercial outputs over all others. "This calls into question the agency of individual citizens, neighborhood communities, grassroots platforms and other non-hegemonic stakeholders in the city." Paredes describes in great detail how this works and proposes a counter practice developed as part of his own academic work. By co-opting the cybernetic paradigm with the aesthetic practices of urban hacking, critical making and play, his experiments offer new ways to perceive and diversify the smart city.

Hanna Husberg and *Agata Marzecová* in their chapter *We Thought It Was Fog, We Thought It Was Just Some Weather: Sensing, Datafication and Governance of Urban Air Pollution* undertake a partly artistic, partly analytical reconstruction of how collective sensing of the environment in Beijing is governed through scientific measurements and smart devices. China's response to the 2013 "Airpocalypse" was to ultimately provide air quality data to their citizens. Through fieldnotes and interviews, Husberg and Marzecová explore how this established a relation with air as "a new arena of care and calculation." Due to the invisibility of air and the fineness of pollutants, sensing its qualities has become as much a matter of technological data collection as breathing it in. Technologically mediated sensing and interpretation of air qualities complements embodied sensing and affective qualities of the air. And this entails a new form governance. It centralizes the ways people perceive and relate with the environment. Withholding or releasing data and sending out recommendations on how to behave, go out or not, wear a mask or not, stay or move away—all this replaces individual sensing and sense-making. Like the cybernetics of smart cities, this management of people's perceptions and movements reduces their agency and inhibits collective action. What Husberg and Marzecová seek to revitalize with their artistic research is a countervailing embodied experience.

5.2 Aesthetic innovation – and collective re-ordering

Antoine Hennion's chapter *How to Better Sense What is Happening? A Political Lesson from Taste and Tasting* opens the second grouping of studies focusing on the innovative potential of aesthetic and political practices. Hennion revitalizes the pragmatist conception of a mutual constitution of objects and subjects in processes of experimental inquiry. Tasting then is a way of sensory attending and affectively opening-up to how things happen while experimentally modulating the relations of heterogeneous elements that jointly constitute the thing and how it is experienced. The practices of amateurs like music or wine lovers serve as an example of the aesthetic approach to the world. The chapter develops this conceptually, first as a combination of semiology with actor-network theory to "let objects speak," and then a combination of actor-network theory with pragmatism to "let tasters listen to and interact with objects." Hennion explores various semantic expressions to capture tasting as a practice of "putting oneself actively in states where the objective is not the control of things, but on the contrary a kind of deliberate loss of control, in order to give things back their hand, and in return to be able to rely on their reactions to increase their virtues ..." With regard to politics he asks: "Is there a more political stance today than to collectively elaborate our ability to better catch and support the propensity of things? Isn't politics, too, an art of making agents and things exist more?" This would then be a shared orientation for invigorating aesthetic and political practice alike: "to get more sensitive to things in process of making."

The chapter *Provoking Taste: Experimenting with New Ways of Sensing* by Jan-Peter Voß, Michael Guggenheim, Nora Rigamonti, Aline Haulsen, and Max Söding picks up and works with Antoine Hennion's pragmatist conception of taste. They report on an exhibition offering an experimental setting for participants to playfully explore the possibility of shaping their own taste experiences by modulating selected elements of an eating situation—not only the food but also elements like memories, framings, body schemes, and atmospheres. They position their project against a diagnosis that the sensory sciences, together with corporate marketing, cultivate an industrialized order of sensing. Gustatory taste is another sense that has undergone industrial standardization and conformity. Can the bonds on our buds be loosened? The exhibition was itself an experiment at giving agency on their own tasting back to the eaters. The chapter describes the design, realization, and effects of this experiment. The authors analyze their undertaking in terms of aesthetic practices, reflexively engaging with sensory experiences of eating by configuring the experimental situation, and in terms of political practices, in a wide sense of problematizing and attempting to re-make collective orders of eating, and in more specific sense of proposing a new collective subjectivity of creative tasting.

Frederike Landau-Donnelly in her chapter *The Beauty of Feeling: On the Affective Politics of Sensing Collectives* investigates how the German art collective Center for Political Beauty (ZPS) articulates a specific collective subjectivity of those who long for politics to become affectively more intense. She focuses on a performance titled *"Thesenanschlag"* where activists on horseback nailed "10 theses for political beauty" to the door of the German parliament. *"Thesenanschlag"* is a German term with a dual meaning. It harks back to Martin Luther's posting of his theses on the church door, which incited the Reformation. But it also translates to "an assault with theses," presumably on the kind of politics practiced within the institutions of the German state. Their "10 theses for political beauty" sought to instigate a new kind of "affective politics" (Brigitte Bargetz). Landau-Donnelly undertakes a "poetic analysis" (Jacques Derrida) of how collectivity is invoked in those theses. This entails the composition of a commentary that is itself written as a poem expressing the affective responses from reading the theses. She reconstructs how ZPS invokes a 'we' that knows and feels the "idea(l) of political beauty as innate to a fairly generalized humankind." Yet, "[w]hile 'the human' as subject and carrier of political beauty is not further specified, the latent understanding of agency and subjectivity developed throughout remains rather individualistic, disembodied, abstract... Crucially, 'we' gain no insight into how 'we' can find to each other in the unstillable longing for other politics." Her analysis questions the universality of such collectivity claims and indeed the extent to which longing is open-ended—an "affective perpetuum mobile"—unmoored from specific issues and matters at hand that normally serve to mobilize.

Sebastian Sommer's contribution *"Wir sind das Volk!" – How the PEGIDA Demonstrations Aesthetically Practice an Exclusive Collective Identity* studies aesthetic practices as constitutive of the German right-wing movement Patriotic Europeans Against the Islamization of Occident (PEGIDA). He employs methods of performance analysis from theater studies to articulate, through his own bodily sensations as participant observer, how the choreography of street rallies in Dresden invoked a united collective subjectivity and its entitlement to hegemony. He positions this case against the background of Occupy Wall Street as an oft-discussed example of protest actions operating aesthetically while at the same time politically performing a specific collective subjectivity (Judith Butler, Jacques Rancière). Politically situated very differently, PEGIDA here appears as a movement that, by similar means, performs a very different collective subjectivity of supremacist nativism. Drawing attention to bodily and material practices of closure to the outside and purification on the inside, Sommer works out the "bio-political effects of performances ... in the sense of aesthetically implementing a desired governmentality ... in 'doing *Volksgemeinschaft*'." With Rancière and his distinction of "politics" (as practices of widening the democratic discourse by making unseen positions visible) and "police" (as practices of closing down arguments by barring unwanted groups), Sommer makes us reflect how and to what extent they are at work in PEGIDA performances.

The chapter *Digital Violence as Affective Disciplining after Feminist Protests: The Case of #NotLikeThatLadies* by *Marcela Suarez* and *Mirjana Mitrović* focuses on affective mobilizations as renewed ways of protesting to resist sexual police violence. Approaching affects as constitutive practices of any social order (Andreas Reckwitz), Suarez and Mitrović analyze these affective practices in political protests as both a site of resistance and an arena for disciplining. Through feminist protests carried out in Mexico City in 2019 to resist sexual police violence, they stress the ways in which fury, anger, and despair were mobilized to create shared ways of sensing and being affected by gender violence, for example, by painting graffiti with the slogan *#Feminicidestate* in historical monuments. They argue that the intertwining of these affects and the political practices transgressed the patriarchal hegemonic imaginary of how women should protest and what kind of affects they are allowed to bring into public spaces. The response to the protests in social networks resulted in practices of disciplining the women's affects, as protesters were the target of thousands of misogynic comments. They were also condemned as violent and dehumanized as irrational. Thus, the authors trace both the arc of affective politics that offer new repertoires for doing feminist politics and the inevitable backlash to reestablish a pre-existing order through affect disciplining.

Rose Beermann in her chapter *Performing Disruptions: A Bodily Encounter with Misogyny in Lifestyle Television* presents a reflection on a dance performance as a "non-discursive, bodily critique" of a sexist TV show. The tackled TV show featured two men sitting on a sofa who casually assess the sex appeal of naked women presented to them in the glow of a spotlight, misogyny in talk-show format. Beermann describes autoethnographically how she had conceptualized, choreographed, and performed a dance performance to problematize the conception of women in this show: "With our bodies as a central means of expression, we wanted the audience to feel our critique... [W]e were looking for a resistant performance of femininity that might allow us to counter the male flow of speech." She reflects on how the critical reenactment actually worked, aesthetically and politically; that is, in how far intended sensory experiences and collective (dis)identifications were invoked in the audience. A key moment was when she realized that the first approach of exposing the objectification of women by simply reenacting the show did not have the desired effect of causing irritations. Beermann ascribes this to an established "affective economy" (Sara Ahmed) in which seeing women as sex objects has become so natural that it doesn't even evoke strange feelings: "In light of my experience as a performer standing naked in front of an audience, I would like to ask: How can I renegotiate the way I want to be perceived? In my experience, the idea of reenactment has limits for establishing another bodily reality. If the affective economies in which the source material is embedded are very powerful and efficient, it is not easy to find gaps for subverting ways of sensory perception." A second approach then was to go beyond caricatural exposure and "not provide emotional clarity" but instead astonishment and confusion by "underperformance" (Lauren Berlant) and letting the performing bodies gradually slip out of their role as sex objects, avert habitualized ways of sensing by taking on strange forms, and gradually take on agency and become willing subjects. She concludes that "performance is a valuable research space to explore the preconditions for being together as a sensing collective."

The chapter *Sensing Collectives as Sensing Selves: Two Artistic Interventions & Two Theories of the Self* by *Jacob Watson* recounts two artistic interventions that were invited to the workshop that served as the basis for this book, making palatable some of the ideas on the agenda: Firstly, Vanessa Farfán's talk on "Collateral Aesthetics" about her experiences in China unintentionally inciting gatherings with her artwork that were deemed potential political agitation. She illustrated her talk with a demonstration for workshop participants to feel the tension of population density vs. personal space. The other intervention by Markus Binner made up the workshop lunchbreak in which all participants took on various roles—sometimes counteractive—to prepare a shared lunch in his "Bitter Mass Cooking" experiment. To make sense and give a sense of what it was like to be part of these two sensing collectives within the scholarly workshop setting, Watson gives a personalized account of his sensory experience as a participant. Using his background in philosophy he analyzes the "self" of a sensing collective as the site of either bundles of sense experiences or an embodied amalgam of will, resistance, and effort, or indeed both.

6. CONCLUDING REMARKS

This book is an opening move, a first foray into a field that stretches out if we look at processes of collective ordering with a view to the intertwining of aesthetic and political practices. In that sense, there is nothing to conclude, but everything emerging from here will be welcomed. We did say, however, that we had set out to assemble contributions in this book in order to explore patterns that may become discernible. This is what we, admittedly very briefly, take up here to conclude. Very briefly only because we do not want to take the analytical evaluation of our explorative case studies too far. They take different approaches and their results cannot adequately be synthesized and escalated too far. Plus, we do not want to close down studies of aesthetic and political practices by impetuously articulating ideal types of patterns and effects, but we, first of all, wish to encourage more open exploration.

Even our small and rather arbitrarily composed sample of cases shows that in the dimensions of both sensing and willing, collective orders are by no means 'natural' or 'accidental.' They are always also reflexively being worked at by embodied human (and non-human) agents, either for building and stabilizing or for disrupting and renewing through engagement in aesthetic and political practices.

In the case studies, we find very different kinds of collective orders engaged with for a wide range of concerns. These are: established orders of (dis-)appreciating diverse cultures and their art styles (Prinz), orders of digitalized techno-capitalism (Austin & Leander), technological infrastructures (Schulte-Römer), commercial packaging (Stewart), smart city management (Paredes), digital sensing of environmental pollution (Husberg & Marcecova), ontological attitudes and ways of relating with the world (Hennion), the tasting of food (Voß et al.), styles of doing politics (Landau-Donnelly), hegemonic political discourse (Sommer), gendered publics and protest culture (Suarez & Mitrović), sexism in popular media culture (Beermann), and the emerging collective order at our own sensing collectives research workshop as shaped by artistic demonstrations (Watson).

The case studies show that both governance and innovation entail the intertwining of specific aesthetic and political practices. We find both kinds jointly stabilizing established and hegemonic forms of governance as well as bringing forward emerging and emancipatory innovations—and often in concert. This thrusts aside the widespread expectation that aesthetic practices are always concerned with disrupting and renewing orders whereas political practices with building and stabilizing them. Even if some case studies start from an interest in stabilizing some collective order and others from their renewal, each study elaborates how efforts at governing and innovating are indeed very closely related. Governance practices often engender their own practices of contestation and renewal, just like innovation practices involve efforts at building and stabilizing new and alternative orders. Table 1 outlines, in a very tapered way, the stabilizing aesthetic and political practices described in each chapter, and the renewing aesthetic and political practices.

Table 1: Chapter overview with specific aesthetic and political practices in governing and innovating collective orders

Author(s)	Governance (established and dominant ordering)		Innovation (new and alternative ordering)	
	Aesthetic practices	Political practices	Aesthetic practices	Political practices
Prinz	Status quo of exclusively appreciating Western modern art as fine art	Elevate Western modernity to a universal standard of civilization	Design from below, nurture and exhibit the specific " topology of forms" of Afro-Brazilian popular culture	Articulate unique Afro-Brazilian collective subjectivity by exhibiting their own modern art
Austin & Leander	Unfurl "aesthetic regimes" of escape/erase/engage to promote Californian Ideology	Invoke collective subjectivities of nihilism/conservatism/commonness in support of corporate strategies	Reflexively and responsibly re-work contemporary technological aesthetics	Mobilize agency against unfettered dynamics of digitalized techno-capitalism
Schulte-Römer	Manage sensory (im)perceptibility of technological infrastructures	Secure public acceptance of technological infrastructures	Bring sensory qualities of infrastructures into perception (brightness of LED lights, impurity of water)	Mobilize resistance against strategies of managing technological infrastructures

Stewart	Design, advertisement, and playful engagement with plastic packaging	Mobilize consumption communities around "unboxing" and joy of rustling	Play-oriented design of reusable packages	Mobilize sustainable consumption communities
Paredes	Digitally sense, represent, and regulate movement in the Smart City	Smart City management performs a collective of "cybernetic selves"	Hack digital sensing tools for counter-mapping collective life in the city	Articulate collective subjectivity of city dwellers as autonomous and creative agents
Husberg & Marzecová	Digitally sense environmental pollution through mobile apps	"Algorithmic governance" performs a collective of centrally steered individual automata	Express human bodily experiences and feelings in relation with environmental pollution and app-data	Articulate collective subjectivity of bodily sensing and affectively communicating human agents
Hennion	Experience objects as static, passive, and independent of human subjectivity	Articulate collective subjectivity of humans detached from objects	Engage in tasting as letting things happen and allowing selves to transform in affective interaction with them	Articulate collective subjectivity of pragmatist experimental savorers (lovers/amateurs)
Voß, Guggenheim, Rigamonti, Haulsen & Söding	Practice the tasting of food as determined by given object and subject qualities (industrialized sensing)	Perform collective subjectivity of eaters seeking the optimal food	Practice tasting as experimental re-assembling of heterogeneous elements of an eating situation	Perform collective subjectivity of eaters creatively shaping situated ways of tasting

Landau-Donnelly	Do politics as soberly and unemotionally assessing and deliberating costs and benefits of options	Perform collective subjectivity of reasonable and realistic members of the polity	Do politics as poetically invoking humanist values and dramatically exposing their breaching	Articulate a longing for political beauty, for passionate and affective ways of doing politics
Sommer	Perform mainstream liberal attitudes of openness, tolerance, and diversity	Articulate collective subjectivity of all-embracing cosmopolitanism	Choreograph street rallies of nationalist-authoritative PEGIDA movement to create "echo chambers" as spaces of felt hegemony	Perform a collective subjectivity of "we, the people" as homogeneous, unified, and powerful
Suárez & Mitrović	Women feel abashed and duck away when falling victim to sexual abuse or they unemotionally claim their objective rights	Perform collective subjectivity of civilized members of a state of law ignoring patriarchal biases	Express rage in street protest, break the image of "good girls"	Perform collective subjectivity of women as hurt, upset, and able to put up a fight against sexual violence
Beermann	Sexual objectification of women in the "masculine gaze," celebrated in a TV show	Perform dual collective subjectivity of active male deciders and passive female bio-material	"Underperform" the female role model, subvert the "affective economy" by weird, maverick, and willful movements and by taking voice in a theatrical re-enactment of TV show	Perform collective subjectivity of women resisting sexual objectification, demanding recognition as interactive subjects

| Watson, Farfán & Binner | Present and discuss papers with PowerPoint projections on a screen in front of rows of chairs | Perform collective subjectivity of competent academics and intellectuals | Stand up and move around to bodily enact the population density of Beijing and to interactively cook a lunch menu | Perform a collective subjectivity of flesh and blood human bodies interactively exploring a possible situational "we" |

In order to further the analytical evaluation of our sample of case studies, we could characterize specific types of aesthetic-political shaping practices with labels like "critical design/design from below," "regimes of aesthetic marketing," "sensory governance and its contestation," "affective design," "hacking datafied sensing," "aesthetic ethnography of digital sensing," "making and feeling things happen," "experimental eating and tasting," "artistic activism for affective politics," "choreography of protest," "feminist protest culture," "feminist theater," "participatory art." This would, perhaps, also be a first step towards articulating more abstract patterns of aesthetic-political governance and innovation in conceptual terms.

Another way to comparatively analyze the case studies would be to cluster them by issues (e.g., technology, digital data, political culture, feminism), styles of engagement (e.g., design, marketing, protest, hacking, performance, experimentation), or scales of engagement (e.g., specific sites like an exhibition, a building, a place, or cities, regional infrastructure systems, national political and media cultures, global marketing strategies, foundational ontological orientations).

All such further approaches of systematically analyzing, comparing, typifying mapping patterns of intertwining are potential avenues that open up from our practice turn in studying relations of aesthetics and politics. However, we do not want to curve in here to close down the multiplicity of aesthetic and political practices and their various ways of intertwining for all too boldly designed ideal types. To do so would be premature. For now, they can be valued for unfurling a diversity of concrete forms of aesthetic and political practices, how they intertwine and jointly contribute to the shaping of collective orders—or the making of sensing collectives, as it were.

If this book is a stimulus for some of its readers to take their own go at tracing how aesthetics and politics intertwine in the shaping of collective orders, we have achieved what we intended. In that sense let's all go for *sensing collectives*—in the two senses implied by the phrase: first, conceiving of collectivity as co-constituted by ways of sensing and feeling and, second, perceiving collective orders empirically with all our senses, by methods of sensory ethnography, artistic research, aesthetic experiments and the like, allowing us to also affectively experience what we study.

References

Adorno, T. W. (1973). *Ästhetische Theorie*. Frankfurt am Main: Suhrkamp.
Ahmed, S. (2013). *The cultural politics of emotion*. London: Routledge.
Alkemeyer, T., & Bröckling, U. (2018). Jenseits des Individuums. Zuir Subjektivierung kollektiver Subjekte: Ein Forschungsprogramm. In T. Alkemeyer, U. Bröckling, & T. Peter (Eds.), *Jenseits der Person. Zur Subjektivierung von Kollektiven* (pp. 17–31). Bielefeld: transcript.
Alkemeyer, T., & Buschmann, N. (2016). Critique in praxis: arguments for a subjectivation theoretical expansion on practice theory. In *Praxeological Political Analysis* (pp. 79–96): Routledge.
Alkemeyer, T., & Buschmann, N. (2017). Learning in and across practices: Enablement as subjectivation. In *The Nexus of Practices* (pp. 20–35). London: Routledge.
Ankersmit, F. R. (1996). *Aesthetic politics: political philosophy beyond fact and value*. Stanford, CA: Stanford University Press.
Arendt, H. (1958). What was authority? In C. J. Friedrich (Ed.), *Authority* (pp. 81–112). Cambridge, MA: Harvard University Press.
Argo, J. J., & Main, K. J. (2004). Meta-analyses of the effectiveness of warning labels. *Journal of Public Policy & Marketing, 23*(2), 193–208.
Aronczyk, M., Edwards, L., & Kantola, A. (2017). Apprehending public relations as a promotional industry. *Public Relations Inquiry, 6*(2), 139–155.
Bachmann-Medick, D. (2016). *Cultural Turns. New Orientations in the Study of Culture*. Berlin: de Gruyter.
Barad, K. (2007). *Meeting the Universe Halfway*. Paper presented at the Meeting the universe halfway, Durham.
Bargetz, B. (2015). The distribution of emotions: Affective politics of emancipation. *Hypatia, 30*(3), 580–596.
Barry, A. (2012). Political situations: Knowledge controversies in transnational governance. *Critical Policy Studies, 6*(3), 324–336.
Bassett, K. (2014). Rancière, politics, and the Occupy movement. *Environment and Planning D: Society and Space, 32*(5), 886–901.
Becker, H. (1953). Becoming a marihuana user. *American Journal of Sociology, 59*(3), 235–242.
Becker, H. (1982). *Art worlds*. Berkeley: University of California Press.
Bentia, D. C. (2014). Sensuous Pageantry: Slow Food Fairs' Alternating Sensory Orders towards Taste Change. *The Senses and Society, 9*(2), 174–193.
Berleant, A. (1970). The aesthetic field: A phenomenology of aesthetic experience.

Beuys, J. (2007 [1986]). *What is art? Conversation with Joseph Beuys*. Forest Row: Clairview Books.

Bevir, M., & Rhodes, R. A. W. (2010). *The state as cultural practice*: Oxford University Press.

Bijker, W. E. (1987). The Social Construction of Bakelite: Toward a Theory of Invention. In W. E. Bijker, T. P. Hughes, & T. J. Pinch (Eds.), *The social construction of technological systems* (pp. 159–189). Cambridge: MIT Press.

Bourdieu, P. (1985). Delegation and political fetishism. *Thesis eleven, 10*(1), 56–70.

Bourdieu, P. (1987). *Distinction: A social critique of the judgement of taste*. Cambridge, MA: Harvard University Press.

Bourdieu, P. (1996 [1992]). *The rules of art: Genesis and structure of the literary field*. Stanford, CA: Stanford University Press.

Bourdieu, P. (2001). *Das Politische Feld. Zur Kritik der politischen Vernunft*. Konstanz: UVK.

Bowen, G. A. (2006). Grounded theory and sensitizing concepts. *International journal of qualitative methods, 5*(3), 12–23.

Brown, M. B. (2015). Politicizing science: Conceptions of politics in science and technology studies. *Social Studies of Science, 45*(1), 3–30.

Brubaker, R., & Cooper, F. (2000). Beyond" identity". *Theory and Society, 29*(1), 1–47.

Bull, M., Gilroy, P., Howes, D., & Kahn, D. (2006). Introducing sensory studies. *The Senses and Society, 1*(1), 5–7.

Burchell, G., Gordon, C., & Miller, P. (Eds.). (1991). *The Foucault Effect. Studies in Governmentality*. Chicago: Chicago University Press.

Burton, S., Andrews, J. C., & Netemeyer, R. G. (2021). Identifying and selecting effective graphic health warnings to prevent perceptual wearout on tobacco packaging and in advertising. *Journal of Consumer Affairs, 55*(2), 609–621.

Butler, J. (1988). Performative acts and gender constitution: An essay in phenomenology and feminist theory. *Theatre journal*, 519–531.

Butler, J. (1990). *Gender trouble: Feminism and the subversion of identity*. London: Routledge.

Butler, J. (2015). *Notes Toward a Performative Theory of Assembly*. Cambridge, MA: Harvard University Press.

Callon, M. (2007). What Does It Mean to Say That Economics Is Performative? In D. MacKenzie, F. Muniesa, & L. Siu (Eds.), *Do Economists Make Markets? On the Performativity of Economics* (pp. 311–357). Princeton: Princeton University Press.

Callon, M. (2010). Performativity, misfires and politics. *Journal of Cultural Economy, 3*(2), 163–169.

Callon, M., Lascoumes, P., & Barthe, Y. (2009). *Acting in an uncertain world: an essay on technical democracy*. Cambridge, MA: MIT Press.

Classen, C. (1997). Foundations for an anthropology of the senses. *International Social Science Journal, 49*(153), 401–412.

Collier, S. J., & Ong, A. (2005). Global assemblages, anthropological problems. In A. Ong & S. J. Collier (Eds.), *Global assemblages: Technology, politics, and ethics as anthropological problems* (pp. 3–21). Malden, MA: Blackwell.

Cosgrove, D. (2003). Landscape and the European sense of sight–eyeing nature. In K. Anderson, M. Domosh, S. Pile, & N. Thrift (Eds.), *Handbook of cultural geography* (pp. 249–268).

Dányi, E. (2015). The Parliament as a High-Political Programm. In A.-L. Müller & W. Reichmann (Eds.), *Architecture, Materiality and Society: Connecting Sociology of Architecture with Science and Technology Studies* (pp. 99–118). London: Palgrave Macmillan UK.

Davey, J., & Ebner, J. (2017). The fringe insurgency. Connectivity, convergence and mainstreaming of the extreme right. *Institute for Strategic Dialogue* (http://www.isdglobal. org/wp-content/uploads/2017/10/The-Fringe-Insurgency-221017. pdf).

De Certeau, M. (1980). On the oppositional practices of everyday life. *Social Text*(3), 3–43.

Debord, G. (1995 [1967]). *The Society of the Spectacle*. New York: Zone Books.

DeLanda, M. (2006). *A new philosophy of society: Assemblage theory and social complexity*: Bloomsbury Publishing.

Deleuze, G., & Guattari, F. (1988 [1980]). *A thousand plateaus: Capitalism and schizophrenia*. London: Bloomsbury.

Delitz, H. (2018). *Kollektive Identitäten*. Bielefeld: transcript.

Dewey, J. (1896). The reflex arc concept in psychology. *Psychological Review*, 3(4), 357–370.

Dewey, J. (2005 [1934]). *Art as experience*. New York: Penguin.

Disch, L. (2008). Representation as 'Spokespersonship': Bruno Latour's political theory. *Parallax*, 14(3), 88–100.

Disch, L. (2010). 'Faitiche'-izing the People: What Representative Democracy Might Learn from Science Studies. In B. Braun, S. J. Whatmore, & I. Stengers (Eds.), *Political matter: Technoscience, democracy, and public life* (pp. 267–296). Minneapolis: University of Minnesota Press.

Disch, L. (2011). Toward a mobilization conception of democratic representation. *American Political Science Review*, 105(1), 100–114.

Disch, L., van de Sande, M., & Urbinati, N. (Eds.). (2019). *The constructivist turn in political representation*. Edinburgh: Edinburgh University Press.

Eagleton, T. (1990). The ideology of the aesthetic. In P. Hernadi (Ed.), *The Rhetoric of Interpretation and the Interpretation of Rhetoric* (pp. 75–86). Durham: Duke University Press.

Easton, D. (1979 [1967]). *A systems analysis of political life*. Chicago: University of Chicago Press.

Edelman, M. (1988). *Constructing the political spectacle*: University of Chicago Press Chicago.

Everts, J. (2016). Connecting Sites: Practice Theory and Large Phenomena. *Geographische Zeitschrift*, 104(1), 50–67.
Foucault, M. (1972). *The archaeology of knowledge*. New York: Pantheon.
Foucault, M. (1980). *Power/knowledge: Selected interviews and other writings, 1972–1977*. New York: Pantheon.
Foucault, M. (1982). The subject and power. *Critical inquiry*, 8(4), 777–795.
Foucault, M. (2020 [1984]). *The history of sexuality, vol. 2: The use of pleasure*. London: Penguin.
Gisler, P., & Shehu, D. (2017). Performative Kapazität der künstlerischen Autonomie–Beobachtungen im Kontext von Kunsthochschulen. In U. Karstein & N. T. Zahner (Eds.), *Autonomie der Kunst? Zur Aktualität eines gesellschaftlichen leitbildes* (pp. 351–371). Wiesbaden: SpringerVS.
Göbel, H. K., & Prinz, S. (2015). *Die Sinnlichkeit des Sozialen. Wahrnehmung und materielle Kultur*. Bielefeld: transcript.
Gomart, E., & Hennion, A. (1999). A sociology of attachment: music amateurs, drug users. *The Sociological Review*, 47(S1), 220–247.
Groys, B. (2008). *Art power*. Cambridge, MA: MIT Press.
Groys, B. (2014). On art activism. *e-flux journal*, 56, 1–14.
Habermas, J. (1981). *Theorie des kommunikativen Handelns. Handungsrationalität und gesellschaftliche Rationalisierung* (Vol. 1). Frankfurt: Suhrkamp.
Hacking, I. (1992). The self-vindication of the laboratory sciences. In A. Pickering (Ed.), *Science as practice and culture* (pp. 29–64). Chicago: University of Chicago Press.
Hajer, M. A. (2010). *Authoritative governance: Policy making in the age of mediatization*. Oxford: Oxford University Press.
Harvey, D. (1989). *The condition of postmodernity* (Vol. 14): Blackwell Oxford.
Hayes-Conroy, A., & Martin, D. G. (2010). Mobilising bodies: visceral identification in the Slow Food movement. *Transactions of the Institute of British Geographers*, 35(2), 269–281.
Heinich, N. (2014). Practices of contemporary art: a pragmatic approach to a new artistic paradigm. In T. Zembylas (Ed.), *Artistic practices. Social interactions and cultural dynamics* (pp. 32–43). London: Rouledge.
Hennion, A. (2004). Pragmatics of taste. In M. D. Jacobs & N. Weiss Hanrahan (Eds.), *The Blackwell companion to the sociology of culture* (pp. 131–144). Malden, MA: Blackwell Publishing.
Hennion, A. (2015). Paying attention: what is tasting wine about? In A. Berthoin Antal, M. Hutter, & D. Stark (Eds.), *Moments of valuation. Exploring sites of dissonance* (pp. 37–56). Oxford: Oxford University Press.
Hennion, A., Meadel, C., & Bowker, G. (1989). The Artisans of Desire: The Mediation of Advertising between Product and Consumer. *Sociological Theory*, 7(2), 191–209. doi:10.2307/201895

Hillebrandt, F. (2014). *Soziologische Praxistheorien: Eine Einführung*. Wiesbaden: SpringerVS.
Hinderliter, B., Kaizen, W., Maimon, V., Mansoor, J., & McCormick, S. (Eds.). (2009). *Communities of sense: Rethinking aesthetics and politics*. Durham: Duke University Press.
Hitzler, R. (2002). Inszenierung und Repräsentation. Bemerkungen zur Politikdarstellung in der Gegenwart. In H.-G. Soeffner & D. Tänzler (Eds.), *Figurative Politik. Zur Performanz der Macht in der modernen Gesellschaft* (pp. 35–49). Wiesbaden: Verlag für Sozialwissenschaften.
Hoggett, P., & Thompson, S. (2012). Introduction. In P. Hoggett & S. Thompson (Eds.), *Politics and the emotions: The affective turn in contemporary political studies* (pp. 1–33). London: Continuum.
Howes, D. (1991). *The Varieties of Sensory Experience: A Sourcebook in the Anthropology of the Senses*: University of Toronto Press Toronto.
Howes, D. (Ed.) (2005). *Empire of the Senses. The Sensual Culture Reader*. London: Bloomsbury.
Howes, D., & Classen, C. (2014). *Ways of Sensing: Understanding the Senses in Society*. Oxon: Routledge.
Hui, A., Schatzki, T., & Shove, E. (Eds.). (2016). *The Nexus of Practices: Connections, Constellations, Practitioners*. London: Routledge.
James, W. (1983 [1890]). *The Principles of Psychology*. Cambridge, MA: Harvard University Press.
Joy, A., & Sherry, J. F. (2003). Speaking of Art as Embodied Imagination: A Multisensory Approach to Understanding Aesthetic Experience. *Journal of consumer research, 30*(2), 259–282.
Kanngieser, A. (2016). *Experimental Politics and the Making of Worlds*. London: Routledge.
Keane, H. (2014). Cigarettes are no Longer Sublime. *Australian Humanities Review, 57*, 1–20.
Kloppers, E. C. (2020). Singing and Sounding the Sacred-the Function of Religious Songs and Hymns in the Public Sphere. *Journal for the Study of Religion, 33*(1), 1–23.
Knorr Cetina, K. (1981). *The manufacture of knowledge: An essay on the constructivist and contextual nature of science*. Oxford: Pergamon Press.
Kooiman, J. (1993). *Modern Governance. New Government-Society Interactions*. London: Sage.
Laclau, E., & Mouffe, C. (2001 [1985]). *Hegemony and socialist strategy: Towards a radical democratic politics*. London: Verso.
Lasswell, H. D. (1936). *Politics: Who gets what, when, how*. New York: Whittlesey House.
Latour, B. (1983). Give me a laboratory and I will raise the world. In K. Knorr-Cetina & M. Mulkay (Eds.), *Science observed. Perspectives on the social studies of science* (pp. 142–169). London: Sage.

Latour, B. (1987). *Science in Action. How to Follow Scientists and Engineers through Society*. Cambridge, MA: Harvard University Press.
Latour, B. (2003). What if we talked politics a little? *Contemporary Political Theory*, 2(2), 143–164.
Latour, B. (2013). *An inquiry into modes of existence. An anthropology of the moderns*. Cambridge, MA: Harvard University Press.
Latour, B., & Woolgar, S. (1979). *Laboratory Life. The Social Construction of Scientific Facts*. London: Sage.
Law, J. (2009). Actor network theory and material semiotics. *The new Blackwell companion to social theory*, 141–158.
Lefebvre, H. (1991 [1974]). *The production of space* (Vol. 142). Malden MA: Blackwell.
Legg, S. (2011). Assemblage/apparatus: using Deleuze and Foucault. *Area*, 43(2), 128–133.
Lerner, D., & Lasswell, H. D. (1951). *The policy sciences: Recent developments in scope and method*. Satnford: Stanford University Press.
Lewis, J. (2013 [1990]). *Art, Culture and Enterprise: The Politics of Art and the Cultural Industries*. London: Routledge.
Lezaun, J., Marres, N., & Tironi, M. (2016). Experiments in participation. In *The handbook of science and technology studies* (pp. 195): MIT Press.
Lindstrom, M. (2005). Broad sensory branding. *Journal of Product & Brand Management*, 14(2), 84–87.
Little, A. (2019). *Politics of Radical Democracy*. Edinburgh: Edinburgh University Press.
Luhmann, N. (1996). *Die Kunst der Gesellschaft*. Frankfurt am Main: Suhrkamp.
Luhmann, N. (2000). *Die Politik der Gesellschaft*. Frankfurt am Main: Suhrkamp.
Lynch, M. (1985). *Art and artifact in laboratory science*: Routledge & Kegan Paul.
Lyotard, J.-F. (1994 [1979]). *The postmodern condition*. Manchester: Manchester University Press.
Mannheim, K. (1995 [1929]). *Ideologie und Utopie*. Frankfurt am Main: Vittorio Klostermann.
Manow, P. (2010). *In the king's shadow*. Cambridge: Polity Press.
Marcus, G. E., Neuman, W. R., & MacKuen, M. (2000). *Affective intelligence and political judgment*. Chicago: University of Chicago Press.
Marcuse, H. (1979). *The Aesthetic Dmension. Toward a Critique of Marxist Aesthetics*. Houndsmill: Macmillan.
Marres, N., Guggenheim, M., & Wilkie, A. (Eds.). (2018). *Inventing the Social*. Manchester: Mattering Press.
Mayntz, R. (1998). New Challenges to Governance Theory. *European University Institute, Jean Monnet Chair Paper RSC, No. 98/50*.
McLuhan, M., & Fiore, Q. (1967). *The medium is the message. A inventory of effects*. Toronto: Bantam books.
Merleau-Ponty, M. (2013 [1945]). *Phenomenology of perception*. London: Routledge.

Mitchell, T. (1991). The limits of the state: beyond statist approaches and their critics. *The American political science review, 85*(1), 77–96.

Mol, A. (2002). *The body multiple: Ontology in medical practice*. Durham: Duke University Press.

Mondada, L., Keel, S., Svensson, H., & van Schepen, N. (2016). Referring to grace, performing grace. In B. Latour & C. Leclercq (Eds.), *Reset modernity! Catalogue for exhibition at ZKM (Center for Art and Media), Karlsruhe* (pp. 395–403). Cambridge, MA: MIT Press.

Nail, T. (2017). What is an Assemblage? *SubStance, 46*(1), 21–37.

Nash, K. (2001). The 'Cultural Turn' in Social Theory: Towards a Theory of Cultural Politics. *Sociology, 35*(1), 77–92.

Nash, K. (2010). *Contemporary political sociology: globalization, politics, and power.* Chichester: Wiley-Blackwell.

Neuman, W. L. (2005). *Power, State, and Society: An Introduction to Political Sociology.* Long Grove: Waveland.

Nicholson, H. (2015). Affective Geographies of the Ballot Box. *Contemporary Theatre Review, 25*(2), 230–241.

Nicolini, D. (2012). *Practice theory, work, and organization: An introduction*. Oxford: Oxford university press.

Nossel, S. (2016). Introduction: On" Artivism," or Art's Utility in Activism. *Social Research: An International Quarterly, 83*(1), 103–105.

Nussbaum, M. C. (2013). *Political emotions. Why love matters for justice*. Cambridge, MA: Harvard University Press.

Penz, O., & Sauer, B. (2019). *Governing affects: neoliberalism, neo-bureaucracies, and service work*. London: Routledge.

Phillips, J. (2006). Agencement/assemblage. *Theory, Culture & Society, 23*(2–3), 108–109.

Pickering, A. (1994). After representation: science studies in the performative idiom. In P. o. S. Association (Ed.), *Proceedings of the Biennial Meeting of the of the Philosophy of Science Association* (pp. 413–419). Chicago: University of Chicago Press.

Pickering, A. (Ed.) (1992). *Science as practice and culture*. Chicago: University of Chicago Press.

Pierre, J., & Peters, B. G. (2000). *Governance, Politics and the State*. Houndsmills: MacMillan.

Pink, S. (2009). *Doing sensory ethnography*. London: Sage.

Plant, S. (2002). *The most radical gesture: The Situationist International in a postmodern age*. London: Routledge.

Prinz, S. (2014). *Die Praxis des Sehens. Über das Zusammenspiel von Körpern, Artefakten und visueller Ordnung*. Bielefeld: transcript.

Rancière, J. (2010). *Dissensus: On politics and aesthetics*. London: Bloomsbury.

Rancière, J. (2015). *Dissensus: On politics and aesthetics*. London: Bloomsbury.

Rancière, J., Panagia, D., & Bowlby, R. (2001). Ten theses on politics. *Theory & Event*, 5(3).

Rebentisch, J. (2012). *Die Kunst der Freiheit: Zur Dialektik demokratischer Existenz*. Berlin: Suhrkamp.

Reckwitz, A. (2002). Toward a Theory of Social Practices A development in culturalist theorizing. *European Journal of Social Theory*, 5(2), 243–263.

Reckwitz, A. (2004). Die Reproduktion und die Subversion sozialer Praktiken. Zugleich ein Kommentar zu Pierre Bourdieu und Judith Butler. In K. H. Hörning & J. Reuter (Eds.), *Doing culture: neue Positionen zum Verhältnis von Kultur und sozialer Praxis* (pp. 40–54). Bielefeld: transcript.

Reckwitz, A. (2008). Praktiken und Diskurse: Eine sozialtheoretische und methodologische Relation. In H. Kalthoff, S. Hirschauer, & G. Lindemann (Eds.), *Theoretische Empirie. Zur Relevanz qualitativer Forschung* (pp. 188–209). Frankfurt am Main: Suhrkamp.

Reckwitz, A. (2010). Auf dem Weg zu einer kultursoziologischen Analytik zwischen Praxeologie und Poststrukturalismus. In M. Wohlrab-Saar (Ed.), *Kultursoziologie* (pp. 179–205). Wiesbaden: SpringerVS.

Reckwitz, A. (2012). Affective spaces: A praxeological outlook. *Rethinking history*, 16(2), 241–258.

Reckwitz, A. (2015). Ästhetik und Gesellschaft – ein analytischer Bezugsrahmen. In A. Reckwitz, S. Prinz, & H. Schäfer (Eds.), *Ästhetik und Gesellschaft. Grundlagentexte aus Soziologie und Kulturwissenschaften* (pp. 13–52). Berlin: Suhrkamp.

Reckwitz, A. (2016). How the senses organize the social. In M. Jonas & B. Littig (Eds.), *Praxeological Political Analysis* (pp. 56–66). London: Routledge.

Reckwitz, A. (2017). Practices and their affects. In A. Hui, T. Schatzki, & E. Shove (Eds.), *The Nexus of Practices. Connections, Constellations, Practitioners* (pp. 114–125). London: Routledge.

Rhodes, R. A. W. (1996). The New Governance: Governing without Government. *Political Studies Association*, 1996(XLIV), 652–667.

Rieff, P. (1953). Aesthetic functions in modern politics. *World politics*, 5(4), 478–502.

Rigamonti, N. (2022). *In(ter)ventive Demokratie? Experimentelle Zukunftsszenarien der europäischen 'Flüchtlingsfrage'*. PhD Dissertation. Berlin: Technische Universität Berlin.

Roberts, J. (1990). *Postmodernism, politics and art*. Manchester: Manchester University Press.

Rockhill, G. (2014). *Radical History and the Politics of Art*. New York: Columbia University Press.

Rosenau, J. N., & Czempiel, E. O. (1992). *Governance without government: order and change in world politics*. Cambridge: Cambridge University Press.

Rosenau, P. M. (1991). *Post-modernism and the social sciences*. Princeton: Princeton University Press.

Ryan, M. (1989). Post-Modern Politics. In M. Ryan (Ed.), *Politics and Culture* (pp. 82–97). Basingstoke: Palgrave.

Sartwell, C. (2011). *Political aesthetics*. Ithaca: Cornell University Press.

Saward, M. (2006). The representative claim. *Contemporary Political Theory, 5*(3), 297–318.

Schäfer, H. (2016). Praxis als Wiederholung. Das Denken der Iterabilität und seine Konsequenzen für die Methodologie peaxeologischer Forschung. In H. Schäfer (Ed.), *Praxistheorie: Ein soziologisches Forschungsprogramm* (pp. 137–161). Bielfeld: transcript.

Schatzki, T. R. (2015). The Spaces of Practices and Large Social Phenomena. *Espaces-temps. net*.

Schatzki, T. R., Knorr-Cetina, K., & Von Savigny, E. (2001). *The practice turn in contemporary theory*. London: Routledge.

Scheffer, T. (2021). Apparate/Apparaturen. Macht und Herrschaft angesichts der Bearbeitung existentieller Probleme. In P. Gostmann & P.-U. Merz-Benz (Eds.), *Macht und Herrschaft. Zur Revision zweier soziologischer Grundbegriffe* (pp. 363–394). Wiesbaden: Springer VS.

Schulte-Römer, N., Bleicher, A., & Groß, M. (2017). *Energy Days 2017 Can you feel the energy? The'Sensory Governance'of energy technologies and systems. Workshop Documentation*. Leipzig: UFZ.

Schwarz, O. (2013). Bending forward, one step backward: On the sociology of tasting techniques. *Cultural Sociology, 7*(4), 415–430.

Shapin, S. (1984). Pump and circumstance: Robert Boyle's literary technology. *Social Studies of Science, 14*(4), 481–520.

Shove, E., Pantzar, M., & Watson, M. (2012). *Dynamics of social practice. Everyday life and how it changes*. London: Sage.

Simmel, G. (1992 [1908/1907]). Exkurs über die Soziologie der Sinne. In S. Georg (Ed.), *Soziologie. Untersuchungen über die Formen der Vergesellschaftung, Gesamtausgabe Bd. 2* (pp. 722–742).

Spence, C., & Gallace, A. (2011). Multisensory design: Reaching out to touch the consumer. *Psychology & Marketing, 28*(3), 267–308.

Stange, R., Rummel, M., & Waldvogel, F. (Eds.). (2018). *Haltung als Handlung – Das Zentrum für Politische Schönheit*. Munich: Edition Metzen.

Steinmetz, G. (1999). *State/culture: State-formation after the cultural turn*. Ithaca, NY: Cornell University Press.

Stoehrel, R. F. (2017). The regime's worst nightmare: the mobilization of citizen democracy. A study of Podemos'(aesthetic) populism and the production of affect in political discourse. *Cultural Studies, 31*(4), 543–579.

Stoller, P. (1989). *The taste of ethnographic things: the senses in anthropology*: University of Pennsylvania Press.

Surmann, F. (2015). *Ästhetische In(ter)ventionen im öffentlichen Raum: Grundzüge einer politischen Ästhetik*. Paderborn: Wilhelm Fink.

Synnott, A. (1993). *The body social. Symbolism, self and society*. London: Routledge.

Teil, G., & Hennion, A. (2004). Discovering quality or performing taste? A sociology of the amateur. In M. Harvey, A. McMeekin, & A. Warde (Eds.), *Qualities of food*. (pp. 19–37). Manchester: Manchester University Press.

Thévenot, L. (2014). Engaging in the politics of participative art in practice. In T. Zembylas (Ed.), *Artistic practices. Social interactions and cultural dynamics* (pp. 132–150). London: Rouledge.

Thrift, N., & Amin, A. (2013). *Arts of the Political. New Openings for the Left*. Durham: Duke University Press.

Vannini, P., Waskul, D., & Gottschalk, S. (2012). *The senses in self, society, and culture: a sociology of the senses*. New York: Routledge.

Venn, C. (2006). A note on assemblage. *Theory, Culture & Society*, 23(2–3), 107–108.

Voß, J.-P., & Guggenheim, M. (2019). Making taste public: Industrialized orders of sensing and the democratic potential of experimental eating. *Politics and Governance*, 7(4), 224–236.

Weber, M. (1992 [1919]). *Politik als Beruf. Zweiter Vortrag in der Reihe „Geistige Arbeit als Beruf" gehalten am 28. Januar 1919 vor dem „Freistudentischen Bund. Landesverband Bayern" in der Münchner Buchhandlung Steinicke*. Stuttgart: Reclam.

Weibel, P. (2015). People, politics, and power. In P. Weibel (Ed.), *Global activism. Art and Conflict in the 21st Century* (pp. 29–61). Karlsruhe: ZKM.

Aesthetic governance – and reflexive engagements with it

Re-designing the Sensory Order
Forms, Practices, and Perception

Sophia Prinz

1. INTRODUCTION

In 1963, the Italo-Brazilian designer and architect Lina Bo Bardi introduced her exhibition "Nordeste," the inaugural show at the Museu de Arte Popular (MAP) in Salvador da Bahia, with the following words:

> This exhibition is an accusation. An accusation of a world that does not want to renounce its human condition in spite of forgetfulness and indifference. It is not a humble accusation, and counterpoints a desperate effort of culture to the degrading conditions imposed by men. (Bo Bardi, 1995, p. 5)

Contrary to what one might expect after such an explicitly political announcement, there were no photographs, texts, or other documentary material on view that gave any literal depiction of the social misery of the region. The exhibition consisted solely of ordinary, everyday objects that Bo Bardi had arranged into a modernist display. But how can an exhibition be an "accusation" if it shows us nothing but things?

Starting from this example, I hope to address the following more general questions: What constitutes the social impact of design and to what extent is the political linked to questions of form? What becomes perceivable through the re-arrangement of existing things that would otherwise have remained invisible? And why is it important to think about design when it comes to social inequality under postcolonial conditions?

To answer these questions, I want to spell out the fundamental relationship between the order of the social and the sensory order of forms in the first part of my paper. For this, I turn to practice theory, following mainly Michel Foucault and Maurice Merleau-Ponty.

My guiding thesis is that the subject acquires not only an implicit practical knowledge but also an implicit *perceptual* knowledge through her repeated bodily interaction with the socio-material surroundings. This bodily interaction—and this is my second thesis—is mediated by the intermingling sensorial and formal qualities or "interface" of the socio-material world, which is to say, its outlines, colors, surfaces, smells, noises, rhythms, constellations, and so on.

As art historians and design theorists have shown in the past, these different formal qualities don't dissolve into an amorphous sensory tangle but assemble into something like a historically and culturally specific pattern or "topology of forms." This topology of forms correlates and interacts with the other elements of the respective governmental dispositive, i.e. with the regularities of discourse, the power relations as well as the technologies of the self. Consequently, forms can't be considered to be neutral; they are always part of social practices and therefore imply cultural valuations, hierarchies, and exclusions.

Against this theoretical framework, I will analyze the general entanglement of power, form, and sensory order more thoroughly using the example of Lina Bo Bardi's "design from below." It will turn out that any design that claims to be critical can't do without an aesthetic. With the term "aesthetic" I neither take up Jacques Rancière's definition of the "aesthetic" as the historically and culturally specific "regime" of Western modern art (Rancière, 2004), nor do I follow Pierre Bourdieu in his assertion that the aesthetic experience is simply a bourgeois invention that aims at social distinction (Bourdieu, 1984).

In my point of view, the aesthetic should be thought of both *more generally* and *more specifically*: it should be thought of as a thoroughly relational practice that explicitly positions itself in dialogue with the prevailing sensory order—and not just in whichever way. As we could say with Adorno, the aesthetic reflects the existing sensory order precisely in the medium in which the sensory order normally reproduces itself—which is to say, in the medium of form. Or to put it another way, what distinguishes aesthetic practices from other modes of critique or reflection is precisely its ability to challenge the sensory order of a dispositive by a re-constellation of its formal elements.

Such an aesthetic intervention is not a privilege of the arts, in the way it has been defined in the West since the Enlightenment. Aesthetic questioning, deconstruction or reordering can take place in all areas of design—including in everyday practices.

2. PRACTICES AND PERCEPTION

One of the central insights of sociological practice theory is that social order is produced neither by anonymous structures nor by a subjective understanding of meaning. Rather, it is reproduced by bodily practices that are conducted mostly unconsciously (Knorr-Cetina, Savigny, & Schatzki, 2001; Reckwitz, 2002; Schäfer, 2016). These bodily practices are guided by a collectively shared, implicit bodily or practical knowledge that the subject performs through repeated and regular interaction with the surrounding social and material environment. However, this is not a uniform conditioning. The implicit practical knowledge is rather to be seen as a type of flexibly applied program or "generative principle" (Bourdieu, 1984, p. 170) that guides the current enactment of practice but doesn't fully determine it. Thus, in the performance of a practice, there can always occur random changes, mishaps, or incoherencies that require spontaneous improvisation or adaptation (Butler, 1990, 1995; Schäfer, 2013).

As for the question of the sensory order of the social and its potential aesthetic provocation by design, we need to clarify to what extent the faculty of perception must also be counted as practical knowledge[1] and what role the socio-material topology of forms plays in this.

First, it must be noted that the social agency of artifacts does not consist only in their material resistance, as actor-network theory and other materiality-centered approaches tend to claim but also in their formal aesthetic qualities: be it the strict rectangular shape of a school desk, the playful typography on a poster, the technical humming of a washing machine, the tactility of textiles, or the spatial constellations of a landscape. All these formal components are part of social practices and its reproduction. Yet how do these forms relate to the perceptual modes incorporated by the actor?

Pierre Bourdieu, one of the thinkers who has strongly influenced practice theory, has astonishingly little to say about this. Though he does speak steadily of "schemes of perception, thought, and action" (Bourdieu, 1990, p. 54) as he describes the functioning of the habitus, he gives no further elaboration of the concept of perception. In *Distinction*, he even tends towards a sociologistical stance, by claiming that the disinterested pleasure of the "pure gaze" (Bourdieu, 1984, p. 3) has nothing (or not primarily) to do with the characteristics of the artwork itself but with the incorporated cultural capital of the viewer, who has learned to distance herself from the necessities of everyday life.[2] Thus, in Bourdieu's view, the concrete practical interaction with the sensory order of the socio-material world does not play a central role in the development of one's perceptual faculties—it's rather the upbringing which shapes the disposition of taste. But also Bourdieu's sociological counterpart, Bruno Latour, is of little help here. Although Latour has laid emphasis on the social agency of things as no other sociologist has, his strict rejection of the subject-object dichotomy doesn't allow him to develop either a concept of the body or a concept of perception. Apart

---

1 For a broader overview of theoretical approaches dealing with the interrelation of sensuality and the social, see also (Prinz & Göbel, 2015).
2 In doing so, he not only falls short of his own claim to want to combine the "external" analysis of the social conditions of art production and reception with an "internal" analysis of the work of art (Bourdieu, 1996, p. 233). As Juliane Rebentisch emphasized, he also overlooks the fact that in the 1960s both art production and the theoretical definition of aesthetic autonomy were no longer based on the ideal of an aestheticism detached from the everyday world (Rebentisch, 2013, p. 167 ff.)

from the term "affordance" (Akrich & Latour, 1992, p. 259), which he adopted from psychologist James J. Gibson (1979, pp. 127–137)[3], the formal and aesthetic dimension of material culture remain quite underdetermined in ANT.[4]

In order to sketch out the interrelation between the "sensory order" of the socio-material forms and the modes of perceptual practices, I therefore take a different theoretical path, namely a re-reading of Michel Foucault's concept of dispositive through the lens of Maurice Merleau-Ponty's *Phenomenology of Perception*.

At first glance, this approach seems to be quite similar to Jacques Rancière's notion of the "distribution of the sensible," which can be interpreted as a further development of Foucault's theory of power (Rancière, 2004). But besides the general claim, that power relations always correlate with certain sensory orders, Rancière doesn't systematically spell out how this connection comes into being, let alone which role design and form processes play in it. Strangely enough, he also defines the aforementioned "distanced contemplation," which Pierre Bourdieu condemned as a bourgeois strategy of social distinction, as a political practice.[5]

In order to gain a more precise theoretical toolbox for analyzing the governmental "sensory order" of a time, I propose to expand Foucault's analysis of discursive formations to the topology of socio-material forms.

In his archaeology writings, Foucault famously distances himself from the classical philosophical assumption that the subject possesses an innate cognitive faculty. Instead, he locates the conditions of possibility of speech and thought in the empirical orders of the external "objective" world: In his view, the empirical formations of statements are what underlie thought, and not the other way round (Foucault, 1972). The cognitive faculty is thus dependent on a subject's empirical conditions of existence and, as a result, is historically and culturally specific.

This basic theoretical figure of inverting the conditional relation between the subject of knowledge and the outer world can also be transferred to the faculty of perception: The perceptible is thus not based on the a priori "forms of intuition" and the innate "power of imagination" (Kant), but also—and analogous to the think-

---

3   Before Latour took it up, the term "affordance" was already used by design theory (Norman, 1988).
4   Nonetheless, the Actor-Network Theory was taken up by some art sociologists to point out the sensory "interactivity" between artist, artwork, and viewer. Strangely enough, the aspect of form, which was of decisive importance for the art-historical debate at least in the 19th and early 20th centuries, was not taken up in this context, either.
5   To be fair, one has to admit that Rancière's argument is more precise: For him, contemplation becomes political when the worker, who isn't normally part of the world of art and aesthetics, lays down his hammer and begins to contemplate the beautiful view from the window. In this regard, contemplation is only political in relation to the social position of the agent and the situational context of practice (Rancière, 2009, p. 71).

able—on an empirical order: namely, the synesthetic "topology of forms."[6] However, in order to clarify the process of incorporation of outer forms into the perceiving body and the development of an implicit perceptual knowledge, Foucault's archaeological model has to be extended.

At this point, it's worth taking a closer look at the *Phenomenology of Perception* by his teacher Merleau-Ponty, from whom Foucault—in a gesture of a philosophical patricide—had sharply distanced himself. In contrast, however, it quickly becomes clear that Merleau-Ponty's writings contain some insights that Foucault and other practice theorists have partially taken up (Crossley, 1994, 2004; Prinz, 2017).

Following from Martin Heidegger's concept of Dasein, Merleau-Ponty already assumes a broadly decentralized subject model, according to which the formation of subjectivity cannot be conceived independently of its particular worldly context. For Merleau-Ponty, the active body plays a central role here, as the body is "towards the world" (Merleau-Ponty, 1962, p. XV) even before the subject has developed the capacity to think and act. More than that, it is only through its active engagement with the practical requirements of its environment that the body acquires a functioning "bodily schema" (Merleau-Ponty, 1962, p. 273) which enables it to orient itself in the world. Consequently, perception holds a primary function, because without identifying individual entities, movement patterns, and contexts, conscious reflection and action are left with no points of reference.

But these units are not present from the outset; rather, proceeding from gestalt psychology, Merleau-Ponty assumes that the body must actively synthesize the polymorphic noise of its environment into individual, meaningful configurations. For Merleau-Ponty, to perceive *something* means being able to perceive forms as such.

This sort of synthesis is necessarily linked to a process of abstraction: Identifying a form as a self-contained, practical unit implies, at the same time, excluding certain sensory information or views that could frustrate this impression of a coherent form. Every perception thus always implies a non-perception. All seeing is, at the same time, blind.

But not all subjects perceive in an equal manner in every place and at any time. The ability to distinguish meaningful forms from their backgrounds depends rather on which stimulus patterns the perceiving body is accustomed to dealing with. In other words, to see the gestalt is contingent upon the synesthetic demands of the world. Or as Merleau-Ponty himself put it: "The sensible gives back to me what I lent to it, but this is only what I took from it in the first place" (Merleau-Ponty, 1962, p. 249).

---

6   Foucault's early texts on painting, which were written parallel to his concept of discourse, are especially helpful in discerning the initial approaches to such a theory on the historical conditions of the visible. (Prinz, 2014)

Even though sociological questions basically play a subordinate role for Merleau-Ponty, he nevertheless seems to adopt a theoretical perspective entirely in keeping with my initial intuition to transfer Foucault's concept of discourse to the topology of forms. And indeed, throughout his writings there are considerations that open up his theory of perception to the question of social practices.

Thus, he makes repeated reference to Marx's concept of praxis, according to which work is to be understood as a concrete "sensuous human activity, practice" (Marx, 1964, p. 421) that creates the social conditions under which man lives. And in the *Phenomenology of Perception* he observes that the subject does not develop an individual facility for perception, but necessarily takes over a cultural "tradition of perception" (Merleau-Ponty, 1962, p. 279) on the basis of his social being "towards the world."

Merleau-Ponty himself names at least three "objective" media of the empirical world through which this tradition of perception is passed on: first, through the bodily movements, performances, and choreographies of the other subjects; second, through "spoken" or conventionalized language; and third—and this is of particular interest for the question of design—through the "silent" world of artifacts. With this in mind, Merleau-Ponty's *Marxism and Philosophy*, states:

> The spirit of a society is realized, transmitted, and perceived through the cultural objects which it bestows upon itself and in the midst of which it lives. It is there that the deposit of its practical categories is built up, and these categories in turn suggest a way of being and thinking to men. (Merleau-Ponty, 1964b, p. 131).

Not only does this mean that the things, technologies, and pictures a society uses can be regarded as a concrete manifestation of a historically specific being "towards the world", but also that they demand a certain perceptive attitude, bodily interaction and practical usage. The synesthetic "affordances" of the socio-material forms thus function as a medium for the reproduction of a collectively shared perceptual knowledge. Or to express it once again in a Foucauldian way, the "topology" of socio-material forms constitutes the historical conditions of the perceptible of a particular time.

Before turning to the example of Lina Bo Bardi, I would like to add some general thoughts on both the term "form" and the term "topology" and how they are used in this context.

3. TOPOLOGY OF FORMS

The concept of "form" and questions of formal aesthetics have a long history in philosophy and art history, but have rarely been discussed in sociology or cultural studies. The reason for this lies not only in the anti-aesthetical and anti-sensual bias of sociology (Reckwitz, 2015) but also in the traditional understanding of form as being opposed to questions of materiality, content, and society.[7] The introduction of the concept of form into the practice-theoretical debate on perception, sensuality, and aesthetics thus also aims to break down these long-established dichotomies. The social order of practices, according to the thesis pursued here, is also reproduced and stabilized through the sensory order of socio-material forms.[8]

As already suggested above, this sensory order of forms can be described as a topology. Drawing on Michel Foucault's concept of the discourse, the term "topology" here means an arrangement of formal elements that exhibit a certain regularity both in their distribution and in their relationship to each other. This regularity is not to be understood as a quasi-metaphysical structure underlying all perceptions and sensory practices. Following Foucault's definition of the cultural archive as a "general system of the formation and transformation of statements" (Foucault, 1972, p. 130), the topology of forms can rather be described as a dynamic "interpositivity" or constellation of heterogeneous elements that constantly (re-)assemble into historically specific patterns and formations on the surfaces of the empirical world.

In this context the term "form" does not simply mean the positively determinable shape of an individual picture, object, or body. Following Merleau-Ponty's late immanence ontological reflections (Merleau-Ponty, 1968) or Derrida's concept of "trace" (Derrida, 1976)[9], becoming form is rather understood here as a fundamental process of differentiation, organization, and ordering through which the socio-material world appears to be perceptually, practically, and intellectually accessible in the

---

[7] The New Art History, which is very much influenced by Cultural Studies, has therefore largely ignored the concept of form, since pure formalist analyses were per se suspected of failing to take into account the necessarily social and political dimension of art. An important exception are the works of the Marxist art historian T.J. Clark (Clark, 1999).

[8] This intuition is in some ways similar to Henri Focillon's vitalist approach to the *Life of Forms in Art* (1948) and its further development by George Kubler in *The Shape of Time*: "History of things is intended to reunite ideas and objects under the rubric of visual forms … From all these things a shape of time emerges. A visible portrait of the collective identity, whether tribe, class, or nation, comes into being." (1962, p. 9) Unlike Kubler, however, I do not assume anthropologically constant processes of becoming and passing away of form, nor would I draw conclusions from a topology of forms to a "collective identity." In literary studies, too, the concept of form has recently been reformulated in terms of a more comprehensive concept that also includes social arrangements (Levine, 2015).

[9] Similar to Merleau-Ponty's late reflection on the self-differentiation of the "flesh of the world" (Merleau-Ponty, 1968), Derrida's concept of the "originary trace" assumes that appearance and meaning can only come into being by establishing a differential order: "It is not the question of a constituted difference here, but rather, before all determination of the content, of the *pure* movement which produces difference. *The (pure) trace is difference.* It does not depend on any sensible plentitude, audible or visible, phonic or graphic. It is, on the contrary, the condition of such a plenitude."(Derrida, 1976, p. 62)

first place.[10] Or to take up the expression of Jacques Rancière, the setting of differential forms is a basic operation of the "distribution of the sensible."

The assumption that forms must be understood as fundamental modes of differentiation leads to another basic insight, namely that socio-material forms can never be analyzed in isolation. Rather, the dynamic interplay, i.e. the rhythms (Lefebvre, 2004), superimpositions, analogies, transitions, limitations, and resonances between the various formal elements must always be taken into account. This formal network of relationships crosses the usual theoretical classifications[11]: On the one hand, it transcends the established dichotomizations of subject/object, body/technology, nature/culture, or analogue/digital. That is, it comprises such diverse phenomena as bodily surfaces, digital interfaces, spatial demarcations, soundscapes, plant structures, landscapes, technical rhythms, writing, social choreographies, movement figures, and so on.[12] On the other hand, the "topology of forms" is not limited by any social or cultural boundary—be it between social classes, milieus or fields or between epochs, nations, or "cultural areas". Even if the formal characteristics of historically specific practice complexes can be analytically distinguished, a "migration of form" (Buergel & Prinz, 2023) always takes place between spatially, temporally, and socio-culturally disparate dispositives.[13] In this sense, the form-finding in design not only gives shape to a single object or image but is necessarily part of a broader orchestration of entangled socio-material forms. Or as Keller Easterling put it in her recent book on design: "Forms orchestrate an interplay between forms" (Easterling, 2021, p. 38).

Thirdly, it can be assumed that materiality does not simply take a passive role vis-à-vis the "active" form, as it has been claimed following Aristotelian hylomorphism, but is involved both directly and indirectly in the process of form making.[14] In particular, the development and processing of new industrial materials such as cotton,

---

10   In this respect, there is also a conceptual overlap with George Spencer Brown's *Laws of Form* (1969), which have been adopted by systems theory. For an application of the systems theoretical concept of form to design, see the works of Sandra Groll 2021.

11   George Kubler also stated that the concept of form makes the distinction between art and non-art superfluous: "The term [visual form, S.P.] includes both artifacts and works of art, both replicas and unique examples, both tools and expressions—in short all materials worked by human hands under the guidance of connected ideas developed in temporal sequence" (Kubler, 1962, p. 9).

12   On the latter, see, for example, Hanna Göbel's forthcoming work on disability, the body, and forms of movement.

13   Global art history in particular has dealt with these transculturalization processes in recent decades.

14   Such a perspective on the activity of the material was especially developed by the Bergsonians Henri Focillion and Gilbert Simondon (Focillon, 1948; Simondon, 2017). The theorists of New Materialism also emphasize the inherent dynamics of non-human materiality but have not yet worked with the concept of form.

steel, or rubber has shown that inherent to materials is not only a certain potential for practical functionalization but also a spectrum of design (im)possibilities and sensory qualities that can introduce new differences and relations into the socio-material topology of forms. The reproduction of forms is thus not solely dependent on human practices, let alone a cultural "will-to-form" (Riegl), but also on the activity and logic of the materials brought into use.

Finally, with reference to Bruno Latour's Actor-Network Theory, it must be taken into account that the sourcing and processing of material is always embedded in larger socio-cultural, economic, and ecological networks, which in turn produce formal effects: Think, for example, of the massive extraction of raw material in the colonies and the power technologies associated with it, the emergence of the chemical industry, which invents new materials, each with its own design possibilities, the exponential expansion of global maritime trade and communication technologies, the rationalization and mechanization of production in the factories as well as the uniformity and sheer abundance of industrially produced goods—all these processes contributed to a literal transformation of modern lifeworlds.

In summary, all dispositives are characterized by a specific differential topology of socio-material forms. This topology does not exist independently but is always interwoven with the other orders of a governmental dispositive. Together they form the historically specific conditions of existence on the basis of which all socio-material practices, and that means also design practices, are carried out. And just as the discursive formation or the technologies of power are not fixed once and for all, the topology of forms is not to be understood as a rigid pattern. Rather, it depends on repeated practices and processes of form-giving, which always hold the potential to change—be it through decay and destruction, through mistakes and mishaps, or through deliberate de- and transformations. But all these changes and transformations do not take place in a vacuum, nor can they simply disregard the topology of the forms as their generative basis.

In this sense, one could say that the existing topology of forms does not fully determine either the modes of perception or the processes of forming but is rather to be understood as a field of formal possibilities that makes some perceptual experiences, formal compositions, and design practices more likely to occur than others.[15] Even more, the formal topologies of various dispositives can differ precisely in whether and to what extent they allow or even provoke certain processes of transformation (as in the case of the creative economy).[16]

---

15   According to Foucault, governmental power is exercised indirectly insofar as it merely structures the field of possible actions (Foucault, 1982).
16   In this sense, Annemarie Mol and John Law's differentiation of social topologies into regions, networks, and fluids could also be examined in terms of questions of form (Mol & Law, 1994).

This sensory "government" by socio-material forms[17]—be it rather rigid or dynamic—is usually not explicitly reflected in everyday perceptions and practices, but rather can be challenged by an aesthetic constellation of forms that deviate from the sensory order of the dispositive.

4. LINA BO BARDI'S ETHNOGRAPHY OF FORMS

Equipped with this theoretical toolbox, I now come back to the initial question of the aesthetics of critical design by taking Lina Bo Bardi's transcultural design from below as an example. Bo Bardi's work is of particular interest in this context as she herself explicitly refers to a practice-theoretical approach, namely the humanist Marxism of Antonio Gramsci, whose ideas were very influential on the Italian intellectual scene of the post-war period. In order to better understand how and in which respect Bo Bardi's design can be interpreted as an aesthetic challenge in the above-meant sense, some details about her biography and intellectual background are crucial. Only on this basis does it become clear how Bo Bardi used her specific "perceptual knowledge"—which she acquired in (post-)war Italy—to push the boundaries of the modernistic "topology of forms" and the sensory order of the Brazilian governmentality of the 1950s.[18]

Two years after the Second World War, Lina Bo Bardi (1914–1992), newly trained in architecture and design, emigrated from Italy to Brazil with her husband, the architecture critic Pietro Maria Bardi. During her studies in Rome, Bo Bardi witnessed not only the rise and fall of the fascist regime, but also the attempts of left-wing intellectuals, architects, and artists to establish, out of the country's ruins and broken political promises, new prospects for a modern Italy. These attempts to articulate a post-fascist vision included debates on modern architecture that went well beyond reciting the myths of rationalist planning.

Edoardo Persico and Giuseppe Pagano, for example, had renounced the megalomaniacal formalism of the fascist party already in the 1930s, proposing instead to take the vernacular architecture of the Italian countryside as a model for a new, people-oriented modernism (Marcello, 2003; Sabatino, 2009). Also, the architect Bruno Zevi, who returned to Italy from exile in the United States after the war, advocated a similar vision: inspired by Frank Lloyd Wright's "organic architecture," Zevi placed

---

17   As Jan-Peter Voß and Michael Guggenheim have recently pointed out, even the way we taste food is governed (Voß & Guggenheim, 2019).
18   This portrayal relies primarily on the works of Zeuler Lima and Silvana Rubino, both of whom have been researching Lina Bo Bardi for many years and helped me to understand the specificities of her work (Lima, 2013; Rubino, 2002).

the interaction between people and their social and natural environment at the center of his architectural theory. Modern architecture should thus fit "organically" into its respective lifeworld and not prescribe certain forms of life (Zevi, 1950).

The debate over architectural theory was flanked by Antonio Gramsci's writings on subalternity, folk art, and modernity, which were widely read in Italy's post-war intellectual circles. Before Gramsci, as chairman of the Communist Party, was arrested and imprisoned by Mussolini in 1926, he had spoken up for the political and social empowerment of southern Italy, which had been subject to exploitation by the hegemonic north. He had criticized, among other things, how the centrally controlled fascist modernization programs overrode local practices and traditions; instead, he advocated for incorporating the knowledge and creative resources of the southern rural population into its political, economic, and cultural restructuring processes (Gramsci, 1985).

Like Merleau-Ponty, Gramsci also referred to Marx's early concept of praxis in order to describe the implicit knowledge reflected in physical labor and cultural products of a time. In this sense, southern Italian folk art, for example, was not simply out of date, as claimed by the apologists of modernism, but has to be understood as a medium for the subaltern "conception of the world" (Gramsci, 1985, p. 189).[19]

When Lina Bo Bardi traveled to her new home of Brazil in the 1950s, she encountered a similar socio-structural problem there: the metropolitan areas of São Paulo and Rio in the south of the country, which were economically and culturally supported by a white European elite, stood in stark contrast to the poor, economically exploited northeast, which was still strongly marked by the feudal systems of colonialism and by the transatlantic slave trade. And much like in post-war Italy, a group of intellectuals, artists, musicians, and theater-makers had come together in Bahia to protest against the planned top-down modernization of the region. In their films, plays, and songs, however, they rather made an effort to pay due respect to local Afro-Brazilian traditions. Paulo Freire's *Pedagogy of the Oppressed* (Freire, 1970) can be considered a central intellectual reference of this movement: like Gramsci's

---

19 In this sense he writes: "Folklore should instead be studied as a 'conception of the world and life' implicit to a large extent ... and in opposition ... to 'official' conceptions of the world ... This conception of the world is not elaborated and systematic because, by definition, the people (the sum total of the instrumental and subaltern classes of every form of society that has so far existed) cannot possess conceptions which are elaborated, systematic and politically organized and centralized in their albeit contradictory development. It is, rather, many-sided [...] if, indeed, one should not speak of a confused agglomerate of fragments of all the conceptions of the world and of life that have succeeded one another in history. In fact, it is only in folklore that one finds surviving evidence, adulterated and mutilated, of the majority of these conceptions" (Gramsci, 1985, p. 189).

model for education, it argued for strengthening subaltern knowledge and the self-emancipation of the poor.

Thus, when the governor of Bahia invited Bo Bardi to set up a museum of modern art in Salvador in 1959, she refused to base it on traditional European ideas of art and aesthetics, especially when it comes to the hierarchizing distinction between fine art and decorative art, modern and pre-modern modes of production, or Western and non-Western cultural forms.

Instead, she decided to build a cultural center that would include a museum of folk art as well as workshops and training rooms where aspiring designers could learn directly from local producers. The aim was neither to romanticize the subaltern material culture, as Bo Bardi accused the elitist "Charity Ladies" of doing (Bo Bardi, 1995, p. 3), nor to preserve it in its present state, as is still common in Western museums. On the contrary, she had no illusions about the humble quality of Afro-Brazilian folk art, which was mainly composed of materials that industrial society had spat out as waste: burnt-out light bulbs, tin cans, scraps of fabric, and old newspapers. According to Bo Bardi, these "objects of desperate survival" stood on the "edge of nothingness" (Bo Bardi, 1995, pp. 3,4) yet it was precisely for this reason that they were a testament to people's unrelenting will to shape their own lives.

Along those lines, Bo Bardi's museum project was clearly future-oriented: Her aim was to support the local producers in developing a distinct Afro-Brazilian design language that did not simply adopt the ideology and social models of European functionalism, as it had happened in Brasilia in Bo Bardi's view. In contrast, the modern Afro-Brazilian design had to be developed out of existing everyday practices. It must, as Bo Bardi herself put it, take into account "how one sees, moves around, stands on the ground."[20]

Accordingly, Bo Bardi, together with fellow scientists and artists from the region, undertook extensive research trips to the arid inland areas of Bahia and Pernambuco in order to systematically collect and document the entire material culture of the region. This fundamental inventory-taking included items such as ex-votos carved out of wood, everyday household objects, material textures, and architectural elements. She documented her journey with hundreds of photographs, unedited and unpublished to this day, tucked in a row of cardboard boxes at the Instituto Pietro e Lina Bo Bardi in São Paulo.

Despite her political emphasis and occasional talk of the innate "creative energy" of ordinary people, Bo Bardi adopted a rather sober research stance. Instead of starting with individuals as the central entities of productivity and meaning, as anthropologists of that time would generally do, Bo Bardi's extensive photo archive re-

---

20   With this approach, she anticipated many basic principles of critical design, which only became established in the USA and Europe in the 1970s. See for example Viktor Papanek's work (Papanek, 1972).

veals that she was mainly interested in the formal aesthetic order of the Afro-Brazilian material culture. Of course, this formalist perspective on socio-material living conditions did not come out of nowhere. As a direct comparison reveals, Bo Bardi adopted her photographic style more or less directly from Giuseppe Pagano, who had conducted an extensive photographic documentation of Italian rural architecture, which was shown in his exhibition "Continuity and Modernity" at the Milan Triennale in 1936. Similar to Bo Bardi's visual ethnography some 20 years later, Pagano's photographs emphasize the efficiency and functionality of architecture rather than its picturesque or romantic aspects.

Thus, you could say that Bo Bardi transferred not only Antonio Gramsci's concept of the subaltern to the Brazilian context, but also a modernist "tradition of perception" (Merleau-Ponty) that she had acquired in Italy during her education years. Because of this specific perceptual knowledge, Bo Bardi seemed to be particularly interested in the formal patterns and regularities that arise unconsciously at the surface of material culture, that is, without any explicitly formulated design intent. And it is precisely in this unintended order, she argues, that the possibility to transform folk art into modern industrial design lies. In 1957, with this in mind, she wrote: "Serial production, which must now be taken into account as a basis of modern architecture, exists in nature itself, and intuitively, in 'popular work'" (Bo Bardi, 2014, p. 95).

Although this may not be how she herself would phrase it, Lina Bo Bardi thus seems to be interested in an interrelationship similar to the one formulated above: namely, the interrelation between the sensory order of socio-material forms on the one hand and its (re-)production or, rather, possible transformation through (unconsciously conducted) practices of design. Thus, the Afro-Brazilian topology of forms can also be interpreted as a manifestation of a collectively shared, implicit practical and perceptual knowledge.

As I will argue in the next section, such an analysis of the socio-material topology of forms is a precondition of any critical design. Only when it works its way through the practices and perceptual habits of a time can it find aesthetic forms that help to reflect and perhaps modify these very habits. Lina Bo Bardi's approach is therefore not only relevant to the historically, culturally, and politically specific circumstances of the Brazilian governmentality of the 1950s; it is also regarded here as exemplary for the inevitable aesthetic quality of critical design itself.

5. CRITICAL DESIGN AND AESTHETICS

The question of whether and how the aesthetic is related to the social and political is one of the fundamental problems of philosophical aesthetics. It should thus be clear that a comprehensive reiteration of the problem field cannot be done here. Instead,

I'll confine myself to formulating some basic thoughts on the critical potential of the aesthetic from a practice-theory perspective on perception.

My approach differs from three common sociological concepts of "aesthetics": firstly, it goes beyond Pierre Bourdieu's understanding of taste. For Bourdieu, the "detached" or "disinterested" gaze that abstracts from the economic and social constraints of everyday life in order to contemplate the formal aesthetic qualities of an artwork has little to do with its actual sensory nature. Instead, it has to be interpreted as a bourgeois attitude or projection that serves the sole purpose of distinction from the lower classes, whose content-based judgments of taste are regarded as illegitimate (Bourdieu, 1984). Because of this fundamental sociological critique of aesthetic formalism, Bourdieu generally tends to neglect both the concrete act of perception and the question of form as an independent medium of the social.[21]

In the course of the cross-disciplinary Material and Practice Turn, some ethnographic analyses of artworks and artistic practices have at least partially filled this theoretical gap. However, a much broader concept of aesthetics has been applied: Following Science and Technology Studies (especially Michel Callon, Bruno Latour, John Law and Madeleine Akrich's Actor-Network Theory), phenomenology as well as pragmatism, the artwork has been reconceptualized as a social actor that stimulates inter-objective perceptions and practices due to its specific materiality and sensual "affordances" (Acord & DeNora, 2008; Born, 2010; Hennion, 2007; Schürkmann, 2017). In this context, aesthetic perception is certainly understood as a specific form of sensory practice, but not—as will be argued here—as an experience that can potentially help to see through collective shared perceptual schemata.[22]

A similarly broad concept of aesthetics can also be found in the more recent sociological debates about an all-encompassing "aestheticization" of lifeworlds in late modern society (Featherstone, 1991; Jameson, 1991; Reckwitz, 2017). Here, aesthetics is understood as a cultural and economic revaluation and intensification of self-referential, sensual experiences and affections, which manifests itself in an individualization of consumption, an increasing medialization of everyday life or the constant expansion of the creative economy. In the face of such a diagnosis, which weakens the critical potential of the artistic, I maintain that the aesthetic can make a differ-

---

21 As Juliane Rebentisch notes, he also misses the fact that both the production of art and the subsequent theoretical redefinition of aesthetic autonomy since the 1960s have long since ceased to be borne by the notion of an ahistorical "transcendental subject," let alone by the ideal of an world-away aestheticism, which is in any case more likely to be regarded as a philosophical misunderstanding (Rebentisch, 2013, p. 165ff.).

22 Although Antoine Hennion emphasizes that experiences of taste are associated with reflexivity, he means primarily the subject's ability to broaden her perceptual capacities through practices of tasting, and not a broader critical reflection on the historical conditions of the perceptible itself (Hennion, 2007).

ence towards the socially established sensory order of forms, even when the latter is committed to a creative imperative.

In order to gain a theoretical understanding of the connection between the sensory order of forms, the collective perceptual schemes, and aesthetic practice, I instead would like to take up some ideas from Theodor W. Adorno's *Aesthetic Theory* (1997). This theoretical move might seem a bit unusual, since critical theory has always been interpreted as an antithesis to phenomenology. But a closer look reveals that Adorno has much more in common with Foucault, Merleau-Ponty, and Rancière than initially thought.

As already described in greater detail, Merleau-Ponty assumes that the bodily subject learns to order the sensory impressions of its environment and to distinguish between form and background, the significant and the insignificant, due to its practical and active being towards the world. However, the perceptive faculty acquired through this is neither ahistorical nor individual. With reference to Foucault, it can be said that the perceptible also depends on the sensory order of empirical, socio-material forms. How and what we perceive is thus connected to our own particular conditions of existence.

However, this does not mean that each individual act of perception has already been mapped out. Depending on the actual social situation, different aspects of the field of perception can be pushed into the foreground or the background, attention can be diverted, or a view can be obstructed. New materials, techniques, and media can be added that require the bodily schema to adapt, or the body may change in such a way that it can no longer perceive as it used to. But these more or less incidental or objective changes within a practice context are not the issue here. What is more crucial regarding the question of the aesthetic is whether and to what extent the subject can influence the conditions of its own perception—in other words, is it in a position to actively engage in the re-ordering of forms?

An initial answer to this can be found in Merleau-Ponty's thoughts on modern painting. Just like the phenomenologist, the painter has to learn to move back behind his incorporated schemes of perception in order to reflect on the way perception functions. The medium of such reflection, however, is not text or language, as in the case of philosophy, but painterly practice, which makes the conditions of the visible itself contemplatable (Merleau-Ponty, 1964a).

Even if it is doubtful from a sociological perspective that such a "pure vision" beyond any cultural shaping can exist at all, Merleau-Ponty's intuition that artistic practice distances itself from an everyday perspective, in order to find aesthetic forms that reveal the underlying schemes of perception, can be made productive for a practice theory reflection on the aesthetic. However—and this would be the difference to Merleau-Ponty—this distinction must be thought of as strictly relational. Accordingly, aesthetic practice must be understood as a highly specific activity that distances itself from the prevailing schemes of perception in order to be able to reveal precisely how these very schemes function. Consequently, aesthetic practices always remain connected to the existing topology of form and thus also to the whole governmental dispositive.

To deepen this argument, Adorno's definition of "art's double character" (Adorno, 1997, p. 5) is also helpful here. Following Adorno, the artwork is both a *"fait social"* and autonomous. In contrast to sociological approaches to art, which locate the social aspect of art primarily in the social rules of art production and reception, Adorno is primarily concerned with the formal and material dimension of the work of art itself: "For everything that artworks contain with regard to form and materials, spirit and subject matter, has emigrated from reality into the artworks and in them has divested itself of its reality: Thus the artwork also becomes its afterimage" (Adorno, 1997, p. 103).

Art thus does not stand somewhere outside the governmental framework of the dispositives since it draws on the existing order of forms as its resource (and this, of course, includes the forms of the art field). In other words: During the artistic process, the producer makes use of her practical and perceptual knowledge as well as of the media and materials available to her. However—and this is the difference to pure commercial products or "art market art"—the aesthetic form does not (or not directly) contribute to the mere reproduction of this order. It instead recombines selected fragments and elements of the dispositive in such a way that other differential divisions of the sensory emerge and thus the historically specific entanglement of power-knowledge, self-technologies and the order of forms itself becomes intelligible: "Form [of the artwork, S.P.] works like a magnet that orders elements of the empirical world in such a fashion that they are estranged from their extra-aesthetic existence, and it is only as a result of this estrangement that they master the extra-aesthetic essence" (Adorno, 1997, p. 226).

The concept of the "constellative" plays a role here in two respects: On the one hand, the formal elements of the dispositive and their respective topologies are the very resource for artistic practice; on the other, the aesthetic can only emerge in a divergent constellation, that is, through the shifting or rearrangement of relations among the existing elements. The aesthetic form thus reacts not only to the individual formal elements of the dispositive as such but also to the way they relate to each other (and to the subject).

The aesthetic difference understood in this sense can explicitly turn critically against the practices, modes of subjectivation and mechanisms of exclusion that correlate with the sensory order—as was the case, for example, with the European avant-gardes. But it can also be designed for the continuous increase and perfection of a program of forms, as can be found, for example, in Chinese pottery or in three-star cooking.[23] In any case, the aesthetic examination, understood as a challenge to the existing sensory order, takes place in the medium of form itself.

In summary, it can be said that all aesthetic practices—whether performed in the art field or otherwise—have a social dimension insofar as they always work their way through the existing topology of forms and, thus, through collective schemes of perception, thought, and action.

Whether and to what extent the forms that emerge in aesthetic practices themselves have an effect on the collective schemes of perception, and are thus able to produce social difference, depends on the context in which they are received and who they are received from. Under certain circumstances, an aesthetic form cannot at all be recognized as such if it is shown incorrectly, if it is withdrawn from the circulation of forms, or if it deviates too far from the implicit perceptual knowledge of its would-be recipients. The aesthetic form thus needs to do both: to stimulate the implicit perceptual knowledge of the recipient and at the same time to introduce a qualitative difference that can no longer or cannot easily be grasped by this very knowledge.

Taking the change of the body schemes of war-disabled persons as an example, Merleau-Ponty shows that the failing of habitualized practices of perception can cause the subject to rework her incorporated "perceptual syntax" and consequently also her entire being "towards the world." Whether and to what extent individual aesthetic forms have similar far-reaching effects is questionable, but repeated interaction with them can undoubtedly help to develop a different perceptual practice. This other perceptual practice provoked by aesthetic forms is not exhausted in the mere irritation of the familiar. In fact, in everyday situations, we are confronted with a lot of puzzles and disruptions that demand some perceptual and practical adjustments. Art, on the other hand, can make the formal organization of social and historical contexts itself contemplatable by using the very medium of form: The irritation of the process of perception is thus not simply a break with the existing order—at the same time, it stimulates a reflexive attitude. Only this double experience of suspending the habitualized perception, on the one hand, and the implicit (i.e. not necessarily cognitively grasped) insight into the contingency of the socio-material order of forms, on the other, turns an experience into an aesthetic experience. From a practice theory perspective, the aesthetic form is thus doubly historically coded: both in its production and in its reception.

---

23   In *Art as Human Practice*, Georg W. Bertram emphasizes that aesthetic difference doesn't necessarily aim at a rejection of the existing but can also mean to confirm or preserve traditions (Bertram, 2019, p. 152).

6. THIS EXHIBITION IS AN ACCUSATION

With these considerations in mind, I'd now like to return to the question posed in the beginning: How can an exhibition be an accusation if it shows nothing but things?

As the title of Bo Bardi's exhibition "Nordeste" already reveals, it was an exhibition with a programmatic claim: one entirely in keeping with Gramsci's concept of the subaltern and the struggles of local cultural movements. Bo Bardi pursued the political goal of wrenching the cultural products of the northeast, which were taken for granted or even deemed worthless, out of their social invisibility and offering them an appropriate public platform. It was not her intention to prove a supposedly "authentic" or pre-modern "primitive" nature of Afro-Brazilian culture, as is the usual case in ethnological museums, for example. On the contrary, her aim was to highlight the modernity and innovative potential of local design practices.

She achieved this through an aesthetic operation in the sense defined here: namely by making the sensory order of the forms themselves the object of contemplation purely through the re-constellation of existing elements of the dispositive.

For the location of the Museu de Arte Popular, Bo Bardi chose Solar do Unhão, a vacant building complex directly at the sea. Due to its architecture and its history of use, it was a powerful example of colonial Salvador: built as a sugar works at the end of the 16th century, it served over the centuries as slave quarters, barracks, ammunition depot, and tobacco factory. With the exception of a large spiral staircase centrally placed in the main building, Bo Bardi refrained from major architectural interventions: The existing structures were cleared, with all superfluous and decayed elements removed, and the walls whitewashed. When redesigning the doors and window frames of the complex, Bo Bardi opted for a red paint to set them apart from the usual blue found in Portuguese colonial architecture.

The complex opened with the "Nordeste" exhibition in 1963. On the two light-flooded floors of the main building, Bo Bardi showed around one thousand everyday objects from the region that she had gathered on her research trips and from the collections of her friends. Although the objects must have seemed familiar to the visitors, who mainly consisted of the local population, here they appeared in a completely different light: Bo Bardi had staged them in such a way that it was not their poverty that stood in the foreground, but their practical functionality, formal aesthetic rationality, and implicit seriality. In doing so, she pursued two goals: first, to make the sensory order of forms transparent, as these form the basis of the collectively shared implicit practical and perceptual knowledge of the local population, and second, to emphasize that this implicit practical knowledge has an intrinsic creative potential that must be supported and activated for a "modernization from below." In other words, she was interested in nothing less than an aesthetic empowerment.

The argument had to function without any texts, since most local visitors were not able to read and write. Instead, the argument was performatively supported by the centrally located spiral staircase, built using a local construction technique. As the architect Aldo van Eyck noted during his visit, the staircase didn't just convey a sense of grandeur to those who ascended and descended it—it also put them in the spotlight: The socially and economically underprivileged people were given a stage on which they can be seen standing tall (Buergel, 2011, p. 56)

Bo Bardi's display thus represents an aesthetic practice insofar as it creates a distance from the familiar by using the existent socio-material forms: a distance that should contribute both to a change in the self-perception of the local population and to a greater appreciation of Afro-Brazilian culture by the cultural and political elite. However, before this experiment could bear fruit, the Museu de Arte Popular was closed shortly after the military coup of 1964, which was then followed by a twenty-year-long dictatorship.[24]

Nevertheless, the short-lived "Nordeste" exhibition should have made one thing clear: The political in design is always a question of aesthetics. And this for two reasons: firstly, all practices are necessarily linked to a collectively shared "sensory order." This means that the incorporated schemes of acting and thinking are inseparably intertwined with incorporated schemes of perception. Therefore, a critique of existing dispositives and power relations cannot help but take into account the historic specific conditions of the perceptible. Secondly, this collective sensory order is reproduced through the topology of forms—how and what becomes perceptible and what is excluded from the field of vision therefore depends on the regularity and distribution of formal elements. Critical design thus cannot escape its aesthetic responsibility: It must challenge the existing topology of forms and the corresponding sensory order and seek for new forms and aesthetic constellations that bear the potential to provoke a change of perception.

References

Acord, S. K., & de Nora, T. (2008). Culture and the Arts: From Art Worlds to Arts-in-Action. *The ANNALS of the American Academy of Political and Social Science*, 619(1), 223–237.

Adorno, T. W. (1997). *Aesthetic theory*. Minneapolis, MN: University of Minnesota Press.

---

24 It wasn't until the 1980s that Lina Bo Bardi, in another project, was able to see her cultural-political ideas more fully realized: In 1976, she was commissioned by the non-governmental organization SESC (Trade Social Service) to convert an old steel barrel factory in the Pompéia district of São Paulo into a public cultural and recreational center.

Akrich, M. & Bruno, L. (1992). A Summary of a Convenient Vocabulary for the Semiotics of Human and Nonhuman Assemblies. In W. Bijker & J. Law (Eds.), *Shaping Technology. Building Society Studies in Sociotecnical Change* (pp. 259–264). Cambridge, MA: MIT Press.

Bertram, G. W. (2019). *Art as Human Practice: An Aesthetics*. London, New York: Bloomsbury Academic.

Bo Bardi, L. (1995). *L'impasse del design. L'esperienza nel nordest del Brasile (english insert)*. Milano, Italy/ São Paulo, Brasil: Charta/ Instituto Lina Bo e P.M. Bardi.

Bo Bardi, L. (2014). Propraedeutic contribution to the teaching of architecture. In C. Veikos (Ed.), *Lina Bo Bardi. The theory of architectural practice* (First edition. ed., pp. 45–192). New York, NY: Routledge.

Born, G. (2010). The Social and the Aesthetic: For a Post-Bourdieuian Theory of Cultural Production. *Cultural Sociology, 4*(2), 171–208.

Bourdieu, P. (1984). *Distinction: A Social Critique of the Judgement of Taste*. Cambridge, MA: Harvard University Press.

Bourdieu, P. (1990). *The Logic of Practice*. Stanford, CA: Stanford University Press.

Bourdieu, P. (1996). *The Rules of Art: Genesis and Structure of the Literary Field*. Stanford, CA: Stanford University Press.

Buergel, R. M. (2011). 'This Exhibition Is an Accusation': The Grammar of Display According to Lina Bo Bardi. *Afterall: A Journal of Art, Context and Enquiry, 26*, 51–57. doi:10.1086/659295

Buergel, R. M., & Prinz, S. (2023). *Migration of Form. Exhibitions for the Global Present*. Zurich, CH: Scheidegger & Spiess.

Butler, J. (1990). *Gender Trouble. Feminism and the Subversion of Identity*. New York, NY: Routledge.

Butler, J. (1995). For a Careful Reading. In S. Benhabib, J. Butler, D. Cornell, & N. Fraser (Eds.), *Feminist Contentions: A Philosophical Exchange* (pp. 127–143): New York, NY: Routledge.

Clark, T. J. (1999). *Farewell to an Idea. Episodes from a History of Modernism*. New Haven, CT: Yale University Press.

Crossley, N. (1994). *The Politics of Subjectivity. Between Foucault and Merleau-Ponty*. Aldershot: Avebury.

Crossley, N. (2004). Phenomenology, Structuralism and History. *Theoria: A Journal of Social & Political Theory, 51*(103), 88–121.

Derrida, J. (1976). *Of Grammatology*. Baltimore, MD: Johns Hopkins University Press.

Easterling, K. (2021). *Medium Design. Knowing How to Work on the World*. London, UK: Verso.

Featherstone, M. (1991). *Consumer Culture and Postmodernism*. London, UK: Sage.

Focillon, H. (1948). *The Life of Forms in Art* (Second English ed.). New York, NY: Wittenborn, Schultz.

Forgacs, D. & Nowell-Smith, G. (Eds.) (1985). *Antonio Gramsci: Selections from Cultural Writings*. Cambridge, MA: Harvard University Press.

Foucault, M. (1972). *The Archaeology of Knowledge*. New York, NY: Pantheon Books.

Foucault, M. (1982). The Subject and Power. *Critical Inquiry*, 8(4), 777–795.

Freire, P. (1970). *Pedagogy of the Oppressed*. New York, NY: Herder and Herder.

Gibson, J. J. (1979). *The ecological approach to visual perception*. Boston, MA: Houghton Mifflin.

Groll, S. (2021). Zwichen Kontigenz und Notwendigkeit. Zur Rolle des Designs in der Gesellschaft der Gegenwart. Bielefeld: transcript.

Hennion, A. (2007). Those Things That Hold Us Together: Taste and Sociology. *Cultural Sociology*, 1(1), 97–114.

Jameson, F. (1991). *Postmodernism, or, the Cultural Logic of Late Capitalism*. London, UK: Verso.

Klein, G. (2017). Urban Choreographies: Artistic Interventions and the Politics of Urban Space. In R. J. Kowal, G. Siegmund, & R. Martin (Eds.), *The Oxford handbook of dance and politics* (pp. 131–142). New York, NY: Oxford University Press.

Knorr-Cetina, K., von Savigny, E., & Schatzki, T. R. (2001). *The Practice Turn in Contemporary Theory*. London, UK: Routledge.

Kubler, G. (1962). *The Shape of Time: Remarks on the History of Things*. New Haven, CT: Yale University Press.

Lefebvre, H. (2004). *Rhythmanalysis. Space, Time and Everyday Life*. London, NY: Continuum.

Levine, C. (2015). *Forms. Whole, Rhythm, Hierarchy, Network*. Princeton, NJ: Princeton University Press.

Lima, Z. R. M. de A. (2013). *Lina Bo Bardi*. New Haven, CT: Yale University Press.

Marcello, F. (2003). Giuseppe Pagano: A Rationalist caught between Theories and Practices of Fascist Italy. *Architectural Theory Review*, 8(2), 96–112. doi:10.1080/13264820309478487

Marx, K. (1964). *Early Writings*. New York, NY: McGraw-Hill.

Merleau-Ponty, M. (1962). *Phenomenology of Perception*. London/Atlantic Highlands, NJ: Routledge & K. Paul/ Humanities Press.

Merleau-Ponty, M. (1964a). Cézanne's Doubt. In *Sense and Non-Sense* (pp. 9–25). Evanston, IL: Northwestern University Press.

Merleau-Ponty, M. (1964b). Marxism and Philosophy. In *Sense and Non-Sense* (pp. 125–136). Evanston, IL: Northwestern University Press.

Merleau-Ponty, M. (1968). *The Visible and the Invisible. Followed by Working Notes*. Evanston IL: Northwestern University Press.

Mol, A. & Law, J. (1994). Regions, Networks and Fluids: Anaemia and Social Topology. *Social Studies of Science*, 24(4), 641–671.

Norman, D. A. (1988). *The Design of Everyday Things*. Cambridge, MA: MIT Press.

Papanek, V. J. (1972). *Design for the Real World: Human Ecology and Social Change* (1st American ed.). New York, NY: Pantheon Books.

Prinz, S. (2014). *Die Praxis des Sehens: über das Zusammenspiel von Körpern, Artefakten und visueller Ordnung*. Bielefeld, DE: transcript.

Prinz, S. (2017). Das unterschlagene Erbe: Merleau-Pontys Beitrag zur Praxistheorie. *Phänomenologische Forschungen*, (2), 77–92.

Prinz, S. & Göbel, H. (2015). Die Sinnlichkeit des Sozialen. Eine Einleitung. In Hanna Katharina Göbel & Sophia Prinz (Eds.), *Die Sinnlichkeit des Sozialen Wahrnehmung und materielle Kultur* (pp. 9–49). Bielefeld: transcript.

Rancière, J. (2004). *The Politics of Aesthetics. The Distribution of the Sensible*. New York, NY: Continuum.

Rancière, J. (2009). *The Emancipated Spectator*. London, UK: Verso.

Rebentisch, J. (2013). *Theorien der Gegenwartskunst zur Einführung*. Hamburg, DE: Junius-Verl.

Reckwitz, A. (2002). Toward a Theory of Social Practices: A Development in Culturalist Theorizing. *European Journal of Social Theory*, 5(2), 243–263.

Reckwitz, A. (2015). Ästhetik und Gesellschaft. Ein analytischer Bezugsrahmen. In A. Reckwitz, S. Prinz, & H. Schäfer (Eds.), *Ästhetik und Gesellschaft: Grundlagentexte aus Soziologie und Kulturwissenschaften* (pp. 215- 247). Berlin, DE: Suhrkamp.

Reckwitz, A. (2017). *The Invention of Creativity: Modern Society and the Culture of the New*. Cambridge, UK & Malden, MA: Polity.

Rubino, S. (2002). *Rotas da modernidade. Trajetoria, campo e historia na atuação de Lina Bo Bardi, 1947–1968*. Campinas, Brasil: Universidade Estadual de Campinas.

Sabatino, M. (2009). Space of Criticism: Exhibitions and the Vernacular in Italian Modernism. *Journal of Architectural Education*, 62(3), 35–52.

Schäfer, H. (2013). *Die Instabilität der Praxis: Reproduktion und Transformation des Sozialen in der Praxistheorie* (1st ed.). Weilerswist, DE: Velbrück Wiss.

Schäfer, H. (2016). *Praxistheorie. Ein soziologisches Forschungsprogramm*. Bielefeld: transcript.

Schürkmann, C. (2017). *Kunst in Arbeit: Künstlerisches Arbeiten zwischen Praxis und Phänomen*. Bielefeld, DE: transcript.

Simondon, G. (2017). *On the Mode of Existence of Technical Objects*. Minneapolis, MN: Univocal Publishing/University of Minnesota Press.

Spencer-Brown, G. (1969). *Laws of form*. London, UK: Allen & Unwin.

Voß, J. & Guggenheim, M. (2019). Making Taste Public: Industrialized Orders of Sensing and the Democratic Potential of Experimental Eating. *Politics and Governance*, 7(4), 224–236.

Zevi, B. (1950). *Towards an Organic Architecture*. London, UK: Faber & Faber.

Escape, Erase, Entangle
Three Aesthetic Regimes Re-composing the Californian Ideology

Jonathan Luke Austin, Anna Leander

1. INTRODUCTION

In 2018, Milan Design Week had an unusual exhibitor: Google. Its first time in Milan, Google's vice president of hardware design waxed lyrical about its reasons for attending:

> People think that aesthetics is making something pretty, and it's really not. Aesthetics is about igniting our senses, to take a moment to sense and feel I think we're all craving that a little bit … My team's job is to figure out what it feels like to hold Google in your hand … We're here at design week. It's the first time Google has a presence in Milan, and we're very excited … As technology progresses, it needs to be closer to us. What is the design language for Google? Bold and optimistic, human in our forms, our colors, our shapes, so we translated that into textures, tactility, fabrics, soft colors, things that are approachable and human to the core … I think technology will eventually be invisible. The design challenge is to make that transition smooth and beautiful. (Google, 2018)

In 2019, Google went back to Milan. And things had escalated:

> Form follows feeling … space actually affects people … design matters … it's why we spend the time making the decisions we do … Those things that we as designers intuit, neuroscience is now proving to have an effect. Google created an exhibition that is showing design's impact on our biology … When you have a heightened aesthetic experience, a sunrise, a piece of music, things that really elevate your everyday experiences, they change you, they change your biology, they change your mood, they change your emotion … The goal [of the Google exhibition] is to see how people resonate with space and to really find out whether what they think they resonate with is what their body is actually resonating with … Where does your physiology feel most peaceful, I think is what people are searching for …

> We've always known this ... but we haven't been able to quantify it ... This is about data used as a mirror back to yourself ... data is just a bunch of numbers and we wanted to make it artistic in its expression ... Technology has the ability to make you know yourself better ... the problems of the future are only going to become more complicated, the solutions have to happen in this collaboration of technology, the arts and science. (Google, 2019)

So: form, function, aesthetics, sensibility, invisibility, beauty, affect, neuroscience, biology, physiology, quantification, technology. Google's description of the centrality of design to its activities is an unusually explicit example of what we explore in this essay: the ways in which the social and political power of technology is fundamentally related to the ways in which a kind of aesthetic 'resonance' is actively generated through its workings. To the ways in which it—indeed—works to "ignite our senses." Put simply, we want to explore how objects do not work upon our bodies and subjectivities solely due their functional capacities, the semiotic meanings they communicate, or their specific material agencies, but also because of their aesthetic form. Of course, this is not the usual view. Typically, Google's focus on "igniting our senses" is considered a kind of ideological gloss to the real (socio-economic and political) bases of their power. As a distraction, as mere advertising. This reading reflects a more general wish to divide the aesthetic and the political into two separate spheres of sociality, maintaining aesthetics as something purer than politics. For example, while social theory has long considered the aesthetic practices of authoritarian polities, it has typically done so in order to stress the danger of that process, arguing that this represents merely an instrumentalization of aesthetics as a form of camouflage that both enables violence and debases the aesthetic. As the power of technology companies like Google continues to grow, this is also a prominent reaction to their deployment of aesthetic sensibilities: 'The aestheticization of technology is dangerous.'

In this essay, we seek to nuance that view. While the (aesthetic or otherwise) politics of contemporary technology certainly poses dangers, our goal is to situate the aesthetic practices at the heart of that politics as something more than a form of instrumentalization. Put differently, we articulate how the aesthetic qualities of technological objects are both reflections of, and increasingly constitutive of, our sense of the troubles facing the world, as well as its future promises. In this view, Google's attention to aesthetics is not simple ideological camouflage but a co-produced vision of an alternative relationship to technology building a 'better' set of human-machine entanglements (Jasanoff, 2004). It is about a struggle to compose a novel kind of resonance with the technological in the face of its current alienating consequences. Now, to make this claim does not imply Google is a place of innocence. When a corporation speaks about how aesthetic experiences "change you ... [and] your biology," the implications are dramatic. More so when we reflect on the ways in which Google's algorithms animate military drones and the dynamics of surveillance capitalism.

In our view, however, addressing those political dangers cannot be achieved by denying the ways in which aesthetics are built into the technological. Instead, examples like Google require we shift our definition of aesthetics. Aesthetics does not refer to an attribute (e.g., an essential quality of art) nor the psychological-emotional-affective states such attributes might evoke. Rather, as underscored in the introduction to this volume aesthetics practices are doing and undoing of sensorial perceptions. More specifically aesthetics refers to "a mode of experience that rests on the directness and immediacy of sensuous perception" (Berleant, 2010, p. 195). For example, goosebumps was Theodor Adorno's favored image for the aesthetic experience (Adorno, 1997, p. 331).[1] Aesthetics is thus something inescapably embedded across social ecologies and the appreciation of which thus demands an "openness to experience while judgement is suspended" (Berleant 2010, pp. 149–53). Such a position requires that the aesthetic be connected to 'sensibility,' 'sensuality' and 'sensations' rather than intellectualist evaluations of aesthetic experience and, more importantly, that "nothing in the human world is excluded" from this understanding of aesthetics (Berleant 2010, p. 46). Following this, the politicality of aesthetics is self-evident in its capacity to produce modes of resonant experience that attract or repel us from particular modes of ordering the world. Seen in this regard, the intimate aesthetic relationship we possess with technology is not simply an imposition upon our lives, artificially placed there by the powerful, but something far deeper and whose consequences—we think—are being underestimated in debates over the future of technological politics.

To explore all this, we move in several stages. We begin by discussing the impression that we are increasingly alienated from the world through our technological enmeshing. But our focus is on the degree of generality of this sentiment and the ways it even extends into those who work at technology companies like Google, not solely as a fear for their business model, but also as a personal experience of those who make real its activities. This move highlights the decline of the socio-political "resonance" once vested in the so-called Californian Ideology (Barbrook and Cameron 1996). To trace that decline, we draw on Hartmut Rosa's conceptualization of resonance, putting it into conversation with earlier discussions of the relevance of a certain "sensual credibility" to the functioning (or not) of society (Kluge and Negt 2016). The bulk of our paper then proceeds discuss how the Californian Aesthetic is

---

1   In his words: "Ultimately, aesthetic comportment is to be defined as the capacity to shudder, as if goosebumps were the first aesthetic image. What later came to be called subjectivity, freeing itself from the blind anxiety of the shudder, is at the same time the shudder's won development; life in the subject is nothing but what shudders, the reaction to the total spell that transcends the spell."

being re-composed and novel technological material aesthetics are emerging in its wake. More specifically, we focus on three examples of aesthetic regimes that are being deployed across the technology industry—which we term regimes of escape, erasure, and entanglement—and unpack the social resonances these regimes generate so to grasp how they are 're-enchanting' the technologies that permeate our worlds. Finally, by way of conclusion, we touch on the politics of these regimes and in particular highlight the ways in which they afford possibilities for contestation and composition. In so doing, we extend the argument beyond the decline of the Californian Ideology and its re-composition in the three epistemic regimes discussed, underscoring the more general implications for our conceptualization of the connection between political agency and aesthetics.

Our analysis of aesthetic regimes informed by an analysis of images, videos, and statements by companies. We have worked bottom up, in quasi-ethnographic fashion, to identify our three regimes. We have assembled something we might term a "cabinet of curiosities" (Latour, 2002, p. 23) that helps us establish how technology is being re-enchanted by the tech industry through its marketing but also through its self-reflections. Working in this manner has allowed us to explore the re-composition of the Californian aesthetic through the multiple media involved but most significantly, through their inter-connections and the manifold connections they therefore open towards their audiences. Such openness to a variety of sources is essential for any approach to aesthetics that sees it at work in affective, contextual atmospheres rather than through an isolated channel. "There are no visual media" as Mitchell puts it (2015, p. 125). The aesthetic regimes we delineate, reflect the processes and relations we found most relevant in our cabinet of curiosities. Other regimes could exist and might emerge. We claim neither exclusivity nor eternity for the regimes we outline. Rather our ambition is to exemplify the political salience of aesthetic resonances that we found to be particularly densely present and to do so in view of underscoring the political openings they afford.

2. THE DECLINE OF THE CALIFORNIAN AESTHETIC

> *If acceleration is the problem, then resonance might be the solution.*
> *– Hartmut Rosa*

Classically, the technology industry has been described as subsumed within a so-called Californian Ideology. This ideology "promiscuously combines the freewheeling spirit of the hippies and the entrepreneurial zeal of the yuppies" achieved through "a profound faith in the emancipatory potential of the new information technologies" (Barbrook and Cameron 1996, p. 45). In our view, however, this image of the technological should not be reduced to 'ideology' but instead to a certain Californian *Aesthetic* which has—we want to say—declined in its socio-political resonance. As Saara Tuusa (2018) has written, the Californian Aesthetic is prominently linked to an aesthetics of futurism and modernism. As she puts it, "futurism's influence on the digital code is undeniable. In the beginning of the 20th century, with the rise of industrialization, the belief in technological progress' ability to emancipate the human race had unprecedented proof." Within this, "the aesthetics of the future" was "defined by the materials linked to industrial progress—chrome, shiny glass, stainless steel, electronic bright colors—and a hard-boiled belief in the perpetual future." These forms were linked to modernist design and its prioritization of "functional requirements instead of traditional aesthetics. As a result, modernist design was simple and clean, based on rationality and functionality, always aiming for a seamless and purposeful experience." This minimalist and functionally-focused aesthetic of the future is directly replicated in the aesthetic design of contemporary technologies. But:

> Today, the dream of the digital has been realized, the aesthetic seeping everywhere. The digital code does not signal a future anymore, it has become the status quo. It reflects the desires and needs of a bygone era, where digitization was only a fantastical dream—not a mundane reality. (Tuusa, 2018)

The result is alienation. A feeling that we have "lost touch" with the world and the realization that utopian visions of the technological were always already myths. A feeling that technology offers no route towards a different kind of future because, well, that future is already here. Importantly, such a perspective is not necessarily reflexively perceived. Indeed, it would be an error to suggest that we can rationally diagnose precisely what is 'wrong' with the technological. Instead, our perception of technological aporia (or danger) seems related to what Oskar Negt and Alexander Kluge (2016) termed "sensual credibility." For Negt and Kluge, this term referred to the ways in which the proletariat could 'sense' something wrong with the world despite being unable to reflexively articulate it: "the masses" who "live with experiences of violence, oppression, [and] exploitation ... possess material, sensual evidence of the restriction of possibilities in their lives ... Accordingly, the resistance to this restriction has a sensual credibility" (Kluge and Negt, 2016, p. 43). In their view, the restrictions that the proletariat's enmeshing in the logic of capitalism places on the possibility of rational or reflexive (i.e. strategic) resistance to that suffering means that their anger and resentment is affectively felt and experienced rather than thought and reasoned. The sensual and affective is therefore located at the core of their resistance. It affords it the 'credibility' required for resistance to be possible. This too seems to be the status quo. We 'feel' that something is wrong with our technological entanglements but quite what 'it' is harder to define. Electoral interference, autonomous weapons systems and surveillance: sure, these are real and pressing problems. But those dangers are things that *could* (bracketing the reasons for why they are not) be dealt with through regulation. The displeasure we feel with the technological, however, goes deeper towards a fundamental alienation with the ontological place of technology in our lives: with its goals, telos, meanings, and—above all—*futures*.

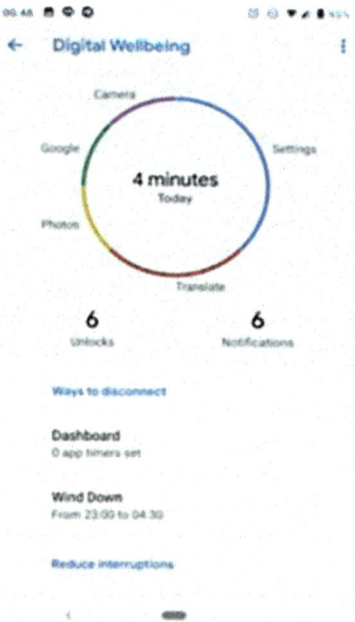

Figure 1: Google's wellbeing (...)
A set of 'digital wellbeing' tools now provided in Google's Android platform.

Source: The Android Open Source Project

What appears to be missing—in short—is Rosa's aforementioned "resonance." For Rosa, the production of resonance is central to overcoming the alienating effects of social acceleration. In his view, the ways in which social systems are—or are not—entangled, fused or knitted together in a meaningful manner rests on whether or not forms of resonance exist therein. According to Rosa (2016, p. 269), humans are "resonating bodies" who find meaning not solely 'in-relation' to the world (that is to other objects, people, and ideals) in a static or fixed sense but in the 'movements' or 'exchanges' that developing resonant relationships with open up. As he puts it, both the subject and her world "are formed, coined by and even constituted in and through their reciprocal relation" (p. 62). In this:

> Resonance is a form of relation to the world that is constituted through af←fection and e→motion, intrinsic interest and perceived self-efficacy, in which subject and world at the same time touch and transform each other. (Rosa, 2016, p. 298)

The arrows in the terms af←fection and e→motion signal the ability to be affectively connected to the world and to actively affect it. They are especially important here for stressing that emotional and affective events require a transformatory dynamic that 'shifts' the locus of the subject. In colloquial terms, we want to be 'moved' by something in the world. As such, "resonance is no echo, but a relation of answer; it presupposes that both sides speak with [their] own voices" (p. 298). Resonance is not achieved through similarity or evoking a known state but, rather, through sensual interactions: the subject and her world must be *"'closed' or consistent enough in order to speak with their own voices, and open enough to be affected"* (p. 298 emphasis added). Resonance is thus about "bidirectional vibration" (p. 279) vis-à-vis corporeality, affectivity, cognition, etc. In all this—to rephrase—"resonance is not agreement; resonance is in between consonance and dissonance" (p. 279).

Now resonance is, we want to suggest, centrally constituted through our *aesthetic* engagement with the world. This becomes clear in the predominant place of art and design in discussions of objects that create affect, emotion, and resonance within individuals. Art is said to 'move' us (for whatever reason). But when we move away from the separation of art into a separate sphere of sociality to politics and technology, it becomes possible to also consider the technological as an object with an aesthetic that does (or does not) produce resonance. And with this, we turn full circle. The critics who originally coined the term the Californian Ideology, Richard Barbrook and Andy Cameron, closed their discussion by offering alternatives to what they saw as its pathologies. Specifically, they advocated for the emergence of new "digital artisans" who would "reconnect themselves with the theory and practice of productive art" to become "artist-engineers" or "designers of the next stage of modernity" (Barbrook and Cameron, 1996, p. 68). In this, they would "create a new machine aesthetic for the information age" in which they would "push beyond the limitations of both the technologies and their own creativity" (Barbrook and Cameron, 1996, p. 68). Notably, they advocated specifically that these digital artisans push away from the Californian Aesthetic's centralization in the social and political culture of the United States (favoring instead a 'European' model) in order to create new forms of resonance that could counter the muting of the world. The goal was to re-infuse the digital or technological with intensity and enthusiasm, countering the anomie, blasé indifference and undoing of affective relations that they diagnosed Silicon Valley as having provoked. What we want to suggest, however, is that despite their diagnosis of a certain "fatalism" within the Californian Ideology, it is paradoxically Silicon Valley that has taken up their challenge (with, perhaps, others in Shenzhen) and begun to actively situate their 'digital artisans' at the center of its activities in order to re-compose the Californian Aesthetic on different terms. The accelerating, capitalist 'de-aesthetization machine' muting society somewhat paradoxically becomes a 're-aesthetization machine' (Reckwitz, 2012, p. 35). Such a suggestion dovetails well with the perspective expressed in the hope that 'digital artisans' may take technology beyond the Californian Ideology. As they pick up the task, they become 'changemakers' not only for the tech industry but also for the mediated, post-modern, contemporary 'digital' society more generally (Arvidsson, 2019). We now proceed to looking more closely at some examples of the aesthetic regimes that are emerging and recovering the resonance that the declining Californian Aesthetic can no longer generate.

3. AESTHETIC REGIMES RE-ENCHANTING TECHNOLOGY

In the wake of the decline of the Californian Ideology, the task is not making technology 'good' but making it feel good. It's not *just* about building ethical algorithms, using technology to better the treatment of the disenfranchised, or diverting its use away from autonomous weapons systems. The trouble is conceiving of a place for technology within the ecological entanglements that cut across the gamut of world politics that gives us a resonant sense of purpose and the possibility of imagining the possible futures that we are moving towards, however contingently and chaotically. The challenge for the tech industry and its digital artisans, to speak with Barbrook and Cameron, is therefore to change our 'sense' of technology. But how do they tackle that challenge? How are technology corporations reacting? In what ways are they re-enchanting our technologically pregnant worlds? How do they make technology speak to us? And how does this contribute (or not) to composing resonance? The answer to these questions could not conceivably be singular. Rather, if we imagine a deeply competitive, constantly shapeshifting tech industry where each company puts digital artisans to work and indeed many of these artisans themselves are (or become) companies in their own right, what we see is more like a small army of artisans, each proposing and marketing its own aesthetics. Instead of a singular aesthetics, we are facing a plethora of aesthetics shifting at an ever-accelerating pace. These aesthetics emerge from the Californian Ideology in decline and so are closely associated with it. They are in close connection with the tech industry. They draw on its aesthetic codes but are re-purposing it, and moving it beyond the image of an unproblematized emancipatory future. Shades and nuances are correcting and masking the defects that made that aesthetic lose its efficacy. This is what we mean by re-composing of the Californian Aesthetic. But, can we be more specific about how this multifarious re-composing is operating and how the resonances it generates re-enchant the world?

To gauge the significance of the re-composing of the aesthetics underpinning the Californian Ideology, and the resonances it is generating, requires fixing it and finding ways of dealing with its complexity. One way of doing so would be to work top down, that is from and with theory, using sharp concepts to "carve out portions of sensible reality" and associating them with specific processes and relationship and so constitute "footholds" from which the significance of the re-composition can be approached and assessed (Brown and Tucker, 2010, p. 235). An opposite way of handling this is to begin from below, upwards as it were, accepting and working with the flux and complexity, embracing the "the messy *informe* of the ongoing-ness of process" (Highmore, 2010, p. 123). Making sense begins with the spaces where the re-composing appears most dense. This latter route is the one we follow. More specifically, we focus on three aesthetics that are particularly densely present in the current efforts by the tech industry to generate resonances for technology beyond the Californian Aesthetic. Our claim is neither that these aesthetic regimes are exclusive and somehow representative nor that they are unchanging. Rather, this is an exploration of densities appearing from our perspective. Working with these densities is a heuristic allowing us to describe the (indeed empirical, material, commercial, political, aesthetic) processes re-composing the Californian Aesthetic and so to open them for analysis and intervention while (and by) accepting their un-containability. To do this, we proceed focusing on how three densely present aesthetics make technology sensible and resonant, and secure sensuous credibility. Connecting these aesthetics to political practices, we sketch the contours of three aesthetic regimes: escape, erase, and entangle and their (respectively) nihilist, conservative, and symbiotic politics.

3.1 Escape

In 2018, Elon Musk's commercial spaceflight venture Space X conducted a test of its rocket Falcon Heavy. Jarringly—however—a Tesla Roadster sportscar produced by another of Musk's corporations was mounted on top of the rocket. A mock astronaut was seated in the car, which now orbits the sun (Figure 1). Generally, these instances of commercial extravagance are seen as symptoms of the narcisic self-perception of those who work in the technology industry as 'visionaries.' Indeed, critiquing Musk's stunt, Alice Gorman has written that:

It feeds into a cult of personality which is at odds with the 'space for all humanity' narrative ... And let's face it, there's no getting away from the fact that a red sports car is all about boys and their toys. The car is a signifier of wealth and masculinity. We've been trying so hard to leave behind the era where the archetypal astronaut was an elite white male, and we've just stepped right back into it. (cited in David, 2018)

Figure 2: Tesla's "Starman" launched into orbit around the sun.

Source: SpaceX, Falcon Heavy Demo Mission, CC0, 2018

The critique here is surely true. Especially given the abundant examples of Musk's indulgence for the misogynistic, meme-ified and flippant. Nonetheless, at the root of this event and the aesthetics it encapsulates is something more. SpaceX encapsulates a growing technological nihilism. Indeed, it is not without irony that so many of Musk's ventures involve a focus on ecological catastrophe. Tesla has done more to promote electrical vehicles than any other corporation, not to mention its development of the Tesla Powerwall: an off-the-grid storage solution for electrical energy. SolarCity is one of the largest providers of solar electricity. And SpaceX is ultimately founded on escaping humanity's reliance on Earth by allowing us to become a "multi-planetary" species, first by travelling to and colonizing Mars. Indeed, Musk once described his motivation for SpaceX as revolving around the fact that there are hypothetically "many dead one-planet civilizations ... out there in the cosmos that never made it to the other planets and ultimately extinguished themselves or were destroyed by external factors" (Biong, 2019). He specially quotes the late astronomer Carl Sagan's words that "our planet is a lonely speck in the great enveloping cosmic dark. In our obscurity, in all this vastness, there is no hint that help will come from elsewhere to save us from ourselves" (Biong, 2019). And, with those words, Musk ultimately proposes himself to be the figure who will save us from ourselves.

There is little romanticism in that venture, however. Musk acknowledges that "your probability of dying on Mars is much higher than on Earth" (Pengelly, 2018). There is a distinct aesthetic shift here from the NASA-era of space exploration. In *Star Trek*, which in popular imaginary perhaps best encapsulates that older aesthetic, expeditions into space sought to expand humanity's knowledge by exploring "strange new worlds" but *not* to abandon the earth. Indeed, in the lore of *Star Trek*, earth "enjoys one of the most advanced, peaceful and materially pleasant cultures of any known." (http://www.trekipedia.com/file/EarthTrekipedia, n.d.). Earth remains home. For SpaceX, its missions to Mars will eventually replace Earth and its immutable problems. If we stay, we will die, so the goal must be to leave. Indeed, Lila Moore (2018) links the symbolism of Musk's Tesla roadster floating around in space to that of biblical revelation through comparisons to the horse, horseman, and rider of the apocalypse. This aesthetics of escape is also firmly situated within a transhumanist perspective at a literal level. Another of Musk's ventures, Neuralink, seeks to create implantable brain-machine interfaces. Neuralink's first goal is to treat neurological diseases but, more broadly, Musk sees it as a means to human enhancement that will create a "symbiosis" between humans and artificial intelligence, with the latter otherwise being seen as a further existential threat to humanity. Again, we must escape ourselves in order to slowly save ourselves.

Notably, the aesthetics of SpaceX are quite literally professionally designed into its products. The spacesuits worn by its astronauts were designed by José Fernández who has more usually worked to craft costumes for films like Men in Black, Black Panther and Ironman, as well as the electronic music duo Daft Punk. Interestingly, Fernández was not aware he was designing spacesuits for real-world space travel, instead assuming he was commissioned to work on another film production (Guy, 2020). SpaceX thus mixes those fictional influences into its aesthetic practices quite directly: a strange mixture between Kubrick's *2001: A Space Odyssey*, with its ultimately sinister gleaming glass and whites, and the Arnold Schwarzenegger-starring *Total Recall*, with its mix of dirt, conspiracy, and sleaze (that is set—not without irony—on a colony on Mars). A set of aesthetic practices constituting a regime simultaneously hinting at dystopia and salvation.

If acceleration is the problem, then the resonance offered as a solution by the aesthetic of escape is that of a grand 'interruption' or 'break' from history. While this echoes to some degree the discourse of disruption at the heart of the Californian Aesthetic, it jettisons the good life. It is the Californian version of Year Zero. Musk personifies this aesthetic. When he embraces the use of cryptocurrencies by 'average' investors, he acknowledges the corruption of the global financial system and situates himself as somehow outside that sphere. When Musk smokes weed with the popular libertarian podcast host Joe Rogan, he does not do so in homage to the Californian Aesthetic's past debt to "the freewheeling spirit of the hippies" but—instead—with a serene sense of self-irony (Barbrook and Cameron, 1996, p. 45). When he posts endless memes on Twitter or produces novelty flamethrowers to advertise his ventures (not least one named the Boring company), he articulates this spirit of meaninglessness that resonates directly with the experiences of many who refer to him as "Daddy Musk" (a trend that even the most skilled of psychoanalysts would have difficulty interpreting given the self-conscious irony in which the term is used). And while it is straightforward to critique the seemingly juvenile nature of these endeavors, they constitute and restore a sensual credibility for technology based on the resonances of an aesthetic of escape and replacement, associated with nihilistic political practices. The image of the successful white, male who can afford to be the provocative and ego-centric boy with toys supports and lends force to this resonance. Indeed, it resonates far beyond other white boys with toys. As such, it would be naïve to belittle or ignore the salience of Musk's aesthetics of escape and the nihilism associated with it. Instead, the power that it holds over many imaginaries deserves to be explored and engaged.

3.2 Erase

In stark contrast to an aesthetics of technological escape is that of technological erasure. If the transhumanist dreams of abandoning the world embraces our 'becoming-technological' in order to save ourselves, an aesthetics of erasure scrubs the technological from visibility. Two seemingly opposed sectors encapsulate this aesthetic: environmental and security technologies. To begin with the environmental, consider the company Beyond Meat, which believes:

> There is a better way to feed our future and that the positive choices we all make, no matter how small, can have a great impact on our personal health and the health of our planet. By shifting from animal to plant-based meat, we can positively impact four growing global issues: human health, climate change, constraints on natural resources and animal welfare. (www.beyondmeat.com).

Figure 3: Example of BeyondMeat's product marketing.

Source: www.beyondmeat.com

Beyond Meat seeks to produce replacements for meat products "without compromise" in the sense that the products will be indistinguishable from the 'real' thing (Figure 3). Going further, Beyond Meat insists that its products *are* meat: "meat is really made up of five constituent parts: the amino acids, lipids, carbohydrates, minerals, and water. They're all actually present in plants. What we're doing is building a piece of meat directly from those plants ... we are delivering meat" (Sexton 2016, 66). The hyper-technological modes through which this 'meat' is produced, however, is seemingly deliberately erased from view. In all this, Beyond Meat is fundamentally conservative, especially compared to alternatives. The traditional environmental approach has been to abandon meat entirely and accept the aesthetic changes this demands to our lives. While often bound-up with romanticism for a less-exploitative past (or images of the 'harmony' of 'traditional' society), this stance is explicitly political and radically so in its requirements to abandon the status quo. By contrast, those more attuned to a Musk-esque aesthetics of escape seek to entirely overcome our reliance on food, advocating for 'meal replacements' that fulfil our nutritional requirements in a functional, utilitarian, and often 'tasteless' way. The development in Silicon Valley of the product known as Soylent) "takes a few things off our plates" while keeping it all. "Protein, carbohydrates, lipids, and micronutrients: each Soylent product contains a complete blend of everything the body needs to thrive" (https://soylent.com). By contrast, and again erasing the presence of technology, *Beyond Meat* plays with an aesthetic of similitude that seeks to subordinate even the most technologically advanced product to human culture. Again, it seeks to address ecological catastrophe "without compromise" in the sense of allowing all to go on as if nothing had changed. Technology gains resonance here for its capacity to assist us in maintain our status quo. Eating meat is not a problem in this utopia.

A second articulation of this aesthetic of erasure is found across security technology. Historically, practices linked to security politics (war-fighting, policing, etc.) have been interwoven with technological imaginaries extensively. This is still evident in the ways governments parade their latest high-tech fighter jets, drones, or weapons systems. However, as security politics has proliferated and infiltrated almost every aspect of our lives, such an aesthetic becomes problematical. Armed drones gleaming in the sky with aggressive names and sharp angles are acceptable when they are flying over far-away places to ruthlessly attack clear-cut enemies. They are less aesthetically acceptable at home where security technologies are increasingly—thus—being erased from view. Virtual fencing technologies, for example, draw on a combination of cameras, sensors, and other technologies hidden discretely around cities to feed data to algorithms that can 'automatically' detect intrusions into protected spaces. In this they allow citizens to 'forget' the politics of insecurity and live a depoliticized life of aesthetic continuity and normality (Austin and Leander, forthcoming). At the same time, these technologies can be 'visibly' articulated in the aesthetic practices of governments, commercial actors and others, who cite their presence in speeches, advertise their effectiveness and reassure publics that technology is working 'behind the scenes' to keep them safe.

Figure 4: Nofence's description of its livestock monitoring technologies.

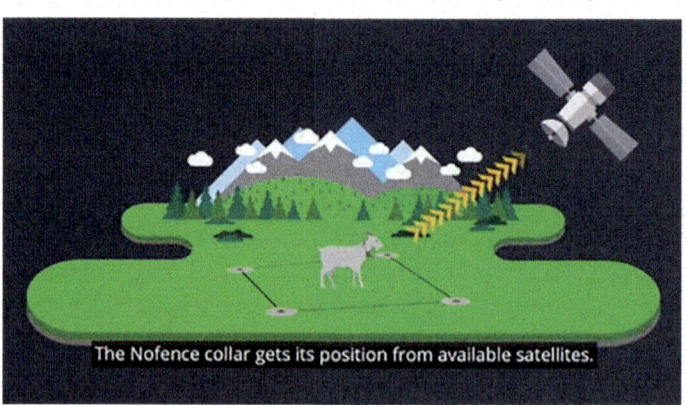

Source: www.nofence.no

Indeed, there is a core tension within this aesthetics of erasure: For the tech industry to produce resonance it must make us 'aware' that it is facilitating the smooth workings of our lives but do so unobtrusively, even invisibly. To see this, consider Douglas Rushkoff's (2019) manifesto *Team Human*, which tackles what he terms the "antihuman" agenda of modern technology. This includes the usual list of fears: robots taking our jobs, algorithms controlling attention spans; social media destroying democracy. Rushkoff's suggests that technology has forced us into a situation in which:

> We begin living as if we were in a shopping mall or casino, where day and night—as well as desire—are programmed by the environment. Everything is strategized by something or someone, even though the walls, lights, ceiling, and signage appear like features of the natural world. We are being optimized by something outside ourselves, toward purposes we don't even know … [The] lighting in the office changes to increase our productivity during the afternoon "lull." Our digital world is like the ultimate casino in this respect. It may have begun as a series of tools for specific purposes—spreadsheets, word processors, calculators, messaging, calendars, contact lists—but these tools went from being analogs or metaphors for real-life activities into being their replacements. Our technologies change from being the tools humans use into the environments in which humans function (2019, section 29).

His manifesto is a plea to reverse this flow: to return technologies to "being the tools humans use." This again is a conservative reading of the (superior) place of the 'human' that more-or-less denies that humans have always been entangled parts of the "environments" in which we function (a house being—indeed—a technology). Against this, the aesthetic of erasure seeks to build resonance in which the 'human' firmly controls the technological and—preferably—banishes it from sight. This is perhaps best seen in an example of its deployment that fuses the ecological (i.e. Beyond Meat) and the securitizing (i.e. virtual fences): the use of technology to control cattle and other livestock. A Norwegian company—Nofence—has developed a technology that allows livestock to graze without fences being installed to contain them. It does so by placing GPS sensors around the livestock's necks. If an animal passes outside a virtually designated 'zone' in which they are allowed to graze, they receive a warning and/or electric shock via their collars. Generally, technologies like these are cited as being useful for reducing labor costs, improving herd management and protecting environmentally-sensitive areas. As Nofence puts it, the tool "safeguards the welfare of the animals and contributes to sustainable agriculture" (https://www.nofence.no/en/). Aesthetically, moreover, they allow for the picture-postcard image of freely and 'naturally' grazing animals to dominate our landscapes. The at first glance amusing but otherwise rather sinister image (Figure 4) of a goat being cybernetically linked to satellites and invisible forcefields is erased in all this, of course. Instead, resonance is generated here by reference to a return to 'traditional' modes of farming and a purer symbiosis between humans and nature. In line with Rushkoff, high-technology is converted here into a tool that can be productively used to manage certain aspect of our lives but which—quite literally in this case—does not 'corrupt' or become our environment.

3.3 Entangle

Back to Google. Its desire to "ignite our senses" represents an aesthetic of 'entanglement' that avoids the more extreme desire to either depart the world and its limits through the technological (the aesthetic of escape) or to return to a purer human realm scrubbed of the technological (the aesthetic of erasure). In part, this is necessitated by the focus of its innovations. Google's tools are very intimate to our lives: smartphones, calendars, mailboxes, search engines, maps. As such, these tools cannot easily be scrubbed from view (at least for the moment) and Google must instead search for a distinct (from the futurism and modernism of the originary Californian Aesthetic) mode of aesthetically resonantly integrating them into our lives. Indeed, at the core of this aesthetic of entanglement is a 'domestication' of the digital that attempts to render the technological an unexceptional object. This is seen—first—in the diversity of Google's design activities. Apparently, only 25% of Google's hardware design team have previous designed electronic devices. Instead, the rest have experience designing bicycles or clothing, and Ivy Ross, Google's Vice President of Hardware Design, began as a jewelry designer. In integrating this expertise, Google seems to aim at situating the digital in symmetrical terms to that which we consider other technological objects that we do not see as being fundamentally dangerous (espresso machines, electric bicycles and so on).

Indeed, it is interesting that Ross has expressed an ontological understanding of human–machine relations that is not in its essence dissimilar to that described by social theorists (among many Haraway, 1991, Bijker and Law, 2004)—focused on the ways the human and the non-human cannot be separated but are instead fundamentally entangled. She writes that though "people are scared of [technological] change" it has to be accepted that *"everything is technology in a way*. We think of it now as screens, but as humans evolve there are new technologies that offer us new things. I want to reshape people's definitions of technology" (Wadsworth, 2018). For Ross, the challenge is thus not returning technologies to "being the tools humans use" but finding a balance in which technology provides greater "sensory experience" because "in some ways we are numbed to feelings in general and technology is reflecting that. The more time people spend on screens, the more they will want three-dimensionality" (Wadsworth, 2018). This is reflected in Google's use of soft color palettes, fabrics (rather than metals) and sounds that evoke the natural world more than the futurist Californian Aesthetic of the technological (Figure 5). However, it is important to stress that Google's arrival at this aesthetic was not a straightforward process but one of constant experimentation.

Figure 5: Early (left) and late (right) designs for Google Glass, depicting the shift from a minimalist and futuristic technological aesthetic (that of the classical Californian Ideology) towards an aesthetic of entanglement privileging soft colors, light, and forms (i.e. sunglasses) that domesticate the high-technological into our lives.

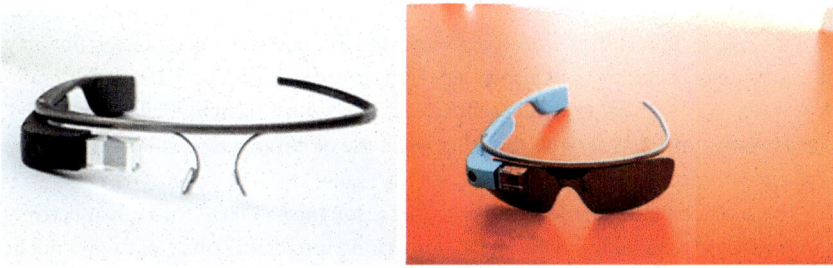

Source: www.google.com

To stay with Ivy, it is notable that she first arrived at Google to take over its development of the now defunct Google Glass. Google Glass was intended to operate as an augmented reality tool in which a small screen built-in to eyeglasses would project information and tools more usually accessed via our smartphones directly in front of our eyes. A true merging of the digital and the physical. Google Glass was not successful, however, in large part because potential consumers were not only uncertain about its functionality (it was originally released in 2012) but more because they disliked its design and fashion aesthetic. As one critique noted, Google Glass faced the problem that wearable technologies:

> Will challenge the tech industry to be more than a pair of white earbuds, to weave themselves even deeper into our clothes and our culture. Could you imagine just one label selling khakis at Macy's? Of course not. Hire a few geniuses, and tech is easy. But fashion is a means of personal expression and identity, making it an infinitely ebbing task that no one company will ever be able to develop alone. (Wilson, 2014)

Ross was hired from the art and design world to help solve these problems, and while she failed with Google Glass, the tweaks she made to that product (shifting it from looking as if it was a *Star-Trek*-esque headset towards integrating more primary colors and soft frames) fed directly into her future roles developing its other products. Indeed, the lessons Google learned fed directly into its establishment of its Design Laboratory that sought understand how it could build resonance through entangling with fashion "as a means of personal expression and identity" (https://design.google). The result was the products it showcased at Milan Design Week, which we opened with, and which have steered it towards an aesthetic of entanglement privileging an ever-deeper expansion of its understanding of human beings at aesthetic, affective, cultural, psychological, and personal levels. Again, Ivy encapsulates that logic in her words that while "some people feel fashion is frivolous" but "if you really tap into society, and can have a feeling of where as a society we want to go, fashion is a way to express that–and I was always looking at technology to get there" (Wilson, 2014). That shift ultimately represented Google conceiving of itself not only as a technology company but also as a design company preoccupied with the 'crafting' of objects: "technology won't eclipse craft. You don't have to make that choice" (Wadsworth, 2018). At least within this aesthetic of entanglement, both should be actively embraced.

The aesthetic of entanglement generates resonance—then—through affectively re-composing technological objects as something intrinsically part of us and not at odds with our taste in fashion, music, decoration, etc. In this, rather than situating technology as a mode of replacing the human (an aesthetics of escape), emancipating the human (in the classical Californian Ideology), or fundamental danger (an aesthetics of erasure), the aesthetic of entanglement seeks to define the technological as something 'neutral' that can be designed happily into our lives, without making grand claims about its possibilities. The political practice embedded here is one then, perhaps, of the 'symbiosis' that is rhetorically characteristic of liberal democratic values in which extremes must be reconciled and the future something that cannot be predefined but which must be negotiated-with. Of course, the usual banal critiques of such a politics being depoliticizing apply. Nonetheless, the 'democratization' of the technological through this aesthetic is clearly one of the most prominent ways in which the technology industry has shifted in the context of its fragmentation of resonance, as we saw in our earlier discussion of moves towards co-design and prod-users. Indeed, it extends far beyond Google. Apple and Microsoft are veering in similar directions, as are innumerable smaller technology companies who explicitly describe their products as 'artisan' objects. Ultimately, the aesthetic of entanglement is one that seeks to design *us* into the technological, and vice-versa.

4. CONCLUDING REMARKS: THE AESTHETIC POLITICS OF TECHNOLOGY

The three aesthetic regimes we have just discussed are re-composing the Californian Ideology, re-enchanting technology in its wake. This said, they vary greatly in terms of the aesthetic resonances by which they do so and so the political practices with which they are therefore associated. Above we drew the contours of three emerging aesthetic regimes to describe this point. Working backwards, we concluded describing an aesthetic that *entangles* technology pervasively in contemporary life. Technology has potential in "every community, every sector and every country," as Microsoft

CEO Satya Nodella put it when introducing the Microsoft Mesh (Microsoft News, 2021). This aesthetics resonates with as symbiotic presence of technology in all political subjectivities and processes. It is an aesthetic regime that sees technology and technological expansion as inexorably connected to any and all politics. Not surprisingly, it is prominent in the big tech industry, including Google, Microsoft, Samsung, and Apple that we drew on to illustrate this point. Distinct from this, an aesthetic *erasing* technology, invisiblizing its centrality to contemporary life. Such aesthetics promise tradition untouched. It mimics, supports, and stabilizes the already existing. In that sense, its politics is conservative. As illustrated by our examples—an aesthetic of technology preserving a meat-based diet as a vegan and a conventional form of farming relying on satellite communications—, this aesthetic works well in areas where technologization is expanding but also resisted and resented as a threat and where, therefore, to misrecognize its significance is to reassure. Lastly, the aesthetic of *escape* we began with, associates technology with the move out and away from the present into an unknown future; a future that is no more problematized or engaged with than is the present. It is a nihilistic politics of sorts associated with a reluctance or refusal to engage politically or even ethically with societal concerns beyond technology itself. We associated this aesthetics with Tesla and Elon Musk's more eccentric projects, underscoring that they resonate with a fascination for and fetishization of technology that is widespread among tech innovators from the hypervisible bitcoin pioneer Vinklevoss twins to the imperceptible hacker.

Nihilism, conservatism, and symbiosis, we do not need to insist, are fundamentally different forms of politics. Engaging the aesthetic regimes that underpin them by re-enchanting technology and redistributing the sensible with regard to its place in contemporary society, therefore, is a correspondingly differentiated challenge. It is a challenge that is particularly exacting, as the aesthetic regimes we have described are never isolated or pure. They are overlapping and fuzzy. Elon Musk is known also for his proposals geared to fix humanitarian crises or move the world to sustainable energy sources that are strong engagements with the problems of contemporary society in both conservative and symbiotic ways. While rendering both analysis and politics more complicated, the fissures and frictions generated by this overlaying of aesthetic regimes are also helpful. They bring forth the contractions in practices of aesthetic politics and so become indicators of possible openings for political agency and change. Driving a wedge into the cracks might widen these openings and so pave the way for responsible and reflective re-workings the of contemporary technological aesthetics and their politics. Even if such agency may be moot for many reasons, directing attention to its possibility is crucial. Indeed, this has been the motivation and ambition of our contribution to this volume and the broader project underlying it. The commercial re-composing the Californian Ideology through commercial aesthetics that we have delved into in this chapter remains mostly overlooked and so unproblematized. Yet, the aesthetic regimes associated with technology are becoming steadily more significant as society is becoming ever more deeply permeated by technology. The aesthetic regimes re-composing of the Californian Ideology permeate processes and practices that extend far beyond those associated with technology markets narrowly defined. Therefore, creating the openness required for prodding, problematizing, disturbing, redirecting, and (why not?) re-composing the deeply commercialized re-composing of the Californian Ideology is a worthwhile endeavor to which this chapter has contributed.

References

Adorno, T. W. (1997). Aesthetic Theory. New York, NY: Athelone Press.

Arvidsson, A. (2019). Changemakers: The Industrious Future of the Digital Economy. London, UK: John Wiley & Sons.

Austin, J., & Leander, A. (forthcoming). The State of the Sublime: Aesthetic Protocols and Global Security.

Barbrook, R. & Cameron, A. (1996). The Californian Ideology. Science as Culture, 6 (1), 44–72.

Berleant, A. (2010). Sensibility and Sense: The Aesthetic Transformation of the Human World. Exeter, UK: Imprint.

Bijker, W. E., & Law, J. (1994). Shaping Technology / Building Society: Studies in Sociotechnical Change. Boston, MA: MIT Press.

Biong, I. (2019, November 20). Elon Musk Disputes Carl Sagan's "Pale Blue Dot": The Answer Is Mars! Inquirer.Net. Retrieved from https://technology.inquirer.net/92462/elon-musk-disputes-carl-sagans-pale-blue-dot-the-answer-is-mars

Brown, S. D., & Tucker, I. (2010). Eff the Ineffable: Affect, Somatic Management and Mental Health. In M. Gregg & G. J. Seigworth (Eds.), The Affect Theory Reader (pp. 229–250). Durham, NC: Duke University Press.

Google at 2019 Milan Design Week: A Space for Being. (2019, June 20). Google. Retrieved from https://www.youtube.com/watch?v=4iA0srfIru0

Haraway, D. (1991). A Cyborg Manifesto: Science, Technology and Socialist-Feminism in the Late Twentieth Century. In D. Haraway (Ed.), Simians, Cyborgs and Women: The Reinvention of Nature (pp. 183–202). London, UK: Routledge.

Highmore, B. (2010). Bitter after Taste: Affect, Food, and Social Aesthetics. In M. Gregg & G. J. Seigworth (Eds.), The Affect Theory Reader (pp. 118–137). Durham, NC: Duke University Press.

Ivy Ross + Hardware Design. (2018, October 9). Google. Retrieved from https://www.youtube.com/watch?v=10ppdFQNl4s

Jasanoff, S. (2004). States of Knowledge: The Co-Production of Science and the Social Order. London, UK: Routledge.

Kluge, A., & O. Negt. (2016). Public Sphere and Experience: Toward an Analysis of the Bourgeois and Proletarian Public Sphere. London, UK: Verso.

Latour B. (2002). What is Iconclash? Or is There a World Beyond the Image Wars? Cambridge, MA: MIT Press.

Leonard, D. (2018, February 9). Tesla Roadster Gets Interplanetary ID [Blog post]. Retrieved from www.space.com/39646-tesla-roadster-gets-interplanetary-id.html

Martin, G. (2020, May 29). The Man Behind America's New Spacesuit: How Elon Musk Took Hollywood Costume Designer Jose Fernandez From Batman To NASA. Forbes, Retrieved from https://www.forbes.com/sites/guymartin/2020/05/29/the-man-behind-americas-spiffy-new-spacesuit-how-hollywood-costume-designer-jose-fernandez-got-from-batman-and-daft-punk-to-nasa/

Microsoft News. (2021, March). Introducing Microsoft Mesh. Retrieved October 21, 2021, from https://news.microsoft.com/march-2021-ignite.Mitchell, W. J. T. (2015). Image Science: Iconology, Visual Culture, and Media Aesthetics. Chicago, IL: University of Chicago Press.

Moore, L. (2018). Technoetic Aesthetics of Revelation and Transcendence: The Horse in the Mind. Preprints. https://doi.org/10.20944/preprints201810.0040.v1

Pengelly, M. (2018, Novemeber 25). Elon Musk Considers Move to Mars despite 'Good Chance of Death'. The Guardian. Retrieved from https://www.theguardian.com/technology/2018/nov/25/elon-musk-move-mars-chance-of-death

Reckwitz, A. (2012a). Affective Spaces. A Praxeological Outlook. Rethinking History, 16(2), 241–58.

Reckwitz, A. (2012b). Die Erfindung der Kreativität. Zum Prozess gesellschaftlicher Ästhetisierung. Frankfurt a/M: Suhrkamp.

Rosa, H. (2016). Resonanz: Eine Soziologie der Weltbeziehung. Frankfurt a/M, DE: Suhrkamp.

Rushkoff, D. (2019). Team Human. New York, NY: W.W. Norton, Incorporated.

Sexton, A. (2016). Alternative Proteins and the (Non)Stuff of 'Meat'. Gastronomica 16 (3), 66–78.

Tesla Roadster in Orbit. (2018, February 6). Wikimedia Commons. Retrieved October 21, 2021, from https://commons.wikimedia.org/wiki/File:Elon-musk-tesla-roadster-solar-system-ecliptic-orbit-projection-20180501.svg.

Trekipedia Entry: Earth. (n.d.). [web log]. Retrieved from http://www.trekipedia.com/file/Earth.

Tuusa, S. (2018, September 18). Re-Designing the Aesthetic of the Future. Medium Retrieved from https://medium.com/the-morrow/the-iphone-7a3cf5da76cb

Wadsworth, E. (2018). "The Tech World Is Jumping on the Design World" Says Google's Head of Hardware Design. Dezeen, 23 May.

Wilson, M. (2014, January 28). Google Glass Gets More Fashionable, But Not Fashionable Enough. Fast Company. Retrieved from https://www.fastcompany.com/3025586/google-glass-gets-more-fashionable-but-not-fashionable-enough

Sensory Governance
Managing the Public Sense of Light and Water

Nona Schulte-Römer

1. INVISIBLE INFRASTRUCTURES AND SENSIBLE ISSUES

Living in a German city, my everyday life is supported and stabilized by sociotechnical systems. Just now, I have switched on a light because it is getting dark, while in front of my window a line of streetlights has switched on to illuminate the street. This morning as every morning, I went to the kitchen and poured myself a glass of tap water and drank it—without worrying about the water quality. If I had not been writing this essay, I probably would not have even appreciated that I have drinking water running into my kitchen sink, electricity supply built into my walls, and a city-wide lighting system out there that illuminates my street via radio ripple control. I have grown up like this, I am used to this. I take public lighting for granted and trust that public water services provide clean drinking water, also known as the "best-controlled product" in Germany (UBA, 2015, December 2). I also had little reason to mistrust these public services. The streets are well-illuminated and the tap water is looking clean, odorless and tastes fine.

My attitude towards tap water and electric lighting can be best described as what cognitive scientists have termed "inattentional blindness" (cf. Zerubavel, 2015). I am not alone. In fact, the wide-spread blindness towards water supply systems and electrical lighting partly explains why they are often described as "invisible infrastructures" (Larkin, 2013) that have "sunk into the background" (Star & Ruhleder, 1996). Such infrastructures are extremely convenient to live with as long as they are properly maintained and work.

However, the invisibility of public infrastructures can also be problematic, if not paradoxical, for three reasons. First, the creation of sociotechnical expert systems and successful delegation of these basic services leaves us dependent and helpless in the event of sociotechnical failure. When the lights go out, as famously described by historian David Nye (2010), we can only hope that they will come back again soon and meanwhile experience the blackout as a state of exception. If water supply systems fail, people are forced to find alternative water supplies and eventually develop their own, often informal infrastructures, which undermines the very concept of modern public services (cf. Gandy, 2014). Second, the "practical invisibility" (Jensen & Morita, 2015) of sociotechnical systems and services can prevent public discourse and democratic deliberation about infrastructural issues (Marres, 2007). As long as experts operate and maintain public infrastructures in exchange for tax payments and yearly servicing fees, we rarely care or ask questions. We might not even know that local and national governments outsource the management and planning of critical infrastructures to private companies (Collier, Mizes, & Von Schnitzler, 2016). Thus, inattentional blindness includes not only the 'invisible' technical infrastructures but also the actual maintenance work and care that keep these systems up and running (Graham & Thrift, 2007; Ureta, 2014). This public ignorance is often convenient, as it leaves experts a free hand. However, it turns into a problem when service providers seek user feedback and participation as they increasingly do in the course of complex sociotechnical transitions towards sustainability (Bogner, 2012; Chilvers & Kearnes, 2015; Dantec & DiSalvo, 2013). Third and finally, a lack of participation can also backfire in uncontrolled ways. Invisible infrastructures and services can resurface and cause undesirable political conflicts and slow down or even prevent sociotechnical projects—either because they fail or because they are transformed or replaced in the course of sociotechnical transitions (Baringhorst, Marres, Shove, & Wulf, 2019; Pohl, Hübner, & Mohs, 2012).

Indeed, current examples of resurfacing infrastructures show that the issues that "spark publics into being" (Marres, 2007) are often *sensitive* in the full sense of the word. In the case of the sustainability-oriented transformation from fossil to renewable energy sources, people protest against blinking wind turbines, the rotating shadows of their blades and infrasound (Pohl et al., 2012). To assume that these sensitivities grow on purely rational grounds, for instance falling property prices, misses the point. Instead, it seems that people develop rational arguments to justify or back-up their subjective sensory sensitivities, for which they have no direct scientific proof or logical explanations. For instance, while local residents might complain about the depreciation of their property when new infrastructures are built in their immediate neighborhood, the falling property prices are also an indicator for a noticeable depreciation of the sensory qualities of a place—in the form of noise, the loss of a cherished, 'unspoilt' or 'natural' view, atmosphere or an "age-old landscape" (Lintz & Leibenath, 2020). To publicly describe or account for this sensory loss is all but easy and often results in objectified techno-scientific responses rather than subjective narratives (cf. Bruner, 1986).

In this chapter I set out to explore how planners and providers of sociotechnical systems respond to and mitigate tangible, but also highly subjective and therefore elusive sensory sensitivities during sociotechnical projects. I further show how they are sometimes challenged by the users of their services. The notion I propose to capture these phenomena is 'sensory governance.' The concept evolved during my ethnographic research on urban infrastructures in the lighting and water sector. Since 2009, I have studied the transition towards sustainable LED street lighting with a focus on Lyon, France and Berlin, Germany. In this period, I witnessed numerous sociotechnical tests and performances. I conducted interviews with lighting experts, primarily in Europe, and visited countless light-related conferences, festivals, LED installation sites and lighting trade fairs (Schulte-Römer 2015). While my own senses were sharpened through my participant observations, I found that most residents of newly LED-illuminated streets entirely overlooked this latest, radical light-technological innovation. This stood in stark contrast to the expert world of lighting, where LED lighting was the dominant topic and focal issue at the time. Looking closer at the paradoxical invisibility of innovative LED light, I realized that in some places, citizens were all but ignorant (see 2.1.). I also found that public attention or ignorance for public infrastructures was no coincidence—but rather closely related to how experts planned, installed, and maintained their lighting system. These insights can be transferred to other public infrastructures (see 2.2. and 2.3.). Around 2016, I observed similar dynamics when I began to conduct research on aquatic chemical pollution, attended expert workshops and visited central and decentral water treatment sites as part of a research project on aquatic micropollutants in German public discourse (Schulte-Römer & Söding 2019). Exploring the phenomenon further the German energy transition proved as another and particularly salient field to study 'sensory governance' (Schulte-Römer, Bleicher, & Groß, 2017).

Theoretically, the focus on practices that govern our sensory experiences and responses to sociotechnical matters taps into and can build on different bodies of literature, including cultural sociology (Lash, 2018; Reckwitz, 2017), human and historical geography (Edensor, 2017; Gandy, 2014), anthropology (Larkin, 2013) and science and technology studies (Bowker & Star, 1999; Hennion, 2004; Michael, 2020) as outlined in this chapter.

In the remainder of this chapter, I will continue with some illustrative examples of sensory engagements with public lighting and water systems (2). Please note, that these examples are not designed to offer robust scientific evidence, but only prepare the ground for my argument: Conflicts over sensory sociotechnical sensitivities regarding infrastructures are no coincidence, rather such conflicts are side effects of what I describe as the 'sensory governance' of sociotechnical infrastructures (3). Sensory governance thereby refers to expert strategies and procedures that are designed to make public infrastructures as unobtrusive as possible, up to the point where they get literally removed from the public eye. These expert ways of governing sensory experiences range from scientific thresholds for sensory nuisances to artistic designs aimed at beautifying sociotechnical infrastructures. I will conclude (4) that these practices, along with the sensory dimension of sociotechnical relations, have not yet been sufficiently addressed in transition research although they directly affect sociotechnical transition processes in a twofold way. On the one hand, they ensure that sociotechnical systems remain what they should be: *Infra*-structures—the Latin for 'below'—that operate unobtrusively and below our attention threshold. On the other hand, objectified sensory governance always leaves space for subjective experiences. This is why infrastructures resurface and cause controversies that are difficult to settle. To deal with infrastructural sensitivities, so my claim, is a governance challenge that has so far received little attention in social-scientific transition research and deserves more reflexive approaches.

2. SENSITIVITIES AROUND LIGHT AND WATER

"The original field of aesthetics is not art but reality," writes political philosopher Susan Buck-Morss (1992, p. 6). "It is a form of cognition, achieved through taste, touch, hearing, smell-the whole corporeal sensorium." Anthropologist Brian Larkin takes up this definition to highlight the "sensorial and political experiences" evoked by infrastructures. "Aesthetics in this sense is not a representation but an embodied experience governed by the ways infrastructures produce the ambient conditions of everyday life: our sense of temperature, speed, florescence, and the ideas we have associated with these conditions." (2013, pp. 336–337). To stress that our encounters with infrastructures are often pre-reflexive, I refer to sensory experiences rather than aesthetic ones, which I consider as a way of knowing.

Public lighting and water infrastructures have ambiguous sensory qualities. The services they provide are highly sensorial, even aesthetic. Illuminations including streetlights shape the appeal and atmosphere of public spaces after dark (Isenstadt, Petty, & Neumann, 2015). The quality of tap water is evaluated based on its clean and pure look, taste and odor (Doria, 2010). At the same time, large parts of the sociotechnical water and lighting systems are hidden to the public eye. Water pipes and electricity lines are buried under ground and water treatment and power plants usually situated in the periphery and hence removed from sight and smell. Nevertheless, there are moments when these invisibilized infrastructures resurface—not only in the metaphorical, but also in a quite tangible, sensory sense. The following example show how system builders not only install and maintain urban infrastructures but thereby also create specific aesthetic experiences. They also show that this sensory governance sometimes fails to meet the taste of their clients and can be contested.

2.1 Keeping lighting invisible

In the past ten years, I have observed and studied the "LED revolution in lighting" (Schulte-Römer, 2015; Schulte-Römer, Meier, Söding, & Dannemann, 2019) and encountered a quite puzzling situation: From 2010 onwards, numerous municipalities have installed innovative LED lighting systems in public streets. Many were eager to hear citizens' opinions about the infrastructural redesign. Yet, unless the transition was accompanied by explicit projects for stakeholder engagement, feedback was non-existent or biased: In most places, residents of LED-lit streets remained silent and appeared indifferent about the technological transition in public lighting. But in some places, LEDs caused a public outcry and citizens publicly complained about or even protested against the new lights. These indifferent and negative responses to local LED projects stand in stark contrast to the worldwide enthusiasm for the innovation. Lighting experts and mass media highlight the unprecedented energy efficiency of LED lighting. In 2014, the Royal Swedish Academy of Science (2014, October 7) awarded the three pioneering LED inventors with a Nobel Prize in Physics for the invention of a new energy-saving and environmental-friendly light source.

The biased public responses are closely related to sensory issues, such as brightness levels, glare, or the color of LED light. Controversies over urban public lighting can be found worldwide from Montreal to Mumbai (Meier, 2018). In both cities, brand-new LED street lights were eventually replaced after public protest. The Indian case can serve as an illustrative example on how sensory aspects of lighting can turn into sensitive public issues. In 2018, my colleagues and I had the chance to interview the head manager of the Indian public-private company EESL (Energy Efficiency Services Limited) (Schulte-Römer, Dannemann, & Meier, 2018). At the time, EESL was carrying out a nation-wide infrastructural program, in the course of which all street lighting infrastructure was to be replaced with LED fixtures in order to considerably reduce the energy consumption for public lighting. As the head manager told us, the planning included not only the calculation of energy savings, but also sensory considerations. In particular, the engineers discussed the question of color temperature with manufacturers. They even did some pilot projects "just to get a feedback." As the head manager told us, "everybody agreed" that 5,700 Kelvin LEDs looked good. This feedback was good news, as cool-white LEDs also consume less energy than LED lights with a warmer color temperature.

Backed by the reassuring feedback, EESL continued their refurbishment work. Everything went well until in January 2015 they replaced the yellow lights that illuminated an iconic boulevard, the Marine Drive in Mumbai, with cool-white LEDs (see Figure 1). To the project managers' surprise, the light color change incited a public outcry and turned into an outright political controversy. Citizens claimed that the new light destroyed the atmosphere of the iconic place and made it look like any newly constructed neighborhood. They also found that the former yellow sodium lights had illuminated the wide pedestrian walkway next to the road and along the water much better than the newly installed LEDs.

Six months after the refurbishment the issue had still not been settled. Eventually, the Bombay High Court recommended that the municipality should change the lights on Mumbai's Marine Drive back to yellow in order to preserve the iconic look and atmosphere of the coastal road and boulevard. News channel NDTV India quoted the Chief Justice suggesting to the municipality that "The Queen's necklace is the pride of Mumbai. Why don't you bring back the sodium vapour lamps?" (Aora, 2015, July 7). The channel further reports that the replacement of the earlier yellow bulbs with LEDs had become "a political flashpoint" between the ruling Indian People's Party Bharatiya Janata Party (BJP) and its alliance partner Shiv Sena, a rightwing Marathi regional party. "While the BJP insisted that the white lamps were energy efficient and would bring down electricity bills by half, the Sena argued that they have stripped the city of its old-world charm." A leading Sena politician, Aaditya Thackeray, stated on Twitter: "Marine Drive is known as the Queen's Necklace. I'm not against LEDs, but that identity known to Mumbaikars and tourists must remain forever."

The conflict nicely illustrates how the resurfacing of an infrastructure can raise contradictory claims to the common good (cf. Boltanski & Thévenot, 2006). While EESL justified their choices on the basis of rational cost considerations, the local politicians highlighted the aesthetic appeal and cultural value of a public spaces. Eventually, the contradiction of efficiency-oriented innovation and heritage-oriented preservation could be mediated thanks to the flexibility of LED technology. As an Indian energy scientist and engineer explained in an interview with the Indian Express "white warm light will be better for Marine Drive... We can switch to warm white LEDs to retain the glow and use diffusers to reduce glare and make the streetlights more omnidirectional. Specialized lens design and adjustable mounting can help address the problem of light not reaching the footpaths, solving all the problems at Marine Drive." (Lukose, 2015). As EESL head manager told us (Schulte-Römer et al., 2018, pp. 100–102), "after a year of hearings, the court decided that the warm white won and we were asked to change the colors of the 6500 lights that we had installed on Marine Drive to warm white." So, they replaced the cool-white LEDs (5,700 Kelvin) with warmer ones (3,000 Kelvin)—not only on the iconic coastal boulevard in Mumbai, but also in religious places where people pray and also objected to the bright and cool-white new LED lighting. In a modern planned city in the North of India, the city government asked EESL to install LEDs with a color temperature of 4,000 Kelvin and so they did. Meanwhile, 90 to 95 percent of the refurbished public streets and squares in India are illuminated by cool-white LED lighting.

The Mumbai example is not the only case where lighting engineers responded to local aesthetic preferences. In Berlin too, citizens protested against the refurbishment of outdated gaslights arguing that their dim warm light Berlin's nighttime streets a unique and historic atmosphere. After fierce public protest, Berlin Senate came up with a LED lighting scheme that mimicked traditional gaslights in design and light color (Schulte-Römer, 2015). In both cases, the new LED light threatened or disrupted citizens' sensory attachments with the familiar look and feel of a particular public space. In both cases, protest groups justified their personal discontent by enacting the cultural or historic value of the lost aesthetic quality. While the Mumbaikars highlighted the iconic value of "the Queen's Necklace," the gaslight friends in the German capital argued that Berlin possessed the worlds' largest gaslight heritage site. Doing so, these citizen initiatives reminded their public services that black-boxed infrastructures still have culturally meaningful sensory qualities that are not considered by technical standards for visual comfort and efficient road lighting.

Figure 1: "Yellow or white?" NDTV reports on and visualizes the controversy over the illumination of Mumbai's iconic boulevard.

Source: Aora, 2015, July 7

The conflicts that occurred in the course of LED refurbishments also confirm the findings and lessons learned from other sociotechnical transitions. Infrastructures resurface when the running system is changed. However, looking at the Indian LED transition, we see that the refurbishments only caused controversies where they challenged a site-specific and tacit, but nevertheless collective sense of comfort and convenience (Bille, 2019; Shove, 2003). Moreover, it seems that public controversies are more likely where infrastructures had already been publicly visible before a sociotechnical transition. This became particularly obvious when I studied the introduction of LED lighting in Lyon, France and Berlin, Germany (Schulte-Römer, 2015). In the German capital, technical failure, privatization, and budgetary constraints had, since the 1990s, created a situation where citizens and tourists could not help noticing the relative darkness and broken street lanterns in the streets of Berlin. In Lyon in contrast, the municipal lighting department had enough resources to plan lighting strategically, carefully test the acceptance of new designs and technologies in small-scale experiments (Deleuil, 2009) or peripheral streets (Schulte-Römer, 2015). Moreover, the annual Lyon festival of lights has become the focal point of public, even worldwide attention while mundane public lighting practices remained in the background (Djaoui & Poirieux, 2007). I consider the Lyon lighting planners' care for their public infrastructures as sensory governance since their strategies and practices had the effect of drawing public attention to the lighting festival while the well-maintained street lighting sunk into the background and remained an invisible infrastructure and service. Ironically, the Lyon engineers were not always happy with their success at invisibilizing and seemed sometimes a bit disappointed that the citizens of Lyon showed so little interested in their faultlessly running, black-boxed lighting service.

2.2 Bringing sewage to the surface

Looking at urban water systems, the focus on the dis/engaging potentials of sensory and affective properties of water infrastructures has gained importance as "changes in the social role of science, complexity and uncertainty, contributed to the emergence of the general public as an important actor in water management" (Doria, 2010, p. 1). There are also several examples of resilience- and sustainability-oriented transition processes where the engagement and participation of water users as citizens was and still is a critical success factor (Ferguson, Brown, Frantzeskaki, de Haan, & Deletic, 2013; Sharp, 2017).

Sensory aspects are particularly obvious when looking at drinking water, which we instinctively check for murkiness or foul smell, and wastewater, which smells repulsive even from a distance. Accordingly, drinking water is associated with positive sensory qualities like freshness and pure flavorlessness. In contrast, wastewater treatment is associated with disgusting features. Coming close to wastewater treatment plants, we cannot help but realizing the bad smell of sewage and sludge, which is officially acknowledged as a "secondary environmental pollution" and "serious nuisance" (Frechen, 1988). Such odor emissions are not just a warning sign that is associated with health risks through foul water. Odor can also cause psychological stress and negative health effects like headaches, nausea, headaches and respiratory problems (Lebrero, Bouchy, Stuetz, & Muñoz, 2011). German regulation tackles this problem with thresholds for odor nuisance. To avoid it, wastewater treatment plants are not built in the midst of residential areas, but are situated in the periphery of communities. However, the assessment of smell as an environmental pollution is all but straight forward. As an environmental expert told me, he relies on a pool of test persons, which he called 'normal noses' as their sense of smell can be described as average—based on European standards. Obviously, such assessments cannot prevent that individual residents who live in the vicinity of water treatment plants have a finer smell and feel disturbed, especially if the wind blows from the wrong direction. Nevertheless, the peripheral placement of wastewater treatment sites has contributed to a situation where the effluents of our modern lifestyle tend to be hidden in plain sight and socially irrelevant (cf. Zerubavel, 2015).

The peripheral placement of water treatment plants is not the only socio-material strategy for making the public service unobtrusive—and invisible to its beneficiaries. Only when looking back in history or when visiting less developed places, where streets are simultaneously used for transport and drainage, are we reminded of how 'multifunctional' urban streets can smell and look like. In 'modern' cities however, we have become used to above-ground cleanliness and underground sewage system (Gandy, 2014; Latour & Hermant, 2006 [1998]). Accordingly, most of us overlook the constant technical care and maintenance that sustain sewage systems despite inevitable decay, changing climate conditions and growing or shrinking urban populations. Most of us also overlook the civil engineering structures, which can well be described as master works. For instance, I was impressed when I learned during a tour around the water treatment plant in Dresden Germany that the pipes of the historic sewage system were not round, but made of V-shaped stones (see Figure 2).

Figure 2: A piece of sewer and a bucket of treated wastewater (photos: Nona Schulte-Römer) and the historical building of the Dresden water treatment plant.

Source: stadtentwaesserung-dresden.de

The tapered shape made the sewage flow faster if there was little water avoiding the blocking of the system—in my eyes a fascinating technical detail.

The tour, which I attended together with a school class, can be understood as part of Dresden's water governance. By making the public infrastructures visible to lay audience, the operators of the water treatment plant aim to shape and raise public awareness for their public services. Sensory experiences are thereby not only inevitable, but also offer sensational highlights.

The Dresden water treatment plant is situated in a peripheral urban area close to the highway. After passing the gate, our group stopped in front of a surprisingly appealing architectural ensemble, which was constructed in the 19th century as explained by the tour guide and on the website of the facility (image 2, right). Today, the buildings that used to welcome and channel the sewage through a large rake have run dry and been nicely renovated to host the visitors center where we assembled to watch a short introductory film about the history of water treatment in Dresden. The accomplished architectural design creates a stark contrast to the stinking excrements and effluents that the buildings used to contain and conceal. After the introduction, we straightly entered the buildings where the water was collected and a large rake retained the solid waste. As we moved around the untreated sewage and the conveyor belt that removed the solid waste the students giggled and covered their noses in a mixture of disgust and a sense of sensation (cf. Michael, 2020).

When we arrived outside at the big basins, the smell faded away and we relied more on our visual sense. As we walked from one basin to the next, the water looked cleaner and cleaner. Our guide made the purification process even more visible by presenting us a bucket of water at every stage of the water treatment. At the first basin, the water was muddy and turbid and it was impossible to see the bottom of the bucket. As we moved on, the water became clearer with every new bucket. As we arrived at the last basin, it was translucent and the guide assured us that the water was now clean enough to release it into the river Elbe and asked a student to smell the water in the bucket. However, he also pointed to a class of substances that are invisible to the human eye and have become known as micropollutants due to their very low doses (Schwarzenbach et al., 2006).

Micropollutants are a perfect example for an invisible environmental challenge that calls for public attention in order to be tackled. Traces of chemical substances can be found in all water bodies, including drinking water reservoirs. Experts are concerned since some plastics and pharmaceutical residues contain hormonal substances that can have adverse effects on water organisms at very low doses (Ternes & Joss, 2006). Although there is no scientific evidence that micropollutants have health effects on humans, they concern us all—as water consumers and even more importantly, as polluters. Accordingly, our Dresden tour guide did not miss the opportunity to raise the teenagers' awareness for the emerging environmental risk. "If you take drugs or the girls take the pill," he told the school class, "your urine will contain traces of these substances." He further observed that facilities like the one in Dresden are not yet prepared to filter out these tiny residues (field notes). Thus, chemical residues are flushed through the toilet into the sewage system, pass through the water treatment plant and accumulate in the water cycle.

The issue of micropollutants nicely illustrates that invisible infrastructures and inattentional blindness can be a challenge when it comes to refurbishing public services in sustainable ways. In order to eliminate micropollutants like pharmaceutical residues, water utilities in Germany have begun to make large investments in infrastructural refurbishments and upgrade their water treatment plants with an additional, energy-intensive fourth purification stage. These sociotechnical and investments are controversially discussed among experts (Gawel, 2015). But there seems little public engagement, despite the fact that the issue concerns everyone who consumes water, pays taxes and uses pharmaceuticals or personal care products (Schulte-Römer & Söding, 2019). Engaging laypersons in this discussion and communicating the environmental risk and is also all but trivial (Jekel et al., 2013). First, micropollutants are per definition tiny and their adverse effects very difficult to grasp. As a result and fortunately, trace substances are therefore imperceptible to our bodily senses. Second, research on the adverse effects of micropollutants is ongoing. While it seems that micropollutants do not negatively affect our health, there is also a lot of non-knowledge and uncertainty (Tobias, 2016). Awareness of micropollutants nevertheless challenges the very idea of entirely pure drinking water. "We used to tell our customers that our drinking water is pure," told me the representative of Dutch drinking water supply services during a conference. "Today, we know better and say that but only claim that it is safe." As my last example shows, not all water consumers are buying that and contest their water providers truths.

2.3 Making drinking water look bad

In Germany, the societal claim for purity beyond health considerations is acknowledged in the drinking water ordinance. The principle of minimizing contaminations of any kind is thereby tied to aesthetic evaluative criteria. Drinking water consumers should not feel disgusted by the sight, taste or smell of tap water (Dieter & Mückter, 2007, p. 329). These "drinking water aesthetics" (Dieter & Mückter, 2007; Dietrich & Burlingame, 2015) are also reflected in the German norm on drinking water supply DIN 2000. According to this norm, "drinking water should be 'appetizing'" and as natural and unadulterated as possible (Klauer et al., 2019, pp. 105, my translation). The following episode illustrates how sensory qualities can undermine the idea of pure water and with it, the idea of trustworthy public water services. It took place in a vegan restaurant in the German city of Leipzig as part of an information event on water filters on a weekday evening in 2017.

Figure 3: A new and a used cotton filter, the rusty inside of a drinking water pipe and an experimental setting with a bowl of tea made with filtered water (left) and one with unfiltered tap water (right).

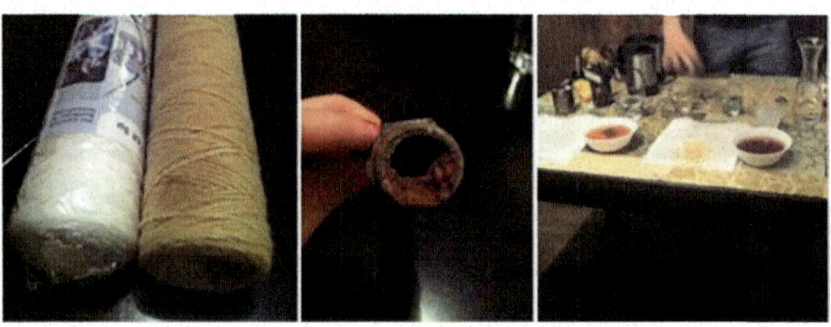

Source: Nona Schulte-Römer

The purpose of the meeting was clear from the start—the promotion of a water filter system by a Berlin company. The host was not employed by the company but an ardent advocate of the filters and convinced of the bad quality of German drinking water. During the event, he eloquently presented what he described as marginalized scientific findings about the bad quality and potential adverse effects of our drinking water. More importantly, however, he exposed parts of urban water supply systems that are usually hidden from view and offered his audience a series of impressive sensory experiences. In particular, he gave us the opportunity to taste with our own mouth and see with our own eyes the differences between the filtered and the ordinary unfiltered, but still controlled and treated Leipzig tap water. While the presentations appeared like quasi-scientific experiments or tests, the framing of the situation was non-scientific. Their purpose was not to explore a specific research question but to illustrate in a sensory way that local drinking water was not pure—irrespective of whether the substances in the water posed a health risk or not.

An acid test, which I faintly remembered from high school, colorfully illustrated that the filtered water is less alkaline than the tap water. The experiment was impressive even if it remained unclear what the coloring really meant in terms of water quality or even health risks. A tea tasting using the two different water samples was even more convincing. As a critical, even skeptical observer of the presentation, I was utterly surprised when I found that the tea from filtered water looked indeed more appetizing and also tasted more aromatic. In addition to these demonstrations focusing on the water, the show also involved the presentation of artifacts that illustrated the detrimental and supposedly non-hygienic state of water supply infrastructures. Our host presented cotton filters that were used in drinking water pipes and already looked disgustingly dirty after only a few days of use, as he said. He also presented a piece of a water pipe that looked utterly rusty and rotten. The presentation did not fail to make an impression on its audience, including me. Although I trust in German water treatment and although I could neither verify the authenticity of these specimens nor the truthfulness of his narrative, these sensory performances made such a strong impression on me that I even briefly considered purchasing a filter.

To conclude, the guided tour in Dresden and the water filter information event in Leipzig both reveal that the sensory qualities of water are suited to engaging water users in techno-scientific issues and sociotechnical matters that shape our daily lives and concern our wellbeing in fundamental ways. In both cases opposing affective experiences of disgust and appetizing purity played an important role. This is very much in line with Mike Michael's account of public and medial representations or "enactments" of fatbergs in London's sewage system and what he describes as "affective infrastructuring"—a way of making both public infrastructures and their audiences (Michael, 2020, p. 377). These public enactments of infrastructures and their maintenance challenges, so Michael, sustain the 'working-ness' of the system "through affective means—by shaping the affects of those audiences in which a problem such as a fatberg becomes, in one way or another, 'acceptable,' 'ignorable' or 'ironicized.'" (Michael, 2020, p. 379). This resonates with my experiences with and observations of sensory engagements with water and lighting infrastructures.

3. SENSORY GOVERNANCE: A CONCEPTUAL PROPOSITION

In order to describe aesthetic practices around infrastructures as sensory governance, it is my conceptual proposition to highlight a particular, politically relevant mode of "infrastructuring." The notion of "infrastructuring" indicates a praxeological, relational approach to sociotechnical systems (Pipek & Wulf, 2009; Star & Bowker, 2002). Sociotechnical systems are analyzed not as structural entities but as the result of "systematically linked and synchronised practices." (Korn, Reißmann, Röhl, & Sittler, 2019, p. 17). Following this methodological line, the activities described above can be understood as practices that concern our perception of public services and mitigate sensory sensitivities around sociotechnical systems and transitions. To conceptualize these practices as sensory governance draws attention to the patterns of public visibility and inattentional blindness that affect how we plan, maintain, and transition our sociotechnical systems—or leave them in the care of– planners, system operators, future-makers. To call this governance 'sensory' rather than 'aesthetic' indicates that the analytical focus differs from "a tradition of thought that understands aesthetics as the key to capturing transcendental truth in sensuous forms" (Black, 2014, p. 101). Instead, 'sensory' refers to a broad spectrum of practices that all enact the relationship between human bodies and their material sociotechnical environment by technical, scientific, aesthetic or other means. The notion 'sensory' thereby also alludes to the techno-scientific means and sensor-based practices that can expand our corporeal sensorium and are key to the (sensory) governance of sociotechnical systems (cf. Gabrys, 2016). These practices are at the center of Foucauldian power-knowledge (Foucault, 1980) and reproduce heterogeneous engagements with sociotechnical systems. Lighting planners and water treatment experts govern light and water based on techno-scientific threshold values and using measuring devices and standardized tests that laypersons neither possess, nor know to perform.

The above-described examples also show that sensory experiences of public infrastructures can vary greatly depending on local contexts and framings. Sensory experiences of sociotechnical systems are not coincidental but enacted in specific situations and institutional contexts and shaped by expectations (Shove, 2003). If sensory experiences contradict these expectations, they can produce quite different senses of water and light. Drinking water is supposed to be "appetizing," wastewater treatment should be unobtrusive. However, if presented in a certain way, drinking water can turn into something unsavory and wastewater and sewage systems can be experienced as sensational—in the context of a guided tour (2.2.) or in an exhibition about fatbergs (Michael 2020). Similarly, artificial lighting can be perceived as 'beautiful' illumination or indispensable in public spaces or else, if we look at it in the context of surveillance or consider its non-visual hormonal effects, especially cool-white light can appear as rather uncanny and even 'dangerous' (AMA, 2016; Hirdina & Augsburger, 2000).

Focusing on the observable effects of sensory governance, we can identify and broadly differentiate between three categories of practices. First, we find normalizing or 'invisibilizing' sensory practices. Their purpose is often to prevent that environmental emissions of sociotechnical systems or their visual appearance compromise their operation or public acceptance. Examples include the above-mentioned creation of and compliance with thresholds for olfactory nuisances from wastewater plants or the prevention of glare and brightness standards for street lighting. Thresholds for noise and ionized radiation also fall into this category. These threshold values are usually created on the basis of scientific experiments, while compliance often involves spatial and material planning and design, e.g., the siting of wastewater plants or LED lighting test sites in peripheral areas, the construction of street lights with a glare-reducing optical system, or the synchronization of wind park lights (Pohl et al., 2012).

Second, we find practices aimed at demonstrating or 'visibilizing' sociotechnical systems in order to reveal how they work, to inform experts and larger lay audiences about their advantages or problems, and to involve stakeholders either in the maintenance and stabilization, or in the phase-out and transition of sociotechnical systems. As outlined, such demonstrative practices can take the form of guided tours through wastewater treatment plants or illuminated urban spaces (Schulte-Römer, 2022). They are also pivotal and common in processes of technological change where stakeholder engagement and public acceptance is paramount and fostered through technology presentations in front of selected or wider audiences (David E Nye, 1996; Pinch, 2003; Simakova, 2010).

Third, aesthetizing practices aim at actively shaping sensory experiences in designerly or artistic ways. They aim at a specific form of "sense perceptions," as Andreas Reckwitz (2017, p. 64) calls it, that are "not embodied in instrumental or normative practice but rather performed for the sake of their affective effects on the subject." (Reckwitz, 2017, p. 64). In the context of sociotechnical transition, aestheticizing can be reflective in the sense that it can open a "reflective conversation" (Schön, 1992) and reveal "the complete range of implications associated with a contending array of ... technological choices," including sensorial sensitivities (Stirling, 2006, p. 137). This can include pleasant decorative illuminations, appealing architectural designs for buildings that contain sewage, the greening of roofs as well as artful approaches to engaging stakeholders in infrastructural projects and visualizations in future-making. On the other hand, aesthetizing sensory governance might also divert attention away from the controversial technical issues or sociotechnical transitions and instead, engage publics in an affirmative spectacle (cf. Debord, 1970 [1967]).

Analytically, the differentiation between normalizing, demonstrating, and aesthetizing practices offers a framework for qualifying the relationship between sociotechnical enactments and sensory experiences. Through this analytical lens, we also see that not all attempts to normalize, demonstrate or aesthetize experiences of sociotechnical systems translate equally well into stable arrangements or desirable transitions. As the Mumbai example shows, the public-private company successfully implemented cool-white LEDs throughout India, but failed to normalize the infrastructural upgrade in Mumbai and at religious sites. In these places, local stakeholder groups opposed innovation by demonstrating its sensory side-effects on the sense of place. The Indian counter-enactments were successful as they were performed by a popular local politician and supported local mass media. In contrast, the maverick who enacted German drinking water as impure and in need of filtering performed from an outsider position in front of a small crowd of about twenty people. Although his sensory demonstration did not trigger a mass movement, he was able to create a momentary sense of unease that challenged the idea of perfectly well-controlled German drinking water. Aestheticizing practices are equally undetermined in their effects. Whether they challenge or maintain the order of a running sociotechnical system strongly depends on the practitioners' position and resources in a field. The Lyon lighting festival, for instance, is part of and supports the city's official urban regeneration strategy (Schulte-Römer, 2011). The Lyon public lighting service thereby actively contributes to what Andreas Reckwitz described as a self-culturalization of cities" (Reckwitz, 2009). Critical reflective conversations that draw attention to social inequalities in public lighting are enacted elsewhere, e.g., in the form of participatory interventions as they are performed by the Guerilla Lighting collective together with local citizens (Sloane, Slater, & Entwistle, 2016). Masato Fukushima describes yet another aesthetic practice, namely the "artialisation" of ugly infrastructures in the form of artistic representations that opens a reflective conversation about "noise in the landscape" (Fukushima, 2020). Historian David Nye (1996) makes a similar point when he refers to modern American infrastructures as performances of the "technological sublime."

Last but not least, the difference between the often successful sensory governance of those in charge of infrastructures, e.g. system builders and public services, and the sensory counter-enactments of their observers resonates with Michel de Certeau's distinction between strategies and tactics (de Certeau, 1984, 2005). In his view, "a tactic is a calculated action determined by the absence of a proper locus" and hence, by the absence of autonomy. "The space of a tactic is the space of the other. Thus it must play on and with a terrain imposed on it and organized by the law of a foreign power" (2005, p. 219). A strategy in contrast, is "the calculation (or manipulation) of power relationships" performed by actors "with will and power (a business, an army, a city a scientific institution) can be isolated. It postulates a place that can be delimited as its own and serve as the base from which relations with an exteriority composed of targets or threats (customers or competitors, enemies, the country surrounding the city, objectives and objects of research, etc.) can be managed" (2005, p.18). Accordingly, experts enact their own sensory relationships with infrastructure and shape the sensory sociotechnical engagements of others from institutionalized positions within their respective techno-scientific fields and in line with established power/knowledge (cf. Lemke, 2001). This techno-scientific "locus" is stabilized and reproduced through institutional settings, standardized methods and procedures, rules, and professional norms. Lighting experts can rely on photometric knowledge and standards (ILP – Institution of Lighting Professionals, 2011), water experts on evidence and norms regarding the organoleptic properties of water (Dietrich & Burlingame, 2015). In short, their sensory governance is based on resources, including standards, measuring devices and expert knowledge that others do not have.

In the face of sociotechnical threats like constant infrastructural decay, system failure and lack of resources, and new challenges like climate adaptation, sustainable development, digitalization, and cyber security, public impression management through sensory governance might appear like a minor issue. However, current public controversies and protest against sustainability-oriented sociotechnical transitions suggest that sensory experiences of sociotechnical environments are all but irrelevant as they shape the ways in which we engage with public infrastructures in transition. This is why I conclude with a call for a more sensorily sensitive social-scientific transition research and more reflexive sensory governance.

3. CONCLUSION: SENSORY BLINDSPOTS OF SOCIOTECHNICAL TRANSITIONS

Artificial lighting and water treatment are only two areas where sensory management practices affect and distinguish the ways in which experts and their larger audiences engage with public infrastructures and infrastructural transitions. There are numerous examples in the context of energy transitions, but also around introduction of 5G telecommunication networks or in the mobility sector where experts and their lay observers do not share the same sensory experiences. While the experts are closely entangled and deeply sensitive to the technology in their care, often aided by sensing devices, lay audiences and users of sociotechnical systems usually pay little attention and take their sensory sociotechnical environment for granted, until something changes. These differences are not coincidental but shaped by sociocultural practices of sensing with all senses, which also produces expert ways of seeing, touching or tasting (Goodwin, 1994; Hennion, 2007; Parolin & Mattozzi, 2013; Vertesi, 2015). But that is not all. As I have outlined in this chapter, system builders, transition managers and their opponents also engage in practices that are designed to shape human sensory experiences. Compared to technological and economic issues, such sensitivities have so far received rather little attention in both theory and practice although they can negatively affect the acceptance and progress of infrastructural projects.

The concept of *sensory governance*, which I have proposed in this article, highlights these practices and allows us to examine how they affect the ways in which we relate and engage with the ubiquitous sociotechnical systems around us. Doing so, we see that in most cases, sensory governance facilitates a very pleasant division of labor, allowing users of public services and infrastructures to remain ignorant of infrastructural work and leave the planning and maintenance to experts. This kind of invisibility is a wonderful sociocultural achievement and makes our lives easier. Yet, it also causes problems or, more precisely, a dilemma: The less we are able to experience public services and infrastructure, the less opportunities we have to engage with them in mundane as well as political ways. If infrastructural issues are removed from the public eye, it becomes more difficult to spark stakeholder engagement and create awareness for risks and critical issues (Kuchinskaya, 2014). The dilemma is even more obvious if we consider sensory governance as a way of *doing* subjective sensorial perception as a basis for collective sense making. Then we see that the predominant *normalizing* sensory practices help stabilize and maintain the taken-for-granted status quo. But they are less suited to opening debates about how outdated infrastructures should be transformed for the common good and what resilience or sustainability means in a specific urban context. Yet, in the course of infrastructural transitions and refurbishments providers of public infrastructure seek and rely on their clients' feedback, acceptance, and cooperation as can be observed in the field of lighting or the water (Deleuil, 2009; Ferguson et al., 2013). After all, infrastructures are planned, built, and maintained with tax money in public spaces and used by the people.

Normalizing practices of sensory governance can also have more serious side effects as it makes it impossible for a population to see the signs of and anticipate system failures. Blackouts hit our digitalized society hard, and failing water infrastructures become a deadly danger in the event of floods, droughts or contamination. In this regard *demonstrating* sensory governance practices gains importance as a means to strategically draw attention to the material, but often invisible weak points of existing sociotechnical systems, e.g., micropollutants that can only be fixed with costly infrastructural refurbishments or more sustainable water and land uses (2.2.). Experts' strategic visibilization of infrastructures can thus play an important role when it comes to raising public awareness, interest, and even pride in local infrastructures (cf. Larkin, 2013; Michael, 2020). At the same time, the example of the Leipzig waterfilter presentation shows that demonstrating practices can also be tactics aimed at contesting existing power/knowledge (de Certeau, 1984; Foucault, 1980). This repertory of contesting tactics also includes *aesthetizing* practices as the case of the Mumbai and Berlin protests against LEDs nicely illustrate. In both cases, opponents of the sociotechnical transition towards LED lighting referred to the pleasure of experiencing a specific atmosphere in what they depicted as a unique, culturally valuable place in order to prevent their governments' plan to modernize existing infrastructure.

Sociotechnical controversies also "provide a plethora of examples for public mobilisation in societies of 'reflexive modernization'...," says political scientist Sigrid Baringhorst (2019, p. 70; cf. Beck, Giddens, & Lash, 1994). In this context, controversies over sensory issues offer an important starting point for analyzing and understanding competing strategies and tactics of sensory governance opening up a space of reflexivity that has been widely neglected in sociotechnical transition processes and transition research (cf. Köhler, Geels, Kern, Onsongo, & Wieczorek, 2017). This lack of reflexivity regarding the sensory dimension of infrastructural projects and sustainability transitions is somewhat surprising as the tangible materiality of infrastructures and sociotechnical systems has always been an issue (Bijker, Hughes, & Pinch, 1987; Latour, 2000), while aesthetic questions have always played a key role in modern critique, from Walter Benjamin to Theodor W. Adorno. In order to explore this untapped potential for reflexivity, I therefore propose to focus on situated practices of sensory governance and to empirically study how they facilitate or undermine societal engagement with infrastructural projects and sociotechnical transitions towards sustainability. The claim is that, if we are to understand public ignorance and opposition, we cannot just focus on the hard facts and objectified indicators. We also need to observe and reflect on how people experience their familiar sociotechnical environment in sensory ways. The history of sociotechnical transitions is full of examples where system builders paid great attention to governing the sensory dimension of their innovations. Just think of Thomas A. Edison, who buried his electricity lines underground and sold his light bulb in lamps that looked familiar gaslight chandeliers (Bazerman, 1999). However, there are also numerous and notorious cases where transition managers manage individual sensory experiences in standardized ways—based on photometric tests or with reference to "normal noses"—and cannot relate to their clients' individual sensitivities. Evidence-based and institutionally established as these practices are, it is difficult to contest the infrastructural realities they constitute. Where the common infrastructural good is at stake, personal unease and sensory experiences that contradict the objectified reality of this established power/knowledge are therefore often dismissed as marginal subjective sensitivities. For instance, the negatively connoted notion of NIMBYism (for "not in my back yard," cf. Devine-Wright, 2014) often stigmatizes people's legitimate protest against a profound and noticeable transformation of their immediate living environment from a rational cognitivist point of view as backward-looking, selfish, and environmentally unfriendly. Likewise, adherence to statistical approaches and the focus on the average sensory experience of populations, passes over the fact that individuals within a population experience differently due to both their physiological and cultural constitution. Accordingly, light-sensitive people who feel heavily affected by LED flicker were extremely disappointed when an EU risk assessment report only accounted for scientific evidence on LED-related health effects on healthy 'normal' people (LightAware, 2020; SCHEER, 2018). Numerous other cases show how hard it can be to gain public recognition and responses for infrastructure-related sensory tangible environmental impacts like the "sick building syndrome" (Murphy, 2006), polluted air or polluted water (Brown, 1992).

All these examples show that people engage with sociotechnical systems and transition in ways that not merely based on reason but also as a result of bodily sensitivities (cf. Marres, 2007). These engagements are relevant as they cause conflicts, slow down or even change the course of well-meant infrastructural projects like the LED refurbishments in Mumbai or Berlin or the installation of wind parks. In this regard, the focus on sensory governance can reveal that experts' and laypersons engagement with sociotechnical systems is not only enacted in different modes (Thévenot, 2007) but also actively shaped in different ways. It can also highlight how less established tactics facilitate public engagements 'by other means,' as outlined in science and technology studies (STS). Such practices can include participatory research, citizen science and environmental sensing techniques (Gabrys, 2016; Gramaglia & Mélard, 2019; Kuchinskaya, 2019), which not only visibilize sociotechnical issues but also affect the ways in which we relate to our sociotechnical environments. They also include artistic performances that enact sociotechnical relationships in aestheticized ways (cf. Mukherjee, 2016).

The theoretical implication of reflections on sensory governance is that it seems worthwhile integrating and considering this sensory dimension as important for "reflexive governance" (J.-P. Voß, Bauknecht, & Kemp, 2006). To put it in Scott Lash's words: "reflexivity must also importantly be aesthetic. That is, that subjectivity is reflective not just through cognitive (or indeed normative) categories, but also through an aesthetic prism" (1993, p. 2). This reflexivity creates and challenges our modern entanglements in sensory rather than purely conceptual ways. They draw out attention to how sociotechnical relationships are facilitated or marginalized in the first place, even before a word has been spoken. Science and technology studies offer numerous and rich accounts and approaches that are instructive for exploring the heterogeneous ways in which sensory engagement and affects are enacted (Parolin & Mattozzi, 2013; Tironi, 2018) and how affective, sensory experiences shape intimate and public engagements (Gomart & Hennion, 1998; Marres, 2012; Michael, 2020). Looking from a legal perspective, Sheryl Hamilton has proposed the notion of "sensuous governance" to explore and question the "particular sensory knowledge-making practices and knowing systems" that form the basis for "the myriad ways in which sensing—embodied being, experiencing, and inter-acting in the world—is integrated into the juridification of social life." (2020, p. 2). However, this research has not yet found its way into transition discourses and research (Köhler et al., 2017). Exceptions include attempts to "remake participation" through more reflexive formats and forms of stakeholder engagement that also reflect the sensorial materiality and entanglements of sociotechnical issues (Le Dantec, 2016; Chilvers, 2013; J. P. Voß & Guggenheim, 2019). Against this background, the notion of sensory governance entails the proposition to reflexively explore the ways in which stakeholders manage sensory experiences and mitigate the subjective experiences with objectified power-knowledge or contest objectified experiences. It implies a mode of reflexivity that comprises aesthetics as well as sociotechnical sensing practices and opens reflective conversations on how we experience the world. The practical relevance of this proposition lies in a better understanding of how people engage, ignore or oppose sociotechnical matters based on subjective sensory experiences.

References

AMA (2016). Report of the Council on Science and Public Health on Human and Environmental Effects of Light Emitting Diode (LED) Community Lighting.

Presented by Luis J. Kraus, MD, Chair. In *CSAPH Report 2-A-16*. https://www.ama-assn.org/sites/ama-assn.org/files/corp/media-browser/public/about-ama/councils/Council%20Reports/council-on-science-public-health/a16-csaph2.pdf.

Aora, N. N. (2015 July 7). In Mumbai, How Queen's Necklace Should Glow Turns into a Battle. Retrieved from https://www.ndtv.com/mumbai-news/court-suggests-return-of-golden-queens-necklace-mumbaikars-happy-778846.

Baringhorst, S., Marres, N., Shove, E., & Wulf, V. (2019). How Are Infrastructures and Publics Related and Why Should We Care? An Email Conversation. In M. Korn, W. Reißmann, T. Röhl, & D. Sittler (Eds.), *Infrastructuring Publics. Medien der Kooperation.* . Wiesbaden: Springer VS.

Bazerman, C. (1999). *The Languages of Edison's Light*. Cambridge, MA: MIT Press.

Beck, U., Giddens, A., & Lash, S. (1994). *Reflexive modernization: Politics, tradition and aesthetics in the modern social order*. Stanford, CA: Stanford University Press.

Bijker, W. E., Hughes, T. P., & Pinch, T. J. (1987). *The social construction of technological systems: New directions in the sociology and history of technology*. Cambridge, MA: MIT Press.

Bille, M. (2019). *Homely Atmospheres and Lighting Technologies in Denmark: Living with Light*. London, UK: Bloomsbury Publishing.

Black, D. (2014). An aesthetics of the invisible: nanotechnology and informatic matter. *Theory, Culture & Society, 31*(1), 99–121.

Bogner, A. (2012). The paradox of participation experiments. *Science, Technology, & Human Values, 37*(5), 506–527.

Boltanski, L., & Thévenot, L. (2006). *On justification: Economies of worth* (C. Porter, Trans.). Princeton, NJ: Princeton University Press.

Bowker, G. C., & Star, S. L. (1999). *Sorting things out*. Cambridge, MA: MIT Press.

Brown, P. (1992). Popular epidemiology and toxic waste contamination: lay and professional ways of knowing. *Journal of health and social behavior, 33*(3), 267–281.

Bruner, J. (1986). *Actual minds, possible worlds*. Cambridge, MA: Harvard University Press.

Buck-Morss, S. (1992). Aesthetics and anaesthetics: Walter Benjamin's artwork essay reconsidered. *October, 62*, 3–41. Cambridge, MA: MIT Press.

Chilvers, J. (2013). Reflexive engagement? Actors, learning, and reflexivity in public dialogue on science and technology. *Science Communication, 35*(3), 283–310.

Chilvers, J., & Kearnes, M. (2015). *Remaking participation: Science, environment and emergent publics*. London, UK: Routledge.

Collier, S. J., Mizes, J. C., & Von Schnitzler, A. (2016). Preface: Public infrastructures/infrastructural publics. *Limn, 7* (July).

Dantec, C. A. L., & DiSalvo, C. (2013). Infrastructuring and the formation of publics in participatory design. *Social studies of science, 43*(2), 241–264.

De Certeau, M. (1984). *The practice of everyday life*. Berkeley, CA: University of California Press.

De Certeau, M. (2005). Making do": uses and tactics. In G. Spiegel (Ed.), *Practicing history: New directions in historical writing after the linguistic turn* (Vol. 217, pp. 213–223). London, UK: Routledge.

De França Doria, M. (2010). Factors influencing public perception of drinking water quality. *Water Policy, 12*(1), 1–19. doi:10.2166/wp.2009.051

Debord, G. (1970). *Society of the Spectacle* (D. Nicholson-Smith, Trans.). Detroit, MI: Black & Red. (Original work published 1967)

Deleuil, J. M. (Ed.) (2009). *Eclairer la ville autrement. innovations et expérimentations en éclairage public*. Lausanne, CH; Lyon, FR: Presses Polytechnique et Universitaires Romandes.

Devine-Wright, P. (2014). *Renewable Energy and the Public: from NIMBY to Participation*: London, UK: Routledge.

Dieter, H., & Mückter, H. (2007). Regulatorische, gesundheitliche und ästhetische Bewertung sogenannter Spurenstoffe im Trinkwasser unter besonderer Berücksichtigung von Arzneimitteln. *Bundesgesundheitsblatt-Gesundheitsforschung-Gesundheitsschutz, 50*(3), 322–331.

Dietrich, A. M., & Burlingame, G. A. (2015). Critical review and rethinking of USEPA secondary standards for maintaining organoleptic quality of drinking water. *Environmental Science & Technology, 49*(2), 708–720.

Djaoui, M., & Poirieux, C. (2007). *Lumières de Lyon. 8 décembre fête des lumières*. Lyon, FR: Édition lyonnaises d'Art et d'Histoire.

Edensor, T. (2017). *From Light to Dark: Daylight, Illumination, and Gloom*. Minneapolis, MN: University of Minnesota Press.

Ferguson, B. C., Brown, R. R., Frantzeskaki, N., de Haan, F. J., & Deletic, A. (2013). The enabling institutional context for integrated water management: Lessons from Melbourne. *Water Research, 47*(20), 7300–7314.

Foucault, M. (1980). *Power/knowledge: Selected interviews and other writings, 1972–1977* (C. Gordon, L. Marshall, J. Mepham, & K. Soper, Trans.). New York, NY: Pantheon Books.

Frechen, F. (1988). Odour emissions and odour control at wastewater treatment plants in West Germany. *Water Science and Technology, 20*(4–5), 261–266.

Fukushima, M. (2020). Noise in the landscape: Disputing the visibility of mundane technological objects. *Journal of Material Culture, 26*(1), 64–84.

Gabrys, J. (2016). *Program earth: Environmental sensing technology and the making of a computational planet*: Minneapolis, MN: University of Minnesota Press.

Gandy, M. (2014). *The fabric of space: Water, modernity, and the urban imagination*. Cambridge, MA: MIT Press.

Gawel, E. (2015). Fighting micropollutants: comparing the Leipzig and the Swiss model of funding quarternary wastewater treatment. *GAIA-Ecological Perspectives for Science and Society, 24*(4), 254–260.

Gomart, E., & Hennion, A. (1998). A sociology of attachment: music amateurs, drug users. *The Sociological Review*, 46(S), 220–247.

Goodwin, C. (1994). Professional vision. *American Anthropologist*, 96(3), 606–633.

Graham, S., & Thrift, N. (2007). Out of order: Understanding repair and maintenance. *Theory, Culture & Society*, 24(3), 1–25.

Gramaglia, C., & Mélard, F. (2019). Looking for the cosmopolitical fish: monitoring marine pollution with anglers and congers in the Gulf of Fos, southern France. *Science, Technology, & Human Values*, 44(5), 814–842.

Hamilton, S. N. (2020). Introduction: Sensuous governance. *The Senses and Society*, 15(1), 1–8. doi:10.1080/17458927.2020.1726059

Hennion, A. (2004). Pragmatics of taste. In M. Jacobs & N. Hanrahan (Eds.), *The Blackwell Companion to the Sociology of Culture* (pp. 131–144). Oxford: Blackwell.

Hennion, A. (2007). Those Things That Hold Us Together: Taste and Sociology. *Cultural Sociology*, 97(1), 97–114.

Hirdina, K., & Augsburger, J. (Eds.). (2000). *Schönes gefährliches Licht. Studien zu einem kulturellen Phänomen*. Stuttgart, DE: ibidem Press.

ILP – Institution of Lighting Professionals. (2011). *Guidance Notes for the Reduction of Obtrusive Light*.

Isenstadt, S., Petty, M. M., & Neumann, D. (2015). *Cities of light: Two centuries of urban illumination*: London, UK: Routledge.

Jekel, M., Ruhl, A. S., Meinel, F., Zietzschmann, F., Lima, S. P., Baur, N., ...Mutz, D. (2013). Anthropogenic organic micro-pollutants and pathogens in the urban water cycle: assessment, barriers and risk communication (ASKURIS). *Environmental Sciences Europe*, 25(1), Article 20. doi:10.1186/2190-4715-25-20

Jensen, C. B., & Morita, A. (2015). Infrastructures as ontological experiments. *Engaging Science, Technology, and Society*, 1, 81–87.

Klauer, B., Aicher, C., Bratan, T., Eberle, U., Hillenbrand, T., Kümmerer, K., . . . Schramm, E. (2019). Arzneimittelrückstände in Trinkwasser und Gewässern. In *TAB-Arbeitsbericht* (Vol. 183). Berlin, DE: Büro für Technikfolgen-Abschätzung beim Deutschen Bundestag (TAB).

Köhler, J., Geels, F., Kern, F., Onsongo, E., & Wieczorek, A. (2017). A research agenda for the Sustainability Transitions Research Network. *Sustainability Transitions Research Network (STRN)*, Manchester, UK: Sustainable Consumption Institute, University of Manchester.

Korn, M., Reißmann, W., Röhl, T., & Sittler, D. (2019). *Infrastructuring Publics*: Berlin, DE: Springer.

Kuchinskaya, O. (2014). *The politics of invisibility: Public knowledge about radiation health effects after Chernobyl*. Cambridge, MA: MIT Press.

Kuchinskaya, O. (2019). Citizen science and the politics of environmental data. *Science, Technology, & Human Values*, 44(5), 871–880.

Larkin, B. (2013). The politics and poetics of infrastructure. *Annual review of anthropology, 42*, 327–343.
Lash, S. (1993). Reflexive modernization: The aesthetic dimension. *Theory, Culture & Society, 10*(1), 1–23.
Lash, S. (2018). *Experience: New Foundations for the Human Sciences*. Hoboken, NJ: John Wiley & Sons.
Latour, B. (Ed.) (2000). *The Berlin key or how to do words with things*. London, UK: Routledge.
Latour, B., & Hermant, E. (2006 [1998]). Paris: invisible city [Paris ville invisible]. Retrieved from http://www.bruno-latour.fr/virtual/EN/index.html. Retrieved 02/10/11 http://www.bruno-latour.fr/virtual/EN/index.html
Le Dantec, C. A. (2016). *Designing publics*. Cambridge, MA: MIT Press.
Lebrero, R., Bouchy, L., Stuetz, R., & Muñoz, R. (2011). Odor Assessment and Management in Wastewater Treatment Plants: A Review. *Critical Reviews in Environmental Science and Technology, 41*(10), 915–950. doi:10.1080/10643380903300000
Lemke, T. (2001). 'The birth of bio-politics': Michel Foucault's lecture at the Collège de France on neo-liberal governmentality. *Economy and society, 30*(2), 190–207.
LightAware. (2020). How does artificial lighting affect human health and wellbeing?
Lintz, G., & Leibenath, M. (2020). The politics of energy landscapes: the influence of local anti-wind initiatives on state policies in Saxony, Germany. *Energy, Sustainability and Society, 10*(1), Article 5. doi:10.1186/s13705-019-0230-3
Lukose, A. (2015, March 4). Explained: LED vs yellow lights for Queen's Necklace. Retrieved from: https://indianexpress.com/article/explained/explained-led-vs-yellow-lights-for-queens-necklace/.
Marres, N. (2007). The Issues Deserve More Credit: Pragmatist Contributions to the Study of Public Involvement in Controversy. *Social studies of science, 37*(5), 759–780.
Marres, N. (2012). *Material participation: technology, the environment and everyday publics*. Basingstoke, UK: Palgrave Macmillan.
Meier, J. M. (2018). Contentious Light: An Analytical Framework for Lighting Conflicts. *International Journal of Sustainable Lighting, 20*(2), 62–77.
Michael, M. (2020). London's fatbergs and affective infrastructuring. *Social studies of science, 50*(3), 377–397.
Mukherjee, R. (2016). Toxic Lunch in Bhopal and Chemical Publics. *Science, Technology & Human Values, 41*(5), 849–875. doi:10.1177/0162243916645196
Murphy, M. (2006). *Sick building syndrome and the problem of uncertainty: Environmental politics, technoscience, and women workers*. Durham and London, UK: Duke University Press.
Nye, D. E. (1996). *American technological sublime*. Cambridge, MA: MIT Press.
Nye, D. E. (2010). *When the Lights Went Out: A History of Blackouts in America* (Vol. 80). Cambridge, MA: MIT Press.

Parolin, L. L., & Mattozzi, A. (2013). Sensitive translations: Sensitive dimension and knowledge within two craftsmen's workplaces. *Scandinavian Journal of Management, 29*(4), 353–366.

Pinch, T. (2003). Giving Birth to New Users. How the Minimoog Was Sold to Rock and Roll. In N. Oudshoorn & T. Pinch (Eds.), *How Users Matter The Co-Construction of Users and Technology* (pp. 247–270). Cambridge, MA: MIT Press.

Pipek, V., & Wulf, V. (2009). Infrastructuring: Toward an integrated perspective on the design and use of information technology. *Journal of the Association for Information Systems, 10*(5).

Pohl, J., Hübner, G., & Mohs, A. (2012). Acceptance and stress effects of aircraft obstruction markings of wind turbines. *Energy Policy, 50*, 592–600.

Reckwitz, A. (2009). Die Selbstkulturalisierung der Stadt. Zur Transformation moderner Urbanität in der "creative city." *Mittelweg 36, 18*(2), 2–34. Retrieved from http://www.eurozine.com/articles/2009-05-20-reckwitz-de.html

Reckwitz, A. (2017). How the senses organise the social. In *Praxeological political analysis* (pp. 75–66). London, UK: Routledge.

Royal Swedish Academy of Science. (2014, October 7). Efficient blue light-emitting diodes leading to bright and energy-saving white light sources. *Scientific Background on the Nobel Prize in Physics 2014*. Retrieved from https://www.nobelprize.org/uploads/2018/06/advanced-physicsprize2014.pdf.

SCHEER – Scientific Committee on Health Environmental and Emerging Risks. (2018). Final Opinion on potential risks to human health of Light Emitting Diodes (LEDs). In R. M. Ion, A. Proykova, T. Samaras, et al. (Eds.), *DG Health and Food Safety, Directorate C: Public Health, Country Knowledge, Crisis management Unit C2—Country Knowledge and Scientific Committees*. Brussels, BE: European Commission. Retrieved from https://ec.europa.eu/health/sites/health/files/scientific_committees/scheer/docs/scheer_o_011.pdf

Schön, D. A. (1992). Designing as reflective conversation with the materials of a design situation. *Knowledge-based systems, 5*(1), 3–14.

Schulte-Römer, N. (2011). Enlightened cities. Illuminations for urban regeneration. In F. Eckardt & S. Morgado (Eds.), *Understanding the Post-Industrial City* (pp. 128–165). Würzburg, DE: Königshausen & Neumann.

Schulte-Römer, N. (2015). *Innovating in public. The introduction of LED lighting in Berlin and Lyon*. (Doctoral thesis). Berlin, DE: Technical University Berlin, http://dx.doi.org/10.14279/depositonce-4908.

Schulte-Römer, N. (2022). Spaces for experience—lighting design as an epistemic approach. In S. Sumartojo (Ed.). New York, NY: Routledge.

Schulte-Römer, N., Bleicher, A., & Groß, M. (2017). *Can you feel the energy? The 'Sensory Governance' of energy technologies and systems*. UFZ Energy Days 2017. Leipzig, DE: Helmholtz-Centre for Environmental Research – UFZ.

Schulte-Römer, N., Dannemann, E., & Meier, J. (2018). *Light Pollution—A Global Discussion*. Retrieved from http://www.ufz.de/index.php?en=20939&ufzPublicatio nIdentifier=21131

Schulte-Römer, N., Meier, J., Söding, M., & Dannemann, E. (2019). The LED Paradox: How Light Pollution Challenges Experts to Reconsider Sustainable Lighting. *Sustainability, 11*(21), 6160. doi:10.3390/su11216160

Schulte-Römer, N., & Söding, M. (2019). Routine Reporting of Environmental Risk: The First Traces of Micropollutants in the German Press. *Environmental Communication, 13*(8), 1108–1127. doi:10.1080/17524032.2019.1592004

Schwarzenbach, R. P., Escher, B. I., Fenner, K., Hofstetter, T. B., Johnson, C. A., Von Gunten, U., & Wehrli, B. (2006). The challenge of micropollutants in aquatic systems. *Science, 313*(5790), 1072–1077.

Sharp, L. (2017). *Reconnecting people and water: Public engagement and sustainable urban water management*. London, UK: Taylor & Francis.

Shove, E. (2003). *Comfort, cleanliness and convenience: The social organization of normality*. Oxford, UK: Berg.

Simakova, E. (2010). RFID 'Theatre of the proof': Product launch and technology demonstration as corporate practices. *Social studies of science, 40*(4), 549–576

Sloane, M., Slater, D., & Entwistle, J. (2016). Tackling social inequalities in public lighting. A report by the configuring light/staging the social research programme. *Configuring Light/Staging the Social*. London, UK: London School of Economics and Political Science

Star, S. L., & Bowker, G. C. (2002). How to Infrastructure. In L. A. Lievrouw & S. Livingstone (Eds.), *Handbook of new media: Social shaping and consequences of ICTs* (pp. 151–162). London, UK: Sage.

Star, S. L., & Ruhleder, K. (1996). Steps toward an ecology of infrastructure: Design and access for large information spaces. *Information systems research, 7*(1), 111–134.

Stirling, A. (2006). Precaution, foresight and sustainability. Reflection and reflexivity in the governance of science and technology. *Reflexive governance for sustainable development*. Cheltenham: Elgar, 225–272.

Ternes, T., & Joss, A. (2006). *Human pharmaceuticals, hormones and fragrances. The challenge of micropollutants in urban water management*. London, UK: IWA publishing.

Thévenot, L. (2007). The Plurality of Cognitive Formats and Engagements. Moving between the Familiar and the Public. *European Journal of Social Theory, 10*(3), 409–423.

Tironi, M. (2018). *Regimes of perceptibility and cosmopolitical Sensing: The earth and the ontological politics of sensor technologies*. London, UK: Taylor & Francis.

Tobias, R. (2016). Communication About Micropollutants in Drinking Water: Effects of the Presentation and Psychological Processes. *Risk Analysis, 36*(10), 2011–2026. doi:10.1111/risa.12485

UBA, U. (2015, December 2). Drinking water in Germany once again "very good." In *Threshold values rarely exceeded—nitrate could become a cost driver for some waterworks*. Dessau, DE: Umweltbundesamt.

Ureta, S. (2014). Normalizing Transantiago: On the challenges (and limits) of repairing infrastructures. *Social studies of science, 44*(3), 368–392.

Vertesi, J. (2015). *Seeing like a rover: How robots, teams, and images craft knowledge of mars*. Chicago, IL: University of Chicago Press.

Voß, J.-P., Bauknecht, D., & Kemp, R. (2006). *Reflexive governance for sustainable development*. Cheltenham, UK: Edward Elgar Publishing.

Voß, J. P., & Guggenheim, M. (2019). Making taste public: Industrialized orders of sensing and the democratic potential of experimental eating. *Politics and Governance, 7*(4), 224–236.

Zerubavel, E. (2015). *Hidden in plain sight: The social structure of irrelevance*. New York, NY: Oxford University Press.

Packaging Pleasures
Design, Play, and Consumer Change

Susan C. Stewart

1. INTRODUCTION

> Loop was here earlier than I expected; so—even though I was really mad about the prices—all of a sudden I'm really excited to open the boxes... I feel like it's Christmas! It's just groceries!" (My Imperfect Zero Waste Life, 2019)

This chapter is about the pleasures of engagement with consumer packaging, especially the packaging of snack foods. It is also about the challenge of change. Change infers a shift in the patterns of expectation, action, sensation, and meaning that underpin a sensing collective. When material systems around which everyday collectives have coalesced are belatedly recognized as toxic, patterns of doing and sensing to which we have become attached are at the front line of change.

Currently most consumer packaging is single-use. Discarded, single-use plastic packaging contributes significantly to the volume of toxic waste that is impacting global bio-systems (Geyer et al., 2017; Simon & Schulte, 2017). The urgency of addressing the problem of plastic waste is recognized in multiple global initiatives to eliminate single-use plastics from our practices (EPA Network, 2017; Ellen MacArthur Foundation, 2017; Kersten-Johnson et al., 2019). Despite significant technological advances in recycling and materials science, complex systemic challenges complicate any easy resolution of the problem (Moreau et al., 2017; Ofrias, 2017; Hird, 2017; Hahladakis & Iacovidou, 2018). Among these challenges one of the least discussed is the hold upon us of embodied habit and sensory reward. Our interactions with disposable packaging trigger deep-seated pleasures that inhere within the sensing collectives of our fast-paced consumer worlds.

Finding a way to interpret patterns of attachment and open them to change is key to addressing the toxicities in which we are entangled. In this chapter I draw upon Roger Caillois's sociology of play (2001) to assist in interpreting our packaging engagements and the sensing collectives they inform. I suggest that the dynamics of play can be harnessed to shift practices. By grasping what is at play within a sensing collective, designers may be able to open pathways into new, less toxic patterns of pleasurable doing and feeling that can help to reconfigure worlds.

Packaging is political. Colorful, shiny, ephemeral plastic wrappers are key actors within the everyday, inconspicuous, and reassuringly routine dramas of unwrapping consumer goods. Gestures of unconcealment and appropriation performed in our daily engagements with packaged commodities, trigger cascades of pleasurable affect. To adopt Andreas Reckwitz's terminology, these colorful wrappers are "affect generators" within our practices of consumption (2017, p.116). They are a locus for endless embroidering of patterns of pleasurable interaction, through which fleeting but heady sensations of mastery flash and sparkle like the wrappers themselves.

Although inconspicuous in their everydayness, the pleasures delivered through packaging interactions have been recognized, captured, and, in some cases, playfully elaborated in unboxing videos. *Unboxing*, an amateur internet video genre, has grown rapidly in popularity since 2008, with YouTube video postings peaking in 2014–15. (Google Trends, 2021; Packaging News, 2018). The majority of unboxing videos adopt a 'product review' approach in which a presenter opens and reviews purchased, packaged products. Of more interest, given our focus, is a sub-genre oriented to the activity of unwrapping and revealing. Here, products are unveiled through protracted dramas of sensuous engagement as their packaging is progressively breached and removed.

To bring to life what is at play within consumer packaging interactions I draw upon two videos from this unboxing sub-genre. Both focus on snack food packaging. Snack foods exemplify the cultures of fleeting, intensely sensuous self-indulgence that are companion to disposability. The selected videos, published on YouTube by EsKannSammeln (2013) and Mairou (2014), have been chosen for the insights they deliver into specific pleasures rather than for their representative character. Both videos have proved popular, as testified by viewing numbers and approval ratings. In this chapter, these videos evidence the presence of Caillois's different types of play and their role in shaping the pleasures and addictions that inform our packaging interactions.

In the last part of this chapter, I turn to the Loop reusable packaging initiative launched in 2019 by TerraCycle (McTigue Pierce, 2019). Loop offers an alternative to disposable grocery packaging by providing a product-based service to manage the return and reuse of purpose-designed, branded, product packaging. The Loop system has been progressively introduced into the United States and Europe, with other countries to follow. An unboxing thread posted on YouTube by "My Imperfect Zero Waste Life" (2019) offers a product review of the Loop system, giving insight into its early consumer reception. Drawing on this and other videos associated with the

Loop launch I ask what we might learn by interpreting reactions to Loop through the lens of play.

2. PLAY AS A LENS FOR INTERPRETING PRACTICES

In his mid-twentieth-century text, *Man, Play and Games* Roger Caillois identified four types of play, referencing them through terms drawn from ancient Greece–mimesis, agon, alea, and ilinx (2001, pp. 12–26). As Caillois observed, these terms provide a starting point for identifying a realm of playful response and interaction within political and practical experience beyond his immediate focus on free play and games (2001, p. 67). Each term in Caillois's fourfold division of play has its own rich history. In what follows I draw on a range of thinkers to communicate the potential of each term to enliven our understanding of everyday practices and the sensing collectives that shape political and aesthetic experience.

For Caillois, mimesis is associated with role-play, imitation, and repetition. A larger literature on mimesis connects it to meaning-making and world-building more broadly (Taussig, 1993; Deleuze, 2014). The constitutive role of mimetic repetition in the formation of sensing collectives is well recognized in the sociology of imitation, contagion, and suggestion (Borch, 2019).

Agon—the Greek term for contest—Caillois associates with competitive play. But our sense of what must be contested reaches beyond play. As Socrates argued in *Plato's Republic*, the agonistic games of the gymnasium should prepare us for contests within the political arena. There, what is tested is our resolution–the metal of our soul–in seeking out and holding to what is right (Plato, 2017, 412 E; Gadamer, 1986a, pp. 95–100). This connection between sportsmanship and ethical behavior lives on, in English traditions of propriety, in condemnation of the unethical as 'not cricket.' Peter Sloterdijk, similarly drawing on this connection in Greek thought, elaborates the role of agon within the political. He attributes to it the cultivation of prideful self-restraint among powerful individuals. Self-restraint opens a respectful space within which others can speak and justice be done (2005, p. 950).

Together, mimesis and agon inform our generative impulses, our making and shaping of worlds and selves. Ongoing iteration, elaboration, and variation of patterns produces coherent worlds. Striving to realize the tangible goods enabled within these patterned worlds orients our energies and gives meaning and direction to our narratives. In these two types of play—mimesis and agon—the cultivation and exercise of human agencies is to the fore. Alea and ilinx, by contrast, point to our engagement with non-human agencies.

Alea denotes luck or fate. For Caillois, luck is the agency engaged in games of chance. In a larger sense, this is the realm addressed by Greek tragedy. The hubris of mortals is laid bare in our encounters with mischance and the fates. Efforts to limit our vulnerability to chance inform both technological striving and our patterning of practice-worlds (Angier, 2010, p.4). We endeavor to craft territories within which predictability and human agency reign and the fates are held at bay.

Ilinx—the fourth of Caillois's types of play—refers to the sensation of vertigo. Ilinx is the experience of precariousness and embodied risk at the limits of physical self-control. Caillois speaks of whirling games and of intoxication. Beyond play, ilinx is ever-present in both exhilarating and disorienting experiences within technology-driven worlds. At its most joyous, ilinx is allied to our experience of the sublime: in speeding, flying, soaring (Dant, 1998, p.83). At its most alienating, ilinx is associated with disorientation, detachment, dislocation, and isolation. Hence ilinx—like the other terms of Caillois's typology—is patterned through experience well beyond his primary focus on free play and games.

Notably, the terms mimesis, agon, alea, and ilinx provide a vocabulary inclusive of both healthy and corrupt states (Caillois, 2001, pp. 43–55). Caillois's mention of unhealthy forms of play is important to recognition of patterns of addiction, alienation, and power-play within our packaging engagements.

When different types of play are mixed—as is usual—they animate and ameliorate each other. The stabilities generated through mimetic repetition are rendered more delightful by an admixture of chance, alea. Alternatively, when the exhilarations of risky destabilization are sought through ilinx we might abandon ourselves to chance or contest the forces that threaten to overwhelm us. In these and other ways, mimesis, alea, ilinx, and agon can work together to variously comfort, delight, challenge or drive us.

Interpreting practices through the lens provided by these terms alerts us to the fertility of the tangible, sensuous experience-worlds that we are immersed in within our everyday doings. Together, mimesis, agon, alea, and ilinx enable recognition of affective registers shaped through creative iteration and striving, through encounters with limits, through shifts between empowerment and precarity. Further, they focus us upon ways our experience-worlds are shared, elaborated, contested, and transformed by their participants. And, when particular practices generate effects that entangle the toxic with the pleasurable, the deadening with the enabling, the inattentive with the social—as packaging practices do—thinking them through the lens of play may also help us to untangle ourselves to some extent, to pick-apart the life-affirming from the problematic and to loosen the hold that current patterns of engagement have upon us.

Unboxing videos are a form of play. They repeat other forms of play. And they repeat the themes, relations, and strategies of the world beyond play. In what follows I draw on unboxing videos to illuminate the playful underpinnings of our snack-food packaging interactions.

3. MIMESIS AND ALEA: UNBOXING KINDER SURPRISE

Figure 1: Unboxing Kinder Surprise; from YouTube uploaded by EsKannSammeln (2013, December 26; 8 mins 39 secs).

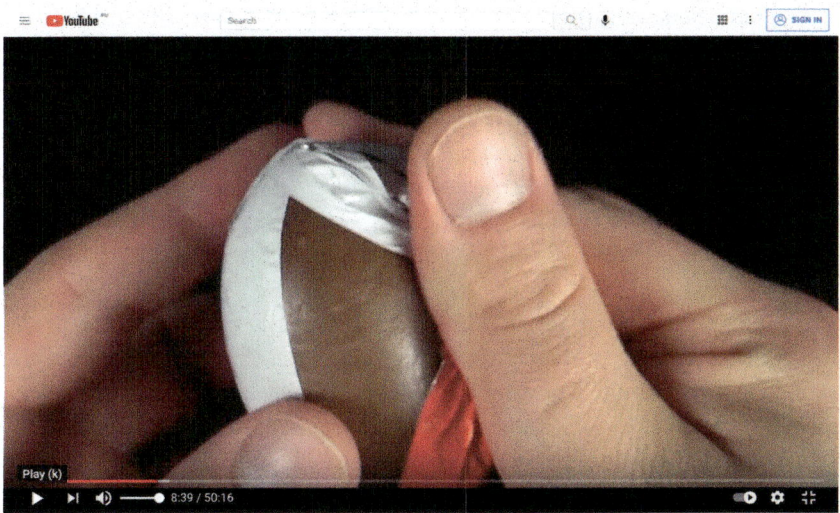

The first video segment I recount is from an unboxing of Kinder Surprise treats posted by EsKannSammeln (2013, 8:31–9:48). It has been viewed more than 11 million times to date. It delivers a play of mimetic repetition and muted alea through successive unveilings of chocolate eggs and their hidden, encapsulated toys. Notable in this drama of unveiling are the attention given to the minutiae of sensuous experience, the hypnotic effects of repetition, the pleasurable modulations between anticipated repeats and myriad small variations, and the satisfaction felt in the revelation of what is hidden as each layer is removed.

On the screen: the focus is on a pair of hands. The camera is positioned as though the hands are those of the viewer. A foil-wrapped egg is held up to the gaze, supported gently by fingertips of both hands. There is silence.
The egg is rotated; quick movements interrupted to pause on each detail of the wrapping. Shaken, it rattles. Then, delicately grasped in both hands, the egg is positioned for opening. The right thumb drags at the foil which parts with sudden release. A smooth curve of chocolate is revealed. The naked surface is quickly rotated into the other hand. The dragging thumb gathers the foil and removes it with a smooth gesture. The wrapper is crushed and dropped.

Now the naked egg is cradled. Thumb and fingers of the left hand delicately grip it top and bottom; the right thumb applies pressure along the vertical seam. The egg is gently squeezed. Slight dragging pressure on the seam focuses the strain along its length. The shell cracks and partly caves in. Shards of chocolate collapse inward. The fractured egg is nestled in one hand while finger-tips gently push pieces of broken shell aside. A plastic capsule is revealed within. This capsule is the prize. It is delicately lifted from the shattered egg. The chocolate shell is set aside.

Fingers either side of its seam, the capsule is gently—then more firmly—squeezed and tugged. It splits. A small plastic toy nestled in a curl of paper is shaken out and the capsule set aside. The curl of paper is picked out and smoothed to reveal diminutive illustrations and text. It is closely examined then set aside. The toy is held up to the camera and rotated to allow leisurely viewing. Fully appreciated it is set aside. A new foil-wrapped egg is selected.

The drama repeats—and again—with slight variation in the movements of the hands, in the tearing of the foil, in the parting of the shell, the opening of the capsule and the assembly of various tiny toys. The only sounds are slight noises made by fingers against foil, by the crushing of foil and breaking of chocolate, by the contents of the capsule clattering lightly onto the table and the occasional clicking together of plastic parts. Variations in the ritual from one egg to the next are myriad but slight and inconsequential. The effect is hypnotic. And there are many eggs.

The breaching of each egg is a choreography of sensuously charged repetitions, of small tugs at resistant surfaces, of rhythmic switches between caressing and insistent movements of finger-tips and thumbs. These repetitions seduce. Remembered touch, sensations of surface—smooth, fragile, resistant but giving way—these are evoked and the viewer drawn into vicarious participation in pleasure-laden interactions.

4. UNBOXING, PACKAGING AND MIMETIC PLAY

Unboxing videos address the gaze. However, their potency depends upon their capacity to conjure remembered sensuous experience. These made-for-viewing enactments of the unwrapping and disclosing of consumer goods are crafted to intensify and repeat sensations that our bodies recognize. The drama of these videos is built on repetition—a repetition that echoes the less-choreographed repetitions of everyday experience. Each opening of a package repeats previous openings.

For the most part our interactions with packaging follow well-rehearsed cues indicated by configurations of form, changes of texture, subtle indentations that meet the fingers. We know where to grip, what to twist. We anticipate the feeling of release as a seal gives way, the slight pop as pressure is liberated. Our bodies have incorporated tacit understandings of how to engage, what to expect, how to react. When an unboxing video repeats, slows, and dramatizes these experiences, the repetition does not belong to the video alone but to the embodied everyday experience that it invokes.

The role of mimetic repetition in our sensuous, embodied, being-within-practices and being-within-collectives has not always been recognized. Rather, within cultures of modernity individual ownership of one's own moves, emotions, experiences, and contributions has been grasped as paramount. However, in 20th century and contemporary thought there have been threads of attention to the potency of imitative repetition. One thread that has recently gained in prominence looks back to the work of Gabriel Tarde. Tarde's thinking took shape amid late 19th century controversies concerning the phenomenon of mesmeric suggestion and the challenge it posed to the concept of free will (Borch, 2019, pp. 13–17). For some among Tarde's contemporaries—including Bernheim, Delbeouf, and Le Bon—the question of manipulation through suggestion pertained not only to the hypnotism of an individual but also to the rippling of suggestion through a crowd. Tarde built on and moved beyond these thinkers. Key to this work was the linking of imitation and contagion.

Contagion within a crowd might seem a far cry from what is at play within everyday engagements with packaging. Undoubtedly there are moments of mutual engulfment in pleasurable affect when, for example, a bag of potato crisps is passed between friends. And, in a different way, this contagious sense of shared affect is also present for viewers of unboxing videos. However, while ripples or surges of shared feeling or response belong to specific engagements—*this* moment of plunging my hand into the glinting, rustling bag that you have passed me—, my interest here is not only in the role of imitation and repetition in shaping such moments. Equally important is the much broader role played by repetition in shaping the milieu within which such surges of shared affect might be triggered. It was in making this shift from the ephemeral to the constitutive that Tarde was so important. He saw beyond the immediate contagion of affect among participants in shared experience. His radical insight was to see society more broadly as "the organization of imitativeness" (Tarde, 1903, p.70). What Tarde grasped was the power of repeated, shared affect to shape, over time, a social milieu.

5. MIMETIC REPETITION AND MILIEU

One vivid image of the significance of shared milieu is provided by Peter Sloterdijk. He imagines a lost text by Aristotle in which a dyer's parable is narrated. Sloterdijk's Aristotle outlines a process for infusing the right pre-conditions—the right atmosphere or mood—into a *demos* prior to their engagement in politics. The parable tells of the immersion "of all citizens of the commonality in the same dyer's vat until they are impregnated to the very innermost fiber of their being" (2005, p.947). This shared immersion in and permeation by a common dye, Sloterdijk emphasizes, does not eliminate differences:

> Far from rendering the city monochromatic and reducing it to some one-dimensional consensus, it is these pre-political 'undertones' that enable those polychromatic layers to be added by dint of which each vibrant city can become a forum for debate. (Sloterdijk, 2005, p. 947)

As Sloterdijk's imagined source is Aristotle, the parable can be read as a re-presentation and extension of the argument of the *Nicomachean Ethics*—now oriented to the formation of a collective rather than focused on the individual soul. Following the argument of Aristotle's *Ethics*, the dyeing process would not be accomplished through a single dip, swirl, and soak. Rather, there would be repeated immersion, a gradual infusion of the dye into the very fabric of the community as it washes through, penetrates, and suffuses every fiber on each successive plunge into the dyer's vat. Over time, through successive immersion, the hold of the dye upon the fabric becomes ever faster. Each situational response that echoes a previous response gives added weight to a tendency to respond in that way, a tendency to repeat that action once again whenever next a situation calls for it (Aristotle NE, Bk2, Ch.1, 1103a-b).

Aristotle gave priority to the rational part of the soul. He sought to school appetitive and emotional responses to be under the direction of reason (NE Bk1, Ch.7, 1098a; Bk1, Ch.13, 1102b-1103a). However, for the most part, it is not reason that directs either embodied experience or the repetitions that play out within everyday engagements. Rather, responses are mapped into the body over time through engagement within an immersive environment that is suffused with ever-shifting variations on the already familiar. The shaping of a sensing and responsive body through repeated, embodied engagements is captured well by another thinker, Levi Bryant, who notes: "A body is not just something that we have, but also something that is formed as a result of the differences that it envelops" (2016, p. 302). To illustrate, Bryant points to those who, like his grandfather, have spent their life at sea:

> My grandfather had implicated or enveloped the waves of the ocean through spending his days on the rocking surface of tug boats and barges and had explicated these differences in a new form of origami constitutive of his disposition to walk and stand in a particular way. He was an embodied wave, a fold of the ocean. (Bryant, 2016, p. 302).

Bryant's grandfather shares, with others who have spent their life at sea, an incorporation of its movement into his body. More, they incorporate particular forms of attention, skilled engagement and care that mark out that life, as well as an aesthetic attunement to the vast, sweeping restlessness of ocean and sky. Those who have spent their lives at sea share an embodied orientation to it that suffuses their entire being.

In these reflections on the shaping power of immersion within a milieu, mimetic repetition is recognized as playing a role. Belonging to a milieu comes about through ongoing immersion within its affective atmosphere. Belonging arises through engagement in a patterning play of repeated themes, gestures, and embodied responses. Hans-Georg Gadamer has likened this patterning play of repetitions to the play of sunlight and shadow beneath the dancing foliage of trees, or the play of light on the rippling surface of water stirred by a breeze (Gadamer, 1986b, pp. 22–23). This play is not dull repetition of the same but ever-shifting variation. It is infused with returns, repeats, re-positionings and re-imaginings. Myriad minor shifts and adjustments play like the endless rushing of a waterfall or the burbling of a brook over stones. It is this play of variation-within-the-same that informs the repetitions of interaction with packaging, repeated again and again in everyday life and again in unboxing videos.

6. MIMESIS AND AGON

Figure 2: Unboxing Doritos; from YouTube video uploaded by Mairou (2014, October 23; 1 min 3 secs).

The second video is a distinctive blend of unboxing drama and conquest narrative. *Doritos Unboxing (Euphoria Overload NSFW)* created by Mairou (2014) has been viewed more than 133,000 times. It is openly playful. But what is at play are tropes of agency, control, and subjugation. Mimetic role-play and agon combine.

The drama unfolds within a bushland setting:

On screen: The camera is attached to and moving with a disciplined body. Purposeful movement through scrubby bushland, the camera focus is on a black-leather-gloved hand that grips a mobile phone in landscape mode. Colorful animations on the phone's screen appear to be informing the tracker's movement. Footsteps crunching unevenly on rocks and plant-debris are the only sound. This is a hunt.

The footsteps pause. The camera focus has shifted quickly from clasped phone to an eye-catching, shiny, parcel-like form set atop a low-lying, semi-distant rock. A focused, deliberate approach to the glinting object is commenced. As it comes more clearly into view the shiny form is disclosed as a packet of Dorito's corn chips, lying face down on the mossy, leaf-strewn surface of the rock.

The camera lens moves in on the shiny packet. A leather-gloved hand reaches to gently touch the gleaming surface then strokes it slowly. The surface is smooth and offers no resistance. The bright, silvery, reflective, metalized plastic packaging rustles and glints in response to the stroking touch. The gloved hand slides quickly and smoothly under and along the edge. The grip closes. With a snatch, flip, and flick, the package is lifted and tossed lightly onto its back, colorful side up, branding fully revealed.

A second approach of hands to the package. One hand carefully grips the package to steady it; the other strokes it again with a soothing, circling motion. The package is gently lifted and briefly transported—rustling, with reflections dancing across its responsive surface. Movements have been choreographed to maximize the crackling and glinting of the surface. The packet is placed with a quick double-movement and released with a flick; hands withdrawn quickly from view. It now lies, face up, on a clearer surface of the mossy rock ....

Thus far, the action might qualify as a playful re-presentation of a Pokémon-Go hunt. The chip-package echoes the role played by shiny Pokémon—the most valuable kind—discovered, captured, and tamed. However, the focus on sensuous interaction with the rustling, metalized plastic surface of the packet intensifies the mood. This is about power. The drama highlights a contrast between masterful, purposive action and the passivity of the package as it shifts and gleams in response to stimuli and to repositioning. The action continues with mounting menace.

With chip packet lying exposed, the hunter removes his hat—it is a plastic, child's-play, bowler hat. We see gloved hands, phone (tucked into one palm), hat, rock, and chip packet. The hat is placed carefully, bowl facing upward, onto the rock beside the chip packet. The phone is placed face down into the bowl of the hat. The play of hands on both hat and phone involves quick touches—a caressing of surfaces: touching, returning, touching again. The leather gloves are quickly removed and placed on top of the phone. Hands, now bared, push the hat away slightly then rub over one another in an enactment of hand-washing. The hand-washing is thorough; gestures attend to the backs as well as the palms and fingers of both hands, rubbing and cleansing. This is a drama of preparation.

Both hands move purposefully. The packet is seized and lifted. A brief pause, then it is swiftly rotated clockwise. Gripping fingers are brought together in the middle of its long side, positioned to tear the package. With fingers twisting and tugging an attempt to breach it is made; the tough plastic-foil compound holds. The package is rotated anti-clockwise and the attempt to breach repeated on the opposite side, again unsuccessfully. With increasing urgency, the package is rotated again and again; each edge tried without success. The package is thrust back onto the rock; hands rubbed quickly in frustration as they are withdrawn.

The drama continues.

A fluffy, pink, child's back-pack is produced and rummaged. Various tools are pulled out, a hammer and then a small saw, each examined quickly then cast aside. A final plunge of hands into the back-pack, and wire cutters are drawn from within. A cutting action is rehearsed. The chip packet is approached.

Without detailing the remaining action, suffice it to say that with the help of the wire cutters the package is breached, ripped asunder, scattering chips which are grabbed and consumed with violent, mouth-stuffing, crunching haste and tumultuous waste. Then the hunter is running—fleeing the scene—and the action has ended (Mairou, 2014).

7. AGON AND THE ROLE OF TECHNOLOGY

Mairou mobilizes technology in his contest with the Dorito's packaging. The wirecutters—excessive for this task—draw attention to the role of technology in shifting power relations.

The tools employed by Mairou and the packaging he tackles are technologies deployed in our everyday world-shaping. Like all technologies, they extend our power, reconfiguring the terrain we inhabit to suit our purposes. Packaging, especially food packaging, is a technology of boundaries. The metalized plastic packaging of the

Doritos chips creates an effective boundary between the contents of the package and the forces of decay—the air and moisture—that would otherwise impact those contents (Marsh & Bugusu, 2007). As a technology of resistance and defense, the packaging is easily appropriated to Mairou's playful enactment of conquest.

The ancient Greeks understood technology—techne—as a way to reconfigure our chances in withstanding the non-human agencies that course through the world, intervening in human fate (Angier, 2010, p.4). Agon, our human striving to overcome the forces that assail or limit us, can be mediated by technologies that shift the balance of power. In games, the greatest fun is had when the powers of contestants are evenly matched. However, in our pursuit of everyday, practical concerns, our aim is often to diminish, as far as possible, any external power that might impinge upon us. Here, technologies are deployed not to balance the contest, as in healthy agonistic play, but to weight the contest in our favor.

Martin Heidegger points to habitual deployment of technological power for the purpose of domination as a dangerous disposition that infects our age (Heidegger, 1977). Ironically, far from delivering control, unrestrained deployment of technological power since industrialization has delivered toxicities, including from packaging waste, that are unbalancing the systems that have hitherto sustained us. Non-human agencies, fueled by our inattention to externalities of industrial production, now threaten our worlds.

Mairou's role-play enacts and celebrates the imbalance of power we have established between active, technology-assisted human agents and the rendered-passive, though resistant, bodies that we seek to subjugate and plunder. Caillois speaks of healthy and corrupt forms of play (1961, 2001, pp. 43–55). The exercise of power for the sake of domination is a corrupt, though intoxicating, form of agon. Concern to redirect this disposition to dominate is behind Sloterdijk's call for a different conception of agon within the political. Sloterdijk, drawing on the Platonic-Aristotelian tradition, recognizes that the most important of contests is that waged in the exercise of self-restraint; when the powerful rein themselves in and allow other powers a place and a voice (2005).

Mairou's unboxing of Doritos confronts us with the sensory euphoria that courses through everyday enactments of technology-enabled dominance. The political challenge, in addressing the toxicities of our times, is to redirect such euphoria to the powerful exercise of self-restraint. And yet, the cultural supports for such restraint are difficult to detect within the sensory register of consumer capitalism, as currently structured.

If we turn to the sensory landscape of consumer capitalism more broadly, not only do we find that unhealthy forms of agon abound. Equally, Caillois's fourth type of play, ilinx, assumes an unhealthy form.

8. ILINX

Ilinx is present to contemporary experience not only in play but also in our everyday addiction to powerful vehicles and swift movement. The connection between the experience of the motorist and the aesthetics of consumer capitalism has been well captured in Venturi, Scott Brown and Izenour's influential text, *Learning from Las Vegas* (1972). There they note that the built landscape of Las Vegas is designed to be experienced from a moving vehicle. Large-scale, simplified forms—signs and decorated sheds—loom into view at intervals within a leveled and utilitarian landscape. The highlights of this landscape, the glittering neon signs dotted along the Strip, present moments of focused intensity and semiotic reduction to the passing motorist. They are seductive, memorable lures, designed for streamlined consumption. Flows of traffic, flows of pleasure-seekers, flows of packaged product, flows of money; the incessant movement of the Las Vegas Strip is an emblem of the capitalist economy.

Adam Smith conceived of growth and accumulation within a capitalist economy as dependent upon the swiftness with which money circulates (Swyngedouw, 2006, p.111). Loss of momentum, he argued, is destabilizing, potentially fatal. Equally, momentum and speed offset instability within ilinx-based play. At speed, through the directedness of their plunge, the hurtling skier or surfer moves responsively and with fine control, directing their thrust, their muscle-power, through the force of their momentum. The world shrinks to a tiny, speeding bubble of focused human agency, aligned with sublime forces in the face of which we are insignificant—catching a ride, giving ourselves over, embracing the precarity. The experience is intensely individual; each actor a focused blur of embodied skillfulness in a tightly defined exercise of responsive self-control. It is exhilarating and terrifying. Ilinx-based play is a saturated version of our experience within the capitalist economy. Like the skier, participants in complex, globalized systems of production and consumption narrow their attention, blurring the wider field to a pre-interpreted, simplified landscape that can be backgrounded within the intensity of focused engagement. Unlike the skier, however, the consumer closes themselves to precarity and risk. They are not exhilarated. Rather, they are desensitized and distanced as complexity and nuance recede from view.

Swiftness of flow, mobility, and speed have become defining experiences within the urbanscapes of capitalism. Speed disassociates the social and material assemblages, that flow through industrialized conduits, from any attachment to situated networks. Erik Swyngedouw ironically notes of such assemblages that speed, movement, and mobility render the field of vision more opaque, transient, and partial: "While the focus is on speed and high-tech networks, the material, socio-environmental connections and the uneven power relations that produce them, remain invisible" (2006, p.113). Through speed, time is banished. The consumer product that circulates swiftly within this system is severed from its past and its future. Seemingly, it arrives from nowhere, is consumed—either in an extended moment of appreciation or in a rapacious gulp—and is lost to view (Griffiths, 1999).

Packaging does much of the work in speeding products through consumption-oriented systems. At point of sale and point of consumption packaging triggers brief, intensely sensuous encounters before passing into waste streams. If mass-produced consumer goods gain little traction in our lives, their packaging has still less. It is this lack of traction that contributes most to the mood of consumer capitalism and to the problem of waste (Han, 2017). In the case of snack food products, rapid consumption is integral to the pleasure of the encounter. There can be no complexity admitted to this experience. A choreography of layers, perhaps, but simplified: smooth to the touch. An intensification of sensory feedback loaded into the moment of encounter and then, nothing. Just satiation.

Our everyday participation in consumer culture bears greater resemblance to the anaesthetizing boredom of a road trip than to the intensity and exhilaration of surfing or skiing. This is a watered-down version of ilinx. As for motorist along the Strip, the rhythms become dull. Even the highlights, though saturated, are repetitive and predictable.

It is not easy to shift expectations and configurations of meaning that are profoundly woven into the milieu within which we operate and which, like the waves ridden by Bryant's seafaring grandfather, have been absorbed into and have shaped our embodied being-in-the-world. So, how do we bring about change sufficient to make a difference to the problem of packaging waste? Appeals to reason and to virtue will not suffice. In the following section I examine a recent initiative by TerraCycle, the Loop reuseable packaging system for groceries (2019).

9. LOOP

Figure 3: Unboxing Loop; from YouTube video uploaded by My Imperfect Zero Waste Life (2019, September 14; 8 mins 27 secs).

Loop, launched in 2019, is the most ambitious of recent reuseable packaging initiatives in the grocery sector. Initiated by TerraCycle, a sustainability focused NGO based in North America whose previous focus has been on recycling, Loop is conceived as a large-scale, global, packaging reuse system. TerraCycle has enrolled, as partners, a number of multi-national grocery manufacturers and retailers. Significant investments have been made in the redesign of product packaging. The supply chain has been reconfigured from one-way flow to a loop between grocery manufacturer and consumer, incorporating the collection, cleansing, and refill of used, reusable packaging. TerraCycle's role is in the management of used packaging, ensuring that containers that can be reused are cleaned and returned to the manufacturer for refilling, while any packaging that cannot be reused is recycled. The goal is a no-waste packaging system (TerraCycle, 2019).

To gain sufficient following to make any real difference to our packaging practices, Loop must either slip smoothly into existing patterns and structures, or lure consumers into new and addictive patterns of action and sensory pleasure. In a promotional video by TerraCycle, their CEO, Tom Szaky, claims the Loop system will allow consumers to "experience a throwaway mentality, but be doing the right thing from an environmental point of view" (McTigue Pierce, 2019, 0:10–0:17). He makes clear that their aim is to play into existing consumer expectations that packaging interactions will be pleasurable, effortless, and inexpensive. However, a closer view of Loop reveals that the sensory experiences expected to deliver pleasure, the systems to deliver convenience and the type of investment expected in order to minimize expense, are all significantly different from those that feed our current habits, addictions, and assumptions. There is a gamble here. Can consumers be lured to commit to this radical translation of their 'throwaway mentality' into material practices that are not throwaway at all?

Early consumer reviews of the Loop experience highlight that the major challenge for the system to gain acceptance lies not in the sensory experiences immediately associated with handling packaged products, but rather in consumer expectations of convenience and affordability of the service as a whole (My Imperfect Zero Waste Life, 2019; Practically Zero Waste Podcast, 2021). Challenged on this, Szaky suggests that the actions required to return Loop containers are "about the same" as for disposable packaging. The containers, when empty, are 'binned' in the shipping container they arrived in. This shipping container, when full, is collected and returned to Loop. The sequence, he argues, involves similar effort to putting out garbage for waste collection. However, the real convenience of the system, Szaky suggests, is in re-ordering. Each product container can be set to trigger reordering when returned: "So it's subscription, but perfectly timed based on your consumption." (McTigue Pierce, 2019, 17:30–19:30). This proposed digital smoothing of the experience of re-ordering groceries plays directly into, and accelerates, the experience of ilinx as detachment (Han, 2017).

The tension, here, between systems designed to reduce consumer waste and those intended to smooth and accelerate flows of consumer goods, is clear. The buy-in from major players within grocery supply chains is likely motivated by not only the reputational advantages attached to participation in an initiative to reduce waste but also the potential for these new systems to further capture consumers within managed flows of goods.

If the convenience of the Loop system is problematically framed as an increase in smoothness of flow, the approach to affordability is equally bedeviled. The stumbling block is the established expectation that packaging should be low-cost and low-responsibility. The Loop system assumes the higher cost of reusable packaging can be distributed over multiple use-cycles. Initial cost to the producer is ameliorated if packaging is retained within the Loop and its life is not shortened by abuse. Thus, cost effectiveness for the producer is tied to consumer behavior. A degree of care is demanded. But this demand is at odds with consumer cultures, in which freedom from care is a key promise (Feenberg, 2017).

To stimulate care for packaging, Loop requires an up-front deposit to cover the value of each container should it not be returned in good order. The potential for financial penalty, and skepticism as to whether Loop delivers 'value for money', undermine enjoyment of the system and its tangible product interactions (My Imperfect Zero Waste Life, 2019; Practically Zero Waste Podcast, 2021). The mood established is more transactional than collaborative.

This transactional mood infects unboxing reviews of the Loop system. Reviewers hold up the packaged products shipped by Loop, rotating them in front of the camera to provide a comprehensive view. Different components of the packaging—the container, label, and lid—are each engaged and tested with finger-tips and nails, tapped, rubbed, or picked at to determine the material type and potential for disassembly. The difference between glass and plastic is detected by tapping and listening, or gripping and pressing. This is a forensic examination, not an appreciative exploration of sensory potential. There is no extended savoring of surfaces, enjoyment of pressure release, delight in pattern, satisfaction with grip. Yet, the containers have undoubtedly been designed to be attractive and to give pleasure in use.

As prospective players within the small dramas of everyday consumption, the reusable jars, tins, and bottles of the Loop system embody the restraint and generosity that Sloterdijk suggests should be brought to political contests (2005). Simple lines and repeated forms bow to the constraints of the system, but without seeming dull. Curved surfaces invite grip. Lustrous finishes on stainless steel and glass offer discrete pleasures (TerraCycle, 2019). These objects are not mean. If non-humans are indeed political players, as Bruno Latour (2005) has helped us to see, then these containers set an example that might, in time, be repeated within their users' dispositions and sensibilities.

Despite the seductive potential of Loop's reusable containers, however, the reviewers seem not to have been seduced. Their mimetic role-play is that of the critic. Agonistic contestation here aims at holding to account. Any anticipation of pleasure upon receiving the first Loop delivery quickly runs aground amid uncertainty as to how the system works, reluctance to invest too much, and suspicion of corporate good faith.

10. LEARNING FROM UNBOXING

Unboxing videos reveal the pleasures attached to unveiling and interacting with consumer goods. Ritualized repetitions, patterned actions and responses, sensuous engagement with surfaces that give way to the touch; in unboxing, human agency is to the fore. We take possession, assert ownership and control of small worlds.

If mimetic repetitions and agonistic assertions of dominance are given rein in our intimate, sensuous engagements with packaging, alea and ilinx—chance and disorientation—are deliberately muted. In EsKannSammeln's unboxing of Kinder Surprise eggs, anticipation of the toy within drives removal of layers of foil and egg. But what is unveiled is not very surprising. A toy that provides more pleasurable interactions than another is a lucky find. A toy identical to one already found is a disappointment. Chance modulates experience, but there is not much at risk. Similarly, ilinx is dulled. Disorientation within a world saturated by brand choice is managed through repetition and reduction.

Everyday interactions with disposable packaging provide micro-assurances of agency and of dominance within a pacified world. Given this, difficulty in recruiting allegiance to reuseable packaging is understandable. Gone is the euphoric sense of dominion and freedom from consequence celebrated by Mairou. In its place is a requirement to take care, and to deal respectfully with objects that are not consumed in the moment of engagement.

The challenge for Loop, or for any other system of re-usable packaging, is to build a patterned world of pleasurable interactions that affirm, through ongoing sensory feedback, the agency of those who use the system. Distributions of power within the system make a difference. The reviewers of Loop were concerned that they were at the mercy of mischance. They feared they were open to financial penalty if the containers should suffer damage. These messages, built into the system, alter the balance in favor of non-human agencies. The play of alea within the system puts participants at risk, and offers little reward.

An opportunity to reconfigure experience of Loop lies in recognition that the system is layered. Indeed, the system is a kind of packaged product. At its heart is a realm of intimate, sensuous, interactions with crafted reusable packaging. But this intimate offering is enclosed by an outward-facing set of interactions and transactions with corporate entities. Perhaps these layers each need a different mood? A different dynamic of play?

The outer layer might draw from Mairou's delight in contestation, reoriented to invert the usual hierarchy of power. Designers of the web-page, financial transactions, the delivery and return systems, might think about how to tilt these technologies toward user empowerment. Can the triumphant euphoria of Mairou be invoked within the Loop-user's interactions with the larger system? Can it be oriented to deliver users a sense of collaborative agency in driving corporations to greater accountability and more responsible behavior? If Sloterdijk's vision of democratic agon is relevant here, it is surely the power of corporations that must be reined in to give place and voice to users within the system.

Conversely, the inner, more intimate heart of what Loop offers might draw upon EsKannSammeln's nuanced unboxing of Kinder Surprise. In crafting a sensing collective disposed to savor Loop's slowing of consumption, designers might draw upon the sensuously charged repetitions of those hypnotic unveilings. Where these interactions would differ from those of the Kinder Surprise unboxing, would be in the robustness, the resilience of the reusable containers. They should communicate to the user a sense of generosity that endures. Materials that age well, that gain in luster through use—and surfaces that continue to be delightful to the touch—these should play their role in cultivating allegiance between users and system.

Recognition of layers of interaction within a system, and the potential to play quite differently within each zone, might be key to negotiating the complex transition from consumer to collaborative culture that Loop attempts.

11. CONCLUSION

This chapter has focused on our everyday interactions with consumer packaging, especially the glinting, light-weight, snack-food wrappers that are so closely associated with moments of indulgence and delight. I have highlighted the role played by these interactions in ongoingly acting-into-being the milieu of consumer capitalism. It is this milieu, in which we have long been immersed, that orients our bodies and senses within packaging engagements. Any initiative for change needs to work with the milieu into which it is introduced. Change can reconfigure, but only from within.

An original contribution to strategies for interpreting sensing collectives, is made by drawing on Caillois' four types of play—mimesis, agon, alea, and ilinx. Each of these terms has been interpreted more broadly than in Caillois's work on play, to unpack how patterns of sensory experience reproduce and give continuance to a milieu. Each type of play, I have suggested, produces a range of aesthetic and political effects. Together, they diversely empower and move us—reassure and stimulate. Different forms and combinations of mimesis, agon, alea, and ilinx, shape the moods, meanings, and aesthetic styles that circulate within a sensing collective.

Evidence of what is at work within our packaging interactions can be found in unboxing videos. I have drawn on videos by EsKannSammeln and Mairou that show our interactions with packaging to be infused with mimesis and agon, the types of play through which agency is exercised and extended. By contrast, their rendition of risk through alea and ilinx is subordinate, tamed. These videos capture and reproduce myriad, small performances through which we assert our dominance within a world of consumer goods.

At the heart of this chapter is a question about relations between sensing and the dynamics of change. The Loop reusable packaging system is an ambitious attempt to address the imperative to shift away from disposable packaging. Early unboxing reviews of Loop suggest a mixed reception of this system. Drawing on the playful insights provided by the unboxing videos of Mairou and EsKannSammeln, as well as on the types of play, I have suggested possible design strategies for better engaging users in this, and similar, reusable packaging systems.

References

Angier, T. (2010). *Technē in Aristotle's Ethics* (1st ed.). London, UK: Bloomsbury Publishing). https://doi.org/10.5040/9781472598035

Aristotle. (1925). *The Nicomachean Ethics*. (W. D. Ross Trans.). Oxford, UK: Oxford University Press.

Borch, C. (2019). *Imitation, contagion, suggestion: on mimesis and society*. London, UK: Routledge.

Caillois, R. (2001). *Man, play and games*. (M. Barash Trans.). Urbana, IL: University of Illinois Press.

Dant, T. (1998). Playing With Things. *Journal of Material Culture, 3*(1), 77–95. https://doi.org/10.1177/135918359800300104

Deleuze, G. (2014). *Difference and repetition* (P. Patton Trans.) (1. publ. ed.). London, UK: Bloomsbury.

Ellen MacArthur Foundation (2017) The New Plastics Economy: Rethinking the future of plastics and catalysing action. Retrieved from https://emf.thirdlight.com/link/ftg1sxxb19tm-zgd49o/@/preview/1?o

EPA Network (2017). *Recommendations towards the EU Plastics Strategy. Discussion paper from the Interest Group Plastics of the European Network of the Heads of Environmental Protection Agencies (EPA Network)*.

EsKannSammeln (2013, December 26). *Kinder Surprise Egg Unboxing – Kinder Surprise Christmas Special (Ultra Super Rare Collections)* [Video file]. Retrieved from https://www.youtube.com/watch?v=kI9BTvw-8Hc (8:31–9:48) (EsKannSammeln's YouTube Channel https://www.youtube.com/user/EsKannSammeln)

Feenberg, A. (2017). *Technosystem: The Social Life of Reason*. Cambridge, MA: Harvard University Press.

Gadamer, H. G. (1986a). *The Idea of the Good in Platonic-Aristotelian Philosophy*. (P. Christopher Smith Trans.). New Haven, CT: Yale University Press.

Gadamer, H. G. (1986b). The Relevance of the Beautiful (N. Walker, Trans.). In R. Bernasconi (Ed.) *The Relevance of the Beautiful and Other Essays* (pp.1–53).). Cambridge, UK: Cambridge University Press.

Geyer, R., Jambeck, J. R., & Law, K. L. (2017). Production, use and fate of all plastics ever made. *Science Advances, 3*(7)

Google Trends (2021) *Evolution of the search term 'unboxing'* Retrieved August 2021 from https://trends.google.com/trends/explore?date=all_2008&gprop=youtube&q=unboxing

Griffiths, J. (1999). *Pip Pip: A Sideways Look at Time*. London, UK: Flamingo.

Hahladakis, J. N., & Iacovidou, E. (2018). Closing the loop on plastic packaging materials: What is quality and how does it affect their circularity? *The Science of the Total Environment, 630*, 1394–1400. https://doi.org/10.1016/j.scitotenv.2018.02.330

Han, B. C. (2017). *Saving Beauty*. (D. Steuer Trans.). Cambridge, UK: Polity Press.

Heidegger, M. (1977). The Question Concerning Technology (W. Lovitt Trans.). In *The Question Concerning Technology and Other Essays*. (pp.3–35). New York, NY: Harper and Row.

Hird, M. J. (2017). Waste, Environmental Politics and Dis/Engaged Publics. *Theory, Culture & Society*, 34(2–3), 187–209. https://doi.org/10.1177/0263276414565717

Kersten-Johnston, S., de Thomas, D., Dearman, S., Harrison, K., Huded, K., Meyers, J., Muouw, S. & Schwarze, C. (2019). *Bridge to Circularity: putting the new plastics economy into practice in the U.S*. E. Martin & L. Brown (external eds.). The Recycling Partnership. Retrieved from https://recyclingpartnership.org/info-hub/?fwp_tags=reports

Latour, B. (2005) From Realpolitik to Dingpolitik, or How to Make Things Public. In B. Latour, & P. Weibel (Eds.), *Making things public: Atmospheres of democracy* (pp. 14–41). Karlsruhe, Germany: ZKM/Center for Art and Media Karlsruhe, Cambridge, MA: MIT Press.

Mairou (2014, October 23) Doritos Unboxing (Euphoria Overload NSFW). [Video file]. Retrieved from https://www.youtube.com/watch?v=VkScAOWw5Z4

Marsh, K., & Bugusu, B. (2007). Food Packaging—Roles, Materials, and Environmental Issues. *Journal of Food Science*, 72(3), R39–R55. https://doi.org/10.1111/j.1750-3841.2007.00301.x

McTigue Pierce, L. (2019, January 24) *Meet Loop, a circular shopping platform powered by reuseable packaging* [Video file], unveiled 24th Jan 2019 at the World Economic Forum in Davos; Interview of Tom Szaky (Founder/CEO TerraCycle) by Lisa McTigue Pierce – Executive Editor of Packaging Digest]. Retrieved from https://www.youtube.com/watch?v=YSxoiF6N2M4

Moreau, V., Sahakian, M., Griethuysen, P., & Vuille, F. (2017). Coming Full Circle: Why Social and Institutional Dimensions Matter for the Circular Economy. *Journal of Industrial Ecology*, 21(3), 497–506. https://doi.org/10.1111/jiec.12598

My Imperfect Zero Waste Life. (2019, September 14) *I Tried Loop: Episode 3 Unboxing* [Video file]. Retrieved from https://www.youtube.com/watch?v=1SoI8sAAyBs

Ofrias, L. (2017). Invisible harms, invisible profits: a theory of the incentive to contaminate. *Culture, Theory and Critique*, 58(4), 435–456. https://doi.org/10.1080/14735784.2017.1357478

Plato (2017). *The Republic of Plato* (B. Jowett Trans.). London, UK: Oxford University Press.

Packaging News (2018) Analysis: YouTube's Influencer Marketing Phenomenon. https://www.shorr.com/packaging-news/2018-11/influencer-marketing-youtube-statistics

Practically Zero Waste Podcast (2021, May 10) Loop-dee-doo, It's my Loop Review! [Video file] Retrieved from https://www.youtube.com/watch?v=6eCZ1f8sagY

Simon, N., & Schulte, M. L. (2017). *Stopping global plastic pollution: the case for an international convention* (1. Auflage ed.). Berlin, Germany: Heinrich-Böll-Stiftung.

Sloterdijk, P. (2005). Atmospheric Politics. In B. Latour, & P. Weibel (Eds.), *Making things public: Atmospheres of democracy* (pp. 944–951).

Karlsruhe, Germany: ZKM/Center for Art and Media Karlsruhe, Cambridge, MA: MIT Press.

Swyngedouw, E. (2006) "Circulations and Metabolisms: (Hybrid) Natures and (Cyborg) Cities." *Science as Culture*, Vol.15, No.2, 105–121

Tarde, G. (1903) *The Laws of Imitation*. (E. C. Parsons Trans.).). New York, NY: Henry Holt and Company. Retrieved from https://monoskop.org/images/3/35/Tarde_Gabriel_The_Laws_of_Imitation.pdf

Taussig, M. (1993). *Mimesis and alterity: A particular history of the senses*. New York, NY: Routledge.

TerraCycle (2019, May 4). *Loop is Reducing Waste by Providing Reusable Containers for your Favourite Products.* [Video file] Posted to YouTube by *Money*, Retrieved from https://www.youtube.com/watch?v=90WoQctzPIQ

Venturi, R., Scott-Brown, D., & Izenour, S. (1972) *Learning from Las Vegas*. Cambridge, MA: MIT Press.

Hegemonic Sensory Practices of the Smart City
And a Collective Remaking of Data-based Urban Commons

Miguel Paredes Maldonado

1. INTRODUCTION

This chapter discusses how urban life is affected by digitally mediated practices of sensing and navigation in the city. It puts forward a project that redeploys those practices to challenge the logics of "computational governance" championed by smart cities and urban platform labor. After describing the project and its proposed interventions, I will discuss how it engages with the city as a "sensing collective" to counter-balance the sensory orders established by hegemonic digital mediations: Whereas smart cities and urban platform labor aggregate and standardize human activity into a reductive model of flows, the described interventions re-introduce individual subjectivity, plurality, and agency as key components of collective life in the city.

The project that constitutes the core contribution of this chapter consists of a case where I worked alongside with student-activists, engaging with the 'models' of digital sensing and navigation prescribed by smart cities and urban platform labor in the urban scenario of Cagliari (Italy). These 'models' (and the attendant sensory orders they instigated) were called into question by creatively appropriating and disrupting their technologies and the data they produced.

This case demonstrates novel modes of engaging with urban data, challenging hegemonic, top-down urban practices in pursuit of alternative, digitally mediated practices that foster a more inclusive and democratic "public commons." In so doing, the project responds to three fundamental questions: What methods might be employed to better understand the relationship between public data and public space in the urban field? Do data-driven infrastructures play a role in restructuring the collective experience of public space, or do individuals forge space through their own data productions? How can citizens be empowered to become performative agents in the production of a data-based urban commons?

From a methodological perspective, the digitally mediated practices presented in this body of work engage two distinct emerging fields: urban hacking, the creative use of digital media to "open up urban institutions and infrastructures to systemic change in the public interest" (Ampatzidou, Bouw, van de Klundert, de Lande, & de Waal, 2015), and critical making, the pragmatic pursuit of critical thinking through actions of goal-based physical making. In that spirit, the work develops by exploring alternative sensing practices that co-opt the cybernetic paradigms of digital sensing and navigation to generate novel perspectives on the collective dynamics of urban life. It makes use of existing open-source databases and original digital data gathered by smartphone apps. These data sources are processed through a custom digital workflow to develop interpretive maps, animations, and drawings that foreground and interrogate collective dimensions in urban life. More specifically, the case presented in this chapter looks into the commuting dynamics of university students into the city center of Cagliari, unveiling their resultant informal patterns of appropriation of urban public space through academic and social activities. Ultimately, the "sensing collectives" that unfold as a result of these processes point to means for urban intervention that overcome the structures of hierarchical, data-based optimization championed by smart city initiatives.

2. THE TRANSFORMATION OF SENSING AND SENSORY ORDERS IN THE CITY

Public space in our cities is woven together with an enormously varied array of elements and features: streets, alleys, and avenues; gardens, squares, and parks; but also, smaller objects (and groups of objects) such as kiosks, benches, playgrounds, bicycle rails, and bus shelters. A lot has been written about the many ways in which these physical components—large and small—organize and regulate our collective experience of the city (see Chapter 1 of this volume by Prinz). As we move about in the urban fabric and negotiate our interactions with its physical system of spaces and objects, we inhabit the city by jointly constructing a network of navigations against the background of public space.

If we consider the above through one of the key ideas presented in this book—the notion that sensory practices play a key role in the organization of our collective social life (Reckwitz, 2016)—, we can say that collective practices of urban navigation are part of this "sensory order" inasmuch as they generate specific forms of collective life in the city. As an example, upon approaching a busy city center by foot, we may decide to join (or to avoid) the crowds of people assembling alongside with others to partake in different activities. If we venture further into the main streets, the lights of shopfronts may invite us to enter the premises and purchase some of the goods on offer. Likewise, the smell of food and drink from nearby cafés might lead us to sit down for a short rest and a snack. This may be followed by some further browsing in a nearby market, which may trigger our curiosity upon hearing the rumble of shoppers and sellers from a distance. Finally, a series of conveniently signaled and well-lit bus stops may provide us with a cue to carry our newly purchased goods home in a non-strenuous manner. Throughout our time in the area, and through a series of sensory interactions, we become part of a choreography of shoppers, café-goers and revelers, participating in the kind of collective experience that we often associate with leisure in urban centers. As this paragraph tries to convey, this particular modality of "collective life" is predicated to a large extent on fostering commercial transactions. Our individual navigations both inform and are informed by this organized rhythm of sensory stimuli, subsequently giving rise to a "sensory order" that is established through the amalgamation of our collective movements and interactions in urban space.

However, in recent times this space has also been populated with yet another category of objects: countless "data points" that are mapped against physical locations in the city. These "data points" are dynamic and changeable: Some register and store our individual impressions, for instance restaurant reviews or geo-localized photographs on social media. Others register important changes in our environment, such as live air quality information (see Chapter 6 by Husberg & Marzecová), or live updates to the schedules of bus networks. Using the appropriate digital platforms, we can access mediated collections of "data points," often adding our own data productions in the process. This has become an almost universal practice and, as it turns out, we seem to have gradually transformed into "Data Citizens": Through mechanisms of environmental sensing, surveillance systems and individual interactions with personal digital devices, our navigations in the city are increasingly informed by the production and retrieval of urban data.

Put differently, bodily embedded sensory practices in the city—and the sensory orders they give rise to—are gradually being displaced by digitally mediated forms of "sensing" which are, in turn, predicated on our interactions with a range of dynamic data. Examples of interactions include, but are not limited to, using apps to guide our movements and activities (for instance to choose a commuting route or to check the opening times of an exhibition) as well as to access services or share our whereabouts with others (for instance by ordering food for home delivery or posting our status in a social network). As the examples suggest, digitally mediated sensing in the city works in both directions: we use apps and digital platforms to look into collections of urban data and, in doing so, also add our own data to those collections. In this manner, I argue that digitally mediated practices of data-based digital sensing in the city encompass a distinct range of materials, meanings, and competences, and thus resonate with an understanding of "praxis" as a tool for the production of knowledge (Shove, Pantzar, & Watson, 2012).

3. HEGEMONIC PRACTICES OF URBAN DATA AND COLLECTIVE REPRESENTATION

In the following sections, I will discuss how these digitally mediated practices of sensing follow a particular set of logics (which I will refer to as "computational logics" throughout the text), and how these logics change the sensory orders that regulate collective life in the city. As a starting point, I identify two distinct practices that, at the time of writing this text, emerge as the prevalent models for implementing these data-based sensing practices: *smart cities* and *urban platform labor*.

The term smart cities refers to the overlay of integrated, responsive digital infrastructures that draw on data streams from mobile apps, sensor networks, social media feeds and transport information, with the goal of making urban features more responsive to changing conditions (Coyne, 2017). An example of this is the "live" coordination of motor traffic information with public transportation schedules and the provision of environmentally friendly commuting alternatives (such as rental electric bikes) across the city. Likewise, the broad category of urban platform labor refers to the digital, app-based logistical systems deployed to coordinate the provision of on-demand labor and services in the city—with an emphasis on adaptiveness and responsiveness. Well-known examples of these platforms are Deliveroo and Uber Eats (which organize food deliveries from third-party restaurants and eateries via "freelance" couriers that ride their own bikes or motorcycles) or Uber (which connects private vehicle owners with individuals seeking door-to-door transportation in the city).

Both smart cities and urban platform labor have a strong steer on the configuration of urban life through their data-based sensory orders. Expanding on the examples above, in smart cities the digital mediation or urban traffic data can be used to privilege some particular routes or means of transportation above others—effectively reconfiguring the collective experience of daily commuting. Similarly, food deliveries through Urban Platforms can potentially reconfigure the dining scene in a city—displacing patrons from restaurants to their own homes—while simultaneously forming a precarious ecosystem of "freelance" urban riders and "dark kitchens." Thus, by changing the ways in which people move about in the city smart cities and platform labor applications also affect how people performatively represent the "polis" as a collective subject.

Among the two hegemonic practices of digitally mediated urban sensing introduced here, the smart cities paradigm holds a particularly strong claim to collective representation—and consequently also to the articulation of the "polis." Therefore, I will use it as the basis for a further discussion on how performative, collective representation in the city is transformed by digitally mediated sensing. As the examples above suggest, smart cities constitute a form of urban governance and decision-making: Waste management and recycling can be optimized on the basis of waste volume data. Crime and policing can be controlled through systems of digital surveillance. Energy consumption for urban lighting or district heating can be adjusted on the spot according to live energy use indicators, and energy sources redirected to minimize their environmental impact.

All of these interrelated urban aspects, and many others, can be jointly and synchronously addressed through the well-oiled, responsive mechanisms of the smart city. This only became possible in recent years through the combination of pervasive computing (the embedding of computational capability into everyday objects) and ubiquitous data (that emerging in a decentralized way from many different, partially overlapping sources). For architectural historian Mario Carpo, the widespread abundance of spatial data combined with an exponential increase in computational power led to a "digital turn" in spatial practice throughout the past decade (Carpo, 2017). In this process, the embedded logics of computational thought were transposed into planning, design, and governance across a broad range of scales. In the urban field, this resulted in the substitution of bodily, embedded sensory practices by computational logics that undertake decision making on the basis of the insights provided by digitally mediated sensing, as exemplified by smart cities. In that respect, it is worth noting that the second-order cybernetic theories of the 1970s have been identified as a precedent for the smart city paradigm, to the extent that the latter can be regarded as a direct re-materialization in space of the former (Krivý, 2018).

As I noted in the previous paragraphs, the digitally mediated sensing practices of smart cities are not just a means of governance and decision-making: They also construct performative representations of collective life in the city and, in so doing, they can be regarded as political forms of representation. Cities constitute "entities of meaning" that are formed collectively and grounded on their very own "intrinsic logics"—the structures of their everyday life that are specific to them (Löw, 2012). Likewise, collectively assembled individual actions in the city—often manifested by movements in urban public space—do have performative qualities which, in turn, can lay claim to political representation (Butler, 2015, pp. 71–72).

Following this line of thought, if the digitally mediated sensing practices of the smart cities change the way in which people move about in urban space, they also change the ways in which they construct performative self-representations of the city through their collective subjectivities. In so doing, the city is manifested as a "polis"; a space for the unfolding of political action or, perhaps more accurately, a "spatialized politics" (Latour, 2003). This, in turn, raises important questions about the new collective representations that may emerge within the data-based sensory orders brought about by smart city practices.

4. DATA-BASED, DIGITALLY MEDIATED SENSORY ORDERS IN THE SMART CITY

In what follows I will provide a more detailed account of the sensory orders that emerge from the hegemonic, data-driven sensing practices that constitute the repertoire of the smart city paradigm. I will argue that these practices articulate three sensory orders, which I will respectively refer to as an "order of singularity," an "order of vertical hierarchization," and an "order of optimization."

The "order of singularity" refers to a "metabolic" reading of urban systems, inherited from second-order cybernetics and based on a metaphor of the city as a "circulatory body." In this conceptual framework, the subject of urban queries is the city-body. Consequently, any smaller, individually heterogeneous components of the urban are "blended" into the larger, homogeneous whole. This reading of the city gained significant traction in architectural theory throughout the "projective turn" of the 1990s (Krivý, 2016). It has also been successfully carried forward into the 21st century: Architect and theorist Kas Oosterhuis has conceptualized cities as infrastructural "bodies," recalibrating humans as "carriers" of matter, energy, and information within urban metabolic structures (Oosterhuis, 2017). This framework has also been explicitly articulated as a result of computational logics, with an insistence on the "metabolic" character of computational processes as they tackle spatial problems pertaining to the urban scale (Segraves, 2013; Weinstock, 2013).

A key aspect of this framework is that it represents the city as an "urban body" that is both "sensed" and "activated" by means of differential "flows" of matter, energy, and information. If "infrastructure governance is enacted through the representations of the infrastructural system" (Offenhuber, 2017) this circulatory metaphor, which posits fluidity as the central principle of development, has important implications: If a particular aspect of the urban cannot be readily expressed in terms of "flow" (which is to say, expressed as a dynamic differential), it cannot be "sensed" (i.e. captured as data) and therefore it escapes urban decision-making (Krivý, 2018). This is immediately apparent in the representation of urban public space: It can be captured as a "flow" only when "sensed" through the marketized notion of "footfall." Hence, this representation of the city as a circulatory body with "inputs" and "outputs" clearly privileges some urban narratives above others. Moreover, this "sensory order" ignores fine-grain practices that either operate below the scalar range of the "whole," or cannot be easily reduced to a logic of differential exchanges.

The second order, the "order of vertical hierarchization," refers to the top-down logic that characterizes design and governance in smart city practices. This logic is based on highly centralized decision making, which is subsequently "cascaded down" to a strict hierarchy of urban agents (Paredes Maldonado, 2020). It should be clarified that "top-down" refers to the direction in which the agency of data-driven representation progresses: From institutions or corporations towards individual citizens. Conversely, I refer to bottom-up logics when the agency emerges from individuals and is disseminated "upwards" into larger constituencies. Whereas this is usually presented as a clear-cut distinction (Picon, 2015) it is often the case that data-based urban processes operate in a range between the entirely top-down and the entirely bottom-up (Offenhuber, 2017).

Notwithstanding this, it is apparent that the operation of the hegemonic digitally mediated sensory practices in the urban field is fundamentally top-down: Data flows in multiple directions between stakeholders (regardless of their relative size or power), but decision-making is highly centralized. Be it in smart cities or in platform labor, individuals (either citizens or workers) have little scope to intervene in this decision-making. Whereas in the case of platform labor this poses challenges to the establishment of fair labor relations (Gregory & Paredes Maldonado, 2020) it is more difficult to disentangle its implications in regards to institutional governance. On the one hand, it can be argued that this orientation follows the structure of political power in representative democracies, and therefore it is important that its conditions are not bypassed. On the other hand, such degree of vertical hierarchization defeats the purpose of establishing a meaningful direct dialogue with citizens. This conflict is exemplified in institutional "Civic Tech" initiatives, which articulate channels for citizens to communicate and report simple issues related to urban governance (for instance by reporting the location of potholes via SMS messaging) but offer little insight into the actual decision making that determines which actions are taken forward.

Finally, the "order of optimization" refers to a focus on quantitative standards of efficiency in the practice of digitally mediated sensing and its attendant performative representations of collective life in the city. As a direct result of this, any qualitative aspects of social life in and around public space are overlooked (Greenfield, 2017a; Haque, 2017). This preoccupation with quantitative optimization is often linked to flow-based urban resources such as electricity networks (Ratti & Claudel, 2016), public transportation infrastructures (Szell & Groß, 2014) and telecommunication services (Greco, 2014) but it also appears to have pervaded many other dimensions of urban life. Interestingly, even some of the most vigorous advocates of smart cities have reservations about the ability of the numerical optimization of differential flows to capture the full spectrum of urban phenomena (Ratti & Claudel, 2016).

To sum up, the practices of the smart city, platform labor and their attendant processes have installed hegemonic, digitally mediated sensory orders in the urban field. Under these practices, the urban is collectively performed and represented as a singular "regime" of inputs and outputs, balanced dynamically through an imperative of maximum performance. This calls into question the agency of individual citizens, neighborhood communities, grassroots platforms and other non-hegemonic stakeholders in the city.

5. COUNTER-PRACTICES OF URBAN DATA SENSING

As elaborated in the previous section, in order to foster more democratic means of digitally mediated sensing, performativity, and representation in the urban field, we must first understand the socio-political agendas that are implicit into different data-based sensory orders predicated. Likewise, we must also understand the processes of algorithmic design and distribution of civic resources they give rise to (Greenfield, 2017b; Gregory & Paredes Maldonado, 2020). Put differently, whereas hegemonic data-driven practices such as smart cities and platform labor are primarily lauded as unprecedented technological achievements, I argue that their success lies somewhere else: The complete pervasiveness of the ontological model they advance.

In contrast to this pervasive technocratic model there are other alternative frameworks that tap into available data sources to drive design, performativity, and representation in urban spaces, albeit in a more socially responsible manner. A well-developed contribution along these lines is the Local Code project (de Monchaux, 2016). This body of work identifies and repurposes inner city infrastructures through data-driven strategies of fine-tuned adaptive reuse and urban biosphere remediation. However, whereas it succeeds in overcoming some of the top-down, mechanistic strictures of the smart city framework by paying attention to a broader, qualitative range of design factors, Local Code offers citizens no means to engage with its data-driven workflow in order to intervene as co-creators of their public urban landscapes. Likewise, Civic-Tech initiatives represent a more nuanced, alternative framework of data-driven spatial intelligence, predicated on using distributed citizen participation as a means to inform institutional decision-making. Such initiatives are augmented through the notion of the "hyperlocal," which champions a focus on the experiential aspects of the algorithmic engagement with Civic-Tech tools (Bullivant, 2017). In both cases, the explicit goal is to open up alternative technological modalities of collective urban dialogue that capture needs and subjectivities beyond the scope of hegemonic data-driven systems.

In an attempt to expand on the lines of work explored by these alternative models, the following sections will put forward a body of research-by-design work developed as part of my own academic practice. As noted in the introduction, this body of work is presented through a case where I worked alongside with groups of student-activists to challenge the hegemonic practices of digitally mediated sensing championed by smart cities and platform labor. The goal was to engage with those practices to subvert their attendant sensory orders, unveiling novel forms of bottom-up, performative urban representation in the process. Throughout the development of the case, this "subversive engagement" was carried out through collective actions of creative redeployment of the technologies and the data produced by these platforms.

The resulting set of "alternative sensing practices" explore civic data through urban hacking and critical making in an attempt to identify and capture fine-grain urban phenomena that are inflected by individual subjectivities and their attendant actions in urban space. To that extent, they pay attention to urban issues that explicitly tackle social friction, collective experiences and contested shared resources. This entails privileging a qualitative interpretation of quantitative raw data sources, leveraging "sensory orders" where data is used as a means to unpack frictional, messy, creative forms of representative citizenship (Haque, 2017). In this manner, the smart city practices of top-down, totalizing, optimized objectivism are countered with practices that re-situate individual subjectivities as the fundamental agents within the urban millieu, identifying the domain of the commons as a "site" of representation that emerges both gradually and collectively.

As explained earlier, the hegemonic sensory order of the smart city follows a hierarchical approach, seeking to optimize urban resources for a limited set of stakeholders. Contrary to this, the methods of urban hacking promote a creative use of digital media to "open up urban institutions and infrastructures to systemic change in the public interest" (Ampatzidou et al., 2015). In so doing, "urban hackers" use data to develop bottom-up collaborative interventions that unveil contested issues within the public commons, with a view to addressing them critically (de Waal, de Lange, & Bouw, 2017). Importantly, urban hacking does not prescribe specific "solutions," but rather "tinkers" with the urban field, testing incremental steps for data-driven action, and endeavoring to privilege collective knowledge and curiosity above strict functionality (Pe, 2017). The practices presented in this chapter mobilize the sensibilities of urban hacking through critical making: Designing and testing small interventions in actual urban contexts constitutes an ideal approach for establishing collaborative practices of participation in design (Ratto, 2011), and also articulates avenues to collectively unpack and explore the politics of such participation (DiSalvo, 2014).

A fundamental aspect of the alternative sensing practices presented here is that their goal is, above all, the production of shared knowledge. The stakeholders involved position themselves as active citizens—wary of dominant urban narratives—working collaboratively to organize alternative networks of digital civic collaboration (Townsend, 2014). Their traits and attitudes resonate with the figure of the "amateur" as described by sociologist Antoine Hennion (2005): They engage with a particular practice (mediated digital sensing) in a dedicated, inventive, experimental manner and—critically—they do that socially, that is, in reference to other members of their collective. Their creative and intimate relationship with particular aspects of the world is mediated by their activities and their endeavors, and subsequently presented to the wider world as an open invitation for others to join the conversation.

The "sensing practices" that underpin the case presented in this chapter develop around two particular themes: circulation and play. Framed as urban phenomena, both themes appear to yield themselves well to interrogation through data-driven methods, offering fine-grain insights into human activities in the city. The first theme pertains specifically to the circulation of individuals, recorded by the individuals themselves as part of a collective exercise. It should not be confused with the notion of "flow" discussed in earlier sections. Rather than illustrating a differential displacement, the theme of circulation is framed as a critical form of agency for urban citizens. It is linked to other, non-digital practices in the city that attempt to break away from the conventional representations of the urban subject. In that spirit, Ignacio Farías and Stefan Höhne (2016) invite us to consider "… the power of circulation to unleash processes of desubjectification, enabling human bodies to enter a plane shaped by the movement and rest, the speed and slowness of de-stratified bodies, a field of vectors and particles intersecting in new ways, becoming something else." As discussed in the work of Michel de Certeau, circulation can also be a "tactic" to overcome functionalist structures in the city (see also, Schulte-Römer in Chapter 3 of this volume). By simply "moving about," one develops "unrecorded and un-recordable productions" (Beltzung Horvath & Maicher, 2016). As de Certeau noted "[T]rajectories trace out the ruses of other interests and desires that are neither determined nor captured by the systems in which they develop" (de Certeau & Rendall, 1984).

In the context of this body of work, the theme of "play" can be considered as a subtheme of "circulation." This draws from the well-known practices of play through serendipitous displacements in the city carried out by members of the Internationale Situationniste (Andreotti, 2000; Smith, 2005). Such practices are best exemplified in the practice of urban "drift" or "*dérive*" as originally theorized by Guy Debord (1956). Here, urban circulation is turned into a game, which individuals agree to play collectively by purposefully recording their movements and productions in the urban field. Play becomes a tactic to undermine attempts to represent the city as a singular, monolithic subject that is activated through the inescapable logics of optimized resourcing. Instead, it renders the urban as a multiplicitous accumulation of collective productions in space, which incorporates the unpredictable, the serendipitous and the creative experiences embedded into everyday life. This tactical use of play is best described by Beltzung Horvath and Maicher (2016): "to free the city from its organization, if only temporarily by games, can be a practice of liberation … Instead of encounters between subjects communicating on a plane of significance, the stripping down of subjectivity, of organization and significance allows for the becoming of a new swarm of multiplicities, a new collectivity."

6. COUNTER-HEGEMONIC URBAN PRACTICES: A CASE STUDY IN CAGLIARI, ITALY

The set of "alternative sensing practices" that constitute this case was developed in the context of a visiting professorship at the University of Cagliari in Sardinia during the spring term of 2017. As part of a broader discussion on their collective experiences of the city, I invited a group of 79 architecture students working under my supervision to install a GPS-tracking app on their smartphones (Figure 1) and share their accumulated trajectory logs for a specified period of time. No specific ad-hoc software was developed for this purpose. Instead, the immediacy, accessibility, and ease of use of freely available tracking apps for smartphones—mostly catering to cycling and jogging enthusiasts who use them to keep records of their progress and share them with fellow cyclists and runners—allowed all group members to get ready for the proposed activity in just a few minutes. The only requirement was to use an app that could record and share trajectory logs in the GPX file format (also known as GPS Exchange Format). This is a simple, open-source file system where a sequence of time-stamped "track-points" with location data (latitude, longitude, and height) are stored in tags and can be interchanged between GPS devices and software. Critically, this extremely simple setup allowed the group to leave technical considerations aside, and to focus on agreeing paths of performative action instead. To that extent, a declared goal was to performatively test out the spatial potentials of "circulation," as outlined by de Certeau and Rendall (1984), and tactical "play," as conceptualized by Beltzung Horvath and Maicher (2016) in relation to the group's navigations in the city.

The group agreed to uninterruptedly record their position data logs for a full day, and to collate the resulting log files together afterwards. The log files were numbered sequentially with no reference to the student that originated them. They did not reveal any personal information other than the recorded positions at a series of points in time. This exercise effectively tapped into the data sources and processes that make up a key component of smart city and platform labor practices: The distributed accrual of location-specific information, obtained from individual smartphones as their users access online services to improve their experiences and navigations in the city. Planning a driving route that accounts for live traffic conditions, finding a nearby coffee shop that offers takeaway services within a certain price range, or sharing our live location with a friend for a limited period of time are some of the functions that both draw from and partake in the structure of these data platforms. However, whereas hegemonic smart city and platform labor practices tend to "flatten" the friction caused by local conditions to ensure that urban experiences remain consistent with expectations, the goal of our exercise was precisely the opposite: To foreground these conditions and the "messiness" of the individual and collective negotiations they trigger. Put differently, the underlying objective of this experimental "sensing practice" was to help revert the prevalence of quantitative information identified by Greenfield (2017a) and Haque (Haque, 2017) in hegemonic models of digitally mediated sensing, positing an alternative that resituated the qualitative components of social life in the urban public realm as the principal means for collective representation.

Figure 1: Screenshot of GPX Logger, one of the Android-based free GPS tracking apps used by participants to record their displacements in the city.

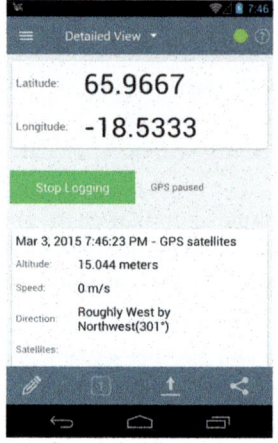

Source: GPX Logger

Once log files were collated, their position data points were imported into CAD software and assembled as trajectory curves. Each individual curve in the resulting CAD file represented one of the anonymized trajectories recorded by members of the group. Using this base material, three time-stretched animations were produced, showing all trajectories being gradually traced from the beginning to the end of the agreed recording time span. I call these animated urban plans as they are 'plans' in the architectural sense, delineated descriptions of space through vertical projection.

Each animation focused on a particular scale of observation: metropolitan, urban, and local. The resulting animations reconstructed the fabric of Cagliari and its surrounding territory through the subjective urban geographies of the participants. As noted before, the intent of this practice—formalized as an exercise of collective performance—was to steer the visual representation of urban data away from the focus on optimizing the 'flow' of resources, directing it instead towards the social orders emerging from the assemblage of many heterogeneous individual subjectivities. This, in turn, revealed some of the social patterns that characterized the community of architecture students in Cagliari as they were manifested in space.

The first animated urban plan of Cagliari produced through this collective 'practice' (Figure 2) focused on the metropolitan scale. This animation revealed the most salient geographical features of the region, such as the coastline and the locations of subsidiary urban nodes. More importantly, it also revealed the strikingly broad territorial spread of the student population, informed by a distinctive culture of daily commuting into the city center from the parental homes in neighboring towns. This commute routinely took up a very substantial proportion of the working day for many of the participants. In that sense, it had become a 'place' for them; a consistent realm of space and time defined by scheduled displacements across the regional landscape. The first animated urban plan provided a visual representation of this 'bracketed' construct of space and time, foregrounding its very long physical range and suggesting that, to some extent, the commute contributed to inform the social-academic life of the students at least as much as their actual on-campus experiences.

A second animated urban plan focused on the central districts of Stampace, Marina, Villanova, and Castello—where the central university buildings and the School of Architecture are located—revealed finer-grain patterns of urban access that emerged from the specific assemblage of geographical, infrastructural, and social conditions affecting both the city and the participating students. These patterns foregrounded—among many other aspects—important issues of access and accessibility into the central campus (located at the top of an ancient fortified citadel). They also highlighted a markedly gendered experience of space and personal safety as the quaint, labyrinthine alleyways of the city center and its citadel were navigated. The snapshot image of this animation (Figure 3) shows an amalgamation of paths in and around the central urban hub of Piazza Yenne, which gradually extended towards the cluster of buildings –located in the old citadel- that comprise the School of Architecture.

A third, close-up visualization (Figure 4) showed the immediate surroundings of Piazza Yenne and the walking routes to the school of Architecture towards the Torre dell'Elefante—an historical entry point into the old citadel of Cagliari. It yielded a very accurate reconstruction of the physical configuration of the urban fabric in that particular fragment of the city. The thick amalgamation of paths revealed in this third animated urban plan foregrounded the social range of the urban university campus, assembled from a multiplicity of daily individual narratives that involved acts of commuting, shopping, studying, resting, and socializing—all of them manifested through a rhythm of displacements and stationary moments; an "urban choreography" of sorts.

Figure 2: Snapshot from the metropolitan-scale animation of student routes in Cagliari based on GPS-traced displacements; Figure 3: Snapshot, intermediate urban scale. Animation of student routes in Cagliari based on GPS-traced displacements; Figure 4: Snapshot, close-up into the surroundings of Piazza Yenne. Animation of student routes in Cagliari based on GPS-traced displacements.

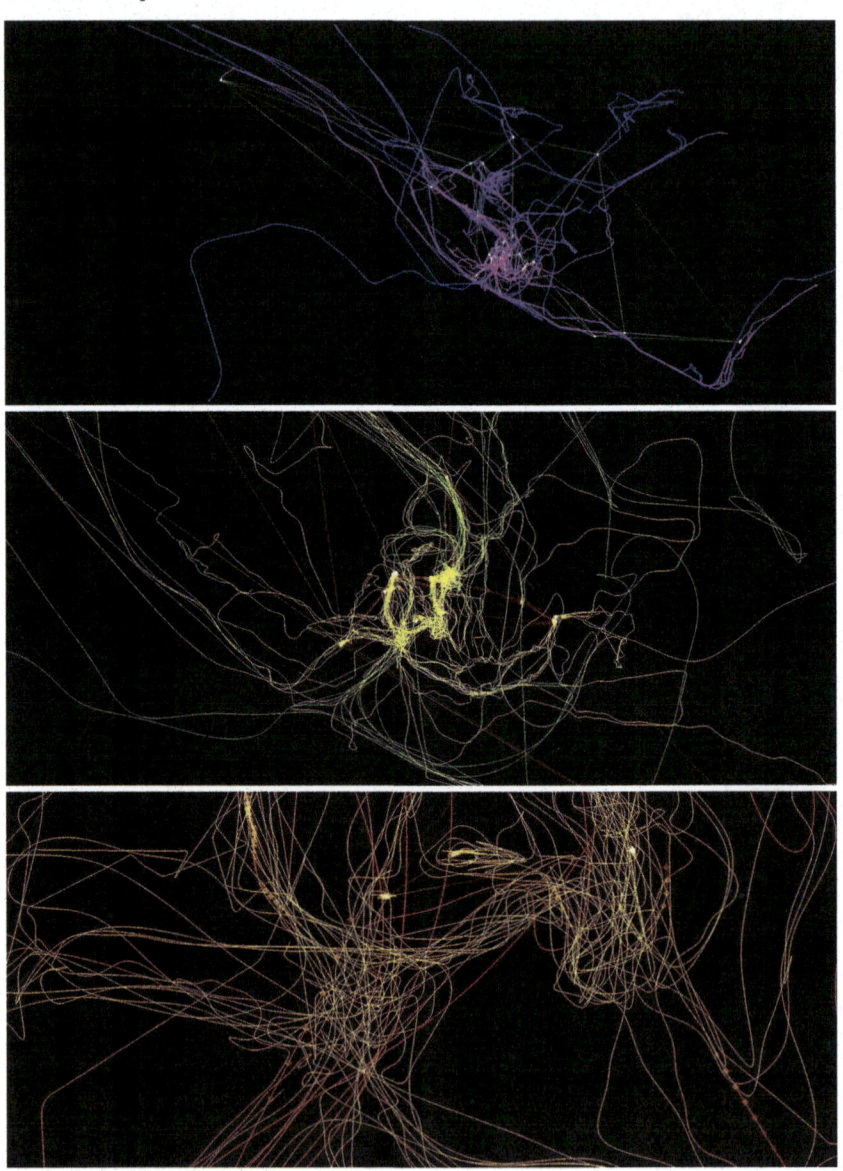

Source: Miguel Paredes Maldonado

Considering the three visualizations as a single, consistent body of work, it seems clear that—much like in Debord's circulatory practice of urban *"dérive* [or drift]" (1956)—quantitative parameters of efficiency play only a limited role in the collective organization of this emerging, multi-scalar landscape of navigations. Social detours, shortcuts, leisurely stops and renegotiations of the individual routes at stake play an important role in the circulation of students across the city and the territory, to at least the same extent as more quantifiable parameters such as bus schedules, traffic routes and teaching timetables.

As the account of the working methodology that led to these visualizations suggested, the agency of participants was not restricted to their own data productions, but also involved coordinated input into the collectively assemblage of trajectories into a single CAD file. The authorship of the resulting visualization was, thus, distributed and flattened. This aligned the work with the tradition of critical counter-mapping practices, inasmuch as the purposes of the spatialized visualizations were rendered transparent, and collective decisions were made on the specific aspects of the data collection that were to be foregrounded (Genz & Lucas-Drogan, 2018). In that sense, the collective politics of this collaborative process—from learning to capture and map smartphone data to determining the rules for the recording of trajectories—constitutes the core act of "critical making" as defined earlier in reference to the works of Ratto (2011) and DiSalvo (2014). Working dedicatedly, pragmatically and with a spirit of invention to digitally 'sense' the information they accumulated collectively, the participants also aligned themselves with Hennion's (2005) figure of the "amateur." Furthermore, in resonance with Townsend's views on the production of shared knowledge (2014) and by partaking in this alternative, digitally mediated sensing practice, the student-activists organized a platform of civic collaboration that cast a critical gaze on established smart city narratives.

It is worth emphasizing how the bottom-up, multi-scalar urban narratives discussed above give rise to an instance of performative self-representation that emerges from a distinct social group: For the students involved in the project—and paraphrasing Latour (2003)—the political space of the city unfolds in a very specific manner. At the same time, it is also important to acknowledge that the group of participants represented only a very small subset of the population of Cagliari, and therefore the insights gained by the exercises of data collection and subsequent mapping could not be extrapolated to other, larger urban constituencies or groups. In other words, and drawing from the theoretical discussion developed earlier this chapter, their claim to collective representation is necessarily limited. Notwithstanding this, their value can be found along the lines advanced by Butler (2015, pp. 59–60): highlighting social modes that exist at the critical edge of the recognizable in the urban field. In doing so, the sensory orders emerging from this alternative sensing practice offer a practical model of collective, bottom-up appropriation of urban data, which leverages self-awareness of the range and extent of our shared productions as a data-citizens.

Moreover, this work also offers potential vectors for exploration and collective action towards a more democratic, socially responsible governance of the urban commons. Some of the urban insights revealed in the Cagliari experiment deal with pervasive issues and concerns that, while difficult to render visible, have a strong bearing in our experiences of the urban commons. In that respect, the methods outlined in this "sensing practice" offer avenues for further testing, increased visibility and eventual action.

7. CONCLUSIONS AND REMARKS

Using the themes of leisure, play, and circulation as drivers for generating and interrogating performative representations in the urban field, the case introduced in this chapter demonstrates alternative modes of collective engagement with urban data. These novel modes of engagement challenge the computational logics of digitally mediated sensing championed by smart cities and urban platform labor. In contrast to the top-down, standardized sensory orders instigated by these two hegemonic paradigms, the set of "alternative sensing practices" developed in Cagliari take a bottom-up approach to foreground the subjectivity, plurality, and agency of individuals in urban space. Thus, these practices engage social life in the city as a "sensing collective" where the movements, activities, and performances of people can become digitally mediated data productions, assembled collectively to construct more inclusive and diverse forms of political representation in urban space.

In doing so, these alternative sensing practices demonstrate that multiple, novel "sensory orders" can be activated through critical, creative engagements with urban data. In Cagliari, the particular sensory order that emerges through the collected smartphone data of participants paints a distinct picture of academic life: An endeavor that is no longer associated with the classroom or the university buildings, but rather described as a choreography of movements into the city, within the city and out of the city, spread throughout the totality of the working day. As demonstrated throughout the discussion of the case, these novel "sensory orders" can be effectively encapsulated through collectively assembled representations of digitally mediated sensing, which tap into some of the productive processes that generate urban data in the first instance. Their attendant sensing practices also demonstrate how these representations unpack and manifest a range of "social orders," expressed as collective urban narratives that intersect the spatial fabric of the city with their own, thematized data productions.

Ultimately, the case presented in this chapter advances viable alternatives to the sensory orders championed by the computational logics of smart cities and platform labor in the urban realm. First, it dispels the notion of the city as a self-consistent "aggregated body," instead putting the focus on the constellation of individual agencies that make up urban life. Second, it resists the top-down narratives of "computational governance" by offering a range of tools to collectively generate bottom-up instances of performative representativity. Third, it exposes the limitations of numerical optimization as a driver of digitally mediated urban sensing by uncovering otherwise hidden qualitative insights into a range of social functions in everyday city life. Although the claims to collective representation afforded by the alternative practices that constitute the core of the Cagliari case are necessarily limited—and could be the subject of substantial debate—they are nonetheless successful in pointing us in the direction of more transparent, democratic forms of data-based urban praxis.

Acknowledgments:

Elisa Pilia, Donatella Fiorino and Caterina Giannattasio (Università degli studi di Cagliari) provided invaluable input and support during the development of the body of work presented in this chapter. This work was also made possible through funding from the Erasmus+ program and a Visiting Professorship at the Università degli studi di Cagliari. This chapter includes a small proportion of material that had already appeared (albeit in a different form) in the earlier publications noted below. This material has been substantially revised, updated, and synthesized for inclusion in this chapter (Paredes 2020).

References

Ampatzidou, C., Bouw, M., van de Klundert, F., de Lande, M., & de Waal, M. (2015). *The Hackable City: A research manifesto and design toolkit*. Amsterdam, Netherlands: Amsterdam Creative Industries Publishing.

Andreotti, L. (2000). Play-Tactics of the "Internationale Situationniste." *October, 91*, 37–58. Retrieved from http://www.jstor.org/stable/779148

Beltzung Horvath, L., & Maicher, M. (2016). Rethinking the City as a Body without Organs. In H. Frichot, C. Gabrielsson, & J. Metzger (Eds.), *Deleuze and the City* (pp. 33–45). Edinburgh, UK: Edinburgh University Press.

Bullivant, L. (2017). The Hyperlocal: Less Smart City, More Shared Social Value. *Architectural Design, 87*(1), 6–15. https://doi.org/10.1002/ad.2126

Butler, J. (2015). *Notes Toward a Performative Theory of Assembly*. Harvard, MA: Harvard University Press.

Carpo, M. (2017). *The second digital turn: Design beyond intelligence*. Cambridge, MA: MIT Press.

Certeau, M. de, & Rendall, S. (1984). *The practice of everyday life*. Oakland, CA: University of California Press.

Coyne, R. (2017). Share city | Reflections on Technology, Media & Culture. Retrieved January 10, 2018, from https://richardcoyne.com/2017/09/12/share-city/

De Monchaux, N. (2016). *Local code: 3,659 proposals about data, design &the nature of cities*. New York, NY: Princeton Architectural Press.

De Waal, M., de Lange, M., & Bouw, M. (2017). The Hackable City: Citymaking in a Platform Society. *Architectural Design*, 87(1), 50–57. https://doi.org/10.1002/ad.2131

Debord, G. (1956). Théorie de la dérive. *Les Lèvres Nues*, 9.

DiSalvo, C. (2014). Critical Making as Materializing the Politics of Design. *The Information Society*, 30(2), 96–105. https://doi.org/10.1080/01972243.2014.875770

Farías, I., & Höhne, S. (2016). Humans as Vectors and Intensities: Becoming Urban in Berlin and New York City. In H. Frichot, C. Gabrielsson, & J. Metzger (Eds.), *Deleuze and the City* (pp. 17–32). Edinburgh, UK: Edinburgh University Press.

Genz, C., & Lucas-Drogan, D. (2018). Decoding mapping as practice: an interdisciplinary approach in architecture and urban anthropology. *The Urban Transcripts Journal*, 1(4). Retrieved from http://journal.urbantranscripts.org/article/decoding-mapping-practice-interdisciplinary-approach-architecture-urban-anthropology-carolin-genz-diana-lucas-drogan/

Greco, K. (2014). Seeing the City through Data / Seeing Data through the City. In C. Ratti & D. Offenhuber (Eds.), *Decoding the City: Urbanism in the Age of Big Data* (pp. 125–142). Basel, Switzerland: Birkhäuser.

Greenfield, A. (2017a). Practices of the Minimum Viable Utopia. *Architectural Design*, 87(1), 16–25. https://doi.org/10.1002/ad.2127

Greenfield, A. (2017b). *Radical technologies: The design of everyday life*. London, UK: Verso.

Gregory, K., & Paredes Maldonado, M. (2020). Delivering Edinburgh: uncovering the digital geography of platform labour in the city. *Information, Communication & Society*, 23(8), 1187–1202. https://doi.org/10.1080/1369118X.2020.1748087

Haque, U. (2017). VoiceOver: Citizen Empowerment Through Cultural Infrastructure. *Architectural Design*, 87(1), 86–91. https://doi.org/10.1002/ad.2136

Hennion, A. (2005). Pragmatics of Taste. In M. D. Jacobs & N. W. Hanrahan (Eds.), *The Blackwell Companion to the Sociology of Culture* (pp. 131–144). Oxford, UK: Blackwell. https://doi.org/https://doi.org/10.1002/9780470996744.ch9

Krivý, M. (2016). Parametricist architecture, smart cities, and the politics of consensus. *Ehituskunst: Investigations in Architecture and Theory*, 57, 22–45.

Krivý, M. (2018). Towards a critique of cybernetic urbanism: The smart city and the society of control. *Planning Theory*, 17(1), 8–30. https://doi.org/10.1177/1473095216645631

Latour, B. (2003). What if we Talked Politics a Little? *Contemporary Political Theory*, 2(2), 143–164. https://doi.org/10.1057/palgrave.cpt.9300092

Löw, M. (2012). The intrinsic logic of cities: towards a new theory on urbanism. *Urban Research & Practice*, 5(3), 303–315. https://doi.org/10.1080/17535069.2012.727545

Offenhuber, D. (2017). *Waste is information: Infrastructure legibility and governance*. Cambridge, MA: MIT Press.

Oosterhuis, K. (2017). Emotive Embodiments. In A. Radman & H. Sohn (Eds.), *Critical and Clinical Cartographies* (pp. 168–183). Edinburgh, UK: Edinburgh University Press.

Paredes Maldonado, M. (2020). Reconstituted Smart Citizenships Hacking Data-Based Urban Representations of the Public Domain. In L. P. Rajendran & N. D. Odeleye (Eds.), *Mediated Identities in the Futures of Place: Emerging Practices and Spatial Cultures* (pp. 153–172). Cham: Springer International Publishing. https://doi.org/10.1007/978-3-030-06237-8_9

Pe, R. (2017). Suburban Resonance in Segrate, Milan: The Language of Locative Media in Defining Urban Sensitivity. *Architectural Design*, 87(1), 78–85. https://doi.org/10.1002/ad.2135

Picon, A. (2015). *Smart cities: a spatialised intelligence*. London, UK: Wiley.

Ratti, C., & Claudel, M. (2016). *The city of tomorrow: sensors, networks, hackers, and the future of urban life*. New Haven, CT: Yale University Press.

Ratto, M. (2011). Critical Making: Conceptual and Material Studies in Technology and Social Life. *The Information Society*, 27(4), 252–260. https://doi.org/10.1080/01972243.2011.583819

Reckwitz, A. (2016). How the senses organise the social. In M. Jonas & B. Littig (Eds.), *Praxeological Political Analysis*. London, UK: Routledge.

Segraves, D. (2013). Data City: Urban Metabolic Decision Processes. *Architectural Design*, 83(4), 120–123. https://doi.org/10.1002/ad.1628

Shove, E., Pantzar, M., & Watson, M. (2012). *The Dynamics of Social Practice*. London, UK: SAGE Publications.

Smith, D. (2005). Giving the Game Away: Play and Exchange in Situationism and Structuralism. *Modern & Contemporary France*, 13(4), 421–434. https://doi.org/10.1080/09639480500329473

Szell, M., & Groß, B. (2014). Hubcab – Exploring the Benefits of Shared Taxi Services. In C. Ratti & D. Offenhuber (Eds.), *Decoding the City: Urbanism in the Age of Big Data* (pp. 28–39). Basel, Switzerland: Birkhäuser.

Townsend, A. M. (2014). *Smart cities: big data, civic hackers, and the quest for a new utopia*. New York, NY: W.W. Norton & Company.

Weinstock, M. (2013). System City: Infrastructure and the Space of Flows. *Architectural Design*, 83(4), 14–23. https://doi.org/10.1002/ad.1614

We Thought It Was Fog, We Thought It Was Just Some Weather
Sensing, Datafication, and Governance of Urban Air Pollution

Hanna Husberg, Agata Marzecová

1. DO YOU EVER THINK ABOUT AIR?

If you do, how do you come to notice it? Is it material, spatial, sensorial, digital, relational, spiritual, chemical or other?

Do you live in Beijing?

Do you think there is something such as "urban air"?

I heard there's a word "wumai" which didn't exist before. Do you remember when fog became smog in China?
How do you think it became perceptible? Do you think air is governable?

These open-ended questions served as an entry point to collect embodied experiences and imaginaries of air in Beijing during an artist residency at the Institute for Provocation (IFP) in autumn 2016. Whereas many other cities in China, India, and elsewhere face even worse air pollution levels, Beijing has over the last decades become notorious for its health-hazardous smog. Since the 2010s (and in particular after the January 2013 Airpocalypse event), a new term for smog, wumai, was adopted by the Chinese general public. In China, this shift in terminology coincided with a spread of technoscientific concepts, such as the National Air Quality Index or AQI (providing an assessment of the estimated health risks in relation to air pollution exposure) as well as PM2.5 (minute particulate matter emitted from cars, industries, fires, etc.) often referred to as the most health-threatening element of the AQI index. Because they can be automatically sensed by digital sensors, both AQI and PM2.5 are readily distributable, and in 2013 when air pollution was finally recognized in China, and official access to air pollution levels in many major cities was granted by China's Ministry of Environmental Protection, several smart-phone apps giving access to real-time air quality index values soon appeared. As a result, Beijingers became early adopters of historically novel, real-time modes of sharing environmental data. This technological shift was made possible thanks to digitalization and automation technologies that transformed all aspects of the air pollution monitoring apparatus. In a short period, ubiquitous automated environmental sensors, automated real-time data transitions, and smart real-time social networks entered the lives of millions of people affecting the ways they receive information about pollution, and in extension, how they go about their everyday lives.

Figure 1: A screenshot of the air quality data from a smartphone application. Different colors indicate different levels of health risk and the infographics illustrates recommended actions.

Figure 2: An example of scaling up air quality (AQI) maps from city to planetary level with the commercial AirVisual Earth application which covers pollution airflows across the world by combining data from public government air quality stations, satellite data and the community.

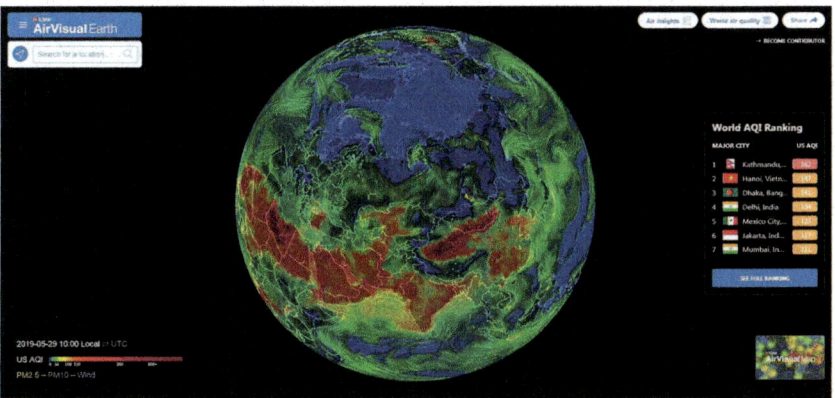

Informed by conversations with local inhabitants, embodied experience, field notes of daily air pollution data collected during a three-month period in Beijing, interviews with experts on atmospheric particulate pollution as well as our long-term transdisciplinary dialogue, this chapter examines the entanglements between the aesthetics and politics of making the toxic but invisible particulate air pollution perceptible to human senses. More specifically, using the Beijing air as a starting point, we focus on the emergence of digital practices for sensing and communicating about air quality, which have become indispensable tools for managing and surviving in the particle-filled urban atmospheres of many metropolitan areas worldwide. As the fluxes of data generated by automated air quality indexes and new practices of digital environmental sensing open new spaces of perception, we observe how this contributes to novel imaginaries of a datafied urban air, which risks suppressing the heterogeneous but incalculable realities from which the numbers were inferred, while at the same time reconceptualizing the urban air and our relation to it as a "new arena of care and calculation" (cf. Liu, 2017; Whitehead, 2011; Husberg and Marzecová, 2021). In other words, we notice that the aesthetics (the doing of sensorial perception) of new collective ways of sensing urban air in the digital era is generative of a new 'sensing' mode of governance, and thereby inherently political as it radically shapes collective subjectivity and agency.

To support our argument, we will first share excerpts from field notes—kept by Husberg throughout her three-month sojourn—that accompanied daily measurements of PM2.5 collected every morning, evening, and during movements within the city, and provide some insights into the practice of monitoring air quality data using an AirBeam (the U.S. produced open-source portable monitoring device), as well as available apps using Chinese air quality data. Bearing witness to the tediousness of data collection, and incorporating annotations on the embodied and felt experience of spending time in the dense Beijing air, the field notes shed some light on the context in which the dialogues with Beijingers that inform this chapter were collected. To denote them from other people (and also not to foreclose the full names of people expressing what may be perceived as sensitive opinions), the discussants are assigned initials, rather than their full names. Second, we provide an outline of the starting points and conceptual framing that have informed this technoecological investigation into the sensing of urban air pollution. Third, we share three vignettes from a broader selection of thirty-five transcribed dialogues or aerial accounts, which illustrate the broader material and highlight the life-structuring effects of air pollution on city inhabitants. These are then followed by a discussion on the technoecological sensing of air and pollution, and the wider impacts of a new 'sensing' mode of governance. Finally, the conclusion highlights the irreducibility of sensing into the singular form of data-sensing, exemplified by real-time air quality data, not only because the effects of pollution cannot be reduced to numerical representation—but, more specifically, because the digital sensing of air pollution does not merely inform of pollution but significantly provides a new (political) terrain for the distribution of governance.

2. THE BEIJING FIELD NOTES, AUTUMN, 2016 (excerpt)

29.8 Arrival. First view of the North China Plain from the plane—clusters of high rises interwoven with lower constructions, next to small sections of fields in different tones, all surrounded by mountains.
My first breaths felt somewhat coarse—acidity in the air, not too much humidity.

30.8 $PM_{2.5}$ measurement 35 in my room.
Took a walk north of the residency, along the hutongs, and towards the towers, $PM_{2.5}$ values between 50 and 70. It jumped to 120 as I entered a bar. A girl was smoking.

1.9 $PM_{2.5}$ 12 in the room.
First metro trip. Above ground the air is good—a bit cloudy, and pleasant with cooler weather—entering the tunnels $PM_{2.5}$ levels went up to 100, ten times higher than outside. The app crashed, so I might have lost the data.

4.9 PM2.5 124 in the morning, at the lunch place PM2.5 190, PM2.5 54 in the eve.
High PM2.5 levels. Have been coughing since morning.
I followed Corinna to 798 art district, a 40-minute bike ride along some highways. The pollution was quite bad, I felt it in the throat. Still not that bad values, peaking around PM2.5 70.
Some issues with the AirBeam, I had to reinstall the VPN on the phone.

6.9 PM2.5 20 in the morning, during the evening PM2.5 levels rose from 50 to 90.
Still very hot, I'm told it's nothing compared to a few weeks ago, however. Humidity is low, not as in the summer.
Coughing a lot although the air has been "good" since I arrived.

10.10 PM2.5 70 in the morning.
A bit hazy again, the pollution is back after a short break. Often quite big variations even in the room, the levels climb up and down.
Went with CSY and Kyo Lee to meet a Daoist master and his wife at Fragrant hills.

11.10 PM2.5 levels between 90 and 165, a bit better in the evening.
I'm getting more sensitive to pollution, I can feel how it gets into the respiratory system. It is enveloping, like a blanket.
I met XG at Chaochangdi. I managed to engage her in a discussion on air, and finally got my first aerial account.

13.10 Very hazy, a bit of a sore throat.
Biked to the visa center with DL, then to Qi master with Corinna, CSY and XL. Had a long discussion with XL after. Her father used to complain about how the water was no longer sweet.
She also told me they issued a red alert warning for three days.
Air quality apps are showing much higher PM2.5 levels than my device is.

14.10 The Airpocalypse app is showing PM2.5 271 and "Baijiu for your lungs," my AirBeam device is still stuck at 182.
My throat feels stuffy, and there's like a numbing sensation around the head.
Yellow heavy fog and haze warning for Beijing. The color codes were apparently revisited in spring 2016.
Visited the urban planning museum in the morning. Then biked to Sanlitun and back to meet VN. Got some air masks on my way back.

15.10 The air is a little better, water drops in the air already in the morning. Other air quality apps are at PM2.5 250, my device 100 below that... Impossible to wear the air mask if I wear my glasses, the exhaled air that slips through the little holes, dimming

the glasses at each breath.
I transcribed the discussions with VN and WG, an artist who uses air ventilation fans to build large installations, and sent them to Agata.
Got a response from the AirBeam developers: "Hi Hanna. Thanks for reaching out. The fact that you're topping out at around 190 is due to limitations in both the sensor and the firmware."

8.11 Good air. Beautiful weather, rather cold, but sunny and blue sky.
Skyped with Agata. She asked whether pollution was a Western concept and if they used it in China.
AA mentioned an object yesterday, a container, that is supposed to protect you from pollution. He talked about food, how it's much more than food, like medicine. There's an idea that if you survive Beijing you build up your immune system, at least when it comes to food scams.
DXY helped me pose my air questions to TGB, a theater director who was visiting.

9.11 American elections.
The pollution is up again, around PM2.5 300.
There's a strong smell of coal.
Visited Renmin University, passed by XMF's office for a short discussion as he wasn't very comfortable in English. Followed a seminar in order to catch another professor, HS, with whom I had a good discussion.
The air is very hazy. Although it's dark, it produces a shimmer as the light is reflected on all the particulates.

10.11 Grey and dull atmosphere, the city is covered by thick layers of floating particles.
Took a taxi to Caochangdi to meet KK.
Air got a bit better towards the evening. I'm still coughing, though.

16.11 Coughing and quite tired. Orange alert.
Lunch meeting with Prof. ZG, an urban planner working on urban air quality, at a vegetarian place (not like the lifestyle ones) at her university. She mentioned that there used to be a public website where you could download free air quality data, but it shut down, and how now only current levels are communicated, so they buy data on Taobao instead.
Met LLL at the gated community in Sanlitun where she works. She mentioned an app one can use to predict pollution based on how it feels, and how it's actually very accurate if a large number of people participate.

18.11 Strong smog all day. PM2.5 levels over 300.
Very obvious pollution, even in the studio the air felt coarse, full of particles.
The glow effect was there again, softening the outlines of objects and buildings.
Grayness, but a magical light.
Long chat with DXY. Huo Wei stayed in, ordered food, didn't want to face the weather.
Small droplets towards the evening

3. STARTING POINTS

Air pollution is classified as one of the deadliest environmental health risks. Even so, because it is largely imperceptible to human senses, and because it operates as slow violence with impacts that are "pervasive but elusive" and mostly surface slowly over the course of years, even decades (Nixon, 2011), its critical analysis has to a large extent been limited to scientific expertise. Air pollution is, however, not merely a scientific phenomenon, but a life-death defining and thus political concern. Therefore, our approach to air pollution argues for more-than-scientific exploration and methodologies. In extension, accessing and making accessible the predominantly technoscientifically defined atmospheric terrain calls for a critical consideration of how pollution is sensed and thus understood. However, how can one study (and make sense of) sensing? Especially such an elusive and evasive element as air? As social theorist Andreas Reckwitz has argued, whereas sensible orders or sense regimes are inherent to any social order, the forgetting of sense is still widespread in social theory (Reckwitz, 2016). Moreover, considerations of sensing often have recourse to optical metaphors that are largely inadequate, not least in the big data paradigm (Agostinho, 2019; Chandler, 2018).

Arguably sensorial engagements with polluted air, which is mostly invisible, ask for a different, technoecological approach that acknowledges the immanent relationality between body, technology, and ecology (see, for example, Liu, 2017; Murphy, 2017). Similar to praxeological approaches, practice-based artistic research allows for sensuous or sense-driven and material approaches and inquiries in which the senses and the body are valid sources of research (Hannula et al. 2014). In line with this, this chapter makes use of excerpts of field notes and transcribed dialogues gathered during an artist residency in Beijing, positioning them not only as an affective and aesthetic reference but equally as valid sources of knowledge. Acknowledging that the bodily sensing of polluted air requires time, Husberg set out with the intention to gather experiences of Beijingers who have a long-term practice of breathing what they have recently come to realize is toxic air. For this, she adopted dialogue as the main practice and central methodology for gathering insights into local imaginaries of air (and its pollution) producing, as a result, a rich set of sound recordings and transcriptions providing wide-ranging and varied perspectives about the experiences of living in the hazy Beijing air. The thirty-five discussants include both people who had a specific interest in the topic through their profession (urban planners, healthcare workers, environmental policymakers, academics, cultural workers), and locals, who had a long-standing relationship with the Beijing air.

While attesting to a diversity of ways through which the air and its pollution was sensed and experienced, all interlocutors emphasized the importance of technoscientific indexes, numbers, and data in navigating the toxic air, both at an individual and societal scale. And yet, while broadly circulated and used, the numbers or indexes retained a level of opacity contrasting with their ubiquitous presence and social importance. Here, it is important to stress that this lack of transparency is not limited to Beijing but represents an integral characteristic of the reliance on technoscientific and corporate modes of sensing pollution that, in the words of feminist science and technology studies (STS) scholar Michelle Murphy, externalize the complex bundles of extensive relations, rendering chemicals as disconnected functionalist molecules (Murphy, 2017). As a result, the chemicals and chemical relations that surround and make us largely reside in the "realm of the imperceptible" thereby remaining inaccessible to non-experts (Murphy, 2006). To make sense of this prevalent, yet exclusionary approach of registering (or sensing) pollution, this chapter developed through art-science dialogue, productively combines artistic research and scientific-epistemological perspectives, to highlight the tensions, entanglement, and uneven coexistence of different forms of sensing aerial pollution. Specifically, by approaching the doing of sensorial perception as a technoecological practice between body, technology, and ecology, this chapter foregrounds the embodied use of numbers and data or, in other words, the entanglement of the technoscientific modes of pollution sensing with human perception, more broadly. The role that air pollution and its sensing through digital sensors and data play in structuring people's lives is emphasized—however not in order to naturalize technoecological entanglements (by treating technology as a natural extension of the embodied sensorium). Rather, drawing on critical analysis of the digital sense and the datafication of governance emerging at the interception of geography (Gabrys, 2016), media theory (Parisi, 2009; Hörl, 2017) and governance analysis (Chandler, 2018; Rouvroy, 2013) helps us to identify the realm of novel air sensing as a critical terrain of the (sensory) politics, not only of air pollution but of urban life more broadly.

4. SENSING POLLUTED AIR
(excerpts from aerial accounts)

Air is part of my memory. It's a very important ingredient of my memory. We breathe in and out; we collect things, emotions, that linger in our realities, we take it in. We breathe all the time, in and out, but we don't notice it. It's almost as how we take in reality and transform it to memories that we recall sometimes.

Of course, for the worst days, if I'm not wearing a mask I can already feel something after so many years. My lungs and my throat are really telling me something is not all right. It's just like people who have pain in their ankles during rainy days.

The thing is that it has become such an issue that it influences everyone's life and health, and people's decisions whether to stay here or not. From this issue, you can definitely see the layers of the city. Even if we are trying to avoid saying middle class in China, I do think it's a very big social class that has the proper education and young children with a future and security in life. I think these people are the most stressed group in this city, they are more aware of the environmental condition than some other Beijingers. Also, because the middle class has the ability to change their lives, a lot of them are thinking about moving out of China or moving out of Beijing. But actually, it is not very easy to do that.

There's this word "Sharing the faith, breathing the air together." It comes from political propaganda. It means if you breathe air together you share the same destiny, the same faith. You are heart-to-heart connected, and you should fight for the same purpose. So that's a very ironic expression now. If we're breathing the same bad air now, what future will we then share together?
—CSY, architect and curator working at IFP

The first thing I do, like the routine, is usually to check my email, my WeChat, everything, but the second thing is: what's the air quality today? Can I still see out through the window? What does it look like? And then I check the weather report. It's kind of like a routine for me, sometimes it makes me feel really, really bad, but you have to know because it impacts how you live. It's just the way I feel. It should be very natural, you know, breathe in, breathe out, but you have to think about it all the time.

When we were children there was already some smog like this, but we didn't know it's smog. We thought it was fog, we thought it was just some weather. Because when we talk about wumai we use this thing PM2.5. It's very, very technical, not a normal word, and it's really bad for your health.

Maybe because it's the season now, it's November, it makes me really, really scared. Because it's the beginning of pollution, it's the beginning of the smog. So maybe because it's November, I'm really worried about that… It's coming, it's coming, it's coming. Like every day, I have to check it.

We don't even need a weather report, you can just see if there is a big event or something, and you know if the weather is good or not. For the national golden week, for example, the weather is definitely beautiful. If there is some important international meeting, and presidents come from all over the world, of course, the weather is beautiful, but when they go… Some of my friends have a joke, maybe the government has big fans outside the city to blow away the bad air. So, for big events, they control the weather, but it doesn't last, afterward it all comes back.
—JJO, marketing officer met at a Halloween party by I-project art space

We're basically all living with machines at home, cleaning machines that run more or less the whole day.

Since three-four years I've been very affected by this weather. I was not in the beginning. I was more thinking it's a moral issue and a health issue. My kids are under control all the time, they have check-ups, and we try to go to Japan three-four times a year, to fly them away for holiday. As soon as it's beautiful, when the weather is good we bring them out. But lately, I've also taken it to myself. When there's a whole week like that I feel there's something really affecting my mind and my perceptual reality. There's a sense of depression, heaviness. This was not so clear before, but lately, I've started feeling a bit disturbed by this aspect.

The level of smog was already high around 2006,7,8, but it was not so visible. There were white skies, it was not this fog or smog you can see. I would say it became visible with technology with the apps. Because, all of a sudden, you're being introduced to this mechanism. Then the apps are measuring this and telling you it has already been three years that you've been exposed to very high standards. You called them white skies, but actually it is pollution. Now the pollution is getting bad and you see people around always checking these apps and comparing the numbers of the Chinese government with the numbers of the American embassy.

Even if the internet is controlled, Weishin, WeChat, and things have become very important tools for the government, especially because it's not a very democratic government, so you need to have feedback, you need to have big data. One of the strategies the government uses dealing with a billion and six hundred people is that whatever you throw at them you have big data. Because of how people react to a problem. Do they all migrate, do they remain? It's the same as if you block Google, what do they do? It seems that the government is very attentive to this kind of feedback and data.
—AR, artist and writer met through IFP network

5. FROM SENSING TO (SENSING AS) GOVERNANCE

While heavy smog is indeed perceptible, minute and toxic airborne particles are mostly imperceptible to human senses. Corporeal sensations such as smell, taste, or the shimmering of light hitting small particulates, as well as respiratory and pulmonary reactions, headaches and other bodily responses mostly occur only when PM2.5 concentrations significantly trespass levels deemed safe by the WHO. A foul smell is not necessarily indicative of hazard, and even if it was, exposure to air pollution affects the health of people over time and in various ways. Moreover, sensing and feeling cannot be disentangled from cognitive and mental states. As the vignettes above attest, the realm of the sensual and the social are connected; how the senses are mobilized, what is perceived or dismissed, and in what way things, people, and environments are sensed and perceived are related to socio-cultural practice (Reckwitz, 2017).

However, as the Beijing accounts indicate, new sensibilities about invisible but toxic particulate air pollution are not only a matter of different attunement by the bodily senses. Indeed, we learned from our interlocutors that while Beijing's air was long troubled by other sources of pollution (such as dust storms) and never deemed good in the first place, the reconceptualization of fog as smog, or wumai, was largely reliant on novel modes of sensing. Significantly, along with the material presented above, our larger pool of discussants echoed the importance of air quality data communicated through the increasingly prevalent digital technologies. They pointed at how Beijingers in the last few years learned a lot of new "technical" and "chemical" words, like wumai, AQI, and PM2.5; at the emergence of a "new air," "the one we talk about a lot" and which is communicated through the "numbers" and air quality indexes of apps; and at how these new datafied imaginaries of air has triggered new patterns of behavior, influencing choices such as where to live (for those who have the options and means) and where to meet. However, air pollution is not one thing, neither is it perceived as a gradient of exposures. For some, it is barely noticeable, either because they are not sensitive or because they are occupied by more urgent things. For others, atmospheric pollution is paralyzing, affecting their body ("my lungs and my throat is really telling me something is not alright," CSY), their sensing apparatus ("the second thing is: what's the air quality today? Can I still see out through the window? What does it look like?" JJO), and their mental states ("there's a sense of depression, heaviness," AR).

These complexities of embodied sensing enmesh with the unprecedented ways of sensing air enabled through technoscientific modes of observation and digital infrastructures of sharing information. While representing only one of the multiple ways in which citizens and governing bodies have gained awareness of the air's toxicity, the indexes have played a critical (and authoritative) role in determining both the personal but also societal sense of pollution. Air quality data have become omnipresent but still remain opaque and difficult to engage with. In Beijing, as well as in other smog-ridden cities across the world, people have learned to use and rely on continuously updated air quality data streams and their supporting technologies which together reveal new spaces of perceptibility. People have accepted, refused, or repurposed the indexes for their ends. Still, the numbers and data have become firmly established as the dominant means for communicating and making sense of air pollution. In effect, by making the invisible, yet toxic, air pollution perceptible and experienceable through interfaces, such as smartphone apps, screens, and smart sensors installed on air cleansing equipment or air monitoring devices, the data and its technologies seem to become naturalized extensions of the human senses.

Crucially, we argue, the data-informed and technological experience of making sense and responding to pollution events through air quality indexes and data constitutes an entirely new arena of (technoecological) sensing. In Technoecologies of Sensation Luciana Parisi discusses the formation of a technoecology of information sensing in cyber capitalist culture, arguing that "changes in technical machines are inseparable from changes in the material, cognitive, and affective capacities of a body to feel" (Parisi, 2009:182). Taking the example of bionic (biologically inspired electromechanical implants) sensors she describes the interaction between environment, body, and machine not as simple transmission between separate entities but as an entire ecology of information sensing, indicating not only an extension of sensory perception but "a mutation in sensations all together" (Parisi, 2009:182). Sensors of air pollutants are external to human bodies, however, thanks to automation and digitalization, air quality data are delivered to personal devices in near realtime, generating a novel digital sense (of air) that resonates with Parisi's analysis. Moreover, the trend of digitalization and automation of sensing is not limited to air. In recent years, cities, ecosystems, even the whole planetary environment, as well as human bodies, movements, and responses have been instrumented with sensors that capture, analyze (and also modulate) their processes and behaviors (see, for e.g., Gabrys, 2016). Increasingly, the data-intensive monitoring of Earth processes (and human behavior) is understood as one of the core areas of scientific research, the governance of environmental change, and a necessary means for the survival of humanity.

Significantly, as summed up by media theorist Erich Hörl, digital environmental technologies do not merely inform us about the environment we inhabit. Rather, cybernetics and the spread of digital technologies have been essential for the 20th-century ecologization of thinking that appeared simultaneously with a new apparatus of capture (Hörl, 2017). Hörl's analysis highlights that the resulting logic of capture and control unfolds through "managing and modulating behavior, affects, relationships, intensities, and forces" (Hörl, 2018) and is indicative of a new mode of governing by structuring the milieu of individuals in order to obtain specific conduct

(Gabrys, 2014). In line with this, reflecting on the effects of technological advances (driven by big data technologies, algorithmic machine learning and ubiquitous sensing) in a postmodern world framed as complex and thus essentially unknowable, media scholar David Chandler (2018) formulates "sensing" as becoming one of the prevalent modes of governance. Following Chandler, under the sensing paradigm, governance employs big data technologies to detect disturbance or change in its emergence and to minimize the impact by facilitating real-time responses, rather than focusing on the prevention of always emergent problems and their complex permutation. In other words, this approach to (environmental and societal) governance sees the ubiquitous data from sensors of all kinds as a means to make subjects respond to and become sensitive to the world and its environment. Effectively, however, this mode of combining technology and governance aims at dynamic stabilization of the status quo rather than offering venues for acting upon the world to change it (Chandler, 2018). Once again using an optical metaphor for the essentially post-optical processes of datafication (Agostinho, 2019), sensing as governance uses data to make the unseen "seeable." In opposition to abstractions and representation—produced through fallible interpretation—data is taken as reality itself.

The sensing of urban air pollution represents only a small part of the 'sensing as governance' paradigm, which operates with data from every arena of the urban realm, including human behavior, health data, online habits, and much more, at regional and planetary scale. Nevertheless, highlighting these digital practices of air quality sensing as consistent with the logic of sensing (and algorithmic) governance is important, precisely because it underscores that the data-driven sense of air pollution it has generated is not merely a technological extension of the human sensorium but, rather, a terrain for the distribution of governance mechanisms.

The sensing mode of governance promises efficiency and actionability in a complex world. However, cautioning against the consequences of subsuming policy decision under big data and algorithm automation, legal scholar Antoinette Rouvroy has argued that the computational turn, and what she calls algorithmic governmentality "does not address individuals through their reflexive capacities, nor their inscription within collective structures, but merely through their 'profiles'" (Rouvroy, 2013:2). Instead, using automated, a-semiotic, pre-political and always emergent big data to construct models of behaviors and patterns, human actors are spared the burden and responsibility to transcribe, interpret and evaluate, and consider cause or intention. Importantly this erodes the possibility of critique and dissensus, as well as the legal construction of norms through laws, regulations, and due process, thereby leaving the distribution of power and domination unexamined (Rouvroy, 2013). Whereas Foucauldian notions of biopower and biopolitics operated on the lives of real populations—governing bodies by norms—algorithmic governmentality operates on virtual populations, constructed for the capture by algorithms (Rouvroy and Stiegler, 2016). Rouvroy's critical analysis focuses primarily on data produced from human behavior. However, it is also relevant for the arena of atmospheric sensing. This is because the technoscientific approach to defining the scale of exposures is based on a reductive understanding of pollution (focusing mainly on particulates but less so on other substances and their interactions) and, especially, a debatable notion of what constitutes human health, and who counts as human (as the idea of human body or population used in air quality indexing is inferred from epidemiological and medical studies). In other words, while situated in the historically and geopolitically specific context of Beijing, the life-structuring effects of air pollution data conveyed in the aerial accounts also reflect a broader epochal shift in how the sensing of environmental phenomena is organized and recognized.

Gathering different experiences of pollution, this chapter highlights the singular importance of conveniently capturable, digitizable and communicable modes of data-sensing, and asks: What are the impacts of this datafication of air pollution, that reduces the relations between city dwellers and urban air to a question of responding to pollution events in response to risk assessment? And what are the effects of its integration into the data-driven ecosystem and the managerial governance of the city? We argue that by bringing air into sense and sensibility, the data do not merely function as objective information but operate as a distinct technology of imagination–with concrete material consequences and political implications. In this context, it is crucial that the politics of air pollution critically engages with how air pollution is sensed (digitally), and asks what is at stake?

To some extent, the ubiquitous technological sensing of air has allowed for new levels of environmental awareness and public scrutiny. It has enabled (middle-class) citizens to minimize health risks, organize into communities and engage with the problem, predominantly to develop adaptation strategies. These strategies are, however, reflective of the neoliberal rationality, that instead of enforcing strict collective regulation of large polluters or complex calculations accounting for the real costs of prevailing modes of production, are equated with highly privatized individual choices in relation to exposure to toxic air. Thus, by framing agency as responsive capacity, sensing as governance evades questions of accountability and causation. And, pointedly, pollution risks losing its status as a problem to be resolved and instead becomes an event that needs to be sensed and responded to. As AR puts it, while the political agency is reduced to investment in privatized care (air monitoring and cleaning technologies, check-ups for the kids, travels abroad) and the comparison of numbers, the role of the state has shifted to governance through feedback from big data. As air quality data streams enable fast responsivity between toxic air and the citizens, eliciting their response (even if inadvertently), it contributes to the datafication not only of the atmosphere, but more broadly to data-driven (that is, digital sensing based) urban governance. In this move towards sensing as governance the 'raw data' of computation—used by different governing bodies in the monitoring of environmental processes, logistics, smart city management and a range of other uses, and which is generally presented as always already there—might appear as more objective and impartial, in part because it disregards individual singularity of people, whereas humans inevitably perceive through categorical biases inscribed in singular lives. Data is, however, produced through sophisticated methods of 'rawification' (through reformatting, cleaning, and ungrounding) and dependent on material conditions of optimization that foreclose anything that escapes calculation (Denis and Goëta, 2014).

One of the main problems of sensing or algorithmic governance is the reduction performed in the automated equation of reality with data. This applies both in the case of pollutants (limiting pollution to what it can be measured) and to citizens (limiting citizenship to the activities of adaptation and response management). Indeed, while air pollution management includes citizen practices, the data-driven sensing mode of governance risks diminishing the agency of citizens (perceived as sensing individuals) to behavior that is capturable and predictable, and not subjectivity. In the process sensing as governance bypasses real (embodied and situated) subjects, replacing them by probabilistically constructed populations, thereby impoverishing subjects who are no longer inscribed in any collective context (Gabrys, 2014; Rouvroy, 2013). Indeed, sensing as governance doesn't empower people in need of social change nor does it resolve environmental threats, instead it advances the responsibilization of individuals who need to monitor the continually emergent patterns of air pollution data and adapt, leaving no time to imagine collective political agency vis à vis pollution.

6. CONCLUSIONS

The different sections of this chapter trace the intrusion of a novel datafied sense of air. On the one hand, the Beijing accounts have made us aware that both the potentially empowering and problematic aspects of technoscientific air quality indexes stem from their 'datafied' nature. It is their volume, their velocity and their digital character that allows them to be integrated into algorithmic models of sensing, distribution, and forecasting. The simultaneously digital and environmental nature of air quality data (PM2.5 and AQI) connects two lines of inquiry: the critique of algorithmic governmentality, relating to the impacts of automation (including sensing) and algorithms on democracy, and the critique of governing through environmental distributions of power and cybernetization of environments (and the atmosphere). In line with a broader interdisciplinary concern about the impact of big data and sensing on governance, the Beijing accounts converged around the recent focus on numbers, highlighting air quality data and digital sensing as one of the critical terrains for contemporary environmental distribution of governance. This is perhaps best exemplified by AQI, which reframes air quality as the expected health response of a population, attesting to the intricate intermingling of technological and neoliberal rationalities in the framing of air, and its pollution.

Scientific and technological formulations of pollutants are rightly considered efficient and evidentiary tools for addressing the problems of atmospheric toxicity. However, what if toxic air can be sensed in different, perhaps incommensurable, ways? And, what if sensing has multiple functions and effects, including the establishment of specific terrains for the distribution of governance? Originating in sense-driven artistic research around the technoecological imaginaries of air, and its pollution, this chapter retains references to other sensorial and perceptual entanglements with pollution posing the question of what information matters and what does not. It follows the researcher navigating the city using air monitoring devices, apps, and her own sensory apparatus; several divergent, yet also complementing, narratives of inhabitants coexisting with pollution over long periods, who have come to monitor air quality and structure their everyday lives accordingly (for those who have the means), or on the contrary, surrender to the consequences of exposure. Whereas usually deemed irrelevant, these perspectives highlight that sensorial perception by different people or through different sensorium is not the same, neither is it equal, by providing concrete everyday examples of the social and political implications of novel modes of data-sensing and the underlying rationality that, rather than addressing the causal relations of air pollution, positions it as an individual risk to be managed. In addition, giving attention to fragmentary and disparate narratives exposes how datafied conceptualizations of air not only normalize but also neutralize the actual world; the irreducibility of the corporeal experience of air (breathing, smelling, tasting, being touched and permeated by, or feeling the heat and humidity of air) that grounds most of our human senses as well as societal decision-making and discussion are sidelined by a computable data-world.

The doing of data-sensing is necessarily a reduction of the heterogeneous materiality of air. In no way do we want to imply that digital air quality sensing and automated data flows cannot be used for (radical) political ends and citizen empowerment. We also do not want to indicate that they have not contributed to improvements in air quality. Indeed, PM2.5 measurements have dropped significantly in the capital since the start of the *war on pollution* and the 5-year Air Pollution Action Plan of 2013. Even so, building on a critical reading of our case study and in solidarity with the legitimate concerns of citizens living in toxic air this chapter argues that radical political projects attending to air need to find means for addressing the prevailing condition of algorithmic forms of governance, precisely because it dematerializes urban bodies and their agency into quantified nodes of planet-scale digital infrastructure. Resonating with Haraway's call for an embodied, embedded, and situated reclaiming of the technologies of perception (and relatedly also sensing) this loss of political agency—which we argue is associated with the novel perceptual regimes of capture and control and strongly shaped by neoliberal rationality—manifest an urgent need to reclaim more caring and politically aware technological modes of sensing (Haraway, 1988).

References

Agostinho, D. (2019). The Optical Unconscious of Big Data: Datafication of Vision and Care for Unknown Futures. *Big Data & Society 6 (1)* (January–June), 1–10.
Chandler, D. (2018). *Ontopolitics in the Anthropocene: an introduction to mapping, sensing and hacking*. London, UK: Routledge.
Denis, J., & Goëta, S. (2014). Exploration, Extraction and 'Rawification.' The Shaping of Transparency in the Back Rooms of Open Data (SSRN Scholarly Paper No. ID 2403069). Rochester, NY: Social Science Research Network. Retrieved from https://papers.ssrn.com/abstract=2403069
Gabrys, J. (2014). Programming environments: environmentality and citizen sensing in the smart city. *Environment and Planning D: Society and Space 32, no.1* (February), 30–48.
Gabrys, J. (2016). *Program Earth: Environmental Sensing Technology and the Making of a Computational Planet* (Vol. 49). Minneapolis, MN: University of Minnesota Press.
Hannula, M., Suoranta, J., & Vadén, T. (2014). *Artistic Research Methodology: Narrative, Power and the Public*. New York, NY: Peter Lang Publishing.
Haraway, D. (1988). Situated knowledges: the Science Question in Feminism and the Privilege of Partial Perspective. *Feminist Studies 14, no. 3* (Autumn), 575–599.
Hörl, E. (2017). "Introduction to general ecology." In E. Hörl and J. Burton (Ed.), *General ecology: The new ecological paradigm*. London, UK: Bloomsbury, 1–75.
Hörl, E. (2018). The environmentalitarian situation: Reflections on the becoming-environmental of thinking, power, and capital. *Public Culture 14, no. 2* (July), 153–173.
Husberg, H., & Marzecová, A. (2021). Changing Imaginaries and New Technoecologies of Urban Air. In H. Rogers, M. Halpern, D. Hannah, & K. de Ridder-Vignone, (Eds.), *Routledge Handbook of Art, Science, and Technology Studies (1st ed.)* (pp. 627–638). London, UK: Routledge. https://doi.org/10.4324/9780429437069
Liu, X. (2017). Air Quality Index as the Stuff of the Political. *Australian Feminist Studies* 32 (94), 445–460.
Murphy, M. (2006). *Sick Building Syndrome and the Problem of Uncertainty: Environmental Politics, Technoscience, and Women Workers*. Durham, NC: Duke University Press.
Murphy, M. (2017). Alterlife and Decolonial Chemical Exposures. *Cultural Anthropology* Vol. 32(Nov), Issue 4, 494–503.
Nixon, R. (2011). *Slow Violence and the Environmentalism of the Poor*. Cambridge, MA: Harvard University Press.

Parisi, L. (2009). Technoecologies of Sensation. In B. Herzogenrath (Ed.), *Deleuze/Guattari & Ecologies* (pp. 182–199). London, UK: Palgrave Macmillian.

Reckwitz, A. (2016). How the senses organize the social. In M. Jonas & B. Littig (Eds.), *Praxeological Political Analysis* (pp. 56–66). London, UK: Routledge.

Reckwitz, A. (2017). Practices and their affects. In A. Hui, T. Schatzki and E. Shove (Eds.), *The Nexus of Practices. Connections, Constellations, Practitioners* (pp.114–125). London, UK: Routledge.

Rouvroy, A. (2013). The end (s) of critique: Data behaviourism versus due process. In M. Hildebrandt & K. de Vries (Eds.), *Privacy, due process and the computational turn* (pp. 157–182). London, UK: Routledge.

Rouvroy, A., & Stiegler, B. (2016). The digital regime of truth: from the algorithmic governmentality to a new rule of law. *La Deleuziana: Online Journal of Philosophy 3*, 6–29.

Whitehead, M. (2011). *State, Science and the Skies: Governmentalities of The British Atmosphere*. London, UK: John Wiley & Sons.

Aesthetic innovation – and collective re-ordering

How to Better Sense What is Happening?
A Political Lesson from Taste and Tasting

Antoine Hennion

> What really exists is not things made, but things in the making.
> —William James, A Pluralistic Universe, 1909

1. WHAT DOES TASTE HAVE TO DO WITH POLITICS?

To me, there is great interest in the intriguing expression "sensing collectives." At first, it is a suggestion to investigate any kind of groupings that are sensing around, that are feeling beings, things or events, or even that are sniffing out opportunities—those collectives including various people but also devices, organizations, procedures, etc. (Callon, Law, 1982; Law, Hassard, 1999). But "sensing collectives" may also read in the other sense as an endeavor to make ourselves capable of sensing our own heterogenous collectives (Voß, Guggenheim, 2019; Voß et al., 2018; Teil, 2004; Teil, Hennion et al., 2013), of approaching them through our senses. Finally, I also convincingly endorse that catchphrase for another reason, namely because it points out not at an object but at an on-going process—as does my use of the gerund tasting rather than taste in the title of this chapter. It is precisely the angle of attack I had adopted to investigate "tasting amateurs" (or fans, enthusiasts, and so on), as drawing up an uncertain and reflexive activity (Hennion, 2007), that requires training and devices, for an always uncertain result. By that, I don't mean a quest for some unreachable object, as aesthetics complacently tends to put it, but rather a minute collective and corporal work in order to make the object of taste "exist more," as Souriau beautifully put it (Souriau, 1956; see Latour, 2014).

If one considers all objects as being open, unachieved, "in process of making" (James, 1909b), all still to be made by relying on a heterogenous assemblage of bodies, collectives, devices, and things, then the relationships between esthetics and politics get crucial indeed, especially in that if forces social sciences—or cultural studies, or empirical philosophy—to better catch how objects enter the game. This is what this chapter will try to clarify, from the lessons given by taste and tasting. It is true that in inquiring such an open, self-producing and often polemical process, I had for my part put the stress on esthetics, corporality, and sensuality, not on politics or social protests. Even if tastes are harshly debated, the frequent use of a revolutionary vocabulary by amateurs and critics does not cost much to the fiercest opponents. More crucially, in the case of tastes, options do not exclude each other. Ignoring the other is always possible; pluralism and non-exclusive fanaticisms are the rule, not the exception. One can dream of a similar picture of politics, except that if it were the case there would be no politics but endless debates and no decisions.

The problem here may be that such great categories as esthetics and politics—or science and technology—are too big to fail. Or rather they are giants with feet of clay. Their solemn obviousness may be a blinding clarity, creating too sharp partitions. If one gets down closer to situations and people, in any of those activities one just sees variously committed members, more or less reliable organizations, trained bodies and unequal competencies, all that framed through rough records or minute reporting, depending on tinkered-with equipment or on more or less sophisticated devices, and so on. But all this is brought together *for something*. What does such a commonplace imply? What if, instead of taking it for granted, we also take the object of any activity as being uncertain, open, still to be made? To say it pompously, what if those gradually shaping, fragile stakes of the activity are themselves neither predetermined nor a remote ideal, but self-defined through their own process of instauration? The big names above only pick the bet after the play.

This is precisely what referring to amateurs may help grasp. Both wordings "sensing collectives" and "tasting amateurs" stress the importance of feelings and sensations and aim at investigating them empirically; both point at collectives, devices, organization, procedures; but the main difference between lies in the focus the latter invites us to put on that common thing which matter so much to amateurs, the object of their passion. The word object itself comprises all the ambiguity at play, as its meaning ranges from a target of any human action (an *objective* to be achieved), making it a quasi-synonymous of issue, or concern, to being on the contrary a quasi-synonymous of thing, in its unhuman *objectivity*. Indeed, the same ambivalence about "object" is true about the word "sense." Its incredible polysemy, ranging from signification or meaning to naming our five organs of perception, has long since been pointed out. To me, it provides a good line to catch the "sensing collectives" project here: to make sense isn't merely a matter of signs. Reciprocally, it also questions how things signal us (*"faire signe,"* as French puts it), as much as we target them. Sensing is a way of connecting those two crucial issues, the status of things in social research and a material and sensual approach to meaning, taken as a matter of bodies, of feelings, of collectives and of devices, including signs themselves. Thus posed, the question is less to articulate esthetics and politics than to better catch their intertwined instauration, before or under any ready-made institutionalization.

To address this, drawing on my past work on music (Hennion, 2015), amateurs (Hennion, 2001) and attachments (Gomart, Hennion, 1999; Hennion, 2017), I will emphasize one specific issue: What kind of reset did social research have to implement in its genes to make itself both more hospitable for objects and, let's say, more sensitive to senses? In a kind of backward rewriting of the story, I will trace back the relationship between sense and things in the French social sciences, from the more abstract and symbolic understanding of the expression "to make sense" by semiology—the science of signs—to the more material and bodily one, to which opens the present project. I do not focus on the French side of the tale only because I am French but because from Durkheim's positive understanding of "the social" as an ignored reality hidden behind natural things to the long structuralist passage from the 1950s to the 1970s that radicalized a purely symbolic understanding of culture, and eventually the negative rewriting of both as a process of denial in Bourdieu's critical sociology, French social scientists of the 20th century had a heavy responsibility in widening the Great Divide between Nature and Culture. It is not by chance that authors who did not follow this wide avenue and fought against the Great Divide, as ANT founders and notably Stengers and Latour, were deeply influenced by American pragmatists or by Whitehead, beside some original French strong personalities as Souriau, Deleuze or Serres—the author of *"Les cinq sens."*

First, I will thus review the relationships between semiology, social sciences and pragmatism, with regard to one crucial issue: the place they give to objects. For my part, after having worked on music and mediation, I undertook to elaborate what I called a pragmatics of taste (Hennion, 2004; 2020), that I will present before developing what it may imply for politics—more specifically I make a wager: Research on taste and tasting/testing are well placed to advance the question of how we collectively sense things that are not yet clearly defined.

2. SOCIAL SCIENCES STRUGGLING WITH TASTE

2.1 Let objects speak!
(completing semiology with Actor-Network Theory)

I start from a criticism of the way social sciences deal with taste. One reason for this is that I belong to the *Centre de Sociologie de l'Innovation de l'École des Mines de Paris*. This research center is the place where the "sociology of translation" was created, which aimed to revise the sociology of science and technology in depth (see founding texts reprinted in Akrich, Callon, Latour eds., 2006). It was the way its French founders had called this approach, then re-labeled Actor-Network Theory, following the fruitful collaboration with John Law—in French, la *"théorie de l'acteur-réseau."* Under the acronym ANT, it spread like wildfire throughout the Anglo-American world from the 1980s onwards.

Critical of some basic postulates made by sociology, this theory has from its beginnings relied very directly on borrowings from semiology: some quite explicit concepts, as *actants* or *débrayage/embrayage* (disengagement/engagement) taken from Greimas (Greimas, Courtès, 1982), or Latour's first article written in collaboration with semiologist Paolo Fabbri, published at the time in Bourdieu's review *Actes de la recherche en sciences sociales* (Latour, Fabbri, 1979); but also, more broadly, the central role given by ANT to the spokesperson as well as to the very notion of translation; all that, later on, has finally brought some of the center's researchers, including myself, closer to pragmatism.

On this last point, through our debates with other centers interested in the pragmatic approach, such as the *Centre d'études de mouvements sociaux* (CEMS) and the *Groupe de sociologie politique et morale* (GSPM), we were certainly more concerned with re-reading Dewey on public debate and inquiry theory (Dewey, 1927; 1938), and also, at least in our case, James's views on ontological pluralism and radical empiricism (James, 1909a; 1912). But Peirce's semiology was very much present too, in the background, through his radical rejection of the dualism between signs and things: The idea that things themselves are signs for an interpreter and that the roles between these three terms are not predetermined seemed to us to be tailor-made for our project.

But there are two ways of reading this initial proximity between semiology and ANT, with regard to reconceptualizing the subject-object relationship. The stumbling block, and this is the problem around which I will focus this intervention, is the status given to things. Is it a question of integrating other objects into semiology, in order to place more and more of them under the banner of "everything is language"? Or, conversely, is it to take semiology out of the world of signs while recovering the tools it has forged, in order to endow the objects themselves with a capacity to propose, address, and call: in short, to give them a voice? Was ANT a generalized semiology, or a completion of semiology, in every sense of the word completion—both a prolongation and an end? Since aesthetics is about taste, and taste is about a relation of things with humans, I recall the development of ANT as an approach radically rejecting any dualism of nature and culture or of things and signs. This excursion lead to re-appreciate taste as a process, a happening, which hopefully may help us discuss its relation with politics in new ways.

With hindsight, even if, as good Frenchmen fighting against the structuralism in which we had been immersed since childhood, we were no doubt simplifying and reinterpreting the pragmatists' theses abundantly for the needs of the cause, it still seems to me indisputable that there already were many points in common between our program and pragmatist and semiotic approaches, particularly in the way they treat the subject-object relationship in direct opposition to those of classical or critical philosophies.

2.2 Let tasters listen to and interact with speaking objects! (completing Actor-Network Theory with pragmatism)

Following this, I will get to the ways by which I developed a pragmatics of taste, closely linked to and embedded with how ANT reconceptualized objects as alive and speaking, rather than deadly passive and mute. The core is to develop a new understanding of the ways human relate to objects as alive and speaking. The key is that this is where taste emerges as what happens when humans engage attentively, reflexively, and experimentally with live objects—appreciating them as being alive and speaking: listening to them, playing with them, provoking them.

It is worth mentioning here that the main idea of this approach met fiercer resistance from sociologists than it did from an audience of semiologists or pragmatist philosophers: The former are so obsessed by the need to show that taste is socially determined—a reality that in fact nobody disputes—that the slightest effort to take seriously both the properties and reactions of the objects tasted and the skills and practices of the tasters makes them stiffen up and pull out the heavy artillery.

3. THE GREAT DIVIDE

Let us first look at semiology, sociology, and the theories of taste as disciplines. This makes the gaps between them widen. As soon as the theories are established, they harden, while investigations in the field force them to compose. I do not pretend here to retrace their history, but only to note selectively their relationship to taste (by which I mean both the things tasted and the taste for them). Until the 1970s, from Saussure to Durkheim, from Lévi-Strauss to Lacan, from Foucault to Bourdieu, sign and symbolism reigned supreme over the French university. The most opposed theories agree on the basic postulate, the Great Divide between nature and culture, physical objects and social realities (Latour, 1983, 2005; Descola, 2013). Dualism always leads to quarrels between doubles: Conversely, on the side of the natural sciences, the refusal of their human colleagues to accept that things intervene in their analyses opens the way to an inverse and symmetrical dualistic reduction—no longer going from things to the meaning that one projects on them, but from the meaning to the matter.

France in particular has given in to the irresistible seduction of "everything is language" to which I alluded. Proud heirs of the founding principle of structuralism, semiotics, and semiology have been enthroned under various banners as absolute kings of the social sciences for more than half a century. Paradoxically, such a sociological reductionism has left the field wide open for the "hard" sciences on taste to extend their empire and build a systematic metrology of taste, whether on the object side by measuring the components of tasty products or on the subject side by mapping our physiological and neurological sensors. This was only the shepherd's answer to the shepherdess: to the arrogance of social sciences, echoed the slow and meticulous extension of the domain of positivism.

But the story doesn't end there. If, on the contrary, Bourdieu radicalizes the great dualistic odyssey by adding to it the necessity of criticism and the idea that social domination is essentially achieved through its own denial (Bourdieu, 1987), the relationship to things becomes even more tense: From the "reification" of the Marxists to the "naturalization" of sociologists, it is then no worse crime than taking things for granted. In sociology in particular, a formidable machine for sucking up all objects has been set up. Even today in France, the apprentice sociologist trembles at the mere idea that he may be suspected of having "naturalized" his object, of having taken our "social constructions" for the reality of things. How, then, on the basis of such premises, could the young researcher sharpen his sensitivity to perceiving what things propose? Why would s/he really pay attention to what amateurs tell her/him, when deep down, s/he thinks they believe that the moon is made of green cheese, taking the game of social differentiation for the beauty of things and the refinement of tastes?

It was by drawing on other disciplines, themselves heavily influenced by semiology, that I then found tools for better thinking about objects in continuity with their meaning, for example in Michel de Certeau's work on the writing of history (de Certeau, 1988), or in Louis Marin's one on mediators in the art of the Quattrocento (Marin, 1989). After sensitizing us for the challenges of knowing taste I will end with a discussion of what this means for relating esthetics and politics and studying their intertwining in practice.

4. WHAT IF THINGS WERE NOT SO PASSIVE?

This is the first point that I would like to establish here. If there is so much blindness in matters of taste, it is in no way due to the social character of the construction of taste and its objects, which every amateur recognizes as soon as she describes her path. On the contrary, it is on the side of the social sciences themselves and the binary definition in which they have locked themselves. More precisely, they are the ones who have taken things for things—that is to say, in their eyes, inert objects, without capacity, good to be left to the microscopes of the "natural" sciences. Nothing could have prepared the French social sciences less to recognize pragmata, those "things in the making" (James, 1909a), "in their plurality," as William James also put it (James, 1909b, p. 210). Hence, in my opinion, their collapse in very few years, when, from climate to biodiversity, from gender to race, from diseases or procreation to GMOs or nanotechnologies, critical questions all politically arose around uncertain objects, while materiality and the body burst in, reaffirming their irreducible presence in every social struggle.

It is no coincidence that pragmatism, even in its very disparate finery, became one of the controversial issues in France just at that time, at the turn of the 1980s. Initially confined to the criticism of the overhanging position of the social scientist, to the recognition of the pluralism of values, and to the revival of the notions of inquiry and trial as the means by which things are defined, it initially served more as a method than as a philosophy. The "pragmatic sociology" of Boltanski and Thévenot (2006), notably, has always carefully maintained a watertight boundary between humans and non-humans. At the CSI, where we discussed a great deal with these researchers, the aim was quite different: It consisted, on the contrary, in reintegrating objects into sociology, the latter making only pretexts of them, if they were cultural objects, or raw facts, if they were natural objects. It is at the same time that we rediscovered with astonishment the radicality of James's ontological pluralism, that of things themselves in the process of being made, in an open, indeterminate world, without exteriority, whose accomplishment depends on the commitment of all: Anachronistically, we read there not only the hypotheses that ANT had in its own way defended before knowing the authors in question, but also how much the rejections and indignant arguments raised at the time by this radically anti-dualist pragmatism resembled those that had been opposed to us. It is not by chance that by now, most of ANT-readers are not sociologists but rather belong to cultural studies, gender studies, climate studies, etc., mixing activists, concerned actors, artists, philosophers, and researchers around emerging problems.

5. LETTING THINGS SPEAK FOR THEMSELVES

I will now take the problem through the other end of the lens. The idea is to start from the very ways in which taste and tasting are expressed, both by amateurs and by social scientists. This returns to semiology, but in a quasi-instrumental way, to make it a resource, a bit like in the early days of ANT: Can it help to shift the analysis of taste from a theory of action to an attention to the propensity of things? This leads me to emphasize the performative role of language: to take it less as a means of saying than as a tool that makes people think, that makes them "realize" things, as the double meaning of this verb puts it so well.

A pragmatics of taste starts with the recognition that we don't like things like that, by just snapping fingers. We have to laboriously make ourselves like them (Teil, Hennion, 2004). In return they themselves provide us holds, but holds that are only holds if we grasp them. This goes far beyond the common idea that we love what we hated and hate what we loved, which would only describe the slow apprenticeship of the real quality of sophisticated objects. No, it is true of any kind of objects, the amateur and what she likes are done by each other. The vocabulary of choice and willingness is too active, the one of sudden revelation or love at first sight too passive: The question is less about what we do than about what we more or less deliberately both let and make happen and about what things themselves express, if we make ourselves sensitive to them. Throughout this sinuous process, made of unexpected infatuations and tenacious passions, it is nowhere a question of mastery, but of responding to the call of things; but also of provoking them, by relaunching them and relaunching oneself. Finally, all this process can only take place if a collective has been able to create the space for common sharing and the material organization in which they unfold.

It is important to underline that there is nothing passive about this *"se laisser faire,"* letting oneself be done (Gomart, Hennion, 1999). Learning to let things "express themselves—*"laisser les choses se faire"*—" through the attention we pay to them requires, on the contrary, a meticulous collective experimentation, based on our bodies and on the objects themselves, mobilizing writings and devices. Taste is constantly rewriting its own history, in a slow process of cross-fertilization of each person's skills ... but no, that would still be saying things wrong, the formulation is too dualistic: For it is less a question of developing the tastes of the amateur and the qualities of the object as two realities that would respond to each other, than of maintaining the very relationship that produces both and continuously makes both be reborn (on the case of Bach in 19th century France, see Fauquet, Hennion, 2000).

A comparison with sport can help understand this point. Indeed, contrary to what the word taste leads us towards, in sport the body dimension and the collective dimension take precedence over the very object of the activity (whether the ball crosses a line, a bar is crossed, a ball is sent back, or a mountain pass is climbed ... what does it matter, in itself?!). This detour makes it clear that soccer does not exist without its rules, its equipment, its audience, the passion it unleashes, but also the very art of moving a ball between two teams, or jumping to unlikely heights at the end of a pole, or sending balls into the holes of a billiard table, it is neither the arbitrary invention of a game, nor the methodical exploitation of available resources, but rather an art of making skills and possibilities "exist more" (Souriau, 1956): both human and non-human capacities, both individual and collective ones, while realizing what things can do, if they are made to do so ...

To describe this, the word "virtual" does not seem adequate to me, it acts as if these properties were already there, latent, just waiting to be exploited. The athlete's body does not exist before the sport he or she practices, any more than the touch of a racket on a ball of regulated caliber and properties, or the ability to take advantage of improbable holds to climb walls, with feet clenched in a Spanish rubber boot ... It is the accumulation of training and techniques, or even the experience of the thing itself, that develops a relationship that is increasingly well adapted between bodies that were unaware of each other. Isn't this also an excellent definition of taste? Wouldn't it be just as inaccurate to believe that wine was "already there" in the vineyards before man cultivated it, as it would be to say that man created it with his own hands? Wine is the long shared history of what grapes have been able to do, and what man could do with them (Teil, Hennion et al., 2013) ... but beware, the word "could" itself is ambiguous, here again we have to watch out for the direction in which words take us in spite of ourselves ("men were capable of ... " versus "it could have happened that ..."): This possibility should not be understood in the sense of an initial capacity that would have been left untapped until then. Rather it should be seen as the unpredictable turn that things take, following a series of surprising interactions and unpredictable resumptions: in short, constantly re-elaborating the unforeseen. But what else is cooking?

6. A GRAMMAR OF THINGS BEING DONE
"In process of making" towards an art of *"faire faire"*

In order to better define taste, I have deliberately, above, linked without measure some turns that are grammatically rather heavy, even in French but even more so in English, this language obsessed with the matter of fact, to which it is always suggestive to confront French. In a way, we are getting back to semiologists here. They would help underline how much work is required on language itself, to formulate "what it is about," "what is happening," "what is going on" in the emergence of things. French is a very rich language for this purpose; it has many tricks up its sleeve to get around the dualistic trap. Notably, it is very fond of the curious "impersonal reflexive" form (here, *"ce dont il s'agit," "ce qui se passe"*), that I have used a lot. Such ambiguous formulas neutralize any subject and any object, or even any action, while grammatically using only these functions; in many turns, it also plays on the finesse of the infinitive double, as in *"faire faire," "laisser faire"* (not to mention their combination: *"se laisser faire,"* is it active or passive?). All these language tricks have been a great help, but they are difficult to translate into English: "let it be done," "let things happen," "to make do," "let oneself be taken in," etc. None of those wordings are really satisfying, nor commonly used in English. It is so much so that in English texts the expression *"faire faire"* is most often used without being translated: It perfectly sums up our theory of action—already in Greimas's work, the actant is very exactly *"ce qui fait faire,"* "what makes do."

These expressions all sought to designate something like putting oneself actively in states where the objective is not the control of things, but on the contrary a kind of deliberate loss of control, in order to give things back their hand, and in return to be able to rely on their reactions to increase their virtues ... Somewhat laborious formulas indeed (as are the previous oxymorons, such as "deliberate control"), but they are valuable when talking about taste: the problem is precisely to manage to speak beyond or below the murderous efficiency of the dualistic division between subject and object, redoubled by the opposition between the active and the passive. Echoing the form of the middle voice in Ancient Greek and the constant use of the gerund in English (who is born, when is born? becoming, is it active or passive? and what about thinking, loving, and of course tasting?), we have had to forge adequate expressions to replace this "voice" that has unfortunately disappeared from modern languages, indeed quite modernistic: No, the "middle" is not "in the middle" of anything; it does not come to take its place between two pre-existing voices more clearly defined than it (the active and the passive ones); it is first, on the contrary. It designates "what happens" before any preconceived distribution of roles. In order to account for the formation of taste (everyone has pointed out that the word taste is itself a middle word, designating both the taste for things and the taste of things, the one we have and the one they have), we have therefore explicitly exploited the resources that French offers—but at the point we have reached, I would gladly say the opposite, as Annemarie Mol has shown with regard to *"lekker"* in Dutch (Mol, 2014): that nothing teaches us better to speak, to weigh up the meaning of words as if on a trebuchet, than to talk about taste.

7. A FINAL WORD: DID YOU SAY POLITICS?
Taste as a lesson in the art of learning from things

The contrast between our two languages is not so anecdotal. It helps to identify these formulation issues. I like to use the example of the conductor. In English, he "conducts" his orchestra; in French, "il le fait jouer," he makes it play. Shifting from the linearity that is too clear subject-verb-complement, this double infinitive opens up the whole range of possible distributions of the action, or more precisely of "what is going on": directing or giving a direction, indicating what to do or getting into condition to go where one wants to go, or even, as with a horse, letting oneself be carried by the orchestra but giving the little signals that accentuate the finds and erase the banalities ... As in the case of education (there are a thousand ways to make a pupil learn his lesson!), the formula does not distinguish between the dictator conductor, for whom making people play means forcing everyone to do what he wants, and the pedagogical conductor or, better still, the discreet stimulator of what emerges as the most pleasant or original in the course of things, to give it more consistency. Those long detours through sports, the orchestra and, above all, language did not come to me by chance in this text on taste: What other object offers a reservoir so full of experiences and practices, entirely turned towards the slow sculpture of the objects to which we are attached?

Is there a more political stance today than to collectively elaborate our ability to better catch and support the propensity of things? Isn't politics, too, an art of making agents and things exist more—or better, or less, or no longer ... (Latour 2014)? For my part, on line with the lessons taste may give to politics, I would conclude in an open way by gladly adapting to the present and pressing social and ecological issues this beautiful and suggestive phrase by René Char: "[The things] that are going to come up know things about us that we do not know about them"—except Char was referring to words, not things: "Les mots qui vont surgir savent de nous des choses que nous ignorons d'eux" (Réné Char, Chant de la Balandrane, roman étranger, 1977). I didn't write this text in order to encourage social researchers to take a renewed interest in taste. In the opposite direction, I rather hope that revisiting this rich history of taste and tasting may help any committed social actors—be they researchers, artists, activists or simply concerned citizens—to get more sensitive to things in process of making.

References

Akrich, M.,Callon, M., & Latour, B., (Eds.). (2006). *Sociologie de la traduction: textes fondateurs*. Paris, FR: Presses des Mines.

Boltanski, L., & Thévenot, L. (2006). *On Justification: Economies of Worth* (C. Porter, Trans.). Princeton, MA: Princeton University Press. (Original work published in 1991).

Bourdieu, P. (1987). *Distinction: A Social Critique of the Judgement of Taste*. London, UK: Routledge. (Original work published in 1979).

Callon, M., & Law, J. (1982). On Interests and their Transformation: Enrolment and Counter-Enrolment. *Social Studies of Science, 12*, 615–625.

De Certeau, M. (1988). *The Writing of History* (T. Conley, Trans.). New York, NY: Columbia University Press. (Original work published in 1975).

Descola, Ph. (2013). *Beyond Nature and Culture* (J. Lloyd, Trans.). Chicago, IL: University of Chicago Press. (Original work published in 2005).

Dewey, J. (1927). *The Public and its Problems*. New York, NY: H. Holt & Co.

Dewey, J. (1938). *Logic. A Theory of Inquiry*. New York, NY: H. Holt & Co.

Fauquet, J.-M., & Hennion, A. (2000). *La Grandeur de Bach. L'amour de la musique en France au XIXe siècle*. Paris, FR: Fayard.

Gomart, É., & Hennion, A. (1999). A Sociology of Attachment: Music Amateurs, Drug Users. In J. Law & J. Hassard (Eds.). *Actor Network Theory and After* (pp. 220–247). Oxford, UK: Blackwell.

Greimas, A. J., & Courtés, J. (1982). *Semiotics and Language: An Analytical Dictionary*. Bloomington, IN: Indiana University Press.

Hennion, A. (2001). Music Lovers. Taste as Performance. *Theory, Culture, Society, 18*(5), 1–22.

Hennion, A. (2004). Pragmatics of taste. In M. Jacobs & N. Hanrahan (Eds.). *The Blackwell Companion to the Sociology of Culture* (pp. 131–144). Oxford, UK: Malden – Blackwell.

Hennion, A. (2007). Those Things That Hold Us Together: Taste and Sociology. *Cultural Sociology*, 1(1), 97–114.

Hennion, A. (2015). *The Passion for Music. A Sociology of Mediation* (M. Rigaud & P. Collier, Trans.). London, UK: Routledge. (Original work published in 1993).

Hennion, A. (2017). Attachments, you say? ... How a concept collectively emerges in one research group. *Journal of Cultural Economy*, 10(1), 112–121. doi: 10.1080/17530350.2016.1260629

Hennion, A. (2020). From ANT to pragmatism: A Journey with Bruno Latour at the CSI. In R. Felski, & S. Muecke (Eds.). *Latour and the Humanities* (pp. 52–75). Baltimore, MD: Johns Hopkins University Press.

James, W. (1909a). *A Pluralistic Universe*. New York, NY: Longmans, Green & Co.

James, W. (1909b). *The Meaning of Truth*. New York, NY: Longmans, Green & Co.

James, W. (1912). *Essays in Radical Empiricism*. New York, NY: Longmans, Green & Co.

Latour, B., & P. Fabbri. (1977). La rhétorique de la sciences. *Actes de la recherche en sciences sociales 13*, 81–95.

Latour, B. (1983). Comment redistribuer le grand partage?. *Revue de synthèse 110*, 203–236.

Latour, B. (2005). *Reassembling the Social – An Introduction to Actor-Network Theory*. Oxford, UK: Oxford University Press.

Latour, B. (2014). Agency at the time of the Anthropocene. *New Literary History*, 45, 1–18.

Marin, L. (1989). *Opacité de la peinture*, Paris, FR: Éditions de l'EHESS.

Mol, A. (2014). Language Trails: 'Lekker' and Its Pleasures. *Theory, Culture & Society*, 31(2-3), (93–119).

Souriau, É. (2009). Du mode d'existence de l'œuvre à faire. In I. Stengers & B. Latour (Eds). *Les différents modes d'existence* (pp. 195–217). Paris, FR: PUF. (Original work published in 1956).

Teil, G., & Hennion, A. (2004). Discovering Quality or Performing Taste? A Sociology of the Amateur. In A. McMeekin, A. Warde, & M. Hervey (Eds.). *Qualities of Food* (pp. 19–37). Manchester, UK: Manchester University Press.

Teil, G. (2004). *De la coupe aux lèvres. Pratiques de la perception et mise en marche des vins de qualité*. Toulouse, FR: Éditions Octarès.

Teil, G., Hennion, A., Barrey, S., & Floux, P. (2013). *Le vin et l'environnement. Faire compter la différence*, Paris, FR: Presses des Mines.

Voß, J.-P., Rigamonti, N., Suarez, M., & Watson, J., (2018). *Workshop: Sensing collectives – aesthetic and political practices intertwined*. Retrieved from http://sensing-collectives.org.

Voß, J.-P., Guggenheim, M. (2019). Making Taste Public: Industrialized Orders of Sensing and the Democratic Potential of Experimental Eating. *Politics and Governance, Vol. 7(4)*, 224–236.

Provoking Taste
Experimenting with New Ways of Sensing

Jan-Peter Voß, Michael Guggenheim, Nora Rigamonti, Aline Haulsen, Max Söding

1. INTRODUCTION

A man sits at a table in a museum and tastes something he has never seen before. He is not sure what it is, but he is prompted to taste orange-red jelly-like cubes—and to do so as if it were an honor to eat such a thing. He hesitates, he looks at it, then, he closes his eyes and slowly takes a bite. He writes down some notes. He takes another bite. He reads along in a document, where he is told to taste again, but this time as if he were ashamed. After completing a series of other, similar experiments, he creates a new dish from the ingredients assembled in front of him, and writes down a title for the dish in his tasting notes. This is the setting of an exhibition called "Schmeck!" (German for "taste!"), that we set up in autumn 2020 at the Museum of Natural History (MfN) in Berlin.[1]

Why did we create an exhibition in which we asked people to taste unknown foods as if they were honored or ashamed? We sought to first explore how taste changes in relation with various elements of the eating situation (such as sounds, previous knowledge about ingredients and expectations) and, secondly, to use these experiences to provoke participants to create new tasting practices and dishes. In the introduction to this volume, the editors develop the notion of "sensing collectives" to study the intertwining of aesthetic and political practices. In this chapter, we discuss the exhibition as a case of engaging visitors in experiments that were at the same time aesthetic (i.e. inducing and shaping sensory perceptions) as well as political (i.e. inducing and shaping collective subjectivity).

---

1 The exhibition was embedded in the larger project "Schmeck! Practices and aesthetics of eating in the governance of a sustainable transformation of food systems." This project was directed by Jan-Peter Voß and Nina Langen and received funding by the Executive Board of the Berlin University of Technology from 2019 until 2021. It was set up as a transdisciplinary project with sociologists and food scientists and 25 citizen scientists working on the question how taste can be studied as it happens and how taste can be experimentally shaped (www.schmeckprojekt.de).

The aesthetic dimension is rather obvious, as the exhibition engages practices and experiences of tasting food. For the political dimension, it is relevant to establish how different ways of tasting are constitutive of social groups and identities – and vice versa, how social groups are constitutive of ways of tasting. Becoming a "we" is often closely connected with certain shared ways of perceiving (food) and of being affected in certain ways: To taste means to (dis-)like and shared (dis-)likes build collectives. The literature in the sociology, anthropology, and history of food and taste can be read as repeated attempts to theorize this link through studies of, among many others, French and American ways of tasting (Barthes, 2013 [1961]), of specific ethnic and religious ways of tasting (Fischler, 1988), of class- and gender-specific ways of tasting (Bourdieu, 2013 [1979]), of specific ways of tasting practiced by collectives of food and wine lovers (Teil & Hennion, 2004), and of social movements forming around specific ways of tasting (Hayes-Conroy & Martin, 2010).

Against this background, we presume that tasting is political, not only in the broad sense of being a collectively practiced reality that excludes other possible realities (Latour, 1983; Mol, 1998; Stengers, 2010; Jonas & Littig, 2016). Tasting is also political in a narrower sense of constituting collective subjectivities by articulating a uniting identity or will for mobilizing collective agency (Latour, 2003; Saward, 2006; Disch, 2008; Disch, 2010).

In the following, we present the concept, setup, and outcomes of the "Schmeck!" exhibition as well as empirical observations on how participants engaged with the exhibition, through the notes they took on their tasting experiences, and interviews we conducted with some of them afterwards.

For making the case for such an intervention, we refer to an earlier article (Voß & Guggenheim, 2019) where we have problematized a concentration of power with the food industry and sensory sciences in the "aesthetic governance" of modern Western eating practices. In this article we argued that democratizing the politics of food would require challenging this dominant mode of "tasting like industry." Our proposal was to democratize the aesthetic governance of food and eating by strengthening the agency of people to re-invent and shape their own ways of tasting. We sketched the concept for a participatory exhibition that would seek to dislodge industrialized tasting practices by inviting and prompting visitors to explore their own creative capacities to experimentally re-configure and shape their ways of tasting.

In this chapter, we discuss how we turned this concept into an exhibition and the effects it had. In the next, second, section, we give some conceptual background on how we understand the very engagement with industrial orders of tasting as both an aesthetic and a political challenge. In the third section, we describe the actual experimental setup of the exhibition. The fourth section reports on the effects of the exhibition, specifically how it generated new tasting practices and experiences. In the fifth and concluding section, we discuss insights: Were we successful in disrupting industrialized orders of sensing and provoking more creative ways of tasting?

2. CHALLENGING INDUSTRIAL ORDERS OF TASTING BY PROVOKING CREATIVE PRACTICES

Classical approaches see taste as either socio-psychologically or biologically determined. They either imply a structuralist understanding of taste as social positions that are inscribed in habitual practices (for example, Bourdieu's concept of a class and gender specific habitus, e.g., 1977 [1972]: chapter one). Or they conceive of taste as biologically evolved predilections functioning for the survival of the species (Katz, 1990). Despite apparent differences both, social and biological determinism, understand taste as a non-reflexive reaction of (specific groups of) human subjects to the given properties of tasted objects. Hence, both are rooted in a "gusto-ontology" that assumes taste results from subjects with given predilections and food objects with given qualities. This logic finds its correlation in the set-up of laboratory experiments with a view to determine average and group-specific ways of tasting specific objects. Tasting, moreover, is usually described in quantitative terms by allocating scores on given scales (Lahne, 2016; Lahne, 2018). Taste, then, is reported as a fixed personal trait aggregated into the taste of the average consumer or of any statistically relevant group.

In contrast, recent studies in anthropology and sociology focus on tasting as embedded in specific situations where both subjective predilections and objective food qualities are merely two elements that are not fixed but constituted in relation with other elements of a more complex configuration of the situation, including, for example, specific culturally established meanings, interactions with other people, specific trained bodily practices of eating or tools and atmospheres (Hennion, 2004; Teil & Hennion, 2004; Hennion, 2007; Hennion, 2015; Mol, 2009; Paxson, 2010; Korsmeyer & Sutton, 2011; Mann, 2015; Mann, 2018; Spackman and Lahne, 2019). Rooted in pragmatism and ethnomethodology, tasting is studied here as an aesthetic practice, a "reflexive and performative capacity, opposed to any possibility of seeing it as an objectified reality which scientific knowledge could account for from the outside" (Teil & Hennion, 2004, p. 27). By reconstructing tasting practices ethnographically in everyday situations and amateur rituals, such studies highlight creative capacities and autonomous ways of tasting that undermine and counter the subject-object mechanics of industrialized orders of sensing. They reveal an alternative "gusto-ontology" of taste as a highly situational, relational, and complex practice in which tasted objects and tasting subjects are mutually constituted as a contingent outcome open to experimental and creative intervention.

With the exhibition "Taste! Experiments for the senses," we drew on this alternative gusto-ontology articulated in recent studies of taste. We conceptualized the exhibition as a public intervention in established collective orders of sensing with a view to induce and enable the practicing of an alternative way of tasting: tasting as creative agency rather than a reproduction of habits and conventions largely shaped by industrialized ways of knowing and doing taste. The exhibition therefore comprised a series of experiments for participants to explore the malleability of taste by actively intervening in the specific situation in which they taste. The experiments were meant to provoke participants to reflexively engage with their own ways of sensing and to become agents of aesthetic practice by creatively shaping their own sensory perceptions.

As such the exhibition was obviously an engagement with aesthetic practices. But to what extent was it also an engagement with political practices? We may differentiate here between a wider and a narrower conception of politics. First, in a wider conception of politics as "cultural politics" (Nash, 2001), "ontological politics" (Mol, 2002), "Dingpolitik" (Latour, 2005), "cosmopolitics" (Stengers, 2010) or "material politics" (Marres, 2012), the exhibition was a political intervention as it engaged with specific ways of collectively knowing and doing taste enacting a specific reality of taste and excluding other possible realities. Here, the exhibition was political because it created a situation for participants to explore how tasting can be done differently, according to an alternative, ecological ontology: It allowed to experience tasting as 1) complex and dynamic, 2) constituted relationally by a diversity of elements 3) malleable, prone to be reflexively shaped by active tasters. We did not offer this alternative ontology in the form of an intellectual treatise or a political manifesto, but as a setting to be engaged with, an experiment to be performed an experience to be made. In this sense, the exhibition was a material political intervention providing an arrangement to invite, induce, and enable participants to realize a creative rather than the industrial style of tasting. This would be the political dimension of our engagement with aesthetic practices in a broad sense of engaging with collectively practiced realities of taste ("queering taste" we might say).

Second, in a narrower conception of politics, the exhibition would also be political as it contributed to inducing and shaping a specific collective subjectivity, a new 'we' of tasters conscious of their shared will to taste differently. Was there also anything like that happening as part of our engagement with practices of tasting? Did we, in any way, articulate a "representative claim" (Saward 2006) on behalf of a collective will to taste differently that could performatively bring into existence a new collective subject with collective agency (Latour, 2003; Saward, 2017; Disch et al., 2019)?

As we did not articulate any such claim in words, we would need to turn to representative claims articulated in more bodily and material ways. Judith Butler, in her "notes towards a performative theory of assembly" (Butler, 2015), proposes to study political speech acts also in the media of material designs and architectures, in body movements and choreographies. For the case of the Occupy Movement, for example, she argues that a representative claim is to be found in the material and bodily arrangement of public camps on city squares that performed a collective subjectivity of "precarity." By analogy, we may also investigate the material and bodily arrangement of our exhibition as a political representative claim beyond words. We may interpret it as the articulation of a collective will to taste autonomously, experimentally, and reflexively. In that sense, our design of the exhibition would also count as political in the narrower sense. The crucial question is, however, if such a representative claim was at all perceived and adopted by the participants, if there are any indications of them feeling part of a new 'we' of creative tasters after having taken part in the exhibition. Towards the end of this chapter, we will come back to discuss the actual aesthetic and political effects of the exhibition as it was taken up and enacted by participants.

3. DESIGNING A PARTICIPATORY EXHIBITION WITH PERFORMATIVE TASTING EXPERIMENTS

How is it possible to create new forms of tasting with an exhibition? We take a cue from methods for "Inventing the Social" (Marres et al., 2018) that "involve an active search for alternative ways of combining representation of, and intervention in, social life" (p. 18): "If we want to really grasp social processes we must somehow invite, persuade or (to put it more strongly) provoke actors and situations to generate accounts, and to produce expressions and articulations of social reality" (p. 28). For the case of taste, this meant for us to move away from documenting how tasting is usually or unusually done in all kinds of different already existing situations,[2] and instead create a new and very specific situation that would provoke participants to trial new ways of eating and tasting. The exhibition was to become a place for "making taste public" by opening it up for collective experimentation. We thus thought of the exhibition as an experiment in fostering new kinds of participation in the shaping of taste via a new kind of sensory research (Lezaun et al., 2016). As an exhibition experiment (Macdonald & Basu, 2008), we had to move away from trying to explain taste as reflexive practice through visual and textual displays. Instead, we had to find ways how visitors could themselves understand taste as reflexive practice by reflexively practicing it.

The experiments allowed participants to experience how our sensory experience depends on the complex interplay of many different elements. In this vein, the experiments are geared to disassemble usual tasting situations into selected elements that relationally constitute a specific tasting practice and experience (Roehl, 2012). We took inspiration from Garfinkel's ethnomethodological breaching experiments

---

2 This is what we did in another part of the larger project "Schmeck!" in which the exhibition was embedded, where we developed the method of "gustography" to account for tasting experiences situated in everyday life (see our online event "How Can We Study Taste as It Happens?" in March 2021 with Antoine Hennion here: https://vimeo.com/521563587).

(Garfinkel, 1964): For these, he asked students to perform surprises on unwitting participants to make visible implicit knowledge of social orders by provoking them to repair normality. While we take up the logic of breaching, we are not interested in how this reveals the taken-for-granted-ness of social life. We invert the approach to make visible the openness and situated complexity of tasting and to provoke capacities of creatively inventing new orders of tasting.

Accordingly, we designed six different experiments to offer a range of access points to doing taste. The six experiments were all presented at one workstation. The exhibition comprised eight such workstations, so that eight people could do the six experiments concurrently. Going through all six experiments usually took participants around 45 minutes. Upon entering the exhibition, participants were greeted by a steward, who guided them to their place and gave them written instructions on a clipboard. The instructions guided the participants through the process of each individual experiment.

We settled on the final set-up (detailed below) after we went through several trials with our extended research team in the project "Schmeck" which included 25 citizen scientists (see endnote 1). The exhibition was supposed to open in May 2020 but had to be adapted for hygiene regulations during the Covid-19 pandemic. The first version provided for a separate station for each experiment with participants moving from one to another. It included two stages where they gathered for interaction (e.g. observing or feeding each other). The second Covid-19 version had to abandon such interactions and guarantee disinfected workplaces and 1.5 meters of physical distance. For reasons of hygiene and available infrastructure, all food had to be served cold and had to be prepared off-site.

The exhibition eventually opened for three weeks in September and October 2020 and was attended by about 1000 visitors. Located at the "Experimental Field for Participation and Open Science" of the Berlin Museum of Natural History, it met a curious audience.

In each of the six experiments, participants were invited to taste one or several ingredients and to take notes regarding their tasting experiences. In doing so, the participants engaged in the observation and reflection of this experience. One central challenge was to use as many unknown ingredients as possible or at least to prepare them in a way that it would be difficult to know exactly what it is in order to circumvent assumed given predilections and embodied, pre-reflexive taste knowledge, while keeping a balance of tastes, smells, colors, and textures.

The first part of the exhibition (exercises 1–5 as detailed below) thus *disassembles* tasting by offering experimental variations on selected elements of an eating situation. Trying them out and exploring their effects helps participants to leave any habitualized ways of tasting behind and experience variability. The second part (exercise 6) then asks participants to *re-assemble* selected elements they have tried. This is the moment of creatively composing not only a dish, but a situation, and to realize the taste experience that it generates.

Figure 1: At the experimental station each phase is marked by a symbol, a color and a corresponding field on the table with utensils and ingredients.

Source: Schmeck!Project ©

Figure 2: In every phase, the form gave instructions on how to conduct the experiments.

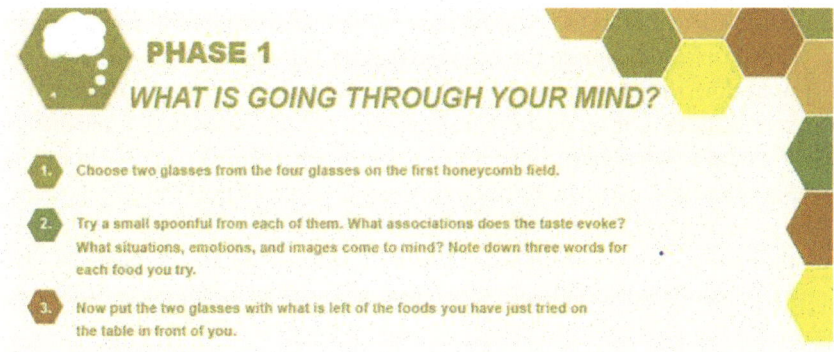

Source: Schmeck!Project ©

The disassembling phase consists of the following five experiments:

(1) *Mental associations* and *memories*: We began by focusing on how taste objects trigger taste memories. Participants were encouraged to select two out of four ingredients (all cubed and slightly cooked vegetables – potatoes, celery, cucumber, parsnip – lightly flavored with various coloring spices to make them visually and in terms of taste unidentifiable), taste them and describe the memories they elicit. This first experiment also served to prime participants for paying close attention to their taste experiences.
(2) *Bodily orientations*: The second experiment moved away from the taste object and focused on how the body of the tasting subject informs taste. Participants had to repeatedly sample a leek compote and imagine they were tasting not as themselves, but with a different body, choosing two out of four creatures (snake, tiger, hamster, fairy).
(3) *Frames* and *information*: The third experiment focused on general frames within which we search for and make sense of taste experiences. Here, participants were asked to sample Goji berries thrice, each time within a different general framing given through written background information. The first framing, "eating is political" gave them information regarding the production context in China, including pesticide use and working conditions. The second framing, "eating is pleasure" informed them about how famous people enjoy Goji berries for the creative mood they trigger. Lastly, the framing "eating is health" informed the participants about the nutritional value and health benefits of eating the berries.
(4) *Expectations*: The fourth experiment played with expectations we have towards the effects of eating. Participants had to choose two out of four ingredients that they had never sampled (mealworms, dried sweet potatoes, spicy Indian "Chakri" snacks, dried apples). They thus had to deal with an absence of specific expectations and focus on the unknown. They had to sample the chosen ingredients twice, once for expected physical effects, tasting as if it were delicious but unhealthy, then as exceedingly healthy. Secondly, they had to taste for expected social effects, as if eating the ingredient were morally embarrassing and then as if it were a major honor.
(5) *Sound* and *atmosphere*: In the fifth experiment, we moved from imagining, knowing, and bodily doing to exploring how changing atmospheres affect taste. Here the participants repeatedly tasted Labneh (thickened yoghurt) and were asked to listen to different sounds (classical music, heavy metal, traffic noise, birdsong).

After this first stage of disassembling a tasting situation into different elements and testing them separately, the second stage consisted of a single sixth experiment. It prompted participants to reassemble the ingredients and experiences from the first phase to create their own dish and tasting situation. Based on their notes taken during the first five experiments, participants were encouraged to compose a dish from the various ingredients and experiences, along with an orientation and a setting within which they would eat it. This last step also included the choice of additional elements: (6) *Utensils* and *social interaction*: They could choose between a variety of utensils (chopsticks, Western cutlery, their hands) to eat with and a base to arrange ingredients on and to eat from, either a ceramic plate, a paper plate, or a cabbage leaf. They were encouraged to think of a title for their dish and once they had finished composing their dish we would take a photograph. Finally, they could decide whether they want to eat by themselves or join other participants at communal tables.

At the end, we gave participants a booklet containing background information, further ideas, exercises and experiments to continue the topics of the exhibition at home (Figure 3).

Figure 3: Excerpt of our booklet.

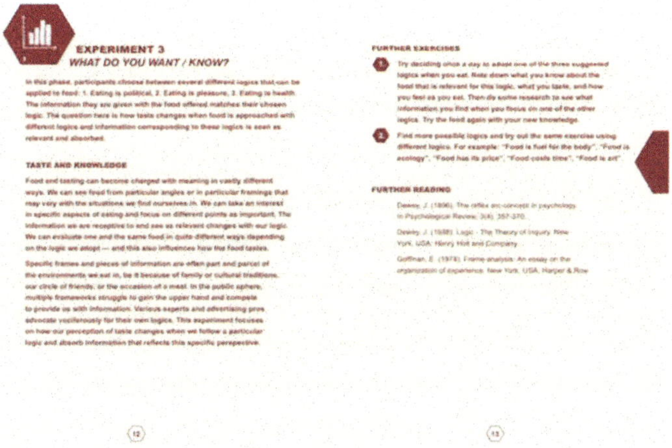

EXPERIMENT 3
WHAT DO YOU WANT / KNOW?

In this phase, participants choose between several different logics that can be applied to food: 1. Eating is political, 2. Eating is pleasure, 3. Eating is health. The information they are given with the food offered matches their chosen logic. The question here is how taste changes when food is approached with different logics and information corresponding to these logics is seen as relevant and absorbed.

TASTE AND KNOWLEDGE

Food and tasting can become charged with meaning in vastly different ways. We can see food from particular angles or in particular framings that may vary with the situations we find ourselves in. We can take an interest in specific aspects of eating and focus on different points as important. The information we are receptive to and see as relevant changes with our logic. We can evaluate one and the same food in quite different ways depending on the logic we adopt — and this also influences how the food tastes.

Specific frames and pieces of information are often part and parcel of the environments we eat in, be it because of family or cultural traditions, our circle of friends, or the occasion of a meal. In the public sphere, multiple frameworks struggle to gain the upper hand and compete to provide us with information. Various experts and advertising pros advocate vociferously for their own logics. This experiment focuses on how our perception of taste changes when we follow a particular logic and absorb information that reflects this specific perspective.

12

FURTHER EXERCISES

1. Try deciding once a day to adopt one of the three suggested logics when you eat. Note down what you know about the food that is relevant for this logic, what you taste, and how you feel as you eat. Then do some research to see what information you find when you focus on one of the other logics. Try the food again with your new knowledge.
2. Find more possible logics and try out the same exercise using different logics. For example: "Food is fuel for the body", "Food is ecology", "Food has its price", "Food costs time", "Food is art".

FURTHER READING

Dewey, J. (1896). The reflex arc concept in psychology. In Psychological Review, 3(4), 357-370.

Dewey, J. (1938). Logic – The Theory of Inquiry. New York, USA: Henry Holt and Company.

Goffman, E. (1974). Frame analysis: An essay on the organization of experience. New York, USA: Harper & Row.

13

Source: Schmeck!Project ©

4. EFFECTS OF OUR INTERVENTION: PROVOKING MULTIPLE PRACTICES AND EXPERIENCES IN DOING TASTE

How did the participants conduct and experience the experiments? What ways of knowing and doing taste could we observe and identify? Did participants also take these into their daily lives, beyond the setting of the exhibition? What insights did we gain about our central intention to open-up industrialized orders of sensing for more creative ways of tasting?

To answer these questions, we first describe some central observations of doing taste in the exhibition. We will complement these observations by drawing on two kinds of empirical data: First, the notes on the instruction sheets that participants filled out during the exhibition. Second, a set of interviews with participants that we conducted two months after the exhibition.

The notes on the instruction sheets were collected on eight A4 sheets held together on a clipboard: The first sheet contained an introduction, followed by 6 sheets, one for each experiment. These gave instructions on how to conduct the experiments and contained fields to write down the outcome of each experiment. The last sheet contained a feedback form. The feedback form asked whether the participants discovered or experienced anything new, what insights and questions they gained from the exhibition, which experiments they found hard to follow, which experiments they would have liked to explore in more depth, what they were missing from the experiments and what we could do to improve the exhibition next time. Although about 1000 people carried out our experiment, we received only 566 clipboards, because many participants conducted the experiments in groups of two or more people. However, from these 566 clipboards with notes, we only received 328 feedback forms, because some participants stopped their notes once they finished the experiments. We then conducted interviews with 18 people selected from 109 persons who left their contact details.

We conducted the interviews a couple of months after the exhibition, between December 8th, 2020 and January 6th, 2021. Only 12 of these interviews, however, could properly be recorded and transcribed. During the interviews we asked (a) whether since their visit, participants remembered the exhibition, (b) whether they remembered specific practices learned during the exhibition, (c) whether the exhibition lastingly influenced how they taste, (d) whether they talked with other people about the exhibition, (e) whether it changed attitudes towards exploring new foods, and (f) how they experienced the design of the experiments.

The participants came from a broad range of professions and educational backgrounds. There were also many young children and students among them that account for almost three-quarters of the participants. Interestingly, even though we designed the exhibition for one person per experimental station, many of the participants conducted the experiments together, mostly in pairs but up to groups of five, as can be seen in the following images:

Figure 4: Experimenting in public.

Source: Schmeck!Project ©

There were only a few dropouts or people who abandoned the exhibition before they completed the experiment (often because they participated with children who were too small to concentrate for the duration of the experiments). For many of the participants the aforementioned industrialized orders of sensing and standardized ways of tasting had been indeed challenged and dissolved, although not always exactly in the way the exhibition was intended and designed. That means some did not—or at least not fully—experience reflexively the creative agency of inventing one's own tasting practice and situation which we will elaborate on in the following.

The intensity with which reflexive engagement took place was the most surprising, most striking outcome, but also the most difficult to document. According to our participant observations most people were sucked into a world of taste that they had never experienced before—despite the fact that most people were completely unaware of what they would encounter.

Not only this, as can be glanced from the images above (Figure 5), participants dedicated themselves exclusively to tasting as activity, as a practice, at the expense of any other sensory attention. People would close their eyes, focus with their nose and mouth, hunch forward, and just dedicated themselves to the experience of taste. Throughout the exhibition, the atmosphere was a concentrated silence, as in a school test, except that it was punctured by laughter and gasps of unexpected experiences. Faces spoke of expectation and distrust that would soon make way to surprise and exhilaration.

Figure 5: Tasting practices.

Source: Schmeck!Project ©

A second proof that this focused exploration worked very well, can be seen from the care, creativity, surprise, and variety of dishes that participants created in step 6. As we have outlined before, during the final phase the participants were asked to combine and arrange elements gathered and investigated separately in the previous five phases. Thus, all the compositions were created from the same 10 ingredients that were offered before during the experiments. All differences between the compositions result from leaving out some ingredients, from the way they were arranged, and, most importantly, from the specific memories, body schemes, framings, expectations sounds that were chosen after experimentally exploring their effects on the tasting experience. What stands out (and what cannot be documented here without listing all photographs of the individual dishes) is that despite the fixed ingredients list, and their pre-prepared form, participants really leaned into the task and each came up with their own dish (see Figure 6), reflecting at least some of their specific experiences and their own dish-creating talents.

Figure 6: Creative (re-)compositions with a self-chosen title.

Source: Schmeck!Project ©

This focused attention cannot easily be captured in evaluative statements, but we can derive from the feedback forms a positive overall perception and assessment of the exhibition by the participants. When we asked which impressions they took away from the experiments (multiple answers possible, n=300), they describe it in the forms as good (85 answers), interesting (70), great (62), new regarding experiences gained (53), exciting (36) or even funny (18).

Though, for 24 participants the underlying ideas remained vague. For them, the exhibition failed to connect the experiments to everyday tasting practices. The experiments remained in a different social space, maybe reminiscent of school experiences, where they were prompted to do something that proved challenging and fun, but whose ultimate aims they failed to understand. The artificiality of the tasks caused a distance to their everyday tasting experiences that they found difficult to overcome.

Some participants noticed that they discovered a new taste (36 answers). Experiences in supervising the exhibition can support this supposition: Some people tried mainly to figure out what they were eating. For these participants an *object-related comprehension of taste* was still important. While 65 participants said that they learned something new without specifying what, 118 persons learned that taste can be influenced in some way. Out of these 101 report insights on *particular elements influencing taste*. Often, they relate to specific experiments: the sounds heard (39 answers), the associations and emotions triggered (18), specific expectations and knowledge or information they obtained (13) or their physical state (2) while tasting.

Obviously for these participants specific experiments stood out, while others worked less well. In particular, experiment 5 with sound stood out (231 mention this experiment for "Which experiments would you like to have explored in more depth?"), while experiment 2 (imaging and practicing different bodies like that of a hamster or a fairy) often did not work (255 mention this experiment for "Which experiments did you find hard to follow or to stick with?). We can read this in multiple ways: It may demonstrate that some experiments were better designed than others; we may simply have failed to construct all the experiments in a way to make them work for the participants. We can also read it as a difficulty of making specific elements of tasting practices amenable to intervention. Experiencing sound as changing the atmosphere is straightforward and its interference with taste was readily understood by participants. Imagining and enacting a different body shape and related way of eating, in contrast, is much more demanding.

We also asked whether participants could think of further elements influencing their taste that were not thematized in the six experiments. Seven mentioned elements like the visual appearance of food, its color, the amount or combination of ingredients as well as the frequency with which the ingredients were eaten. With regard to new insights and understanding of how they individually approach their own tasting, 17 participants responded that the exhibition has helped them to learn how tasting is related to fun, pleasure, health, concentration, appearance, attention, or with their own openness to explore new taste experiences without bias. Two of them mention the relevance of how the food is placed in the mouth, such as that they would slow it down or taste the same ingredient repeatedly.

Asking for the insights and questions the exhibition left the participants with (multiple answers possible, n=250), the majority stated that they learned something new. Also, some participants intended to continue the experimental approach beyond the setting of the exhibition (27 answers). These intentions are related to different aspects: Some mention intentions to eat and taste with more attention to details, such as the specific situation or the political dimension of food, while others intend to be more open to experiencing new tastes as well as to change previous tasting habits. These participants state explicitly that they understood and adopted the approach of the exhibition and the challenge that it poses. They reported that they would *actively shape their taste more consciously in the future*.

In addition to the very positive answers in our forms, two months after the exhibition still nearly half of our interviewees state that by participating in the exhibition they have learned about the relevance of unexpected and unknown elements influencing and thus co-constituting taste which had been completely new or at least unconscious to them. An interviewee described it as follows:

> I would say that this awareness of the changes in the taste experience through these changes of ideas [body, knowledge], I wasn't really aware of it in that sense. So, I created it unconsciously, as we all do, by trying to create nice situations for eating... But I wasn't really aware of the different nuances that are possible. It was more social "what you do," but not such a conscious, detailed design. (Interviewee 1, personal interview, December 12, 2020, translated by the authors)

The other half of our interviewees report an intensification and widening of an already existing awareness of one or more specific elements, such as political or health aspects of particular ingredients, memories, and emotions, sounds or the visual appearance of food. The following statements from two interviewees illustrate this point:

> Again, with the sound as well. I mean, the thought of going out in nature or listening to classical music is setting an ambience. But beyond the idea of ambience, I don't think I've consciously thought, oh, this will literally affect how I taste. So that's quite interesting. ...[since the exhibition] the sound encourages me to slow down a bit and maybe set the mood. (Interviewee 2, personal interview, December 9, 2020)

> So, my wife is, I would say, very health focused and political regarding food. And I am, let's say, more into enjoyment, also politics, but above all enjoyment. And I noticed [in the exhibition] what a difference it makes. So, when I eat and think food is healthy, for me that has also positively influenced my taste experience. And with this mindfulness and meditation, so to speak, ...I can basically decide for myself which focus I take. (Interviewee 1, personal interview, December 12, 2020, translated by the authors)

Again, nearly half of the interviewees say that they have overcome some inhibitions that came with the experimental set-up or the non-identifiability of ingredients. This not only seems to lead to a modified attitude towards the specific ingredient but also towards taste itself: There is no invariable, determined taste—even with regard to an ordinary potato, but rather a highly situated experience depending on multiple factors influencing taste that are presented in each experiment. Another insight is that except for one, all interviewees who conducted the experiments with another person emphasize the relevance of social interaction and related exchange for their tasting experiences. Further, some interviewees mention they have perceived the impact of diverse elements (e.g., associations or the situation) on taste again in everyday life afterwards or have at least continued to reflect on it.

5. COULD WE PROVOKE NEW WAYS OF TASTING? IN HOW FAR ARE AESTHETIC AND POLITICAL PRACTICES INTERTWINED?

We started with the diagnosis that current sensory orders are dominated by the food industry and the sensory sciences: They shape the knowing and doing of taste as a mechanical matching of food product qualities with given subjective perceptions of individuals statistically aggregated into groups and averages. We called this "tasting like industry." As a collectively shared way of doing taste it constitutes a subjectivity which suggests that we are stuck with our individual predilections having to search for the best matching food products in order to enjoy taste.

Our exhibition was an experiment to investigate, if and how we could disrupt this dominant order of doing taste and help to establish a different one, based on a different ontology of tasting: We designed the exhibition to make participants experience that taste is a relationally constituted practice that can creatively be shaped by the tasters themselves. We did not articulate our alternative ontology as an intellectual treatise or a political manifesto, but as a material arrangement and a set of experiments to perform it in practice and immediately experience it as an alternative reality of tasting.

We described in detail how we conceptualized, designed, and realized the exhibition at the Berlin Museum of Natural History, and we gave an account of what actually happened, how our arrangement was taken up by participants and the experiences they made. We found that our setting was to some degree effective in generating a creative style of tasting. A large percentage (40%) of our participants fully embraced and experienced what we had envisioned, explicitly saying that they learned taste can be influenced. Nearly all visitors evaluated the exhibition positively and learned something new about taste. The exhibition brought up questions on how to practice taste, on political dimensions of food or on their own willingness to experience new food. One out of ten participants declares that they intend to continue experimenting with taste. However, some of the tasting experiments that we offered worked better than others. The participants overwhelmingly said that the experiment with sounds made them explore the malleability of their own tasting, while experiments with different body shapes and expectations towards food were difficult to understand or did not have the effect of experiencing creative agency in matters of taste.

In terms of aesthetic practices, our observations show that we could actually change the ways people taste. Of course, this happens only in a limited way, not for everybody, and not far beyond the setting of the exhibition and not forever. But we successfully engaged, triggered, and to some degree shaped the aesthetic practices and experiences of those who were willing to participate. In that sense our exhibition was an engagement with established orders of sensing. Our exhibition partially disrupted them and created a space for alternative orders to emerge. It provoked people to reflexively engage with their own ways of sensing, to become agents of aesthetic practice by creating their own sensory perceptions.

In terms of political practices, we come back to the wide and the narrow notion of politics that we introduced above. In the sense that the exhibition made people perform a way of tasting not based on a mechanical ontology, but on a relational ecological ontology, we may say that we engaged with the "ontological politics" of doing taste. Everybody who participated at least contributed to make an event happen that opened up questions about what taste is and how it works. In that sense the exhibition made taste an issue of public interest and concern. For a considerable part of the participants we can say that taste was not only called into question, but that they collectively performed the creative tasting that we sought to provoke as an alternative reality to the more widespread reality of tasting like industry.

With regard to a more specific concept of politics as the performative representation of collective will and identity, we could investigate the design of the exhibition as a non-verbal representative claim on behalf of a new collective subjectivity of creative eaters. One could look for how this claim was articulated in the material set up and the bodily and experiential experience of the exhibition. For evaluating the performative effects of such a claim, however, we would have to follow-up on how it was taken up by participants and wider audiences in the media and elsewhere. Did tasters recognize themselves as creative tasters after participating in the exhibition? Did they recognize this as a common subjectivity shared with other participants, imagining a new "we" with the will and agency to break out of tasting like industry and to explore different possible realities of tasting? Due to a lack of data we cannot answer these questions, but they hint at interesting future research opportunities.

Thus, while obviously engaging with aesthetic practice (inducing and shaping perceptions) and with political practice in a wide sense (collectively enacting specific realities), it remains open in how far the exhibition was engaging with political practice in the narrower sense (performatively representing collective subjectivity).

By way of conclusion, we would like to highlight some specificities of our approach. What makes it particularly rewarding or challenging to engage with collective orders in the medium of eating and tasting, and in the form of a participatory exhibition?

Firstly, we should highlight that, by focusing on eating and tasting, the project could engage and play with implicit everyday experiences that are very generic and routine for everyone. Everybody eats and tastes multiple times a day. Creating a new politics of taste does not depend on specific experiences that only certain groups or professions make. The task was therefore relatively easy, inasmuch as we did not have to explain the general importance of the issue.

Secondly, because foodstuffs as taste objects are individually stable but varied material objects, their politics can relatively easily be demonstrated. Each ingredient is relatively stable and has its own history, politics, and memories attached to it.

Compare this to for example sound, which is materially fleeting, does not come in defined objects, depends on a technological infrastructure that is invariable and that cannot be easily opened up (classical music and traffic noise are reproduced by the same technologies, and these technologies are not easily opened up to tinkering).

Third, because tasting is a private and bodily experience, related to designated and small tasting objects, it is relatively amenable to an experimental setup. For example, it does not depend on the availability of a large-scale gathering, or overtly complex technological infrastructures. Experimentalizing taste does not necessitate to bring together "society."

Fourth, because tasting is fundamentally a small-scale practice that happens between a tasting subject and a tasting object, it is relatively easy to make it independent of its environment. Further, because tasting is an everyday practice that people know from other contexts, it can relatively easily operate in a different space. Compare this to the problem of the white cube in visual art: To produce visual art as a form of politics has become embroiled in an endless debate where art cannot be seen without its context and where this context is seen to take over the art. In that sense, to experimentalize taste, while unusual, is also easy. To experimentalize other parts of our experience may be a more difficult task.

References

Austin, J. L. (1975 [1962]). *How to do things with words.* Cambridge, MA: Harvard University Press.
Barthes, R. (2013 [1961]). Toward a psychosociology of contemporary food consumption. In: C. Counihan & P. Van Esterik (Eds.). *Food and culture: A reader* (pp. 28–35). Abingdon, UK: Routledge.
Bourdieu, P. (1977 [1972]). *Outline of a Theory of Practice.* Cambridge, UK: Cambridge University Press.
Bourdieu, P. (2013 [1979]). Distinction: A social Critique of the Judgement of Taste. In: Counihan C and Van Esterik P (Eds.) *Food and Culture. A Reader.* Oxon, UK: Routledge, pp. 31–39.
Butler, J. (2015). Notes Toward a Performative Theory of Assembly. Cambridge, MA: Harvard University Press.
Disch, L. (2008). The People as "Presupposition" of Representative Democracy – An Essay on the Political Theory of Pierre Rosanvallon. *Redescriptions: Political Thought, Conceptual History and Feminist Theory* 12(1): 47–71.
Disch, L. (2010). 'Faitiche'-izing the People: What Representative Democracy Might Learn from Science Studies. In: Braun B, Whatmore SJ and Stengers I (eds) *Political matter: Technoscience, democracy, and public life.* Minneapolis: University of Minnesota Press, pp. 267–296.

Disch, L., van de Sande, M. & Urbinati, N. (2019). The constructivist turn in political representation. Edinburgh, UK: Edinburgh University Press.

Fischler, C. (1988). Food, self and identity. *Information (International Social Science Council) 27(2)*, 275–292.

Garfinkel, H. (1964). Studies of the routine grounds of everyday activities. *Social problems 11(3)*, 225–250.

Hayes-Conroy, A. & Martin, D.G. (2010). Mobilising bodies: visceral identification in the Slow Food movement. *Transactions of the Institute of British Geographers 35(2)*, 269–281.

Hennion, A. (2004). Pragmatics of taste. In M. Jacobs and N. Weiss Hanrahan (Eds.). *The Blackwell companion to the sociology of culture* (pp. 131–144). Malden, MA: Blackwell Publishing.

Hennion, A. (2007). Those things that hold us together: taste and sociology. *Cultural Sociology 1(1)*: 97–114.

Hennion, A. (2015). Paying attention: what is tasting wine about? In A. Berthoin Antal, M. Hutter and D. Stark (Eds.). *Moments of valuation. Exploring sites of dissonance* (pp. 37–56). Oxford, UK: Oxford University Press.

Jonas, M. & Littig, B. (2016). *Praxeological political analysis*. London, UK: Routledge.

Katz, S. H. (1990). An evolutionary theory of cuisine. *Human Nature 1(3)*, 233–259.

Korsmeyer, C. and Sutton, D. (2011). The sensory experience of food. *Food, Culture & Society 14(4)*, 461–475.

Lahne, J. (2016). Sensory science, the food industry, and the objectification of taste. *Anthropology of food (10)*.

Lahne, J. (2018). Standard sensations: the production of objective experience from industrial technique. *The Senses and Society 13(1)*, 6–18.

Latour, B. (1983). Give me a laboratory and I will raise the world. In K. Knorr-Cetina and M. Mulkay (Eds.). *Science observed. Perspectives on the social studies of science* (pp. 142–169). London, UK: SAGE.

Latour, B. (2003). What if we talked politics a little? *Contemporary Political Theory 2(2)*, 143–164.

Latour, B. (2005). From Realpolitik to Dingpolitik or How to Make Things Public? In B. Latour & P. Weibel. (Eds.). *Making Things Public – Atmospheres of Democracy. Catalogue to the show at Zentrum für kulturelle Kommunikation, Karlsruhe* Cambridge, MA: MIT Press, pp. 4–31.

Latour, B. (2013). *An inquiry into modes of existence: An anthropology of the moderns*. Cambridge, MA: Harvard University Press.

Lezaun, J., Marres, N. and Tironi, M. (2016). Experiments in participation. *The handbook of science and technology studies* (pp. 195). Cambridge, MA: MIT Press.

Macdonald, S. & Basu, P. (2008). *Exhibition experiments*. New York, NY: John Wiley & Sons.

Mann, A. (2015). Which context matters? tasting in everyday life practices and social science theories. *Food, Culture & Society 18(3)*, 399–41

Mann, A. (2018). Ordering tasting in a restaurant: experiencing, socializing, and processing food. *The Senses and Society 13(2)*, 135–146.

Marres, N. (2012). Material participation: technology, the environment and everyday publics. Basingstoke, UK: Plagrave Macmillan.

Marres, N., Guggenheim, M. and Wilkie, A. (2018). Inventing the Social. Manchester, UK: Mattering Press.

Mol, A. (1998). Ontological politics. A word and some questions. *The Sociological Review 46(S)*, 74–89.

Mol, A. (2002). The body multiple: Ontology in medical practice. Durham: Duke University Press.

Mol, A. (2009). Good taste: The embodied normativity of the consumer-citizen. *Journal of Cultural Economy 2(3)*, 269–283.

Nash, K. (2001). The "Cultural Turn" in Social Theory: Towards a Theory of Cultural Politics. *Sociology 35(1)*, 77–92.

Paxson, H. (2010). Cheese cultures: Transforming American tastes and traditions. *Gastronomica 10(4)*, 35–47.

Roehl, T. (2012). Disassembling the classroom–an ethnographic approach to the materiality of education. *Ethnography and Education 7(1)*: 109–126.

Saward, M. (2006). The representative claim. *Contemporary Political Theory 5(3)*, 297–318.

Saward, M. (2017). Performative representation. In Brito Vierira M (Ed.). *Reclaiming Representation. Contemporary Advances in the Theory of Political Representation* (pp. 75–94). London, UK: Routledge.

Spackman, C. and Lahne, J. (2019). Sensory labor: considering the work of taste in the food system. *Food, Culture & Society 22(2)*, 142–151.

Stengers, I. (2010). *Cosmopolitics*. Minneapolis, MN: University of Minnesota Press.

Teil, G. and Hennion, A. (2004). Discovering quality or performing taste? A sociology of the amateur. In M. Harvey, A. McMeekin and A. Warde (Eds.). *Qualities of food* (pp. 19–37). Manchester, UK: Manchester University Press.

Voß J-P. & Guggenheim M. (2019). Making taste public: Industrialized orders of sensing and the democratic potential of experimental eating. *Politics and Governance 7(4)*, 224–236.

The Beauty of Feeling
On the Affective Politics of Sensing Collectives

Friederike Landau-Donnelly

1. DISENTANGLING AFFECTIVE POLITICS AND POLTICIAL BEAUTY

In this chapter, I approach collectives, and a notion of collectivity that holds collectives together, via a lens of affective politics (Bargetz, 2014a; 2014b). Affective politics, loosely defined, underscore the always-already emotional and passionate elements engrained in the *doing* of politics. Put differently, I understand politics as existentially entangled in individual and collective practices of claims-making, dreaming, desiring, and forging for political collectivities that reflect one's own normative understanding of the good life, a just society, an equitably shared planet. With the objective to explore how notions of collectivity and affective politics intertwine, I study the performance *Re-Formation der Geschichte* (*Re-Formation of History*; 2009) of the Berlin-based artist collective *Zentrum für Politische Schönheit* (*Center for Political Beauty*; ZPS). In a public, unsolicited performance, the artist group delivered ten theses of political beauty to the doorstep of the German Bundestag via a ceremony-like, staged horseback ride (see Table 1 and Figure 1). Their gesture implicitly referenced Martin Luther's famous nailing of 95 theses onto a church door, which contested the religious hegemony at the time. Their *"Thesenanschlag"* (a wordplay to be elaborated below) was deployed by ZPS as a poetic means to disrupt the existing order of politics. By zooming in on specifically three of their theses, I critically discuss the artist group's understanding of collectivity.

Figure 1: Staged horseback ride to deliver ten theses of political beauty.

Source: ZPS 2009a, p. 25

In a previous analysis, I have systematically screened of all ten theses of political beauty (Landau, 2019; see Table 2).[1] In that exercise, I distilled three analytical vignettes which evoke ZPS's understanding of political beauty—captured in the codes of BEAUTY, VITALITY, and LONGING. The ten theses, considered together, request and invoke an intense longing for more aesthetic and affective ways of doing politics. The theses appeal to (re)activate a lost sense of poetry, passion, and beauty in politics. Via a framework of political difference (Marchart 2010; 2013), which differentiates (however not neatly, or definitively) between politics and the political, I captured the ways in which the theses leverage political feelings. While politics points to the more narrowly defined practices of routinized or institutionalized rules and procedures, the political addresses the more encompassing and irreducibly conflictual realm of political life. Along this continuum, I have discussed how political beauty can significantly (re)politicize the realm of politics towards a more affective, encompassing notion in the spirit of the political. While political beauty is suggested as desirable mindset and motivation, political beauty can however never be fully attained or realized. In this lingering dilemma between a universal call to action and individual

---

1   Individual sentences of this chapter have been derived verbatim from my earlier account on the affective politics of political beauty (Landau, 2019). Instead of quoting these sentences directly, I am interweaving them here and take full responsibility for those few identical phrases an algorithm might be able to detect if my two pieces of writing were put into direct comparison.

agency to strive towards more politically beautiful futures, the theses do not specify where and how such political beauty can be attempted or practiced. In addition, it has not been studied *by whom* political beauty shall be advanced. In other words, while aspects of political beauty already indicate how affective and political concerns are multiply interrelated, what remains to be explored is the concrete connection between political beauty and collectivity. Hence, I develop my existing account further and add here a fourth analytical vignette—COLLECTIVITY—to study ZPS's implicit and explicit understanding of collectivity. In relation to their overall manifesto, I critically discuss how ZPS's advocated return to intense, poetic, and passionate politics, which are full of desire, greatness, and life, does indeed lead to more beautiful—or affective—politics, actualized by a politically beautiful collective.

To test and wrestle with this hypothesis, I scrutinize three selected theses from ZPS's performance with regards to the potential of political beauty to create new collective subjectivities, motivate collective political agency, or make politics more affective (again). Briefly, I scrutinize: (How) can political beauty help us to imagine political collectivity? What does a politically beautiful collective feel like? Does the concept tell us anything about the values, goals, or concrete shapes of beautiful collectives? Who exactly is this 'we' that strives for political beauty? And how do 'we' come to know and sense it? Can political beauty only be sensed collectively?

To approach these questions methodologically, I conduct what I call a spectral or hauntological reading of the ten theses. Borrowing from Derrida's (1994) hauntological approach, I assume temporality as constantly "out of joint," precarious and permeated by ghosts from the past. With this framework, I capture the fragmented and polyphonic dimensions of texts, data, and our responses to them. With regards to the concrete case of *Re-Formation of History*, the complicated connection between past and present is provocatively drawn out by ZPS; they conjure specters of the past, nail them to the doors of the Bundestag, thus haunting contemporary German politics. More specifically, I offer a poetic analysis as response to the theses of political beauty, and herewith aim to strengthen poetry in/as research approach (Allen, 2017; Faulkner, 2009). In relation to the theses of political beauty, I explore how affective politics can be mobilized and felt via words, texts, metaphors, images, appeals, warnings—however utopian or dystopian they might be.

Together with my own affective responses and reflections on the theses of political beauty, I build on the concept of affective politics by political theorist Brigitte Bargetz (2014b), and her proposition of a political grammar of feelings in particular. In addition, I draw on political theories of affect (Ahmed, 2014; Anderson, 2014; Bargetz, 2015), and radical democratic concepts of political difference by Oliver Marchart (2010, 2013). I put these notions in conceptual dialogue with Andreas Reckwitz's (2017) analytical account on the role of the senses in social practices. Extrapolating from Reckwitz's claim that "social orders always entail sensible orders" (2017, p. 60), I study the links and disconnects between feelings, or affects more broadly, and orders of politics, the political, and beauty. In line with this volume's shared interest in understanding the trope of sensing collectives, I trace appeals to collective, and not-so-collective, sensible orders via the theses of political beauty. With this, I set out to understand how these affective forms may push political collectives to challenge, disrupt, establish, forget, govern, innovate, irritate, or stabilize collectively sensed social orders.

Table 1: Ten theses of political beauty.

#1	In every human being, there is a profound desire for the beautiful.
#2	Everything great is born from desire.
#3	People are not only moved by causes, but also by goals. Beauty, greatness, and perfection are goals.
#4	Beauty and ugliness are both poles between which life fundamentally takes place.
#5	"Everyone warms their heart in a different way." From this, the moderns have drawn the conclusion to not warm their hearts at all. Without the experience of beauty, human experiences are incomplete.
#6	"He [sic] treats beauty as entomologists treat butterflies. He catches the poor animal, he pins it down, and as its exquisite colors drop off, there it lies, a lifeless corpse under the pin. And what is what they call aesthetics." (Goethe)
#7	Hopes are not there to be abandoned.
#8	What we know depends on what we feel.
#9	A soul that has not experienced beauty commits emotional suicide.
#10	Souls without poetry are an undiscovered form of mental illness.

Source: own translation after ZPS 2009a, p. 26

2. THE *CENTER FOR POLITICAL BEAUTY* BETWEEN AGGRESSIVE HUMANISM AND CONTESTED COLLECTIVITY

The artist activist collective consists of a fluctuating number of up to 70 artists, intellectuals, scholars or "accomplices," as ZPS calls supporters and donors for individual actions. Since its foundation in 2009, and to this day, ZPS has engaged in a variety of performances and public actions which have problematized the political disenchantment, passivity, and assumed indifference of specifically German, and European citizens and politicians. For example, with regards to Europe's admittedly inhumane human rights and refugee politics, ZPS has staged creative protests such as *Mauerkreuze* (Border Crosses, 2014, Landau forthcoming), *Die Toten Kommen* (The Dead

Are Coming, 2015) or *Flüchtlinge Fressen* (*Devouring Refugees*, 2016), in which they address what they perceive as the German government's failure to commemorate past and ongoing death of refugees at European borders. With sometimes grim theatrical scenarios, the artist group has buried dead refugees in front of the German Bundestag, has arguably imported and exhibited the ashes of Auschwitz casualties in central Berlin and has drawn attention to genocides throughout Europe. The *Center for Political Beauty* has repeatedly condemned the insufficient acknowledgement and commemoration of the Holocaust in German politics and commemorative culture, which, according to ZPS, should constitute the backbone of any political action.

In 2009, as one of ZPS's first public actions, the horse-back ride of the ten theses of political beauty was originally planned to nail the theses on the doors of the Bundestag—in historical reference to Protestant reformer Martin Luther. The German term "*Thesenanschlag*" is a play on words on "*Anschlag*," which can point either to the physical process of installing the theses by hammering in a nail or allude to an attack, possibly on the lack of political beauty in dominant German politics. In relation to the hauntological framework of ghostly time, the installation/intervention/attack invokes these voices of the past. Typical for ZPS's interventionist actions, the *Re-Formation of History* assembled a temporary, serendipitous audience (or a however temporary collectivity)—visitors waiting to access the dome of the German Bundestag. However, there are also more structural assumptions about collectivities to be affected by ZPS's actions which I unpack in the following.

Spearheaded by Dr. Philipp Ruch, a philosopher by training, and the most commonly recognizable public face of the ever-morphing collectivity, ZPS continuously evokes controversial reactions in Berlin-based, German and international media. The creation of polyphonic, ambivalent media environments has been described as one of the goals of ZPS's interventionist practice (ZPS, 2019). While many of their actions hover between legal persecution (i.e., claiming that ZPS engages in criminal activity; MDR Thüringen, 2019) and the protected freedom of artistic expression, it is precisely in this ambivalence that affective and political practices are intertwined (ZPS, 2009b). The term "aggressive humanism" (Bayrischer Rundfunk, 2014) is often used either to describe the group's activities, used by group affiliates themselves to identify and describe their actions. The provocative interconnection—and tension—between 'aggressiveness' or 'aggression,' which evokes associations with violence or hostility, and the latter term of 'humanism,' which implies a concern for individual agency, rationality, progress, as well as responsibility, dignity, and care for all human beings, also shines through in the ten theses of political beauty. Aggressive humanism might invoke, on the one hand, a sense of verve and edginess to (self-)identify the group as a radical, critical or otherwise subversive art collective. On the other hand, the term might affectively mobilize a drive towards human flourishing, mutual care and accountability in the spirit of Humanism. In summary, and without further going into detail about the curious term of aggressive humanism, ZPS and its surrounding mediatized reception activate a variety of emotional responses that range, but are not exclusive to guilt, shame, regret, and hopelessness to its precise counterparts of hope, comfort, consolation, and potentially optimism for a better future—described by newspapers, social media comments, and also felt personally.

While it is not my goal here to classify or categorize the aesthetic practices of ZPS strictly as 'art' or 'not art' and I am concerned rather with their affective political impetus, it becomes apparent that public perceptions of ZPS's activities, performances, and activism continue to be controversially debated with every new coup they stage. Yet, before I dive into a poetic analysis to reconstruct the specific constellation of collective subjectivity in the selected three theses that speak to "everybody" in the quest for political beauty, let me briefly situate my understanding of affect.

3. READING AFFECTIVE POLITICS THROUGH POETRY

My understanding of affect is informed by the so-called affective turn in social and cultural theory (Angerer et al. 2015; Gregg and Seigworth, 2011). The latter brings to the fore the crucial importance of feelings, emotions, passions or the trans-individual expression of affect in both analytical and empirical questions of collective subject formation.[2] Notably, feelings or emotions (and affects more generally) are never either just good or bad, appropriate or not, or at least not indisputably so (Cvetkovich, 2007, 2012). Negative feelings such as displeasing states of distress, including anxiety, depression, aggression, sadness, shame, fear, or guilt (Watson et al., 1988) do not feel or affect 'everybody' in the same way. Hence, instead of pathologizing or vilifying certain feelings or emotions as negative, the ways in which we are affected reveal themselves as always multiple, often unpredictable and always to some extent subjective. Accordingly, being affected by politics (or by 'the political' at large) is not automatically a good or beautiful thing. Notably, affective politics can also mobilize and create fear, anger, resentment (see Sommer, this volume). Especially in light of rising illiberal political movements, which notably often instrumentalize culture or cultural policies for nationalist or otherwise oppressive purposes

---

2   Affect and emotion/feeling are interrelated yet different concepts or analytical approaches. Especially with regards to their respective (pre)cognitive and (trans)individual scope, scholars differently assess the similarity or distinctiveness of affects and emotions (Ahmed, 2014; Leys, 2011). Generally, affects can ignite politicizing and depoliticizing, emancipatory and reactionary, conservative and liberal political attitudes and actions (Berlant, 2011). Notably, Hemmings (2005) points out that precisely the relative or situated autonomy of affects illustrates the partial interdependency between affect and individual emotion or embodied experience. In my approach to antagonistic affective politics, this ambivalence is not resolved, but wriggles through my poetic analysis.

such as xenophobia, homo- and transphobia, or racism, connections between passions and politics are to be considered with caution (Bóren, 2020). However, besides divisive feelings such as (collective) anxiety vis-à-vis a more or less visible 'Other' or other forms of exclusion, affective politics might also bring about new forms of encounter, care, compassion, community or collectivity (Bargetz & Freudenschuss, 2012). In sum, affective politics paradoxically hover between dangerously affecting and diving collectivities of people, places, and things, and the potential to stimulate, invent, and invigorate new ways of feeling and being together (Cvetkovich, 2012; Hemmings, 2005).

Political theorist Chantal Mouffe (2006) has underscored that passions are important drivers in political mobilization and clout. Within an emerging scholarship on the affective implications of politics (Bens et al., 2019), or the governing of affect (e.g., Penz & Sauer, 2020), my investigation shall contribute to better grasping concretely felt and practiced connections between passions (or emotions and/or affects) and politics (encompassing both politics and the political, including political claims, rules, laws, institutions, but also political mo(ve)ments, actors, collectivities, and forms of political expression outside of the formalized realm of politics). Following Protevi (2009), I concur that political affects can leverage new forms and articulations of political belonging, agency, community or collectivity.

But how to grasp political affects, or affective politics? As briefly mentioned, I want to foreground the creative practice of poetry as/in research (Faulkner, 2009). While this experimental methodology might constitute a rather ephemeral approach, I consider this speculative, affective, poetic reading as a preliminary step to conduct further empirical analyses on the connections between politics and passions. The implications of this method of affective reading gives insight into one affective response to the theses of political beauty, which hopefully stimulates further discussion of the affective politics of collectivity, and collectives. Loosely following Faulkner's (2009) notion of poetry as method, which suggests using poetry not only in research settings but also as tools for data analysis and discussion, I hope to encounter the theses of political beauty anew as inspiration, instruction, inclination towards politically beautiful collectives.

Deploying a poetic analysis as a way to creatively (de)construct texts as data, I want to elevate the affective quality of texts. Certainly, reading text as affective text, or reading texts affectively, poses methodological challenges of validity, reliability, and generalizability. Yet, this approach assists in considering and analyzing text as much *more*, and significantly *other* than just a text. That is to say that I have read the theses as text, but also as affective matter beyond their textual form (including visual and video data, media reports on the performance etc.). Via the self-designed coding scheme of vignettes, I have sought to annotate or tag recurring analytical themes and references to conceptualize ZPS's specific sense of collectivity. As I have previously attempted such reading as spectral activity (Landau, 2019, pp. 6–7), I am aware of the burden of such haunted reading, bearing the weight of multiple pasts, which also affect us in the present (Slaby, 2017).

4. SENSING COLLECTIVES VIA A POLITICAL GRAMMAR OF FEELINGS

My exploration substantially draws on Brigitte Bargetz's (2014a) political grammar of feelings, which hovers between embodied, bodily practices of feeling politics (i.e., project towards feeling as a verb, a practice, an activity of doing) and politics of feelings (i.e., considering feeling more as a noun, an institution, a tool (or place) of power). Put differently, feeling politics revolve around the emotional, sensory, perceptual, affective dimensions of feeling whereas a politic of feelings points to the power-related dimensions of feelings as constructions or normalizations of affect in collective orders. Notably, these two conceptual nodes cannot be completely separated from each other, but constantly interpenetrate and inform each other. In that sense, the analytic of a political grammar of feeling is similar to political difference, in which politics and the political constantly influence each other, but work in notably different logics. Again, feeling politics mobilize the translation of "relations of power and exploitation into embodied ordinary practices" (Bargetz 2014b, p. 129, my translation). Feeling politics thus underscore the experience of affects as bodily or embodied practices, and inscribe feelings in everyday political practices both in the realm and rationale of politics and the political at large. With regards to the notion of political difference discussed above, which is engrained in the political grammar of feelings, feeling politics could conceptually align both with the ontic, everyday realm of politics as well as the always-changing apparitions of the political. In comparison, the politics of feelings could roughly resonate more with the ontic, construed realm of politics, trying to impose a specific notion or practice of hegemony (Landau, 2019, pp. 4–5). Both politics and the political might make us feel or sense the weight of political decisions that will affect our lives. For example, people get goosebumps during demonstrations (a mo(ve)ment of the political and 'feeling politics' on the streets?), others feel nauseous when they see xenophobic election posters (arguably a materialization of exclusive politics, and in opposition to constricting politics of feeling?), some feel excited and jumpy when seeing politicians giving speeches (again, gesturing towards the manifold forms the political can take). In short, affects can politicize social, sensible, and aesthetic orders for better or worse, depending on who you ask.

To advance an understanding of the politics of feeling as "motor and instrument of the political" (Bargetz, 2014b, p. 119, my translation), I have chosen the path of poetry in and as research practice to approximate the theses of political beauty with a specific focus on the notion of collectivity. With this, I am testing new ways of encountering the text *as* poetry, which has elicited my own responses or analysis also in the form of a poem. Inspired by the growing scholarship on affective methodologies

(Barad, 2003; Blanco & Peeren, 2013; Knudsen & Stage, 2015), I approach the theses as affective data, which can confront us with an afterlife of its own (see Blackman, 2015) and thus might escape us. Since affective data also elicits wonder that "resides and radiates in data" (MacLure, 2013, p. 228), let us finally dive into the nexus between political beauty and collectivity.

5. EXPLORING COLLECTIVITY IN POLITICAL BEAUTY

After reading, re-reading, wrestling with these theses, I came to this poetic reflection on what ZPS' sense of collectivity felt like to me:

collect-if
can you even stop collecti(vi)ng?
the gorge of possibilities
there is nobody outside of practice
yet we are not the horse they rode
I am actually allergic to horses, so how inclusive is that
whose is the collective who is the collective
and why are the butterflies dead
can beauty keep on living?
is it a sense of beauty or sensing beauty together, will we wellness?

Did I just create affective data? Or was it just the brush of a ghostly text?

In addition, have a look at how my affective reading of the thesis flowed into a coding scheme that sought to highlight where and how the different vignettes of political beauty—BEAUTY, LONGING, COLLECTIVITY, and VITALITY—intersect and linger.

Table 2: A spectral coding of theses of political beauty.

	Thesis of Political Beauty	Vignette
#1	In every human being, there is a profound desire for the beautiful.	BEAUTY; LONGING; COLLECTIVITY
#2	Everything great is born from desire.	LONGING
#3	People are not only moved by causes, but also by goals. Beauty, greatness and perfection are goals.	BEAUTY; LONGING; COLLECTIVITY
#4	Beauty and ugliness are both poles between which life fundamentally takes place.	BEAUTY; VITALITY
#5	"Everyone warms their heart in a different way." From this, the moderns have drawn the conclusion to not warm their hearts at all. Without the experience of beauty, human experiences are incomplete.	VITALITY; BEAUTY; LONGING; COLLECTIVITY
#6	"He [sic] treats beauty as entomologists treat butterflies. He catches the poor animal, he pins it down, and as its exquisite colors drop off, there it lies, a lifeless corpse under the pin. And what is what they call aesthetics." (Goethe)	BEAUTY; VITALITY
#7	Hopes are not there to be abandoned.	LONGING
#8	What we know depends on what we feel.	VITALITY; COLLECTIVITY
#9	A soul that has not experienced beauty commits emotional suicide.	BEAUTY; VITALITY
#10	Souls without poetry are an undiscovered form of mental illness.	BEAUTY; VITALITY

Source: own translation after ZPS 2009a, p. 26

Besides my poetic reaction to the theses, the analytical vignettes of VITALITY, BEAUTY, LONGING, and COLLECTIVITY assist in systematizing and analytically structuring the multiple functions, aspects, and directions of political beauty. As the first component of political beauty, I subsumed references to life, birth, death, vitality, and sickness, as well as references to what it is, what it means to be or feel human or alive or 'have' a soul in the vignette VITALITY. This is the most prominent category, mentioned in six out of ten theses. Notably, while affect theory widely draws on Deleuzian discourses on affect, multiplicity, vitality, and vitalism (e.g., Marks, 1998; Massumi, 2015; Uhlmann, 2020), my own reading here is explicitly situated in political theories of difference and antagonism (Landau, 2019). Certainly, a complementary Deleuzian reading of political beauty would provide further interesting insights.

The second trope of BEAUTY in political beauty touches on invocations to beauty, and ugliness as its analytical counterpoint, and also aesthetic experiences or artefacts such as poetry or literature. This appeal appears in seven out of ten theses, underlining how important it is to experience (political) beauty, which might simultaneously be aesthetically beautiful. Third, LONGING aims to capture the German term Sehnsucht, but can only partially reflect that. Longing is both more and other than just desiring, dreaming, hoping of arguably beautiful characteristics such as greatness and perfection. This stretch towards political beauty can be identified in five out of ten theses. Fourth, and crucially for this chapter, COLLECTIVITY is invoked via references to people, humans or the general addressee of 'we.' COLLEC-

TIVITY appears as both aspirational—calling sentient, exclusively human subjects to action—and relational, as some theses are written from a semi-authorial voice in which parts of ZPS appear as part of a collective 'we' that knows and feels. This appeal to collectivity or community is mentioned in four out of the ten theses, out of which I analyze three below (thesis #3 is not discussed in detail as it carries the same tag constellation as thesis #1).

> Thesis #1: In every human being, there is a profound desire for the beautiful.

Thesis #1 opens the manifesto with the universalist address of "every human being," without further specifying who or what a human being is or should be (or why the "profound desire for the beautiful" wouldn't be a concern for non- or more-than-human actors). This first thesis can be tagged with the vignettes of BEAUTY, LONGING, and COLLECTIVITY as it grandly proclaims political beauty to be not only "desire" but "profound" and seemingly inevitable. From this desire, "greatness" is derived (thesis #2). However, neither desire nor greatness are specified with regards to their origin, location, temporal or historical context. While the first thesis appeals to every human being, the statement itself does rather little to activate or affect people. Rather, this thesis seems to be making an assumption or announcement about people. On the one hand, the profound desire and greatness appear as fairly disembodied, abstract notions, as fundamental yet intangible drivers of human existence without concrete (affective) content or direction. To some readers, this might be a discouraging opener—for example, those looking towards specific political practices, goals or collectives on the micro-scale. Bringing in Bargetz's grammar of feelings, this would invoke feeling politics (or possibly a way to counteract the politics of feeling). On the other hand, this empty first thesis might unlock an affective politics of collectivity precisely in its suspense, openness, or absence of any concrete information or definition of what desire for political beauty is made of, who the everybody is, or what it feels like. With that wider-ranging appeal, at best, the first thesis can bring the political to the fore, nudging "everybody" to reflect on their respective affective interpretations and appropriations of their own profound desire. In other words, by starting to think, feel, see where and how every human being, including us, might find him-, her- or themselves in a profound desire for the beautiful, new constellations of collectivity could emerge. Amidst this claim of bottomless desire, ZPS founder Ruch (2012, p. 230) positions political beauty as desire, as "appetite or thirst" which "must be satisfied." However, the sentient readers of the theses will nowhere throughout the document receive any concrete instruction or guidance on how to approach, attain or satisfy this thirst (let alone be informed that is not even possible in the first place). In conclusion, the affective reader is stimulated to think about desire, yet confronted, and potentially irritated, after this initial universal communication to humans, addressed in a very vaguely contoured collectivity.

> Thesis #5: "Everyone warms their heart in a different way." From this, the moderns have drawn the conclusion to not warm their hearts at all. Without the experience of beauty, human experiences are incomplete.

Thesis #5 continues in the normative and universalizing tradition expressed in earlier theses, and uniquely interconnects all four vignettes of BEAUTY, VITALITY, LONGING, and COLLECTIVITY. Here, ZPS appeals again to "everyone" (see thesis #1). Briefly afterwards, the affective practice of heart-warming is qualified as subjective experience and practice. More precisely, ZPS first assumes that everyone warms their heart in notably *different* ways—highlighting and leaving room for individual affective experiences, practices, and encounters—but subsequently criticizes and dismisses the individualism of "the moderns." Difference is not valued as possibility to live together (see Valentine, 2008), but rather dismissed as cold-hearted and thus problematic. With regards to the political grammar of feelings, the attitude of the moderns could be conceptualized as the looming of the politics of feeling (e.g., an institution or collectivity of power, a hegemonic seat of norms, sensible and social orders).

Rather one-sidedly, the practice of heart-warming is presented as in any case favorable to cold hearts, thus urging everybody into a practice of warm-hearting. This comes at the cost of excluding those who do not "warm their hearts at all." This division into a heart-warming, or warm-hearted human population or collectivity (again, what about other species, some of which survive well as cold-blooded animals?), and the not-warm Other (i.e., those who do not warm their hearts) raises important questions about the conditions of possibility for politically beautiful collectives. What about the cold-hearted, excluded ones? Where do they go, are they gone for good? Does one warm the heart via belonging to a collective, or is this an entry criterion to be part of a collective? What can "everyone" do to support the heart-warming of others? What if heart-warming is based on problematic assumptions such as homo- and trans-phobia, racism, and meritocracy? What about those how do not want to, for whatever reasons, not warm their heart in ways ZPS finds politically beautiful? Ultimately, does a collective only emerge if everyone is warm-hearted or simply, does politically beautiful collectivity imply the collectivization of heart-warming?

While thesis #5 unambiguously speaks about "human experiences," it avoids specifying what it takes to qualify as "human." The question whether those who do *not* warm their hearts can still be considered human is left unanswered. Moreover, thesis #5 reveals the paradox between the universalist undertones straddling throughout the manifesto and the attempt at subjective, phenomenological, affective, embodied experience (i.e., Bargetz's feeling politics). The last sentence unpacks another tension: It reveals the rift between the potentially divisive, but also potentially collectivizing consequences of political beauty—those who sense it, those who feel it with their warmed hearts, will be able to feel complete. The others, who do not have warm hearts, linger at the margins; as leftover, excess or abject of the warm-hearted collectivity which consists of (only?) humans. Summing up, the warm inside of politically beautiful people, politics or hearts is premised on this exclusion to create warmth and beauty *within*, offering an illusion of completion or arrival in political beauty (contracting, as a side note, thesis #1)—and at the expense of obliviously leaving behind those with cold hearts, stranded in their own incompletion.

Lastly, thesis #5 takes up the vitalist innuendo that lingers in other theses (see theses #9, #10). There is clear preference and non-ambivalent celebration of life and living over death, captured in the VITALITY vignette. Yet, is this little reflected, conservative-sounding, modernist humanism meant as affective provocation? More bluntly, is ZPS serious? Would the theses then propose a politics of feeling that would favor, and unilaterally equate (political) beauty with moral goodness, greatness, the sublime, life? Uncomfortably vetted in the pathologization of negative feelings or emotional states such as half-warmed heart, the lack of political beauty is almost equated with death (see #9 and #10 theses), this thesis might trigger cruel optimism (Berlant, 2011), prolonging an affective longing for a fully warmed heart that can never be attained.

If life without (political) beauty equals inner death or a cold heart, in return, beauty appears as necessary criterion for human collective experience and life. With this unhalted appeal against political and emotional indifference, ZPS not only mediates a sense of urgency, but also of affective discomfort if we don't collectivize—because, what happens if we don't succeed to warm our hearts?

> Thesis #8: What we know depends on what we feel.

Thesis #8 addresses LONGING by establishing a direct, causal relation between affect and knowledge. It showcases ZPS's affective epistemology of political beauty, which makes knowledge possible only when 'we' feel. Briefly, thesis #8 introduces an account of experiential, affective knowledge. While neuro-psychology and social and cultural theoretical interpretations have been critiqued by feminist scholars for their problematic separation of cognition and feelings (Leys, 2011), thesis #8 establishes knowledge as inseparable from feeling and/or affecting, and being affected. Put differently, knowledge cannot be sensed without being affected or affecting; 'we' cannot know without feeling. Following feminist scholars' rejection to divorce ontology from epistemology (see Barad, 2003; Hemmings, 2005), thesis #8 offers a way to (re)marry affect and knowledge instead of further perpetuating the problematic separation of emotion and rationality (Bargetz, 2014b).

Yet, what does affective knowledge do for the emergence or (im)possibility of collectives? When we know because we feel, will we only know/feel/learn when we are collectivized? To what extent is affective knowledge also knowledge full of desire or LONGING? And most pressingly: If some of us do not feel, will they also not know? The possibility of feeling seems to precede the capacity of knowing as the latter will flow from the former. While this formula might be a relief to some—to know that feeling facilitates learning, thus deconstructing deeply engrained rationalism that lingers in contemporary science and academia—but still, how do we know? I did not know, so ...

knowing the feeling of beauty
knowing ourselves together
collective longing
longing (for) collectives
when we know together, will we feel together?
will we not be human just because we don't know?

Thesis #8 squarely resonates with Bargetz's feeling politics, or politics as a verb and process. However, in contrast to Bargetz's emphasis on the bodily, embodied, sensuous, sensory or otherwise perceptual practice of feeling politics—or if I may extend her claim, feeling knowledge—ZPS only subtly imagines a politics of feeling knowledge. If not felt, knowledge remains barred, thus imposing a fairly restricted account of affective knowledge. In this thesis, the "we" appears again as universal—we know (or feel, for that matter) nothing more or other than what we feel. Thus, we are seemingly not able to transcend much of the invoked sensing, knowing, or feeling of collectivity. Drawing this excursus on affective knowledge to a close, thesis #8 uniquely addresses us as (collective) subject that feels knowledge, and political beauty in the larger sense. Yet, this thesis leaves us dangling in the air about the concrete, felt connections between the vague collectivity of us and knowledge.

6. SYNTHESIS: LONGING FOREVER - TOGETHER?

In summary, the discussed theses assume that the idea(l) of political beauty as innate to a fairly generalized humankind. The theses do not specify what, where, and by whom that political beauty can be attained, sensed, practiced within collective subjectivity, or how a specific collective can act to advance political beauty. While the human as subject and carrier of political beauty is not further specified, the latent understanding of agency and subjectivity developed throughout remains individualistic, disembodied, abstract. Political beauty is affectively mobilized via LONGING and hope for a more beautiful (political) future, but it is unclear what kinds of people desire, and do or do not feel political beauty. Crucially, "we" do not gain insight into how we can find to each other in the unstillable longing for other politics. LONGING in that sense crystallizes both the possibility and impossibility of political beauty. As political beauty is continuously desired, and remains desirable precisely *because* this thirst for beauty can ultimately never be stilled, LONGING invokes a political and affective perpetuum mobile.

Departing from this, what are the implications of a never fulfillable longing for the emergence, dissolution or fragmentation of collective subjectivity? Could such unstillable political affects, or affective politics, maintain the political as radically open and contingent? Does this state of being unsettled produce different political collectivities in comparison to those trans-local collective movements that pursue a concrete and tangible goal (e.g., the end of a specific dictatorship, the shared opposition to a particular law, the request for a specific political goal to be realized)?

It is precisely in these entanglements with the concrete and abstract LONGING that contemporary and future generations might coalesce into more beautiful futures. Claire Colebrooke (2014, p. 116) describes longing as the "force from which social relations emerge; even if all social forms emerge from desire, desire also exceeds the systems that it has generated itself." The first part of Colebrooke's quotation resonates with theses #1 (and #2) and their appeal to radical desire and utter greatness. From this abyss of never-ending desire, social orders—and affective, sensible, and political ones, too—emerge from this excessive, intangible, universal desire. LONGING goes on; it remains besides and beyond our control. We will, in the worst case, forever be trapped in *not* achieving the lust our yearning has pushed us towards—the dangling carrot of political beauty. Affectively speaking, the urge to warm our hearts (see thesis #5) and appeal to hope (see thesis #7), ZPS might induce pressure, insecurity, impatience, anxiety, while, at the same time, offering the possibility for a different future—a future that will have been politically beautiful. And this however vague outlook is exactly what "we" as unsettled collectivity might need in dire times of political disenchantment. In conclusion, the committed drive towards LONGING while accepting that it can never be fully achieved, co-constitutes political beauty with a specifical proposal for a collectivity that LONGS *despite* the impossibility (and failure) to stop desiring. Briefly, political beauty keeps time, place, politics, affect in motion.

7. OUTLOOK: TOWARDS POLITICALLY BEAUTIFUL COLLECTIVES

While the theses of political beauty variously invoke "everybody" and "us" as sensing agents, the individually and/or collectively attempted articulations of political beauty remain vague, wooden, and overly anthropocentric. Also, the universalizing and glorifying of VITALITY complicates a notion of collectivity or collectives. Is there only a collective when "we" are all alive and warm-hearted? What about being in community with the dead (a communion ZPS has been concerned with recently, see Landau forthcoming) or the more-than human (see Larsen & Johnson 2017)? While life might be crucial to enact political beauty in the now to be able to care and sense together, it might not be the only way. Besides unconditional vitalism, LONGING for political beauty sparks an affective unrest and perhaps stimulates a sense of wonder(ing) about such desire for political change and new political subjectivities.

Furthermore, the affective politics of politically beautiful collectivity are mainly narrated without a concrete sense of agency. Instead, they are normatively entrenched sense of direction—towards hope and beauty and life (hence, against death and ugliness). Political beauty is recounted without a historically embedded sense of time, but romantically evokes both pasts and futures that were and will have been better or more beautiful. While political beauty appears as a collective concern, goal, necessity, desire, the operational approach to politically beautiful collectives remains opaque. Briefly, we still do not really know who the "we" that organizes towards political beauty is. The question whether collectivity is desirable after all is left untouched. We are addressed collectively, however impersonally, yet how do we know each other, and how do we organize in the spirit of politically beautiful collectivity? How do we spread it, sing it, fight for or against it?

With regards to the political grammar of feelings, the feeling politics of ZPS's theses become apparent in references to individual and collective appeals to action. Political beauty, on the one hand, unlocks feeling politics in micro-political and micro-perceptual states of affecting and being affected in everyday life and politics (e.g., striving for greatness, warming one's heart). The politics of feeling, on the other hand, criticize or capitalize on political apathy and the lack of political passion and imagination. These politics of feeling, however, might be closely aligned with feelings of irritation about ZPS's all-too-universal celebration of vivacity and moral beauty, leaving the emergence of collectives barred that are less beautiful, absolute, sublime. What about dirty collectives, transitory help, shared pain, vulnerability?

Despite the seemingly easy and uncontestable claims for greatness, beauty, and poetry, political beauty remains structurally paradox. As both possibility and impossibility, fullness and absence, imagined and felt desire, political beauty projects the promise and risk to create new affective relations, found in proximity and distance to each other (Kemmer, 2019). Taking the appeal for political beauty, and for poetry, as potential course for political action might offer us a glimpse at possibilities to experience, feel part of, or simply *sense* collectives. These collectives will be driven by a LONGING for futures that will be, and have been more politically beautiful. Methodologically speaking, I hope that my poetic responses to affective data might provoke other research in/as poetry to analyze further texts about politics and beauty. In a nutshell, we are left to imagine and get to work on our own ways of thinking, sensing, and making the (im)possible. In the quest of wanting to know and feel what "affect *does* politically" (Bargetz 2014a, p. 301), my own wondering about political beauty leaves me wanting to know—yet will I only know when I feel?—can political beauty exist even when we continue to struggle to work, act, long as a collective? I continue to hope, while I also am longing to find beauty in contingency, sometimes conflict, and care.

References

Ahmed, S. (2014). Affect/Emotion: Orientation Matters. A conversation with Sigrid Schmitz and Sara Ahmed. *Freiburger Zeitschrift für GeschlechterStudien* 28(2): 97–108.
Allen, M. (Ed.) (2017). Poetic Analysis. In *The SAGE Encyclopedia of Communication Research Methods*. 1261.
Anderson, B. (2014). *Encountering affect. Capacities, apparatuses, conditions*. Farnham, Surrey, Burlington, VT: Ashgate.
Angerer, M.-L.; Bösel, B.; Ott, M. (Eds.) (2014). *Timing of Affect. Epistemologies, Aesthetics, Politics*. Zurich, Switzerland: Diaphanes.
Barad, K. (2003). Posthumanist Performativity. Toward an Understanding of How Matter Comes to Matter. *Signs: Journal of Women in Culture and Society* 28(3): 801–831.
Bargetz, B. (2014a). Mapping Affect. Challenging of (Un)Timely Affect. *Timing of Affect. Epistemologies, Aesthetics, Politics*, 289–302. Zurich, Switzerland: Diaphanes.
Bargetz, B. (2014b). Jenseits emotionaler Eindeutigkeiten. Überlegungen zu einer politischen Grammatik der Gefühle. *Affekt und Geschlecht. Eine einführende Anthologie*, 117–137.
Bargetz, B. (2015). The Distribution of Emotions. Affective Politics of Emancipation. *Hypatia*, 30(3), 580–596.
Bargetz, B. (2018). Der sentimentale Vertrag. Eine politische Theorie der Affekte und das unvollendete liberale Projekt. *Leviathan. Berliner Zeitschrift für Sozialwissenschaft*, 46(1), 37–58.
Bargetz, B., & Freudenschuss, M. (2012). Der emotionale Aufstand Verhandlungen um eine Politik der Gefühle in Zeiten der Krise. *Femina Politica. Zeitschrift für feministische Politikwissenschaft*, 107–114.
Bens, J., Diefenbach, A. John, T., Kahl, A. Lehmann, H., Lüthjohann, M., Oberkrome, F., Roth, H., Scheidecker, G., Thonhauser, G., Ural, N. Y., Wahba, D., Walter-Jochum, R., & Ragip Zik, M. (2019). *The Politics of Affective Societies: An Interdisciplinary Essay*. Bielefeld, Germany: transcript.
Berlant, L. G. (2011). *Cruel optimism*. Durham, NC: Duke University Press.

Bayrischer Rundfunk. (2014). *Aktionskunst zur Rettung von syrischen Kindern*. Retrieved from https://www.br.de/radio/bayern2/sendungen/kulturjournal/zentrum-fuer-politische-schoenheit-104.html

Blackman, L. (2015). The Haunted Life of Data. In *Compromised Data: From Social Media to Big Data* (pp. 185–209). London, UK: Bloomsbury.

Blanco, M. d. P., Peeren, E.. (2013). *The spectralities reader. Ghosts and haunting in contemporary cultural theory*. London, UK: Bloomsbury Academic.

Bóren, Ts. (2020). Spatializing authoritarian neoliberalism by way of cultural politics: City, nation and the European Union in Gdansk's politics of cultural policy formation. *Environment and Planning C: Politics and Space, 39(6),*, 1–20.

Colebrooke, C. (2014). *Sex After Life – Essays on Extinction*. Ann Arbor, MI: Open Humanities Press.

Cvetkovich, A. (2007). Public Feelings. *South Atlantic Quarterly*, 106(3), 459–468.

Cvetkovich, A. (2012). *Depression – A Public Feeling*. Durham, NC: Duke University Press.

Derrida, J., & Kamuf, P. (1994). *Specters of Marx. The state of the debt, the work of mourning, and the new international*. New York, NY: Routledge (Routledge classics).

Faulkner, S. (2009). *Poetry as Method. Reporting Research Through Verse*. London, UK: Routledge.

Gregg, M., & Seigworth, G. J. (2011). *The affect theory reader*. Durham, NC: Duke University Press.

Hemmings, C. (2005). Invoking Affect. Cultural theory and the ontological turn. *Cultural Studies* 19(5): 548–567.

Kemmer, L. (2019). Promissory things: how affective bonds stretch along a tramline, *Distinktion: Journal of Social Theory*, 20(1), 58–76.

Knudsen, B. T., & Stage, C. (2015). *Affective Methodologies. Developing Cultural Research Strategies for the Study of Affect*. London, UK: Palgrave Macmillan.

Laclau, E. (1990). *New reflections on the revolution of our time*. London, UK: Verso (Phronesis).

Landau, F. (2019). Exploring the Affective Politics of Political Beauty – An Antagonistic Approach. *Conjunctions. Transdisciplinary journal of cultural participation*, 6(1), 1–16.

Landau-Donnelly, F. (2022). *Politics of (Dis)Assembling – (Re)Moving Borders across Europe*. London, UK: SAGE.

Larsen, S. C., & Johnson, J. T. (2017). *Being Together in Place: Indigenous Coexistence in a More Than Human World*. Minneapolis, MN: University of Minnesota Press.

Leys, R. (2011). The Turn to Affect. A Critique. *Critical Inquiry*, 37(3), 434–472.

Marchart, O. (2010). *Die politische Differenz. Zum Denken des Politischen bei Nancy, Lefort, Badiou, Laclau und Agamben*. Frankfurt am Main, Germany: Suhrkamp.

MDR Thüringen. (2019). Vorwurf der Bildung einer kriminellen Vereinigung. Ermittlungen gegen „Zentrum für politische Schönheit" eingestellt. Retrieved from: https://www.mdr.de/thueringen/ermittlungsverfahren-zentrum-poli tische-schoenheit-eingestellt-100.html

MacLure, M. (2013). The Wonder of Data. *Cultural Studies ↔ Critical Methodologies*, 13(4), 228–232.

Marchart, O. (2013). *Das unmögliche Objekt. Eine postfundamentalistische Theorie der Gesellschaft*. Berlin, Germany: Suhrkamp.

Marks, J. (1998). *Gilles Deleuze: Vitalism And Multiplicity*. London, UK: Pluto Press.

Massumi, B. (2015). *Politics of Affect*. Bristol, UK: Polity Press.

Mouffe, C. (2006). Religion, Liberal Democracy, and Citizenship. In H. de Vries & L. E. Sullivan (Eds.), *Political Theologies* (pp. 318–326). New York, NY: Fordham University Press.

Mouffe, C. (2005). *On the political*. London, UK: Routledge.

Penz, O., & Sauer, B. (2020). *Governing Affects. Neoliberalism, Neo-Bureaucracies, and Service Work*. London, UK: Routledge.

Protevi, J. (2009). *Political affect. Connecting the social and the somatic*. Minneapolis, MN: University of Minnesota Press.

Reckwitz, A. (2017). How the senses organise the social. In *Praxeological political analysis* (pp. 56–66). London, UK: Routledge.

Ruch, P. (2012). Beauty in the Political Sciences. The Insufficiency of Contemporary Accounts and the Premature Death of the Category. In J. Cuffe & A. Horvath (Eds.), *Reclaiming Beauty: Collected Essays in Political Anthropology*, 1, 211–237. Florence, Italy: Ficino Press.

Slaby, J. (2017). More than a Feeling: Affect as Radical Situatedness. *Midwest Studies in Philosophy*, 41, 7–26.

Uhlmann, A. (2020). Chapter 8 – Affect, Meaning, Becoming, and Power: Massumi, Spinoza, Deleuze, and Neuroscience. In A. Houen (Ed.): *Affect and Literature* (pp. 159–174). Cambridge, UK: Cambridge University Press.

Valentine, G. (2008). Living with difference: reflections on geographies of encounter. *Progress in Human Geography*, 32(3), 323–337.

Watson, D., Clark, L. A., & Tellegen, A. (1988). Development and validation of brief measures of positive and negative affect: The PANAS scales. *Journal of Personality and Social Psychology*, 54, 1063–1070.

Zentrum für Politische Schönheit. (2009a). Portfolio. Retrieved from: https://issuu.com/philippruch/docs/portfolio_2009

Zentrum für Politische Schönheit. (2009b). Aktionen. Retrieved from: https://www.politicalbeauty.de/reformation.html

Zentrum für Politische Schönheit. (2019, February 27). Personal conversation, Berlin.

"Wir sind das Volk!"
How the PEGIDA-demonstrations aesthetically practice an exclusive collective identity

Sebastian Sommer

1. INTRODUCTION

The aesthetic dimension of political protest has become a growing field of scientific research over the last decade. By semi-permanently occupying urban spaces, the participants of newly emerging movements, such as Occupy (Wall Street), were not only demanding change or expressing their indignation but creating alternative forms of social life, thereby turning the spaces of protest into embodiments of desired social change. These practices have been described as "presentist democracies" (Lorey, 2014) or tangible examples of managing the "commons" and organizing the "multitude" on a local scale (Hardt & Negri, 2017). These assemblies or encampments drew attention to a general "political performativity" (Butler, 2015, p. 18) as a specific mode of acting together in the here and now, as well as highlighting the affective and emotional involvement of the participants.

Every protest event constitutes specific forms of collective action in which the aesthetic and the political are indistinguishably intertwined, not only when it comes to self-ascribed progressive movements or permanent actions. In order to differentiate between different forms of political performativity, Rancière introduces two major principles of how political action (re-)shapes the aesthetic perception of the common world. On the one hand, "politics" describes the attempt to widen the democratic discourse by making unseen positions visible. On the other hand, "police" attempt to close down the argument by barring unwanted groups from it (see Rancière, 2016, p. 69f.). This primarily philosophical distinction can help to widen the perspectives on political movements when analyzing single protest events. For example, far-right protests, like PEGIDA in Dresden ("Patriotic Europeans against the Islamization of the Occident"), often claim to represent "the people." Therefore, what vision of such national collectivity is performatively embodied on the streets?

In general, the global rise of right-wing groups and movements or "(nativist-)authoritarian populism" (Häusler, 2018, p. 14ff.), such as the Brexit campaign, the

Trump presidency, and the electoral gains of parties like the German Alternative for Germany (AfD), can only be understood through the aesthetic dimension of their politics. This is reflected in the emergence of ideological approaches to political action from the right that extend beyond parliamentary politics into the allegedly pre-political social field of everyday life. Cultural practices/performances such as demonstrations are core elements of such "meta-politics" ("Metapolitik" in von Waldstein, 2017) aiming to create political effects through an aesthetic perception of collective action. In this respect, Hochschild describes the substance of a local Trump rally in 2016 in the motivation of an "emotional change" among the participants by evoking feelings of (patriotic) dominance, rather than as a (coherent) presentation of political concepts (Hochschild, 2017, p. 301). Nevertheless, it would be shortsighted to view such events merely as staged and unreal activities—an "aestheticization of politics"—as Walter Benjamin did in his famous interpretation of mass events in fascist Germany (Benjamin, 2008). This perspective tends to overlook the bio-political effects of performances as means of (national socialist) propaganda in the sense of aesthetically implementing a desired governmentality by transgressing the line between fiction and politics in "doing Volksgemeinschaft" (Annuß, 2019, p. 45) and thus embodying the imagined community collectively.

The historical perspective illustrates the importance of aesthetic practices as a vital part of (far-right) politics. This is not limited to campaign rallies and mass meetings, which often directly address the sensory or affective perception of the participants through staged events. Even simple participation in a demonstration can have many aesthetic effects; some interviewees in Pilkington's participant observation of the "English Defence League" allude to the feeling of a "demo buzz" to describe the specific affective sensation of political togetherness or collective identity at their rallies (Pilkington, 2016, p. 181). The creation of such "collectives of emotion" is a central part of what Virchow calls "performance politics" (see Virchow, 2007) with regard to his research on neo-Nazi rallies in Germany between the late 1990s and early 2000s.

Roughly a decade later, the German public was confronted with the biggest protests on the political right since the end of World War II. The PEGIDA demonstrations, with their openly anti-Muslim and anti-immigration ideology, regularly brought thousands of people onto the streets of Dresden. In existing research on PEGIDA, scant attention has been paid to in-depth analysis of the demonstrations as collective performances, their aesthetic perception or their emotional and affective dimensions. Instead, the view of the single protest events has remained on a descriptive level, focusing on their structure (as "rituals" according to Currle et al. 2016) or on the analysis of the various texts presented (s. Daphi et al., 2015). Only Geiges, Marg and Walter (2015, p. 33ff.) have included a separate chapter on the researchers' perception of the demonstrations, but did not connect the various accounts to their subsequent political analysis.

2. RESEARCHING *PEGIDA* AS COLLECTIVE PERFORMANCE

This chapter concentrates on the performativity of nativist-authoritarian populism in Germany using the example of PEGIDA. As it employs the perspective of performance studies, the work focuses less on PEGIDA as a political movement and more on the staging and performativity of the individual protest events as cultural performances in public space. The events are approached with a performance analysis, one of the most common methods in theater science for studying performances in action.[1] Although it may be compared to the field approach of participant observation in social science, performance analysis does not seek to observe and participate in specific social interactions with the participants. Instead, it concentrates on how the collective performance shapes the social situation as a whole and how it evokes corporal, emotional, or affective experiences and stimulates the ascription of meaning. In doing so, the body of the researcher itself becomes the main methodological instrument. Its corporal and sensory perceptions or affective involvements can serve as analytical hints to the performative mechanisms on how those sentiments and feelings were, willingly or unwillingly, evoked and whether the individual perceptions can be inter-subjectively generalized. This can cause methodological problems when it comes to analyzing performances from which the researcher has a certain political or ideological distance, as is often the case with protest mobilizations of the political right. Those events are not addressed to the participant observers and therefore do not necessarily speak to them in the same way they do to regular participants. These possible differences of personal experience could make it substantially harder to draw generalized conclusions, which is why performance analysis needs to include observations of other participants in the sense of a relational phenomenology in order to verify or counterbalance the inevitably personal and therefore subjective perceptions.

Field research was conducted by the researcher as a non-distinguishable participant[2] at six protest events from October 2015 to October 2016. Due to the sensory-ethnographic approach, some interactions, like joining in certain collective chants, had to be made. The main database consisted of the personal observation protocols written usually a few hours after the end of the demonstrations. In addition, external sources, such as local newspaper reports, YouTube videos, and Facebook comments of alleged participants were also included. The following analysis cannot provide a detailed overview on the protests of PEGIDA. It is rather an attempt to shed some light on the characteristics of the protest performances at a certain point in time.

---

1   For a detailed overview on the method: see Balme, 2008 or Weiler & Roselt, 2017.
2   Participant observation as a non-marked researcher is a controversial application of the method. It poses significant ethical questions that cannot be satisfyingly discussed here. The reason for this methodological choice were considerations of personal safety.

3. WHAT IS *PEGIDA*?

The protests of PEGIDA started in October 2014 in Dresden, the capital of Saxony. Whereas the first meetings attracted only a few hundred people, those numbers doubled week on week. They reached the first peak on January 12th, 2015 with an estimated 25,000 participants. The protests were not organized by previously known actors of the far right.[3] Nonetheless, they expressed an exclusionary German nativist nationalism with open cultural racism, targeting mostly people perceived as Muslims or immigrants.[4] Its ideological heart is the populist claim of representing the will of the people by defending German national or cultural identity against an allegedly treacherous government, backed by the mainstream media. Therefore, PEGIDA held mass demonstrations as the embodiment of a growing public rejection of government policies in order to enforce political changes without engaging in a democratic dialog. After some enforced breaks due to governmental lockdown measures, there are still regular PEGIDA rallies in 2021 which attract a few hundred participants (Volk 2021). Regardless of a significant loss of relevance, the PEGIDA demonstrations in Dresden are still the biggest and the most persistent regular protest events from the political right in Germany. As the organizing group is not open to participation, the single protest events are nearly the only way to engage in PEGIDA apart from social media. The protests of PEGIDA play a crucial part in the growing network of authoritarian-nativist populism in Germany. PEGIDA co-founder Lutz Bachmann describes their role as to "increase the pressure on the streets" (COMPACTTV[Video File], 2016, timestamp 3:58:40). Indeed, the demonstrations have fulfilled this goal and have become a blueprint for many other protests in the political field of nativist-authoritarian populism. PEGIDA led the way in a broader practical application of the ideological concepts of authoritarian-nativist populism in Germany, turning mass protest events into the main form of performative practice and thus an opportunity for the aesthetic experience and creation of a nativist collective identity.

---

3   With the growing number of participants at the PEGIDA-events in Dresden, numerous local GIDA-groups were formed independently in other German cities; many of them by neo-Nazis. The organizing circle of PEGIDA could never fully control those dynamics. They approved only a few of them. Officially, PEGIDA has been distancing itself from fascist groups. However, their members could always participate in a private capacity. Because of that, the distancing has to be seen as some kind of masquerade in order to maintain the image of the demonstrations as civilian protests, despite the strong links to ideologies of inequality.

4   The underlying opinial structure in the German public had been showing similar tendencies in empirical surveys for (at least) decades (vgl. Heitmeyer, 2018, p. 140ff.). The open expression in public hints at changes in the overall discourse where cultural racisms (mostly in the form of anti-Muslim racism), for example, have become less challenged.

4. THE DRAMATURGY OF THE PROTEST EVENTS

Despite the changes in the structure and political role of PEGIDA, the general staging of the rallies and their overall dramaturgy have been more or less consistent. Regular events take place on Monday evenings around 6 pm on a public square in the historical center of Dresden. The stage for speeches is the platform of a truck parked at one edge of the gathering spot in front of which participants assemble. They mostly come in small and unconnected groups of friends or co-workers and are usually engaged in private conversation before the rally begins. There is no significant interaction among them and only infrequent chants. This situation changes as soon as the recording of the official PEGIDA hymn is played. The chatter comes to an end, flags are waved and the majority of the participants focus on the stage. Afterwards, the first part of the stationary rally begins with a speech by one of the organizers, followed by one or two other contributions in a predetermined order. During this part of the event, the participants can only react to speeches by collectively clapping, booing, or shouting slogans. Over time, this division of roles in the collective performance has led to the development of a genuine PEGIDA rhetoric. The speeches are often designed to evoke certain reactions at specific moments marked by buzzwords or rhetorical pauses. This creates the impression of call-response chorales where, for example, a passage on the politics of then German chancellor Angela Merkel is answered by collective shouts of *"Merkel muss weg!"* ("Merkel must go!"), which are repeated over and over again until the speaker continues.

The next stage of a regular PEGIDA event is the *"Spaziergang"* ("promenade"), a circular demonstration through the center of Dresden, which is supposed to be a silent march. There are no speeches but a few sporadic chants, and private conversations begin again. After returning to the point of departure, the second part of the rally begins. After one or two additional speeches, it ends with the collective singing of the German national anthem, after which the crowd disperses into the Dresden evening. This short description sketches out the central elements of a typical PEGIDA event. It gives a first insight into how feelings of collective identity are being evoked. The general staging facilitates the performative coordination of the heterogeneous assembly of single individuals and groups into a collectivity that feels able to exclaim *"Wir sind das Volk!"* ("We are the people!").

5. PERFORMANTIVE POLITICS AS AN ATTEMPT AT "DISTRIBUTION OF THE SENSIBLE"

As Judith Butler remarks, the (self-)assignment "We the people!" is to be understood as a claim of the assembling collectivity to be identified as "the people" in order to overcome an experienced precarity (Butler, 2015, p. 181). In this context, Butler extends the concept of precarity beyond the common socio-economic understanding to include general feelings of threatened bodily existence, as well as perceptions of lack of support in leading a livable life free from fears about future needs, such as protection, shelter, nourishment, mobility or expression (Butler, 2015, p. 129). The "bodies in alliance" that performatively constitute the assembly make visible a collectively felt precarity and the demand to be publicly recognized (Butler, 2015, p. 208). This is strongly reminiscent of the concept of the "demos" (the "people") in Rancière's political philosophy: "The one who belongs to the demos, who speaks when he is not to speak, is the one who partakes in what he has no part in" (Rancière, 2010, p. 32). Like Butler, Rancière attempts to think of political action in categories of the aesthetic. For him, the political and the aesthetic cannot be separated. The former shapes the individual and collective possibilities of being in a common space in society in the sense of a shared *aisthesis*. Thus, the political assigns people to a certain bodily and sensory "presence in the world" (Rancière, 2016, p. 18), which determines how they can perceive this world and how they are perceived in it. For example, are certain individuals recognized as legitimate speakers in public discourse, are their voices being heard when uttered, are they being ignored as their voices are only recognized as noise and not as speech, or are they silenced and therefore made invisible? The political which is performatively embodied in political action establishes not only a normative order—who is recognized as a political subject—but also leads to a general "distribution of the sensible."

> This partition should be understood in the double sense of the word: on the one hand, as that which separates and excludes; on the other, as that which allows participation. A partition of the sensible refers to the manner in which a relation between a shared common (*un commun partagé*) and the distribution of exclusive parts is determined in sensory experience. This latter form of distribution, which, by its sensory self-evidence, anticipates the distribution of part and shares (parties), itself presupposes a distribution of what is visible and what not, of what can be heard and what cannot. (Rancière, 2010, p. 36)

Therefore, political action is to be seen as a never-ending struggle over the division of the common world (of the sensible) in the form of the shared public space (of society), which is to define and continually redefine who is included, who seeks inclusion, and who remains excluded from the current regime of perception. From this point of view, staging a demonstration is a tangible way of expressing a formerly invisible collective existence, making it seen and heard through the assembled people who temporarily change the distribution of urban space by occupying public squares: "A demonstration is political not because it occurs in a particular place and bears upon a particular object but rather because its form is that of a clash between two partitions of the sensible" (Rancière, 2010, p. 39). Political action thus seeks to widen the possibilities of participation, as mentioned above, by challenging the existing "distribution of the sensible" and establishing a new distribution from the position of the "demos." The demand for a "part of those who have no part" (Rancière, 2010, p. 33) is an attempt of the currently voiceless to make themselves heard to those who were not listening. For Rancière, the struggle for political participation in the sense of being part of a commonly shared aisthesis is the heart of democracy. This is what he calls "politics." The second form of a "distribution of the sensible" is opposed to such an open-ended dispute. The principle of the "police" is the attempted closure of any argument by neglecting the existence of a "demos."

> The essence of the police lies in a partition of the sensible that is characterized by the absence of void and of supplement: society here is made up of groups tied to specific modes of doing, to places in which these occupations are exercised, and to modes of being corresponding to these occupations and these places. In this matching of functions, places and ways of being, there is no place for any void. It is this exclusion of what-is-not that constitutes the police-principle at the core of statist practices. (Rancière, 2010, p. 36)

But which of these two opposing logic principles is represented in the PEGIDA demonstrations? The protesters' claim "Wir sind das Volk!" ("We are the people!") suggests the collective embodiment of a "demos." This view is already challenged by taking into consideration the composition of the demonstrations. First, all of the empirical surveys on PEGIDA suggest that the majority of participants are German, white, male, on average 51 years old and consider themselves part of the working middle-class (for an overview see Patzelt in Patzelt & Klose, 2016, p. 159ff.). These characteristics imply at least minimum access to social, political, or cultural capital and are not commonly associated with extensive precarity. Second, in his analysis of the political topics and demands of PEGIDA, Heim concludes that most of them were present in previous public discourse (Knopp, 2017, p. 362). These two points, the relatively privileged status of the participants, as well as their discursively well-established demands, seem to suggest that the performative logic of PEGIDA does not follow the principle of "politics" in the sense of making a suppressed subjectivity visible and thus contributing to a diversification of political discourse. Rather, it embodies the "police" in the sense of striving for hegemony and establishing an exclusive order of political discourse. But how does this principle influence the collective performance of the protest event and the aesthetic perception of the participants?

6. EXCLUSIVE SPACES

The temporary occupation of public places, streets, and squares is always part of bodily assemblies. They directly influence the way common urban space can be perceived. With PEGIDA, there is a certain tendency to gather at such places that are literally enclosed on all sides by buildings, wide streets, or natural borders in the city, like the Elbe river. One example is the Theaterplatz, where most of the rallies in the second half of 2015 took place (see figure 1). The gathering spot can only be reached through a limited number of streets in which two more barriers have to be passed before entering. The first is a more or less narrow cordon of small groups of official police forces, who inspect anyone wishing to proceed further. This is followed by PEGIDA's own security staff asking for donations. Therefore, it is nearly impossible to stumble into a PEGIDA rally involuntarily. Accordingly, there are almost no other people to be seen at the gathering spots apart from the participants. Even if there are other persons—such as tourists—they are made very much invisible compared to the sheer numbers of demonstrators. Furthermore, counter-protests generally have to take place at a certain distance from the PEGIDA rallies. Hence, they are usually not visible and can only sometimes be heard in the distance. Yet, even such slight interruptions lead to complaints by the PEGIDA speakers.

All these elements taken together can contribute to a feeling among the participants of being "among one's own." Groups or individuals that are disliked by PEGIDA and most forms of dissensus are widely absent at the rallies. This is not a coincidence. It is the desired effect of the deliberate staging in enclosed areas and the result of the collective performance so that, journalists (as part of the "lying press"), for example, are attacked verbally and physically by the participants in order to make them leave. In effect, PEGIDA rallies tend to turn the ideally heterogeneous public space of the city[5] into an exclusive space for a more or less homogeneous, or more precisely homogeneously imagined, group of participants as the legitimate representation of the "German people." In doing so, the protests temporarily establish a new spatial arrangement. They reshape the possibilities of the perception of urban space in a way that is practically opposed in order to enable a shared aisthesis.

In this respect, Butler argues that the self-assignment of an assembled collectivity as "We the people!" necessarily produces exclusions—at least of those groups or individuals who are not present (Butler, 2015, p. 4). However, it is different if a protest is aware of its own exclusory mechanisms and attempts to minimize them or to make the missing groups invisible to those on the inside. By retreating into enclosed spaces, PEGIDA embodies the latter, corresponding to the logic of the "police":

---

5   "The city creates a situation, the urban situation, where different things occur one after another and do not exist separately but according to their differences. ... However, the urban is not indifferent to all differences, precisely because it unites them." (Lefebvre, 2003, p. 117f.)

"Move along! There's nothing to see here!" (Rancière, 2010, p. 37). The "police" divide the sensible into visible parts—the subject of the shared aesthesis—and parts not worth seeing, just as PEGIDA shields its rallies from outside impressions. For Rancière, not only is political dissensus as the basis of democratic argument excluded from the rallies by the spatial arrangement, but their content is strongly oriented towards presenting a collective consensus. Controversial speeches are rare and most contributions fall within a narrow and popular range of topics and arguments. The constrictive character of the expected presentation of consensus is highlighted by a personal experience at the PEGIDA rally in Dresden on July 18, 2016, where Tony Fleischmann made his debut speech claiming not to like the term "lying press." In the vicinity of my observations, this remark caused vigorous head-shaking and disapproving shouts towards the stage. Taken together, the staging of the protests in enclosed spaces and the absence of argumentative dissensus make the rallies a real-life "echo-chamber" in which only PEGIDA is to be heard and seen. This is not only meant metaphorically. While the walls of the surrounding buildings limit the visible urban space to the rallies themselves, they also reflect the collective chants back to their origins. With a few thousand participants in attendance, the rallies tend to fill the individual range of sensory perceptions nearly exclusively with impressions created by PEGIDA, thus evoking feelings of hegemonic power.

The degree to which such perceptions form the core of the aesthetic dimension of the protest and shape a genuine PEGIDA experience becomes evident when these mechanisms of staging or the dynamics of collective performance fail. With decreasing numbers of participants, it was becoming harder to fill the occupied urban areas and therefore the sensory field of the participants. To counter this development, the protests were moved to narrower squares, like Schlossplatz. However, PEGIDA rallies sometimes had to be held on public squares that were either far too big, leaving the participants scattered across the area, like the second anniversary at Theaterplatz with only an estimated 8,000 attendants, or that were open to the sides, like the Wiener Platz next to the Hauptbahnhof (see figures 1 & 2). In such situations, the participants were constantly confronted with other perceptions, like urban everyday activities, that prevented the emergence of a feeling of hegemonic exclusivity. This resulted in a diminished air of confidence at the rallies. There were, for example, significantly fewer slogans to be heard and fewer people participating in them. Following the aforementioned rally on July 18 at Wiener Platz, participants even complained afterwards in social-media groups that "as usual" few people attended the protest. Such descriptions hint more to a feeling of disillusionment evoked at the event than of collective power.

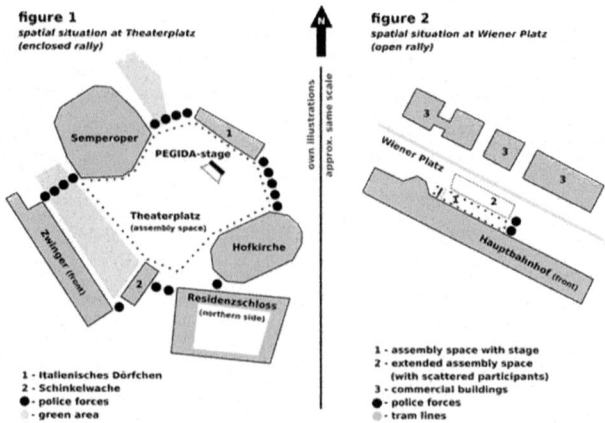

figure 1
spatial situation at Theaterplatz
(enclosed rally)

figure 2
spatial situation at Wiener Platz
(open rally)

1 - Italienisches Dörfchen
2 - Schinkelwache
● - police forces
▨ - green area

1 - assembly space with stage
2 - extended assembly space
    (with scattered participants)
3 - commercial buildings
● - police forces
◎ - tram lines

7. MECHANISMS OF SYMBOLICALLY KEEPING A DOUBLE DISTANCE

Therefore, the specific "distribution of the sensible" of PEGIDA is realized through the symbolic and factual exclusion of unwanted "others" from the sensory perception of the participants. A similar tendency pervades the speeches at PEGIDA rallies, which often follow an overarching narrative of "keeping a distance" from disliked groups (Knopp, 2017, p. 107f.). Besides this horizontal dimension of exclusion, there is also a noteworthy tendency towards vertical distancing—in practice as well as in philosophical theory. The logic of the "police" separates "actual groups defined by differences in birth, and by the different functions, places, and interests that make up the social body" (Rancière, 2010, p. 36). Separation in this case means giving or denying those groups the possibility of political participation or access to the collective exercise of *arkhê*: "The logic of *arkhê* thus presupposes that a determinate superiority is exercised over an equally determinate inferiority" (Rancière, 2010, p. 30). The logic of the "police" as the performance of *arkhê* is based upon and (re-)produces inequality. During the PEGIDA rallies, this is enacted in two ways.

7.1 "Rituals of status reversal" à la Turner

One example is the call-and-response pattern during the speeches, as described above. This can be interpreted as the performative establishment of a vertical relationship between PEGIDA and those mentioned in the speeches by expressing the desire to collectively exercise power over them, for example by "clearing them out." Especially with regard to groups or individuals perceived as superior, like politicians, the chants rhetorically flip the predominant social order as perceived by the participants. Those collective performances (of chanting) resemble the "rituals of status reversal" described by Victor Turner. In these cultural practices, "groups or categories of persons who habitually occupy low status positions in the social structure are positively enjoined to exercise ritual authority over their superiors" (Turner, 1991, p. 167). This derogative tendency has always been present in PEGIDA speeches. For example, Patzelt refers to the protests as a *"Schmähgemeinschaft"* ("Vilifying community") bound together by the expression of disdain towards "a political-medial class" (Patzelt in Patzelt & Klose, 2016; p. 36). In mid-2016, PEGIDA co-founder Siegfried Däbritz even declared that the rhetoric device of irony was one of the main principles of PEGIDA for "unmasking the regime of lies" by "ridiculing the Merkel-system" (Däbritz at the PEGIDA rally on July 18, 2016).[6] This statement provoked a wave of applause among the participants. Just like Turner's "rituals of status reversal" pejorative chants at PEGIDA are used to renew the existing social order (as it is) by (re-)grounding the political rule in the nativist communitas of the assembled German *"Volk."* In the self-image of PEGIDA, the protests (re-)establish a democratic *"Volkssouveränität"* ("Sovereignty of the people").

7.2 Performing "German supremacy"

The argument of a performative status reversal is only applicable to groups or individuals perceived as superior. It must be modified when vulnerable groups, like refugees, are targeted. Their symbolic degradation follows the racist assumption that those groups or individuals are granted more privileges than they are entitled to, based on the omnipresent ideologies of inequality which group people vertically by ascribing a social status based on an attributed cultural, racial, national, or religious identity. In the ideology of PEGIDA, social participation and the nationalist or even nativist imagination of legitimate German-ness are intertwined. Kimmel observed an equivalent mechanism of supremacist thinking in his sociological study on "Angry White Men" in the U.S. about the structure of feelings amongst white working-class males and its cultural forms of expression. Those men, Kimmel remarks, "feel entitled while looking 'down' at the hordes of 'others' who are threatening to take what they believe is rightfully theirs and are being aided in their illegitimate quest by a government that is in their thrall" (Kimmel, 2013, p. 63). Those viewpoints are based on the imagination of an allegedly righteous property based on national or cultural identity, for example in the form of a stock of privileges that

---

6 To be precise, the aforementioned speech was given by Däbritz, but he claimed to have read a letter that was handed to him anonymously before the rally started. The veracity of this claim cannot be proved. The speech is cited from personal notes.

is being taken away or hollowed out illegitimately.[7] Hardt and Negri call the imaginative connection between a racialized property of privileges and identity "race privilege": "Identity and property thus have a double relation in right-wing populisms: identity serves as a privileged means to property and also as a form of property itself, which promises to maintain or restore the hierarchies of the social order" (Hardt & Negri, 2017, 53). The rhetorical degradation of vulnerable groups functions as a means of a social self-elevation. It must, therefore, be seen as a performative embodiment of supremacist thinking in order to restore a desired social order based on racist or nativist ideologies of inequality.

8. FROM SYMBOLIC DISTANCING TO PHYSICAL DOMINANCE

In this respect, the initial rally at each PEGIDA event shows the mechanisms of a "distribution of the sensible" by means of the "police" at work. Its staging tends to turn the heterogeneous public space into an exclusive real-life echo-chamber in which mechanisms of, mainly symbolic, double-distancing are exercised. This creates an atmosphere of supremacist hegemony against the background of a collective performance of nativist identity. The following demonstrations seem to oppose this logic as they exit the enclosed protest space. However, the participants enter the urban lifeworld not as individuals but as a part of a protest collective. The underlying collective identity has been performatively evoked during the rally just previously. Moreover, the demonstrations present a, potentially massive, collective presence of protesting bodies that dominate the streets in the absence of a comparable opposition. They become the manifestation of the claimed hegemony, extending their air of supremacy over the enclosed rallies and into the wider city. Hence, the political dimension of the demonstrations does not derive from the expression of demands or opinions, since they are mostly "silent marches." They are mainly political in their aesthetic effects on the collective perception of the urban space.

During the marches, the formerly exercised position of symbolic supremacy transforms into direct acts of verbal and physical exclusion and dominance. For example, on November 30th, 2015, PEGIDA passed the state parliament of Saxony

---

7   Kimmel (and also Hochschild) point out that, due to socio-political upheavals favoring a re-distribution of social wealth from bottom to top, the socio-economic situation of many U.S. citizens (even from those segments formerly untouched by the threat of social descent) has deteriorated in recent decades, exposing them to a growing risk of precarity or at least blocking their social advancement. This is the objective (and empirically studied) background of similar feelings of deprivation (see Kimmel, 2013, p. 282) to which (cultural-)racist or nativist (in the sense of supremacist) positions, as a way of making sense of the world, can be politically attached. Heitmeyer (2018, p. 98ff) describes similar developments for Germany.

and the "House of the Press." Despite both locations being mostly empty, the participants shouted angry slogans in their direction. The thin line between symbolic and physical aggression is tested each time the PEGIDA demonstrations pass rallies of counter-protestors. Those were normally attended by only one or two hundred people. Nonetheless, they were heavily guarded by riot police. With their clearly minoritarian position, they could easily have been ignored by the passing PEGIDA demonstrations. Instead, the participants started to shout at the counter-rally as soon as it came into sight. Some even waved fists or approached the counter rally angrily to insult individual participants. In those situations of confrontation with opposed groups, PEGIDA participants were actively enacting the logic of the "police" by trying to collectively suppress dissensus. The effects of such a performance, which combine symbolic distancing and the exercise of physical dominance, can be seen at the end of the PEGIDA event. The mass singing of the German national anthem completes the creation of the German *"Volk"* as a collective body in performative synchronicity. Afterwards, the participants leave the rallies. Unlike the individualized gathering process, there are now collective chants to be heard and flags are being waved. Taken together, this creates the impression of small demonstrations heading away from the PEGIDA rallies. Therefore, the atmosphere of supremacist hegemony based on the performatively enacted collective identity extends over the main event. This could be interpreted as the realization of a right-wing political concept of "meta-politics." The nativist publicist Thor von Waldstein describes the effects of PEGIDA in the sense of creating a "weekly increasing courage of the people and confidence in their own strength" which will eventually reduce trust in "established politics" (von Waldstein, 2014, p. 33). Potentially, the staging of collective protest performances might enable an actual anti-democratic empowerment of the participants through aesthetic and affective experiences.

9. FUELING A NOSTALGIC ANGER-PERFORMATIVE EXCERISE OF A NATIVIST HEGEMONY

PEGIDA claims to embody the unheard voice of the German "people" currently unrepresented in the legislative system. It seems to mirror the logic of the "demos" in the political philosophy of Rancière. However, analysis of the protest performances showed a significant tendency to act according to the logic of the "police" by symbolically and physically barring unwanted groups from the common ground of a shared aisthesis (here the urban space). Hence, the PEGIDA events enact the desired social change as collective protest performances by creating temporary spaces where the political utopia of a supremacist hegemony may not be fully realized but can be affectively perceived in the overall atmosphere that has been collectively produced. There are no Muslims or (illegal) immigrants at the rallies. Politicians are rhetorically degraded to their supposed role as representatives in the sense of servants to a majoritarian will, who are told by the crowd what to do, even if they will not listen. Moreover, even if there is some dissensus, it can be silenced by acts of verbal or even physical domination.

The PEGIDA protests exercise a political dominance in the form of a "distribution of the sensible" through collective action based on supremacist ideology. This leads to a performative re-installation of a social order based on "race privileges" that have supposedly been lost, since they are no longer a guarantee of social advancement (see Kimmel, 2013, p. XII or Hochschild, 2017, p. 188f.). In the eyes of PEGIDA, the protests reclaim what should belong to them "naturally." This logic of re-appropriation follows the emotional structure of anger about an unjust loss of property—even an immaterial one like privileges—through no fault of one's own. Simultaneously, guilt is projected onto certain vulnerable groups, which become targets for feelings of revenge—a mechanism that has been described in the previously mentioned study by Kimmel:

> Aggrieved entitlement can mobilize one politically, but it is often a mobilization toward the past, not the future, to restore that which one feels has been lost. It invariably distorts one's vision and leads to a misdirected anger—often at those just below you on the ladder, because clearly they deserve what they are getting far less than you do. (Kimmel, 2013, p. 24)

This orientation towards the past is also present in the PEGIDA movement. The protest is not centered around the political management of the current diverse socio-political situation to foster the future opening of the democratic argument to a wider variety of people. Instead, it enacts the closing of democratic debate by means of the "police" and returning to an imagined socio-political "lost paradise" where the bond between identity and privilege still existed. Bauman calls this nostalgic re-creation of a patchwork backwards utopia "retrotopia" (Bauman, 2017, p. 17). For PEGIDA, this means the re-installation of a hegemonic German "Volk" which is, in effect, the supremacy of the white, German (male). The performative enactment of a backwards utopia makes the Dresden protests an ideal example of "the reduction of politics to the police" as described by Rancière in the sense of a return to the, allegedly, "normal state of things" (Rancière, 2010, p. 42f.). However, the staging of the desired social order that builds upon affective management of anger over the perceived loss of "race privileges" is only temporary. As Kimmel pointed out, anger is a "hot emotion" that has to be fueled constantly (Kimmel, 2013, p. 36f.). This is what the PEGIDA protests do by regularly taking to the streets of Dresden. They constantly renew the projection of perceived injustices to vulnerable groups and their supporters in state legislation and the media. On top of that, they enact a symbolic revenge which opens spaces of aesthetic perception to feel at least a small amount of affective satisfaction.

10. CONCLUSION

It is this "metapolitical" dimension of collective action in populist movements that leads Kimmel to conclude that populism is rather "an emotion, not a political ideology" (Kimmel, 2013, p. 64). In the end, it is important to remember that the specific "distribution of the sensible" that shapes the aesthetic perception at those protest events is not virtual. It enables real corporal and sensory experiences and evokes emotional and affective movements. Therefore, the constant exercise of feelings of a hegemonic collective identity and the resulting regular (re-)creation of a "sensing collective" can have consequences. The events around October 3rd, 2016 have shown this. Around this date, when the official festivities of "German Unity Day" were being held in Dresden, PEGIDA and similar groups tried to crash them. Their supporters appeared at different events of the festival, sometimes with a few hundred people, and began to insult and even attack politicians and attendees. The mainly symbolic re-appropriation of the urban space that has been exercised or drilled regularly on PEGIDA Mondays then turned into actual acts of political dominance by trying to police large parts of the city. This development is not a unique attribute of the protests in Dresden. Similar mechanisms of aesthetically exercised collective dominance that turned into political vigilance could be observed throughout the authoritarian protests against the state measures to control the COVID pandemic in Germany. Therefore, the questions remain concerning how democratic forces can politically react to the growing attempts by authoritarian forces to police urban space by means of protest and reinforce a "distribution of the sensible" that enables the aesthetic perception of more diverse collectivities or "sensing collectives."

References

Annuß, E. (2019). *Volksschule des Theater: Nationalsozialistische Massenspiele*. Paderborn, Germany: Wilhelm Fink Verlag.
Balme, C.B. (2008). *The Cambridge introduction into theatre studies*. Cambridge, England: Cambridge University Press.
Bauman, Z. (2017). *Retrotopia*. Berlin, Germany: Suhrkamp.
Benjamin, W. (2008). The work of art in the age of mechanical reproduction. In H. Ahrend (Ed.), *Illuminations* (pp. 217–252). New York, NY: Schocken Books.
Butler, J. (2015). *Notes toward a performative theory of assembly*. Cambridge, MS: Harvard University Press.
[COMPACTTV]. (2016, November 5). COMPACT-Konferenz 2016: Offensive für Meinungsfreiheit [Video File]. Retrieved from https://www.youtube.com/watch?v=qWuJNfRANoY.
Daphi, P. et al. (2015). *Protestforschung am Limit: Eine soziologische Annäherung an Pegida*. Berlin, Germany: ipb working papers.

Geiges, L.; Marg, S & Walter, F. (2015). *PEGIDA: Die schmutzige Seite der Zivilgesellschaft*. Bielefeld, Germany: Transcript.

Hardt, M. & Negri, A. (2017). *Assembly*. New York, NY: Oxford University Press.

Häusler, A. (2018). Die AfD: Partei des völkisch-autoritären Populismus. In A., Häusler (Ed.), *Völkisch-Autoritärer Populismus: Der Rechtsruck in Deutschland und die AfD* (pp. 9–20). Hamburg, Germany: VSA.

Heitmeyer, W. (2018). *Autoritäre Versuchungen: Signaturen der Bedrohung I*. Berlin, Germany: Suhrkamp.

Hochschild, A.R. (2017). *Fremd in ihrem Land: Eine Reise ins Herz der amerikanischen Rechten*. Frankfurt am Main, Germany: Campus.

Kimmel, M.S. (2013). *Angry White Men: American masculinity at the end of an era*. New York, NY: Nation Books.

Knopp, P. (2017). Abstand halten: Zur Deutung gesellschaftlicher Krisen im Diskurs Pegidas. In T.,Heim, (Ed.). Pegida als Spiegel und Projektionsfläche: Wechselwirkungen und Abgrenzungen zwischen Pegida, Politik, Medien, Zivilgesellschaft und Sozialwissenschaften (pp. 79–110). Wiesbaden, Germany: Springer VS.

Lefebvre, H. (2003). *The urban revolution*. Minneapolis, MN: University of Minnesota Press.

Lorey, I. (2014). Presentist democracy: Exodus and tiger's leap. Retrieved from https://transversal.at/blog/Presentist-Democracy.

Patzelt, W.J. & Klose, J. (Eds.). (2016). *PEGIDA: Warnsignale aus Dresden*. Dresden, Germany: Thelem.

Pilkington, H. (2016). *Loud and proud: Passion and politics in the English Defence League*. Manchester, England: Manchester University Press.

Rancière, J. (2010). Ten theses on politics. In S., Corcoran (Ed.). *Dissensus: On politics and aesthetics*. (pp. 27–44). New York, NY: Continuum Books.

Rancière, J. (2016). *Politik und Ästhetik: im Gespräch mit Peter Engelmann. Passagen Gespräche 5*. Vienna, Austria: Passagen Verlag.

Turner, V. (1991). *The ritual process: Structure and anti-structure* (7th ed.). Ithaca, NY: Cornell University Press.

Virchow, F. (2007). Performance, emotion, and ideology: On the creation of "collectives of emotion" and worldview in the contemporary German far right. *Journal of Contemporary Ethnography*, 36 (2), 147–164.

Volk, S. (2021). Die rechtspopulistische PEGIDA in der COVID-19-Pandemie: Virtueller Protest für

"unsere Bürgerrechte". *Forschungsjournal soziale Bewegungen*, 34 (2), 235-248

von Waldstein, T. (2015). Metapolitik: Theorie – Lage – Aktion. Schnellroda: Verlag Antaios

Weiler, C. & Roselt, J. (2017). Aufführungsanalyse: Eine Einführung. Tübingen & Basel: Francke UTB

Digital Violence as Affective Disciplining after Feminist Protests
The Case of #NotLikeThatLadies

Marcela Suárez and Mirjana Mitrović

1. INTRODUCTION

In Latin America there is a severe crisis of violence against women. This situation is aggravated due to the high level of impunity enjoyed by perpetrators and, further, the institutional violence directed at women seeking justice, leading in most cases to revictimization. Feminist protests against said violence have exploded throughout the region. They carry the banner of common slogans such as #NiUnaMenos (NotOneMore) as a way of demanding an end to the impunity. A renewed feminist agency that brings the affects to the forefront has emerged, and with it the affectations of violence, as a way to enrich the political repertoire of the fight against sexual violence (Baer, 2016; de Souza, 2019). An exemplary series of protests of this kind took place in Mexico City after two cases of minors raped by the police went public in August 2019. To protest police impunity, women painted red circles symbolizing blood outside the police station, dumped pink glitter on the head of Mexico City's security secretary and graffitied historical monuments with feminist slogans. Black-masked women also smashed bus station windows and mixed the shards with pink glitter to call attention to these sites of violence against them. These affective interventions permeated with fury, anger, and despair over the devastating situation of gender violence, created shared ways of sensing and being affected by violence.

The responses to the women's mobilizations have been quite ambivalent: On the one hand, there is a tangible euphoria and solidarity among women, as a form of collective resistance, but this is met with increasing *corrective threats* on social networks, on the other. The hashtag #AsiNoMujeres (NotLikeThatLadies)—created in response to feminist protests in 2019—is evidence of that. It was the women who were then condemned as violent and even irrational—not police impunity or the society that tolerates it. These forms of digital violence show the currently contested character not only of female bodies but also of their affects, revealing the deep intertwinement of how gendered hegemonies are both vulnerable to aesthetic interventions but tend to resort to reciprocal cycles of violence, too.

Cultural expectations have widely been considered in feminist literature as a form of symbolic violence to discipline women by designating the ways women 'ought to behave' as well as by mobilizing the penalties they must pay for their public role (Savigny, 2020). In the same way, with the praxeology analysis of aesthetics, Reckwitz (2016) points out that aesthetics is always bound up with the mobilization of affects. The response to the protests in the media and social networks resulted, however, in practices of disciplining affects (Reckwitz 2016).

In spite of the fact that the public opinion largely denigrated the protests because of women's rage, the protest did find resonance in public policy. The government indeed responded by activating a "gender alert" in November 2019, which implies that a series of measures focused on addressing gender violence must be taken. Moreover, amendments to the penal code were also approved to criminalize digital violence. In the end, feminist protesters have found a way to turn such vicious cycles into virtuous paths toward countering digital post-protest behavioral critique and affect discipline.

This article aims to analyze the intertwining of the aesthetic and political practices that emerged in the protests both as a site of resistance but also as discipline. To do that, we engage with the literature of violence against women in politics and affect theory. We claim that the great diversity of aesthetic-political actions accompanying the protests render visible the evocation of rage as a shared collective subjectivity and thus a renewed feminist agency that is verbalized in the slogan "*Somos malas; podemos ser peores*" (We are bad; we can be worse). We further argue that the intertwining of affects and political practices in these performances and protests characterized by bringing the women's affects to the political arena have transgressed the affective order and political imaginary of how women should protest and what kind of affects they are allowed to bring into public spaces. We read the interventions of collective rage as a revolt against the cultural expectations of women violated feeling ashamed and having to endure it. Due to these expectations, women protesters are routinely punished for showing anger in the public arena—and not articulating their demands (as they "should") in "rational" and "intelligent" ways. Thus, they become the targets of hundreds of misogynistic posts on social networks where users expressed shame and hate toward feminism. Women are also accused of corrupting the meaning of femininity and, finally, provided with male role models and ways in which they should protest.

Methodologically, we undertook a digital ethnography understood as a research strategy that is not limited to the digital space but also includes on-site participant observation and interviews (Murthy, 2011). The main sources of our research comprised field notes of participation in the protests (including the multi-sensory perceptions and the affects they generate) (Pink, 2009) and the collection of various audiovisual materials, such as photos, videos, and reviews of the protests. The digital ethnography also included on-site field periods in Mexico City to conduct in-depth face-to-face interviews with activists from the feminist collective Luchadoras. This is a feminist collective that promotes processes of personal and collective political transformation by narrating and disseminating women's stories. Their mission is to build an internet free of violence and to create political spaces for women's empowerment (Luchadoras, 2020). Our digital ethnographic approach was combined with the analysis of posts containing the hashtag #NotLikeThatLadies on the social media platform Twitter. Through data mining techniques, we collected 2172 tweets in the period from August 16th—31, 2019. This hashtag was trending as users mobilized their opinions and expectations for women protesting against violence affectively. Field notes, interviews, and the tweets were analyzed with content analysis (Hernández, Fernández, & Baptista Lucio, 2010).

This article contributes to the literature on violence against women in politics and affect theory by analyzing, in a more integral way, the public demands on women to control their affects as a medium of gender politics and patriarchic power, that is, to be civilized and rational—but at the same time it is arising as a source of new ways of resistance against impunity. We also document evidence of the digital violence and the discipline that activists and human rights defenders face in social media in the wake of feminist protest. In the next section, we draw on contributions about violence against women in politics and affect theory to address practices of resistance and how they in turn face discipline. In section three, we discuss feminist strategies to subvert affective governance during the protests. In section four, we focus on the media response, the digital violence directed at the activists and their bodily reactions. Section five centers on the subsequent affective disciplining that followed the protests by focusing on the #NotLikeThatLadies as a political site. A final section offers our conclusion that women's fear turning to rage has entered the political repertoire of affective feminist politics despite any reactionary discipline to put women back 'in their place,' effectively turning a corner in Latin American feminist politics. Feminism at large has learned to use #NotLikeThatLadies-type disciplining as a source of inspiration billowing up in clouds of pink glitter.

2. VIOLENCE AND AFFECTS

Gendered violence is a contested concept (M. Krook, 2020). New discussions are directed toward questioning the focus on physical violence and changing it to the diverse ways in which violence against women is also perpetrated. These include symbolic, semiotic (use of symbols, language, and images), cultural violence and, more recently, digital violence. All these practices take their toll on women's' bodies, professional careers, and their status in society, with considerable physical, psychological, moral, and even economic losses (Bardall, Bjarnegård, & Piscopo, 2020). Particularly, current discussions of our platform society have prompted literature on digital violence to explode (Jane, 2014; Jane, 2016; Powell & Henry, 2017). Many other authors have conceptualized digital violence in a broader sense, as any acts of gender-based violence that are committed via the use of information and communication technologies (APC, 2015; Henry & Powell, 2018).

In this article, we focus on digital violence against women protesters. We rely on the conception of violence against women in politics as a distinctive phenomenon from violence against women in general. While the objective of the first concept is to disqualify women (politicians, human rights defenders and activists) as political actors (M. L. Krook & Sanín, 2020), the second is meant to sustain and reinforce women's subordination (Bardall et al., 2020). The literature on violence against women in politics has focused on women politicians to date; we thus claim that there is a research gap about the ways in which women human right defenders and activists are affectively disciplined through digital violence—for in fact mobilizing their own affects as a way to prompt new political repertories in collective action. In this article, we approach digital violence—not as just another type of violence, but rather we understand internet as a social space (Proctor, 2020) where violence is enmeshed into the digital realm.

The literature on violence against women in politics states that misogynistic comments impose a division between 'correct' and 'incorrect' ways to behave and is directed at women as a way to punish them for violating traditional gender roles and stereotypes (Manne, 2017). For instance, by reinforcing the idea that women's place is the kitchen (Jane, 2014), meaning that women should remain 'docile,' because, traditionally, women are seen as being emotional and not rational—but also needing to keep that affect at home on the fainting couch, so to speak—any show of affect in public both plays into the stereotype and simultaneously transgresses it. This transgression in turn invites corrective measures to re-reinforce the stereotype, that is, a form of cultural violence that constructs a morality, one that tends to carry more implications for women than it does for men in patriarchal societies (Al-Rawi, Chun, & Amer, 2021). This means that although men may also be subject to affective discipline, the implications for women are different. These kinds of comments are focused on women's bodies—specifically debasement of a woman's 'looks' or threat of physical violence—or gender scripts undermining women's competence in the political sphere (M. L. Krook & Sanín, 2020). Moreover, misogynistic comments on social media result in symbolic aggressions (M. L. Krook & Sanín, 2020; Savigny, 2020). The violence is expressed in abusive language, implicit irony, and sarcasm, explicit derogatory commentaries or verbal abuse (Fuchs & Schäfer, 2020). Although male activists may also experience disciplinary actions in the wake of their protests, these mechanisms are directed toward the men's actions *and* not based in gender roles or bodily images (Citron, 2014). Digital violence against protesters altogether inflicts a violation of their political rights (such as the right of freedom of expression, the right of protest) (M. Krook, 2020). These practices have further implications—dangerously stigmatizing and stifling activists—and thus open further possibilities for the state to criminalize such actions and for society as a whole to repress dissent (Amnistía Internacional, 2021).

Social media has been thoroughly analyzed as an affective social space where publics can be mobilized and connected through *feelings* (Hiilis, Paasonen, & Petit, 2019; Papacharissi, 2016). While social movements theory has focused on the emancipatory potential of affect (Castells, 2015), feelings are a site of both discipline and resistance (Bargetz, 2015; Di Gregorio & Merolli, 2016; Reckwitz, 2016). Affect theory has discussed the dichotomies that exist between the celebration and critique of affects and the opposition between rationality and affects (Kahl et al., 2019). Moreover, feminist contributions to affective politics literature have also argued that the relation of certain affects to categories such as gender, race, and class—and thereby their (d)evaluation—tend to confine women to certain affective regimes of oppression that play rationality off against emotionality (Bargetz, 2015; Penz, Sauer, Penz, & Sauer, 2020). It also disputes the idea that some societies are more affective than others, for example non-Western societies (Hynnä et al., 2019; Kahl et al., 2019).

Drawing on the literature of violence against women in politics and affective politics, our contribution here follows three lines of argument: First, we present evidence of the attempts to discipline activists and human rights defenders through digital violence, and in doing so the article seeks to put to rest rational and affect binarisms. Secondly, since we base our evidence on feminist protests in Mexico City and the affective discipline, we also seek to contest the idea that women generally are more inclined toward affectivity. Affective regimes of governance are efficacious as part of the practices that sustain violent practices, particularly in the aftermath of large feminist mobilizations. Finally, this article contributes to the literature on affective feminist politics by analyzing performances and interventions at historical monuments *guided by rage* as a strategy to hold the state accountable for the situation of impunity prevailing in the country.

3. THE AFFECTIVITY OF GENDERED VIOLENCE

A context of structural violence prevails in Mexico (Franco, 2013; Rodríguez, 2009). While it is true that violence is generalized for both men and women, it should be noted that gender violence is not related to drug trafficking, which is the main cause of violence in general and is perpetrated by men. Feminicides are, in turn, the extreme case of gender violence that implicates both the state (direct and indirectly) and individual perpetrators (Fregoso & Bejarano, 2010; Lagarde, 2008). This type of violence is rooted in gender inequalities and misogyny because it is expressed in the killing of women just because they are women. In spite of the increasing trend of feminicides, there are still several difficulties in classifying the murders of women as feminicides, so that some estimates indicate that there could be as many as 20 a day (Linares, 2021). Moreover, not only is violence a problem but also impunity, since 94.8% of all crimes—including gender-based violence—go unpunished (Linares, 2021), because many victims have serious obstacles to accessing formal justice. Faced with this situation, women articulate their resistance via interventions in public spaces—the internet being one of those spaces—showing rage, fed-up-ness against the violence and solidarity with other women. August 2019 was a historic moment for feminist mobilizations in Mexico. First in the protests under the hashtag #NoNosCuidanNosViolan ("They don't take care of me; they rape me") and then the following Glitter Protest. In the next subsections, we will analyze the feminists protests and the affective repertoires they mobilized.

3.1 The #NoNosCuidanNosViolan protest of August 12th, 2019

This protest followed the two abovementioned rape cases of minors at the hands of police officers in Mexico City (Jímenez, 2019). The protesters' anger was ignited not merely by the act of violence perpetrated by police officers. A series of irregularities occurred when one of the minors went to file a complaint, namely, the minor's identity was exposed by none other than the authorities themselves (Ruíz, 2019). In addition, the authorities alleged that the minor's statement presented contradictions. These types of practices, like leaking personal data in an effort to discredit or invite threats, are common ways for women to get blamed in a double victimization and for police offenders to evade responsibility (Arjona, 2019). The leaks resulted in the minor dropping her legal claim (Pradilla, 2019). The irregularities continued, such as the fact that the doctor did not follow rape case protocol in examining the minor for three whole days after the rape—allowing evidence to disappear. There were also contradictions between the statements of the police chief that the allegedly guilty police officers were still working, and the mayor, who stated that they had already been suspended (Ruíz, 2019). Only three days after this rape, a second case became known of another minor who was raped by an on-duty policeman inside the Museo Archivo de la Fotografía in Mexico City. Claudia Sheinbaum, the mayor of Mexico City, was cautious in her response, stating that a proper investigation would be carried out. In response, various feminist collectives called anonymously for a first demonstration outside the police station in Mexico City on August 12th, 2019.

The protest's slogan—#NoNosCuidanNosViolan—can be read as a statement implying that police officers not only do not observe their duty to provide protection, but instead they themselves commit sexual violence. The protest began at the Secretaría de Seguridad Pública and ended at the Procuraduría General de Justicia, both of the main judicial institutions in the city. The call to protest in social media was simple: the hashtag, the date and place, and the plea that only women attend. Some women wore black, some wore only miniskirts and bras. Some were carrying banners showing a pig's head, while still others protested performatively by dressing up as police officers with a sign that read "Police Rapist." Others painted blood stains and graffiti outside on the stairs at the entrance of the institution. When the head of the Secretaria de la Seguridad Pública was being interviewed by the press, women threw pink glitter at him. They also broke the glass door of the Procuraduría General de Justicia to demand due diligence in the investigations as well as a stop to the revictimization through leaking victims' personal information.

Mayor Sheinbaum—herself a woman—issued a press release that same day. She stressed that fighting violence against women is part of the government's agenda. At the same time, she called the protests a provocation and said that she would not fall into it. The outrage at Sheinbaum's statement resulted in a rapid, spontaneous, and decentralized response from feminist activists. Immediately, there was a call for a new protest in various Mexican cities for Friday night, August 16, 2019, just five days after the "provocation" protest. As if by magic, glitter was present almost everywhere: Photos with glowing pink glitter were sent from smartphone to smartphone, and feminist memes were created parodying the idea of glitter as an extremely dangerous provocation based on the incident with the secretary. For example, one meme shows a soldier presenting 14 tons of seized contraband—not of drugs, but glitter (Figure 1). The call to protests in over 30 cities in Mexico said bring pink glitter. Thus, glitter became an extremely important symbol of feminist resistance in Mexico.

The group Resistance Femme shared the event via Facebook under the hashtag #NoNosCuidanNosViolan, accompanied by the demand "We want justice!" On the morning prior to the protest various collectives published a statement addressed to both Mayor Sheinbaum and the Secretary of Municipal Security. In the text, they denounced the government's inability to "identify and punish those who violate women's human rights" and declared that "our protests arise because it is the State itself, through its police and military forces, who perpetrates the crimes of sexual abuse, protects the offenders, silences the victims and humiliates them" (Femme Resistencia, 2019).

Figure 1: Glitter meme on Twitter.

Source: Redón, P. (2019) "– Already seized 14 tons, boss. – Of drugs? – No, of pink glitter."

3.2 Fieldnotes from the Glitter Protest of August 16, 2019: "We are bad, we can be worse"

On the day of this protest, we met at the office of the feminist collective Luchadoras. The office was calm and welcoming. Feminist posters, flyers, and symbols decorated the white painted walls of the room where they had also produced some of the content for their website and social media. Luchadoras made a homemade version of—non-polluting—glitter (sugar and crushed pink eye shadow). Together we walked to the place where the protest would start. We walked until the Insurgentes Avenue, a big street that goes in a circle, a roundabout with various metrobus stations. In the middle, there is a square with the entrances to the metro station. When we arrived, the square was already full of women and journalists. It was impossible to understand a word of what was being shouted through a megaphone. Walking around, the pink glitter was present everywhere, girls were passing around big plastic bags full of it. Purple smoke ascended into the air. In general, it was a good vibe, some women were chanting, but in general it felt like the calm before a storm. The phrase "Demanding justice is not a provocation" was written in a circle of flames on the ground (see Figure 2). In addition, a hooded woman dressed in black with an aerosol can in her hand shouted loudly in the direction of the press representatives, "This protest will be a spectacle!" and thus set the atmosphere of the night.

The black-clad and -masked women of the so-called "autonomous black block" were relatively few. Various feminist movements, groups, and collectives were present. The majority of the women seemed young, schoolgirls or young students, but also other generations came out, from small children to elderly women. Some attended together, like mothers and daughters. Different groups prepared performances.

A member of the feminist collective Luchadoras portrayed the atmosphere of that afternoon in the following way: "the mood was very heated and what was planned was a sit-in, not a march; but with so much rage, it was not possible to have people standing in one place" (Luchadoras, personal communication, October 14th, 2019).

The people began to move; they filled the streets. The situation was a bit chaotic; nobody seemed to know where to go, but the need of the mass to move was clear. When we moved upstairs to the roundabout, women started walking around in circles. There was the building of the Secretaría de Seguridad Pública. The atmosphere was tense, becoming more and more aggressive. The chants in front of the building were getting louder; purple fireworks were fired against it. Black-masked women smashed the bus station's windows, which they had previously covered with graffiti. Most of these actions were supported with applause by the women protesters; only on rare occasions did they shout out for the masked women to stop. All the while, pink glitter floated in the air.

Figure 2: Demanding Justice is not a Provocation;

Figure 3: Protesters Walking with Purple Smoke | Figure 4: Only Female Police Officers Were Visibly Present During the Protest.

Figure 5: Broken Glass and Pink Glitter.

Source Figures 2–5: Mirjana Mitrović (2019), Exhibition "Pink. Glitter. Violence."

Figure 5, a picture of smashed glass and pink glitter, expresses the unique mixture of rage and celebration. The glitter was also used by the young women to "attack" men in general—not just the head of the Secretaria de la Seguridad Pública, as during the march of August 12th. This tactic was also used to push out of the protest potentially supportive men, who tried to enter, because men had expressly not been invited.

After nearly all protesters had left Insurgentes Avenue and moved on to the Angel de la Independencia, a historical monument, the press documented the damage to the metrobus station. On their way, the protesters passed a police station. Only then, when glass was broken and fires were set at this police station, did the fire department intervene. Before that, only female police officers had been present during the protest (Figure 4), and they seemed to have the order not intervene whatever happened. They just stepped back and observed. It is not common in Mexico to just have female police officers at protests, but this was a protest against sexual violence executed by male police officers. It can be read as an acknowledgment by the authorities that something was wrong. Some protesters, however, saw it as an attempt to control the optics. And they saw it going hand in hand with a second tactic used by the city government: erasure. Already the next day, all broken glass had been swept up and replaced. New glass panes and advertising signs were placed in bus stations. The graffiti had been removed as best and as quickly as possible. This cleanup practice was surprisingly fast in the context of Mexico City. It was interpreted as an attempt to render the protest invisible.

The tactic of cleaning up the broken glass and glitter as a symbol of rage did not work at the historical monuments, where the protesters arrived later that night. They graffitied all over the pedestal of the Angel de la Independencia and the Hemiciclo a Juárez. This can be understood as tactic of "overwriting," not erasing the powerful symbols but attacking and using them for their political claims. After the interventions at the historical monuments, the collective "Restauradoras con Glitter" was formed. Its purpose was to demand that the graffiti should not be removed until the safety of women in Mexico was guaranteed (Restauradoras con Gliter, 2019). In a statement, the collective alluded to graffiti as an aesthetic practice of collective memory to subvert the hegemonic meaning of historical monuments linked to male memory, respect, union, and progress. In the same document, the collective demanded an end to the prevailing impunity for gender violence, through the implementation of public policies with a gender perspective designed in conjunction with civil society, with the mobilization of the hashtag #MujeresNoParedes (women not walls). The collective recognized the aesthetic, historical, and social values of the monuments; however, they pointed out that these values cannot take precedence over the most important value, which is the life of women in full exercise of their human rights. At the end, they called on society to "look, read, reflect, and empathize with the terrible situation of violence against women, remembering that heritage can be restored, violated women will never be the same, while murdered women never return home" (Restauradoras con Gliter, 2019).

4. MEDIA RESPONSES, DIGITAL VIOLENCE, AND BODILY REACTIONS

Although the deadly gender violence in Mexico did garner attention after the protests, public opinion mostly focused on the women's rage. In the wake of most protest, there is usually an initial corrective attitude that circulates in response, but this is different than environmentalists being chastised for occupying treetops and disabling machinery or even black-block anarchists being condemned for burning private cars. The wave of threatening responses—not merely calling for behavior correction but rather physical and sexual violence—was arguably unlike anything faced by other groups. In addition to the usual gender-based recriminations of the newspapers, women who protest face threats of rape and murder online.

As noted by a member of Luchadoras (personal communication, October 14, 2019), after the protest there was a massive wave of hate against feminist activists. This collective alone received 300 comments in just two days following the protest of August 16, 2019 as a result of coordinated actions. The collective received disciplinary and corrective threats in the form of images of women's bodies cut into pieces. This provoked a series of affectations in the protesters' bodies: fear, nervousness, desire to vomit, intimidation, and crying (Luchadoras, personal communication, October 14, 2019) . Luchadoras was not the only target. Several other activists had also experienced digital violence as a form of correction and intimidation, as well as to instill fear to prevent future mobilization actions (Sanín, 2020). The Mesoamerican Initiative of Women Human Rights Defenders issued a statement in which it spoke out against the defamation and criminalization campaign, alluding to the legitimate right to protest and arguing that these types of practices only contributed to continue normalizing and justifying the gendered violence that prevails in Mexico (IM-Defensoras, 2019).

However, press reports and social media discussions focused in the days that followed on the graffiti on historical monuments and the broken glass of the bus station in the days that followed, paying little attention to the women's demands. The predominantly young women, with bags full of pink glitter in their hands, shattered any societal expectations of how they should protest. To one big misunderstanding about what is violence—smashing things or killing women—some feminist protesters might have responded: 'As long as you talk more about destruction of objects instead of femicides, we will continue to intervene in public space.' It can be said that they held true to this statement, as this repertoire of protest now permeates feminist civic actions in Latin America.

Subsequent feminist demonstrations on November 25, 2019 and March 8, 2020 and 2021 in Mexico replicated the practice of making fire circles in public spaces. The strategy of "aesthetically intervening," not only at historical monuments but also outside of the Government Palace in downtown Mexico City, by painting the door red with stains simulating blood on the walls, was repeated over and over. In such protests, female protesters evoked the image of the 'good girl' who likes pink glitter and subverted it by mixing glitter with broken glass on the asphalt or using spray-paint. The tactic of overwriting was widely used by protesters at this monument, as well as at the Hemiciclo a Juárez, a historical monument that the current government has appropriated as a symbol of its political project of transformation. The monuments were painted with feminist symbols and slogans blaming the state, which were then turned into hashtags, becoming themselves symbols of resistance. By smashing the glass, painting feminist graffiti on the walls and the streets, and above all by throwing pink glitter, they change the aesthetics of public space, often a space of fear for them. Aesthetically and practically they turn it into their space and reclaim it as a feminist space, at least for a moment.

5. DIGITAL VIOLENCE AS AFFECTIVE DISCIPLINING

The social networks and major newspapers discredited the aesthetic practices of graffiti at historical monuments and the damage to the bus and the police stations by claiming that it was irrational to ask for the cessation of violence with more violence. DataPopMx (2019), a social data analysis organization, found that most media outlets made on average 51 daily comments about the graffiti on the Angel of Independence and described it as violent, while only 5.6% referred to the main cause of the protest, which was the more serious act of violence—physical, sexual violence by police officers against women. In social networks, the corrective hashtag #NotLikeThatLadies began to trend on Twitter just two hours after the protest had started. From August 16–31, 2019, 2172 posts appeared with this hashtag. The literature on violence against women in politics explains this phenomena, calling it "cultural violence," which employs a double standard by tolerating the sexual violence of police against two minors while decrying the women protesters' vandalism as violence (M. L. Krook & Sanín, 2020). We analyze here the hashtag #NotLikeThatLadies as a site of affective politics (Bonilla & Rosa, 2015; Papacharissi, 2016) where hegemonic constructions about gender roles, in this case shaping public opinion, were mobilized. Out of our content analysis of the tweets, we were able to identify four main categories of the digital violence against protesters: 1) affects that the public opinion evoked toward feminists after the protest, such as shame and hate; 2) affects vis-à-vis rationality; 3) expectations for "femininity" in protests; and 4) models and ways in which women "should" protest.

5.1 Affects mobilized after the protest

In the analysis of the tweets, we could identify a pattern in which users evoked affects, such as shame, pity, and hate, as a way to construct shared ways of feeling about the feminist protests, thereby shaping public perception against the protest (Petersen, 2011). The following tweets are examples of that:

#NotLikeThatLadies I get the impression that what they really generate with their protests and destruction is that we hate all these bitches.

It is serious #NotLikeThatLadies who are setting such a deplorable, sad, pitiful, ignorant, low intelligence example. While laws are not enforced and there is insecurity in what head fits that this would produce a change.

The first tweet mobilizes hate in a misogynistic way of referring to protesters as bitches. The literature on violence against women in politics states that the use of denigrating words such as "bitch" has the objective of silencing women, reflecting the idea that women should be seen and not heard, and is thus a way of rendering women's voices inaudible (Nadim & Fladmoe, 2021; Savigny, 2020). The second tweet evokes the pity and shame these women 'should feel' by imposing a moral standard between the correct and the incorrect or out-and-out good and bad ways of protesting (Manne, 2017). It also implies that women should be exemplary in protesting; however, because they chose the bad ways, the protest would thus have no impact in producing political change. The idea that women should be exemplary also resembles what is discussed in the literature regarding related expectations according to gender (Sanín, 2020). Both tweets give evidence that affects are mobilized to shame women for the ways they protest, creating at the same time an hostile affective environment in platforms (Di Gregorio & Merolli, 2016). These misogynistic comments can also be understood as a means to discipline women who had entered into the public sphere and a warning to other women to stay away from protesting like that, *or else* face similar consequences (M. Krook, 2020; Wagner, 2020).

5.2 Affects vis-à-vis rationality

Other ways of denigrating women presented in the #NotLikeThatLadies posts established a division between 'smart' versus 'pointless' protest, as evidenced by these tweets:

| #NotLikeThatLadies, it is regrettable strategy of female primates |
| One must have very, very little gray matter in the brain to defend the actions of feminist troglodytes, #NotLikeThatLadies, shit is what they've got in there. |
| I do not know if it is right or wrong, if it is the wrong way or the perfect symbol of enough is enough, I just hope this does not lead to more violence. I know it's about progress and not staying in resentment #NotLikeThatWomen, #YesLikeThisWomen #TheyDoRepresentMe #TheyDoNotRepresentMe |

These tweets delegitimize the ways in which the women protested because it did not correspond with the cultural expectations of how a feminist social mobilization 'should' be done. The misogynistic comments stating that women have very little gray matter or even accusing them of having 'shit for brains' are ways of disqualifying women for showing rage during the protests. This can be explained by the division between rational and affective politics and traditionally relating 'the rational' with male models and 'the emotional' with women, as in 'they are too emotional' (Kahl et al., 2019; Liljeström, 2015). According to the literature on women in politics, these attacks toward protesters can be traced back to the women having challenged traditional gender stereotypes (M. L. Krook & Sanín, 2020).

The last tweet in particular reflects the usual antagonism between progress and resentment with the assumption that women are resentful. The tweet implies that there cannot be progress when women have these affects. Likewise, the tweet alludes to the binarism of positive and negative affects (Kahl et al., 2019), whereby resentment, besides being negative, does not allow societies to progress. It highlights in particular the linear and rational idea of progress implied by the division between affections and rationality (Latour, 1993). Moreover, the tweet is also inscribed in the binarisms that reinforce the idea that certain groups of societies, in this case women and non-Westerners, are more affective than others (Hynnä, Lehto, & Paasonen, 2019).

Further tweets along the same lines condemned the affect of rage in public spaces by pointing out "that they [the tweeter] have also had family members disappeared or murdered but they do not vent their anger in the public arena." Another tweet claimed that "women caused hatred toward the movement by showing irrationality, calling for intelligent women to demonstrate with class." All these tweets have in common the practices of affective disciplining (Reckwitz, 2016) that, on the one hand, disapproved of the womanly ways of the protesters and, on the other, command women that they should protest in a certain way and above all what affects they are allowed to show in public. This is basically the meaning of the hashtag #NotLikeThatLadies.

5.3 Expectations of femininity in protests

Cultural violence literature has stated that the construction around femininity operates as an form of social control and discipline (Savigny, 2020). In the #NotLikeThatLadies tweets, there were different ways in which users rendered visible their expectations of femininity for the protesters. The following tweets show examples of constructions of femininity:

| An authentic woman is one who does not lose her values, not feminazi women. |
| It is shameful that they are women. My gender should show intelligence and class. This denigrates my gender there are ways to demand our rights even if they are not women. |

The first tweet reveals what users relate with femininity, for example "values," and then uses the word "feminazi" as a way to delegitimize the feminist protests by comparing them with an authoritarian fascist regime that uses extreme practices of violence. The second tweet evokes shame toward women protesters. It clearly shows that women should protest with "intelligence and class" to demand rights. These tweets show cultural constructions based on gender scripts of how women are expected to behave (Sanín, 2020). These expectations are the root of cultural sexism and explain why women who transgress these cultural norms of femininity in the framework of protests are punished, shamed, and made invisible (Savigny, 2020).

5.4 Models and ways in which women should protests

Several other tweets the disqualify the actions of women protesters by offering male personalities as role models:

By the way, in the civil protests against corrupt judges: zero violence, no mess, not one graffiti, flagging the cause in a rational way #NotLikeThatLadies
#NotLikeThatWomen #TheyDon'tRepresentMe #NotLikeThat Luther King represented an entire race that was enslaved for centuries, men, women, and children.... He only began his memorable speech by saying "I have a dream." Meme translation: Next time a feminist says that her violent attitude is to make herself heard, introduce her to Luther King. He defended a race without harming anyone.

Figure 6: Martin Luther King, Jr. meme

Source: Elias, R. (2019). #ASiNoMujeres #EllasNoMeRepresentan #AsiNo

The two tweets cited reveal the idea of rationality as another of the expectations for how feminists should protest. In the first, rationality is related to the lack of graffiti left behind by a separate protest against corruption. The second tweet, in addition to the post, includes a meme that was widely circulated after the protest (Figure 6). The meme puts Martin Luther King Jr. forward as a model of protest, a personality with historical transcendence who, in a civilized way, begins his speech solemnly alluding to peace and yet who provokes a radical change. The photo highlights the fact that Luther King is dressed in a suit as a model of how women should raise their voices: well-dressed and through a speech that transcends history. The tweet gives evidence of what Penz and Sauer (2020) point out: Affective regimes are part of society's cognitive schemas. In addition, the tweet also accounts for the binarism that prevails in separating negative and positive affects (Kahl et al., 2019), whereby victory would then only be achieved through positive affects. Finally, the meme also provides gendered ideas of how to protest, placing men above women (Savigny, 2020) and thus resisting gender transformations in the political arena (M. L. Krook & Sanín, 2020). The provision of masculine ideals, in this case to protest, is also an expression of cultural sexism, because they reflect the stereotypes of men that are associated with political transformation of the public space—whereas women are relegated to the private sphere in such thinking (M. L. Krook, 2020).

6. CONCLUSIONS

This chapter has argued that renewed feminist agency as the intertwinement of affective and political practices in the protests transgressed the hegemonic aesthetic and political imaginary of how women 'should' protest and what kind of affects they are allowed to bring into public spaces. This renewed agency conflicted with cultural expectations of women protesting in a "rational and peaceful" way. We have shown that these expectations are based on gendered scripts (Sanín, 2020) that resulted in digital violence that had the objective to affectively discipline women in politics (Reckwitz, 2016). However, the intertwining of the mobilized aesthetic-affective and political practices aimed at contesting the hegemonic affective orders on two levels: first, the domination exercised by men over women in the form of violence; the second, the aesthetic orders of how women 'should' protest and the affections they 'may' show in public.

The slogan "We are bad, we can be worse" showcases the affective politics of rage. The second part of the sentence, "we can be worse," can be read as a threat in the political arena. This slogan expresses the fact that women's fear has become politicized and turned into rage. Women did not isolate themselves in their homes with their affections to cry over the precarious security situation, but rather they transformed anger itself into new repertories for action. This provokes fear in the government, the perpetrators (perhaps even in those women opposed to the protests), because such a basic social affection has become politicized. The "critics" try to reestablish the old gendered collective affective orders by devaluing this anger and by scolding the women like little girls. But the affective repertoires show that the 'little girls' can be also bad, because they do not just throw pink glitter. Their best weapon is anger, which subverts the affections by which they have been ruled (Penz & Sauer, 2020). Finally, the images of mean, angry activists intervening in monuments and breaking glass render visible the affective disputes on the internet. They show that even though new images of affected and affecting women were mobilized in the public arena, affective disciplining practices continue (Reckwitz, 2016). Paradoxically but predictability, these protest practices faced the corrective ways of disciplining protesters' affects as a response, by trying to impose on the women how they 'had to protest'—also by providing male role models for how to do so.

What was thought in 2019 to be just a rabid women's protest that would quickly fade into history when the monuments were cleaned up has instead become entrenched as part of the political repertoire of affective feminist politics. These actions have been repeated in subsequent feminist protests, such as the 8M of 2020 and 2021, to such an extent that the fear-based government surrounded the palace and historical monuments with protective fences, in addition to deploying hundreds of police officers. The implications, however, of the digital violence to protesters is that the criminalization, stigmatization, and the violation of their political rights and ultimately exclusion from the political arena. The research suggests also that further work is needed to investigate the life implications for women and the political trajectories of protesters.

References

Al-Rawi, A., Chun, W. H. K., & Amer, S. (2021). Vocal, visible and vulnerable: female politicians at the intersection of Islamophobia, sexism and liberal multiculturalism. *Feminist Media Studies*, 1–18, online first.

Amnistía Internacional. (2021). *México: La era de las mujeres: Estigma y violencia contra mujeres que protestan*. https://amnistia.org.mx/contenido/wp-content/uploads/2021/03/VF-Mexico-La-Era-de-las-Mujeres-FINAL.pdf

APC. (2015). *Technology-related violence against women. A briefing paper*. https://www.apc.org/sites/default/files/HRC 29 VAW a briefing paper_FINAL_June 2015.pdf

Arjona, J. C. (2019). *Informe sobre las violencias de género en la procuración de justicia en la Ciudad de México*. https://cdhcm.org.mx/wp-content/uploads/2019/09/Informe_violencia_de_genero.pdf

Baer, H. (2016). Redoing feminism: Digital activism, body politics, and neoliberalism. *Feminist Media Studies*, 16(1), 17–34.

Bardall, G., Bjarnegård, E., & Piscopo, J. M. (2020). How is Political Violence Gendered? Disentangling Motives, Forms, and Impacts. *Political Studies*, 68(4), 916–935.

Bargetz, B. (2015). The Distribution of Emotions: Affective Politics of Emancipation. *Hypatia*, 30(3), 580–596.

Bonilla, Y., & Rosa, J. (2015). #Ferguson: Digital protest, hashtag ethnography, and the racial politics of social media in the United States. *American Ethnologist*, 42(1), 4–17.

Castells, M. (2015). *Networks of Outrage and Hope: Social Movements in the Internet*. Polity Press.

Citron, D. K. (2014). *Hate Crimes in Cyberspace*. Cambridge: Harvard University Press.

DataPopMx. (2019). (August, 20, 2019). En promedio, se publicaron 7.6 notas diarias sobre la violación… y 51 sobre el Ángel de la Independencia. Retrieved 21 January 2021, from https://twitter.com/DataPopMX/status/1163718134974570501

Dérbez, F. (2019). Yo no sé si está bien o mal, si no son los modos o es el símbolo perfecto del ya basta, sólo espero que esto no depare en más violencia. Sé trata de progresar y no quedarse en el resentimiento. #ASiNoMujeres #AsíSíMujeres #EllasSiMeRepresentan #EllasNoMeR. 21 February 2021, from https://twitter.com/ultra_violento/status/1163175228085800961

Di Gregorio, M., & Merolli, J. L. (2016). Introduction: affective citizenship and the politics of identity, control, resistance. *Citizenship Studies*, 20(8), 933–942.

Femme Resistencia. (2019). Esclarecimiento de abusos por parte del Sistema Judicial. Cárcel para violentadores sexuales. Décreato de alerta de género para la Ciudad de México. Facebook. Retrieved 8 March 2021, from https://www.facebook.com/ResistenciaFemme/photos/888291611547437

Franco, J. (2013). *Cruel Modernity*. Durham & London: Duke University Press.

Fregoso, R.-L., & Bejarano, C. (2010). *Terrorizing Women: Feminicide in the Americas*. Durham & London: Duke University Press.

Fuchs, T., & SchÄfer, F. (2020). Normalizing misogyny: hate speech and verbal abuse of female politicians on Japanese Twitter. *Japan Forum*, 33(4), 553–579.

Henry, N., & Powell, A. (2018). Technology-Facilitated Sexual Violence: A Literature Review of Empirical Research. *Trauma, Violence, & Abuse*, 19(2), 195–208.

Hernández, R., Fernández, C., & Baptista Lucio, P. (2010). *Metodología de la investigación* (5th ed.). México: Mcgraw-Hill.

Hiilis, K., Paasonen, S., & Petit, M. (2019). *Networked Affect*. Cambridge, London: The MIT Press.

Hynnä, K., Lehto, M., & Paasonen, S. (2019). Affective Body Politics of Social Media. *Social Media and Society*, 5(4), 1–5.

IM-Defensoras. (2019). MÉXICO / Campaña de difamación y criminalización contra defensoras feministas. Retrieved 21 January 2021, from https://www.facebook.com/IMDefensoras/posts/2550376701710012

Jane, E. A. (2014). Back to the kitchen, cunt: Speaking the unspeakable about online misogyny. *Continuum*, 28(4), 558–570.

Jane, E. A. (2016). Online misogyny and feminist digilantism. *Continuum*, 30(3), 284–297.

Jímenez, G. (2019, August 6). Policías someten y violan a menor en Azcapotzalco. *Excelsior*. https://www.excelsior.com.mx/comunidad/policias-someten-y-viola n-a-menor-en-azcapotzalco/1328672

Kahl, A., Lehmann, H., Lüthjohann, M., Oberkrome, F., Roth, H., Scheidecker, G., ... Bens, J. (2019). *The Politics of Affective Societies*. (A. Kahl, H. Lehmann, M. Lüthjohann, F. Oberkrome, H. Roth, G. Scheidecker, ... T. John,Eds.). Bielefeld: transcript Verlag. Retrieved from https://doi.org/10.14361/9783839447628-fm

Krook, M. (2020). *Violence Against Women in Politics*. New York: Oxford University Press.

Krook, M. L. (2020). Violence Against Women in Politics. In M. Sawer, F. Jenkins, & K. Downing (Eds.), *How Gender Can Transform the Social Sciences* (pp. 57–64). Cham: Palgrave Macmillan.

Krook, M. L., & Sanín, R. J. (2020). The Cost of Doing Politics? Analyzing Violence and Harassment against Female Politicians. *Perspectives on Politics*, 18(3), 740–755.

Lagarde, M. (2008). Antropología, Feminismo y Política: Violencia Feminicida y Derechos Humanos de las Mujeres. In M. Bullen & M. C. Díez (Eds.), *XI Congreso de Antropología: retos Teóricos y Nuevas Prácticas* (pp. 209–240). Donostia: Ankulegi Antropologia Elkartea.

Latour, B. (1993). *We Have Never Been Modern*. Cambridge: Harvard University Press.

Liljeström, M. (2015). Affect. In L. Disch & M. Hawkesworth (Eds.), *The Oxford Handbook of Feminist Theory* (Vol. 1). New York: Oxford University Press.

Linares, A. (2021, October 11). Violent crimes rise in Mexico; 94.8% go unpunished. *Noticias Telemundo*. Mexico City. Retrieved from https://www.nbcnews.com/new s/latino/violent-crimes-rise-mexico-948-go-unpunished-rcna2846

Luchadoras. (2020). Somos una colectiva feminista que habita el espacio público digital y físico. Retrieved 4 September 2020, from https://luchadoras.mx/nosotras

Manne, K. (2017). *Down girl: The logic of misogyny. Down Girl: The Logic of Misogyny*. New York: Oxford University Press.

Murthy, D. (2011). Emergent Digital Ethnographic Methods for Social Research. In H.-B. Sharlene (Ed.), *Handbook of Emergent Technologies in Social Research* (pp. 158–179). New York: Oxford University Press.

Nadim, M., & Fladmoe, A. (2021). Silencing Women? Gender and Online Harassment. *Social Science Computer Review*, 39(2), 245–258.

Papacharissi, Z. (2016). Affective publics and structures of storytelling: sentiment, events and mediality. *Information Communication and Society*, 19(3), 307–324.

Penz, O., & Sauer, B. (2020). *Governing Affects*. London: Routledge.

Petersen, J. (2011). *Murder, the media, and the politics of public feelings: remembering Matthew Shepard and James Byrd Jr.* Bloomington: Indiana University Press.

Pink, S. (2009). *Doing Sensory Ethnography.* London: SAGE Publications, Inc.

Powell, A., & Henry, N. (2017). Sexual Violence: A Feminist Criminological Analysis. In A. Powell & N. Henry (Eds.), *Sexual Violence in a Digital Age* (pp. 23–47). London: Palgrave Macmillan UK.

Pradilla, A. (2019, August). Rabia feminista contra las violaciones en Ciudad de México. *Público.* Retrieved from https://www.publico.es/internacional/violencia-machista-rabia-feminista-violaciones-ciudad-mexico.html

Proctor, D. (2020). The Social Production of Internet Space: Affordance, Programming, and Virtuality. *Communication Theory,* 31(4), 593–612.

Reckwitz, A. (2016). How the senses organise the social. In M. Jonas & B. Littig (Eds.), *Praxeological Political Analysis* (pp. 68–78). London: Routledge.

Restauradoras con Gliter. (2019). Comunicado (documento adjunto). Retrieved 21 January 2021, from https://www.facebook.com/restauradoras.glitterMX/photos/100827411293004.

Redón, P. [@pagusredon] (2019, August 13) "– Already seized 14 tons, boss. – Of drugs? – No, of pink glitter." [Tweet]. Twitter. https://twitter.com/pagusrendon/status/1161290803794386945

Rodríguez, I. (2009). *Liberalism and its limits. Crime and Terror in the Latin American Cultural Text.* Pittsburgh: University of Pittsburgh Press.

Ruíz, M. (2019, August). Once días de filtraciones sobre violencia sexual de la policía. *Pie de Página.* Retrieved from https://piedepagina.mx/once-dias-de-filtraciones-sobre-violencia-sexual-de-la-policia/

Elias, R. [@ruthy_em] (2019, August 19). #ASiNoMujeres #EllasNoMeRepresentan #AsiNo "Luther King representó..." [Tweet]. Twitter. https://twitter.com/ruthy_em/status/1163234793032704000

Sanín, J. R. (2020). Violence against women in politics: Latin America in an era of backlash. *Signs,* 45(2), 302–310.

Savigny, H. (2020). *Cultural Sexism – The politics of feminist rage in the #metoo era.* Bristol: Bristol University Press.

Souza, N. M. F. de. (2019). When the Body Speaks (to) the Political: Feminist Activism in Latin America and the Quest for Alternative Democratic Futures. *Contexto Internacional,* 41(1), 89–112.

Wagner, A. (2020). Tolerating the trolls? Gendered perceptions of online harassment of politicians in Canada. *Feminist Media Studies,* online first.

Performing Disruptions
A Bodily Encounter with Misogyny in Lifestyle Television

Rose Beermann

1. INTRODUCTION

In this chapter, I will trace my experience as author and performer of "Strip naked, talk naked," a performance I created in 2014 together with my collaborator Iva Sveshtarova. The performance is itself an intertwining of aesthetics and politics in response to the television show *Blachman*, which was broadcasted in 2013 by a Danish public TV channel. Due to its inflammatory nature, it ignited an international media response. Invented by the Danish jazz musician and X-Factor judge Thomas Blachman, the TV show is structured as follows: In a dark studio without spectators, two men are sitting on a sofa. They are fully clothed. In front of the two men steps a woman who removes her bathrobe and stands naked and fully illuminated in front of them. The men then discuss female beauty, male sexuality and cognate subjects. The camera moves back and forth; the exposed woman stays silent. The TV show's stated goal is to teach men to verbally express their sexuality. The premise is that women and men are no longer allowed to express themselves equally in polite society. In analysis of *Blachman*, I realized that the TV show is not only about representing a particular idea of gender but, in fact, about producing it with enormous intensity. At the same time, a specific heterosexual male subjectivity and a certain form of perception of women and their bodies are produced through this performance. Something in the performative structure of the TV show, however, seemed to effectively obscure the underlying power structures and deprive them of analysis. This very fact brought us reenact the TV show in the first place, aiming at a bodily response (1). With our bodies as a central means of expression, we wanted the audience to *feel* our critique. To do so, we chose *reenactment* as a method, but its main limitation proved to reproduce this gendered argument couched within a sensory order—which I will identify as belonging to *affective economies*—instead of disrupting it, as hoped; so, we turned to two further disruptive means with *micropolitical ruptures* and the concept of *underperformance* to get the audience squirming as much as we did ourselves.

The circumstance that *Blachman* was produced and broadcasted by a public TV channel points to the acceptability of such a misogynist idea of gender by a broad public. How do those images of men (and women) attract an audience? In the rehearsal process for "Strip naked, talk naked," we were looking for a resistant performance of femininity that might allow us to counter the male flow of speech. By understanding *Blachman* as a specific aesthetic practice of sexuality, the critique became about proposing subversive ways of sensory perception. We were searching for forms of sensuous address to re-negotiate the way how we are perceived as women standing naked and silent in front of two men. However, we came up against the limits of the idea of reenactment itself for establishing another bodily reality. Starting by a reenactment that could be read as such, we moved to the boundaries of the form itself as the performance progressed. The question of what I, as a performing artist, can do to counter prevailing forms of perception still occupies me today: How can a rather small-scale and clearly framed intervention like a performance make us experience the *sensing of collectives*?

Following the analysis of the sociologist Andreas Reckwitz that social orders are always sensual orders, I assume here that "sense regimes" operate on the level of bodies, affects and artifacts (2015; 2017; 2017a). This puts the body and the senses at the center of theory making. From my perspective as a performing artist, I wonder if this shift in perspective on the functioning of social orders requires a different form of writing, an embodied form of writing. Building on the work of ethnographer Dwight Conquergood as well as sociologists Norman K. Denzin and Laurel Richardson, I propose autoethnographic writing to reflect on my experience as author and performer of "Strip naked, talk naked." Autoethnography focuses on personal experiences to explore one's own practice, which makes it a promising way to present my case. As an embodied writing about an embodied practice, autoethnography allows me to approach academic writing from the perspective of my artistic practice, and to produce within the reader some of the sensations I hope to produce in my audiences.

To understand, how the sensory perception of a woman's body is done in *Blachman*, I will first analyze its performative structure with reference to the media scholar Gareth Palmer and his critical analysis of *lifestyle television*. Following on from this, I will report from the rehearsal process and the experience of performing the finished piece. I will outline the way we have related ourselves to the original material to identify forms of bodily critique we employed in the performance. Based on the artistic choices we made, I will discuss the potential of performance practice for (un-)doing sense regimes. Building on the work of performance theoreticians Bojana Kunst and Stefan Hölscher, I will explore the idea of micropolitical ruptures and the critical potential of a reenactment. Considering the limitations we have experienced in working with the form of reenactment, I will end by proposing the idea of *underperformance* by queer feminist philosopher Laurent Berlant as a way to perceive each other differently.

2. AUTOETHNOGRAPHY AS AN EMBODIED FORM OF WRITING

Recognizing how much personal experience influences a research process, autoethnography takes into account subjectivity, emotionality, and the researcher's influence on the research itself. This makes the body the first and foremost instrument of research, verbalizing physical perception, emotions, and the capacity for empathy are the base for writing an autoethnography. This approach was articulated by ethnographer Dwight Conquergood (2006/1991) and sociologist Norman K. Denzin, who developed the concept of "performance ethnography." This concept refers to the combination of academic writing and performance practice, often with the goal of communicating research findings through performance (1997, 2003, 2006). However, from my perspective as a performing artist, I am not interested in translating theoretical research findings on stage but bringing my experience creating performances into dialogue with academic writing.

Based on lived experience, autoethnography aims at resonance with the reader's experience, as sociologist Laurel Richardson vividly illustrated in "Fields of play: constructing an academic life" (1997). By including the process of writing in the writing itself, she involves the reader in the creation of her book. To do so, Richardson advocates for the aesthetic value of autoethnography, but not for a specific form (2000, p. 15). Thus, the method is about the search for another language, a way of storytelling that not only names and classifies the underlying experiences, but makes them tangible. This does not mean, however, that it is primarily a matter of autobiographical writing. Richardson suggests the following:

> [T]he central imaginary is the crystal which combines symmetry and substance with an infinite variety of shapes, substances, transmutations, multidimensionalities, and angles of approach. ... Crystallization provides us with a deepened, complex, thoroughly partial, understanding of the topic. (1994, p. 522)

Like the infinite number of shapes, dimensions, and angles of a crystal, different forms of knowledge can be related in autoethnographic writing. But even though a crystal can always look different and even change its shape, it always has a structure. Thinking through sensuous, embodied experience makes it possible to relate different forms of analysis and different genres of writing.

3. AFFECTIVE ECONOMIES IN LIFESTYLE TELEVISION

In the TV show's title sequence, Blachman claims his ambition to "positively recharge the women's view of men's view of women" to meet the circumstance that "the female body is craving words, a man's words" (transcript of the first episode, translation: Matilda Mester). Introducing himself as a "modern man, and therefore more of a woman than any woman ever had the ambition to be, unfortunately" that is not able to face this challenge on his own, Blachman continues by introducing his guest, a different male figure from public live in Denmark for each episode.

Following the media scholar Gareth Palmer (2008), I would identify the TV show as "lifestyle television," a genre which is centered around the neoliberal idea of the flexible self: Mediating the optimization of daily practices, lifestyle television is based on the phantasm that the self is a question of choice, strategically obscuring social, economic, and political dimensions. Furthermore, Palmer draws attention to lifestyle television's tendency to reproduce normative femininity. Questioning the social recognition of such reactionary positions, he identifies the co-existence of a distancing irony, an as-if in a supposedly playful setup, with the simultaneous re-affirmation of normative femininity as the very characteristic of lifestyle television.

Interestingly, all of Blachman's guests are either intellectuals or artists, and, in the conversations, they are asked to use their specific expertise to find a language for his proclaimed project. So, besides its misogynistic character, *Blachman* is deeply problematic in terms of class: A writer, a fashion designer, a visual artist, a songwriter, a rapper and a sexologist are introduced as experts to ensure "striving, discretion and good taste" (Palmer, 2008, p. 6) in expressing heterosexual male sexuality. Palmer points out the role of the expert in this very format as early as 2003, describing a development he will later call life-style television. Aiming at the transformation of selves, the role of these experts is to make this process as entertaining as possible. As with Blachman, their background is in the service industry, committed to consumer culture in their profession to shape the self. At the center of these operations is the body as the venue for the struggle for self-optimization (p. 175 ff.). Palmer conceptualizes the moment of broadcasting as "a shift from the panoptic to the synoptic" (p. 148), opening the possibility for the many to look at the few in how they are made subjects of normalization. As a hook for the TV show, Blachman states the impending loss of heterosexual male identity in a supposedly incomprehensible new living environment. To counter this state of emergency, he presents himself as an expert to establish a "re-naturalization" of gender relations. Instead of dealing with male bodies, perversely, women's bodies are subjected to discipline. Female subjects are silenced and objectified to restore a powerful, oppressive male subject in the synopticum of public television.

Regardless of views affirming or criticizing *Blachman*, discussions that took place with colleagues while developing our performative response to the TV show were characterized by a strange inaccessibility or inability to formulate a clear argument. Discussing the concept of "Strip naked, talk naked" with us, one male dramaturg insisted on his "right to arousal." Obviously, he felt backed into a corner by the mere fact that two women were planning to develop a performance about the TV show (he hadn't even seen a rehearsal yet). According to his impression, there was no space for heterosexual male sexuality in his social environment. Discussing *Blachman* with female friends, every one of them was outraged by the fact that a public TV channel produced and broadcasted a show which reaffirms such a narrow, problematic idea of gender. But in the discussion itself, the arguments seemed to be missing: The conversations were dominated by expressions of anger and frustration, and it was difficult to grasp why the TV show was enjoying such success at the present time.

Using the idea of mediality and the principle of premediation, formulated by the media scholar Richard Grusin, I assume here that media function by producing affective states and, in this way, influence future events (2010, p. 6 f.). In the conversations described, I became aware that representation and production of a certain gender image are deeply intertwined in *Blachman*. Packaged in an entertaining TV format, the underlying misogynistic attitude becomes even more threatening. The gesture of a supposed re-naturalization of the relationship between genders seems to effectively obscure the underlying power structures and deprive them of analysis. The way this TV format defies analysis forces me to acknowledge the power of such affective economies (Ahmed, 2004), shuddering with disgust. The concept of the queer-feminist philosopher Sara Ahmed describes the way, how particular feelings and values become "stuck" to specific notions. The emerging affective economies shape the affective response to particular statements, objects, and actions. In *Blachman*, the woman is constructed as the other by marking her behavior as the cause of feelings of inadequacy, frustration, and unfulfilled desire in heterosexual males and thereby mobilizing feelings of hatred towards women. A fantasy of a collective subjectivity of disadvantaged male heterosexuals is created, who are now collectively reclaiming their right to penetration. The intensity with which *Blachman* succeeds in generating such a fantasy can only be explained by the affective economies in which the TV show is embedded.

4. FEELING NAKED, OR: ARGUMENTS BEYOND WORDS

For the reenactment we wanted to create, the first step was to explore the affective economies of and around *Blachman* practically. Therefore, we started rehearsals with a precise reconstruction of the TV show on stage: Iva Sveshtarova and I analyzed

Blachman building upon our knowledge as choreographers, meticulously tracking every movement, every camera pan, every cut. The intimate atmosphere of the TV show seemed to be produced by close-ups, a handheld camera and slow camera pans of the women's bodies as well as the supposedly casual set-up of Blachman's studio. As in the TV show, the stage remained empty for the reconstruction, except for two side-by-side leather chairs on which our "Blachman" and his guest were placed. To recreate these approaches of the camera to the bodies, we experimented with different theatrical means to direct the gaze of the audience. Therefore, we set points in space for specific camera perspectives. To translate camera pans, we worked with small choreographies. We had performers intensify or weaken their actions to direct the attention of the audience to specific images. Later in the process, our lightening designer also worked to direct the spectator's gaze, recreating the extensive square studio light present in *Blachman* and subtly highlighting places on stage with additional spotlights. To perform cuts, we choreographed freezes to clearly end one camera view, pausing in new positions for a moment before resuming the action. We invited Sebastian König and Daniel Hinocho to perform Blachman and his guest. These performers joined the rehearsal process a little later. Together with our dramaturg Marcel Bugiel, we edited a script out of the six episodes, compiling the most striking dialogues between Blachman and his guests. The reconstruction of the TV show on stage went well and I developed a kind of perverse pleasure in the clever precision with which *Blachman* is constructed.

The central question in the rehearsal process, however, was how to make our audience *feel* our critique of *Blachman*. This became an almost insurmountable task because—and I can only speak for myself here—I literally felt naked, deprived of my expressive possibilities in view of the affect mobilizing machine, I perceived *Blachman* to be.

> Blachman (B): The woman isn't a threat, she is a wonderful counterpart. The woman becomes a threat if she can't take in the man, if she can't deliver her half of the deal. Without crossing the border. You are yourself, and I am myself. You take care of your business, I'll take care of mine. Give me a fucking moment of silence and just be a woman.

Staging this monologue in front of a live audience seemed to create a certain alienation. The reconstruction of *Blachman* on stage would disclose the TV show's mode of production but this was far from the statement we wanted to make. How to disrupt the situation without making the subject of our critique unrecognizable? How to open up spaces for subverting ways to be perceived? We experimented with dance styles, costumes, and props which we associated with a resistant performance of femininity: burlesque dances, living paintings, Duncan technique, dances with particular female body parts, bikinis, nipple pasties, nudes, fake plants, fruits, and many more practices and artifacts we found during our research in the depths of the internet. For a few days, we were even fantasizing about a spectacular showdown between men and women inspired by Western movies. Based on this scenic research, we developed several strategies to disrupt the performative structure of the TV show. I will elaborate these strategies in the following along a description of the finished performance.

We decided to start the performance with a reconstruction of the TV show but slowly moving out of the performative structure. From the beginning, we were breaking with the regime of precision and integrity that usually characterizes a reconstruction. We did not change our appearance to make the men's comments (quoted from the actual show) suit our bodies; so it happened that the two men were commenting on my supposedly short hair whereas I was wearing it long at that time, they did also comment on my tattoos even if there were none visible on my naked body. Whereas the two male performers were asked to stick to the filmic original, Iva Sveshtarova and I did not. These small disturbances point to the fact that the performance was not an affirmative reconstruction of a media event; instead, it was a reenactment created by two female artists.

After the two men entered the stage and sat down on two adjacent chairs, just like the actual show, I entered the stage in a black satin bathrobe. I stopped in the middle of the stage and—unlike the show—looked briefly towards the audience before opening my bathrobe and letting it slide over my shoulders onto the floor. I remember always hearing my heart beating with excitement at that moment, anxiously awaiting how the atmosphere would change with my act of undressing. Most evenings, my act was followed by a tense, fragile silence. I held this tension for a moment and then turned around to the two men who were positioned diagonally behind me and they began to speak.

> B: Such a fine, silent entrance. You could hear that wasn't a man. Like an insect.
> Guest (G): But also... They shouldn't do that... it's a sneaky walk, a tricky walk, where you think: Am I going to be taken by surprise now? Women should stop thinking they have to surprise... to do a good job.

I listened as this dialogue continued and observed the reactions of the audience. I also allowed myself to comment on the dialogue of the two men with a glance at the audience, as well as shooting them a look for their reactions to a certain extent, or by stepping out of my position in front of the chairs or letting go of a pose and performing a relaxing exercise. Reconstructing a close-up of the two men, they were positioned facing the audience, I left the stage for a short break in the meantime and came back when they had changed to the next camera setting. After a few changes of position, my collaborator entered to replace me. We smiled at each other—unlike the show—and I exited backstage while the two men continued talking.

> B: But just look at that ass... [...] what do you prefer?
> G: Ass-wise?
> B: The shape of a drop, baggy or what do you want?
> G: That is a nice ass.
> B: Just simply a nice ass? To the woman: Could you please turn around again?
> G: Legs and breasts are important, I think. They communicate really fast. And the way they move. To the woman: Could you move a little bit? Just walk back and forth.
> B: To the woman: May I see you from the side?
> G: I love asses. To the woman: Turn around, please!
> B: To the woman: May we see the pussy there, just for a moment?

Iva Sveshtarova responded to this request with an ironic smile and a suggested presentation gesture with her arms while turning to the two men. Shortly afterwards, she simply put on her bathrobe and left. Then, we entered stage together to perform a short dance. Obviously, we had departed from the show's format by now. Creating short dances to be performed in between was another strategy to disrupt the performative structure of the TV show. We took on the (passive) TV images of women that appeared in the conversation between the two men, with the idea of countering them with a (lively, dancing) bodily reality. For the transitions between the reconstruction and the short dances, we entered the stage again each time in the paradigmatic black bathrobe, took it off, performed our dance and put it on again to leave the stage. The two men remained sitting in their chairs, seemingly unaffected by what was going on. These short dances left traces on the stage and on our bodies, which remained visible in the further course of the performance.

For one of the dances, we had explored images of a "natural femininity." The dance began by rolling balls made of plastic leaves (the kind used as potted hedge miniatures for hotel décor or other representative architectures). These dark-green, slightly absurd artifacts remained on the stage like a plastic moonscape. Inspired by burlesque dances, we performed another dance where we shook our boobs in every way imaginable. We wore oversized, self-made nipple pasties and moved a little bit too resolutely (in my case) or too pleasingly (in my collaborator's case). The rest of the performance was spent with long colorful threads attached to my breasts that seemed to pop out of my nipples.

> B: That's also the complex and abstract nature of women nowadays, that they have both this feminine ambition... of being overly dressed up and at the same time have a traditional male career. If they could only be completely crazy! All the time. Then they could do whatever they want...
> G: Because then you feel more normal?
> B: No, then I'm entertained, then I'm not bored.
> G: So you just need to be entertained?

B: I need a show from when I get up till I go to bed, I need to ease the pain, call it what you like.

After approximately forty minutes, the two men dropped out of their performance as Blachman and his guest. They undressed silently and started commenting on the audience. Shortly afterwards, we entered to interrupt and ask them to leave the stage. After asking the audience for comments, we announced ourselves as the creators of the performance and outlined the concept of *Blachman*. The performance could have ended here, but we had the feeling that we had not escaped this entertainment machine yet. Interestingly, the majority of our test audience, whom we invited towards the end of the rehearsal process, hardly seemed to question the relationship of our short dances to the original material. Most of them expressed the desire for more intensity and stimulation: more feelings, more dances, more flesh, more sex. However, I did not want to comply with this request, because I had come to the conclusion during the rehearsal process: I could not escape the situation by exaggerating the TV images of women more and more. Where would this end up? In putting dildos rhythmically in my body to some fancy beat?

Because the time until the premiere was short, Iva Sveshtarova proposed to share loosely connected artifacts and related scenic ideas that we had gathered during the rehearsal process. I agreed since this did not seem to me at least to correspond to *Blachman*'s idea of gender. We named the artifacts and brought them in relation to our bodies, for example, we recreated scenes from renaissance paintings with the plastic plants, or my collaborator decorated my folded arms with fruits so that I turned into a living fruit basket. The performance ended after we had dressed in street clothes, cleaned the stage to leave it to our sound and light designer for a little duet of their skills. Avoiding a melodramatic logic that would demand a climax and a resulting resolution of what had gone before, we did what from today's perspective I would identify as underperformance, according to Lauren Berlant:

> Underperformativity, a mode of flat or flattened affect that shows up to perform its recession from melodramatic norms, foregrounds the obstacles to immediate reading, without negating the affective encounter with immediacy. (Berlant, 2015, p. 193)

By performing the unfinished scenic fragments pragmatically, one after the other without further contextualization, and then leaving the audience alone with the technical apparatus of the theater, the last part of the performance eluded a clear interpretation of the situation. Although this artistic decision caused much incomprehension, I still find it interesting today because it allowed us to escape the attributions as "women" called on stage by *Blachman*.

5. A BODILY CRITIQUE?

Discussing the particular temporality of performance, the philosopher and performance theoretician Bojana Kunst (2015) conceptualizes its political potential emerging from its very materiality through which a situative re-ordering, "a micropolitical rearrangement" can take place. Thus, performance practice never addresses specific politics but itself can become a political act: "there is no concept of politics that would suit the practice of performance, and no performance which would give us a satisfactory answer with respect to its politics" (p. 1). Insisting on the singularity of performance practices, which she assumes to be the precondition for their political potential, she ascribes them the power to create micropolitical ruptures. As singular event, a performance forms a temporally and spatially bounded community of shared experience. And yet the perception of the experienced can vary greatly from audience member to audience member. A micropolitical rupture might emerge when something supposedly familiar is perceived in an unfamiliar way and this experience is disruptive. The question of how a disruption of prevailing forms of perception affects a larger context depends primarily on its potential to attract more people to the same cause.

As described above, we explored the idea of reenactment creating disruptions. In response to the performance, the Austrian dance critique Helmuth Ploebst stressed the political importance of reenacting a TV show like this, which he considered to be "essential in a hyper-oblivious time like ours" (2015, my translation). But at the same time, he asked "if the pure reenactment as a documentary performance within the frame of a contemporary theater festival would still be self-explanatory enough—or if explicitly articulated critique would be needed again" (Ploebst 2015). I am still asking myself what "explicitly articulated critique" could be within the frame of such a performance. Indeed, what would be the point of performing if the critique is explicitly articulated?

The performance theoretician Stefan Hölscher (2018) identifies the meaning and purpose of a reenactment not in the faithful reconstruction of the original but in "the breaking up of events" (p. 523, my translation). Following Michel Foucault, Hölscher proposes an idea of event that goes beyond its discursive reading, as something that exists within and through networks of power and knowledge but at the same time has the potential to escape them.

> Unlike reconstruction, which attempts to reconstruct events trapped in facts, reenactment, as presented here, aims at the boundary itself between the order of facts and the disorder of events, at the storm between the sensuous and the intelligible. (p. 531, my translation)

Reenactment, then, can bring to light that which cannot be captured through the practices of writing down and classifying: the unordered, the unclear, the sensual, the dirty, the unhinged. Hölscher develops the idea of an "aesthetic theatricality" (p. 523, my translation) and conceptualizes a surplus of the sensual as critical potential. From my perspective as a performing artist, I would like to pursue the question here of how such a form of non-discursive, bodily critique can be practiced. In light of my experience as a performer standing naked in front of an audience, I would like to ask: How can I renegotiate the way I want to be perceived? In my experience, the idea of reenactment has limits for establishing another bodily reality. If the affective economies in which the source material is embedded are very powerful and efficient, it is not easy to find gaps for subverting ways of sensory perception. Building upon the work of queer-feminist philosopher Lauren Berlant, in what follows I would like to suggest another way to counter prevailing forms of perception.

6. DANCING IN A SPACE OF BROKEN FORMS

Berlant uses the term "flat" or "flattened affect" for exploring the possibility of resisting dominant genres of sense and feeling. She conceptualizes affective structures "as beneath the surface of explicit life that is collective, saturating atmospheres of held but inexplicit knowledge" (2015, p. 194). This understanding refers, on the one hand, to the question of how these structures emerged historically and, on the other hand, to the emergence of growing social structures. Questioning the supposed connection between high intensity and importance, she disagrees with any "self-evidence of excess" (Berlant 2015, p. 195). Adapting the concept of interpassivity by the philosopher Slavoj Žižek (1998), she claims:

> In this remodeling of the concept, interpassivity is the condition of relationality as such; and affective activity communicates first as inexpressive form, presuming that we no longer know it when we feel it, and vice versa, whether or not it seems to provide a neutral or holding space for assessing situations of being-with. (Berlant 2015, p. 196)

Berlant advocates for underperformance as a mode of encounter that does not anticipate its perception and therefore invites an aesthetics of apprehension. These forms of (non-)expression, she finds in "performance modes that do not provide emotional clarity but, whatever else they do, dramatize the process of sociality by wedging open what shapes the encounter as such" (Berlant 2015). How to invite more of those minor forms of being together? Which practices do not presume the event in the space of an encounter? After writing this narrative inquiry in spring 2021, I feel the desire to explore practically how to create that very style of underperformance: How to escape "that modality of performance that attaches feeling stated to their gestural inflation in bodily performance" (Berlant 2015, p. 191)? Inspired by Berlant's demand for "living in a space of broken forms" (2016a), I would like to explore dancing in a space of broken forms, creating bodily realities that might allow us to sense each other differently. How could one inhabit a space of broken forms? Being there, I understand as the refusal to express certain feelings and values excessively and comprehensively, so that their dominant forms collapse like empty shells. Therefore, in my bodily research I would look not for physical forms of expression but for the underlying physical states and atmospheres and affects related to such states. As a temporary microcosm, performance is a valuable research space to explore the preconditions for being together as a sensing collective. Thus, the basis for exploring underperformance would be considering performance primarily as a social situation. For this is where I see the political potential of performance: Speculating about resistant forms of being together and hereby creating micropolitical ruptures, through which we might catch a glimpse of possible futures.

Endnote

(1) I would like to note here that this text only reflects my perspective, since I wrote it without Iva Sveshtarova. The "we" I use here is in no way meant to render invisible the differences that are always part of a collective authorship, rather they are not the focus of this contribution. Therefore, I have chosen to use "we" to refer either to shared decisions within our collective authorship or to the temporally and situationally limited community as female performers on stage.

References

Ahmed, S. (2004). Affective economies. *Social Text*, 22(2), 117–139.
Ahmed, S. (2014). *The Cultural Politics of Emotion* (2nd ed.). Edinburgh, UK: Edinburgh University Press.
Berlant, L. (2015). Structures of Unfeeling: *Mysterious Skin*. *International Journal of Politics, Culture, and Society*, 28, 191–213.
Berlant, L. (2016a, November 28). *Lauren Berlant Interview / IPAK Centar*, [Video file]. Retrieved from https://www.youtube.com/watch?v=Ih4rkMSjmjs&ab_channel =IPAKCentar
Berlant, L. (2016b). The commons: Infrastrucure for troubling times. *Society & Space*, 34(3), 393–419.
Bochner, A. & Ellis, C. (2016). *Evocative autoethnography: Writing lives and telling stories*. London, UK: Routledge.
Conquergood, D. (2006). Rethinking ethnography: Towards a critical cultural politics. In D. Soyini Madison & J. Hamera (Eds.), *The Sage handbook of performance studies* (pp. 351–366). London, UK: Sage Publications, Inc. (Original work published in 1991)

Denzin, N. K. (1997). *Interpretive ethnography: Ethnographic practices for the 21st century.* London, UK: Sage Publications, Inc.

Denzin, N. K. (2003). *Performance ethnography: Critical pedagogy and the politics of culture.* London, UK: Sage Publications, Inc.

Denzin, N. K. (2006). The politics and ethics of performance ethnography: Toward a pedagogy of hope. In D. Soyini Madison & J. Hamera (Eds.), *The Sage handbook of performance studies* (pp. 325–337). London, UK: Sage Publications, Inc.

Ellingson, L. (2009). *Engaging crystallization in qualitative research: An introduction.* London, UK: Sage Publications, Inc.

Ellis, C. (2004). *The ethnographic I: A methodological novel about autoethnography.* Lanham, MD: Altamira Press.

Ellis, C., Adams, T. E., & Bochner, A. P. (2011). Autoethnography: An Overview. In *Forum: Qualitative Social Research*, 12(1), Art. 10. https://doi.org/10.17169/fqs-12.1.1589

Grusin, R. (2010). *Premediation: Affect and Mediality after 9/11.* London, UK: Palgrave Macmillan.

Guattari, F., & Rolnik, S. (2007). *Molecular Revolution in Brazil.* Semiotext(e).41

Hölscher, S. (2018). Reenactment ist keine Rekonstruktion, sondern das Aufbrechen von Ereignissen. In O. Ebert, E. Holling, N. Müller-Schöll, P. Schulte, B. Siebert & G. Siegmund (Eds.), *Theater als Kritik: Theorie, Geschichte und Praktiken der Ent-Unterwerfung* (pp. 523–531), Bielefeld, Germany: Transcript.

Palmer, G. (2003). *Discipline and Liberty. Television and governance.* Manchester, UK: Manchester University Press.

Palmer, G. (2008). Introduction – The habit of scrutiny. In G. Palmer (Ed.), *Exposing lifestyle television: The big reveal* (pp. 1–24). Farnham, UK: Ashgate.

Kunst, B. (2015a). *Artist at work. Proximity of art and capitalism.* Winchester, UK: John Hunt Publishing.

Kunst, B. (2015b). The Trouble with temporality: Micropolitics of performance. *Stedelijk Studies 3.* Retrieved from https://stedelijkstudies.com/journal/the-troubles-with-temporality/

Ploebst, H. (2014, November 7). Supernettes Sonnenbankerltanzen: Nacktes und Intimes zum Auftakt des Freischwimmer-Festivals im Brut-Theater. *Der Standard.* Retrieved from http://derstandard.at/2000007869188/Supernettes-Sonnenbankerltanzen

Reckwitz, A. (2015). Ästhetik und Gesellschaft – ein analytischer Bezugsrahmen. In A. Reckwitz, S. Prinz S. & H. Schäfer (Eds.), *Ästhetik und Gesellschaft. Grundlagentexte aus Soziologie und Kulturwissenschaften* (pp. 13–52). Berlin, Germany: Suhrkamp.

Reckwitz, A. (2016). How the senses organise the social. In *Praxeological political analysis* (pp. 68–78). London, UK: Routledge.

Reckwitz, A. (2017). Practices and their affects. In A. Hui, T. Schatzki, & E. Shove (Eds.), *The Nexus of Practices. Connections, Constellations, Practitioners* (pp. 114–125). London, UK: Routledge.

Richardson, L. (1994). Writing: A method of inquiry. In N.K. Denzin & Y.S. Lincoln (Eds.) *Handbook of qualitative research* (pp. 516–529). London, UK: Sage Publications, Inc.

Richardson, L. (1997). *Fields of play: Constructing an academic life*. New Brunswick, NJ: Rutgers University Press.

Richardson, L. (2000). Evaluating ethnography. *Qualitative Inquiry*, 6 (2), 253–255.

Spry, T. (2001). Performing autoethnography: An embodied methodological praxis. Qualitative Inquiry, 7(6), 706–732.

Spry, T. (2017). Autoethnography and the Other: Performative Embodiment and a Bid of Utopia. In: N.K. Denzin & Y. S. Lincoln (Eds.), *Handbook for Qualitative Research*, (5th ed.) (pp. 1090–1129). London, UK: Sage Publications, Inc.

Williams, R. (1978). Structures of Feeling. In D. Sharma & F. Tygstrup (Eds.), *Structures of feeling: Affectivity and the study of culture* (pp. 20–25). Berlin, Germany: De Gruyer.

Žižek, S. (1998). *The Interpassive Subject*, http://timothyquigley.net/vcs/interpassive.pdf

Sensing Collectives as Sensing Selves
Two Artistic Interventions and Two Theories of the Self

Jacob Watson, Vanessa Farfán, Markus Binner

> All in all, the creative act is not performed by the artist alone; the spectator brings the work in contact with the external world by deciphering and interpreting its inner qualification and thus adds his contribution to the creative act.
> —Marcel Duchamp, 1957 (as cited in Klanten et al. 2011)

1. WHAT HAPPENED - TO WHOM?

My contribution[1] to the Sensing Collectives volume first and foremost documents two artistic interventions that pertain to the topic at hand and, secondly, to offer a simplified 'philosophical' inquiry into a central feature of all the work done in this book, but not always addressed directly. That feature is the *self* and more importantly the idea of a collective self, collective will, or the gathering together of multiples of willpower, which translates into 'political will.' Such a collective self would be that which an individual understands or projects herself to be a part of, one could almost say the group identity. Now, in a book that espouses a praxeological approach to studying aesthetics and politics, to want to look at—or rather look for—the self that does the practicing seems to be at odds with the premises stated in the introduction. I contend that the notion of a self, or lack thereof, is where one might best plumb the depths of the practice at hand, for that is where sensing and willing happens.

---

1   Vanessa Farfán and Markus Binner are listed as co-authors of this chapter as it is their artworks that I treat and thus they are authors of the experience I (Jacob Watson) describe as the writer of this chapter.

I am a translator who studied philosophy, and do not consider myself an academic in the traditional sense; nevertheless, my identity has been shaped by my experiences in this field of research and editing this book. Thus, my method in this chapter shall be to give a personal account of the two artistic interventions from our two-day Sensing Collectives workshop in November of 2018 by artists Vanessa Farfán for her "Collateral Aesthetics" and Markus Binner for his "Bitter Mass Cooking" experiment. In this account, many actors come into play, there are people and things, sensory impressions and complex affectations.[2] What I will present here is how the entire situation *in*fluenced me, flowed into my very being to mess with my *identity* and my *will* somehow, i.e. I will describe my experience of 'sensing' the situation. Why is this important to our Sensing Collectives project? I feel that the self is a collection of sense inputs, sensory experience, and affects, perhaps more primarily so than even conscious reflection. The combination of those inputs and affects gives the self a certain shape, and that shape can determine our conscious awareness of ourselves. If I have a bad night's sleep, it certainly affects my sense of self in the morning (if that thing called "self" here is even there, as we will get to). That shape can be then fit a class of things that other individuals see themselves as belonging to—or that others deem them to belong to, be they amateur enthusiasts of some activity or a political movement. Just as with a bad night's sleep, a few delicious meals and extraordinary eating experiences may help one who had merely been a consumer to identify with slow-food enthusiasts, for example. More radically, being assaulted during a protest may push a peaceful participant into an extreme camp.

But what is it that gets affected? What experiences the sense, does it do the *sensing*? The very fact of the sensual nature of the self is paramount to that collective belonging. This is where social science of the senses takes a view of sensing that is active, done by someone or someones, who then together become a group of sensers and willers. The degree to which sensing is active or passive here is indeed, however, an aspect that must be explored philosophically, as I do in my analysis below. As with the chicken and the egg, the philosopher always wants to know which came first. Since the self is an order of sorts, to my mind, of sensory experience and bodily affections driven by phenomena (for our context of a mostly social interaction origin), it is important to give some theoretical foundation to the idea of the self as a sensory being.

In my analysis of the two artistic interventions, I will work with two theories of identity, those of the Enlightenment philosophers David Hume (1739, 1748) and Maine de Biran (1802 and posthumously 1834, 1859), that could be analogous to what—I think—goes on in a sensing collective. In short, Hume's focus is on sensory

---

2   These are all topics that are handled in much greater detail elsewhere in this book. Since these topics are not my focus but constantly cloud the background of what I've written here, I have not cross-referenced in order to clear the fog for my own thoughts.

experience and the lack of an experience of self, arriving at identity as purely a bundle of one's sensual impressions and simple cognitive ideas; meanwhile, Biran perceives the effort in willing as the primary fact of his existence. While Hume perceives no sense of willpower, ergo no self to will, Biran's self is a trifecta of will, bodily resistance, and the effort that connects them. Whether shell or feather is primary here, I sadly cannot answer, but my exploration of the two discussants in exploration of where and what is will and power, and hence self, at least gives us a framework to think about the question of what a sensing collective is. It is also highly interesting to me that these two modern philosophers took more or less a praxeological view to interrogate the self. Arriving at wholly different theories, they nevertheless explored effects above and beyond all other considerations. This also gives me a lens for looking back at what brought me to co-edit a book on the subject:

What happened at our Sensing Collectives workshop—two artistic interventions described below—will be the object of my self-reflective study on how sensory experiences turned our individual selves, i.e. rather cerebral workshop attendees, into a sensing collective. The two artistic interventions helped the workshop participants to coalesce into a group brought together through shared sensory and affective experiences which arouse a sort of will to delve in further.

This is also a crucial political moment in that the self feels embedded in some form of collective subjectivity and volition, ready to collaborate, to follow a joint agenda, to act in concert. This circles back of course to the self and—through further processes of identity formation—into group adherence, i.e. belonging to a sensing collective based on common sensual experience.

2. FIRST ARTISTIC INTERVENTION: COLLATERAL AESTHETICS

Now, I will turn to the first case of an artistic intervention by Vanessa Farfán, which she entitled "Collateral Aesthetics." This name certainly intrigued us, organizers, when she applied to the workshop. The idea that she had stumbled into a problematic and political 'space' while creating artworks on the streets of Beijing seemed to be right up our alley. Farfán describes her experience as follows, accidently arriving at a clash between how people gather and the political consequences:

If I could speak Chinese, maybe my experience of the city would have been less experimental and I could have found out more about how the physical closeness affected social dynamics. However, my lack of knowledge of Chinese language led me in an apparently purely aesthetic direction: to focus on the aspect of the Chinese characters, especially on the ones embossed on drain covers in the city streets. Sometimes flanked with stars, those relief characters in which one could probably read something like, "Beijing City Drainage" fascinated me. I would have liked to take them with me to Berlin but stealing strainer covers would surely be highly punishable. Thinking on ways to "take" these symbols and realizing that I only had a notebook with me, I decided to "take them out" by embossed them on paper. I spend many days looking for all different drain covers in the city. As soon I found a new one, I would kneel on the street and placing a sheet of cotton paper on the metal cover, I would begin to emboss the symbols. This operation could take several minutes. I repeat this action in different zones of the city including the Embassy's Area of the city. This area, is in an exclusive neighborhood where the streets are usually empty of pedestrians but full of luxury cars. Once, while looking for new drain cover in front of the Swedish Embassy, the gate guard of the embassy run out to me. He spoke to me in Chinese, I guess he was trying to figure out what I was doing. Fortunately, I had with me a badge that I got at the residence with the word, "Artist" wrote in Chinese. I showed it to him together with the series of prints I had made earlier. For sure he understood what was about, since without straying too far from his work station, he helped me enthusiastically, to find other new sewers.

I continued my drain cover search in more crowded areas. There, it was common that groups of people would gather around me to watch what I was doing. As soon as the police arrived, the people moved away. I didn't understand what the problem was until I performed this near to Tiananmen Square. As usual a few minutes after I started, a bunch of people gather around me, some even started recording with their phones. The group of people around me grew up. Some seconds later three policemen came and tried to dissolve the group. First in Chines and after with signals they try to say that I should stop doing my embossings. Despite this, I moved out to repeat the action on another place, the result was the same: as soon as a small group of people gathered around me, the police came to break up to the group of people. Sometimes friendly, sometimes aggressively they try to stop me from continuing embossing the drain covers. Some days later, through a friend I have found out what the problem was: After the Tiananmen Square Protest of 1989 and the so-called, "June Fourth Incident," where a thousand of demonstrators were injured, and hundreds were killed, the assembly regulations in public spaces in Beijing change drastically. In 2014, gatherings of more than three people in public spaces were forbidden.

How can the grouping of more than three people in an overcrowded city like Beijing, where masses are bumping into each other all the time, be forbidden by the state? Why are subway queues not dissolved as a political gathering? There's a common purpose and a gathering of definitely more than three! What Vanessa Farfán accidentally found out with her artistic experiment—her collateral insight—is that a gathering becomes political when more than three people's attention is drawn to a common focus. This makes them a sensing collective. And only then they become political in their gathering. And that is something the Chinese state seems to fear. But is the political a collateral of the aesthetic? Or are these aesthetic restrictions a collateral of political considerations?

These last two are questions that pertain directly to our workshop, and the way Farfán proposed to convey this experience of unavoidable proximity to one another for our workshop was to go beyond talking and showing pictures in a typical presentation. She wanted the participants to partake, to feel something with their bodies—knowledge transfer via corporeal affect. What follows is my perspective on how she did this:

Before the intervention, we had already put out the seating in careful rows, as a typical frontal presentation calls for. But, Farfán came with masking tape. Her idea was to tape out square meters of space to stand in, so that everyone could feel what it is like to be somewhere with at least one person per meter, like in urban China.

My personal experience of her experiment was quite involved. As an organizer, and the non-university-affiliated member, i.e. with less paperwork to deal with, I had taken up the task of setting up the workshop space. It was the large open room of the TU's Hybrid Lab, which offered lots of freedom. The choice of where to place the 'stage' and the 'audience' was completely arbitrary. We had to come up with a conference design in the most basic sense, and at first we were fairly basic in our conception. Vanessa—now on first name terms—and I had to move all the chairs, draw a grid on the ground large enough for at least a fair number of participants to partake in the affect knowledge on offer. What would it feel like to stand so close to a bunch of strangers? Pre-pandemic, the thought gave me[3] chills; now, I involuntarily start to sweat at the notion; but at the time of the conference we were intrigued. Would this intervention indeed give us the feeling of a Beijing resident?

My answer is yes and no. Most clearly, we did not experience the threat of 'becoming political' in this way that would be a problem in China. There were no police marching into our conference to intervene in her intervention. And there is no way that simply standing too close to another person give a person a precise understanding of the multilayered sensorial, spatial, cultural norms of such a different world—as Farfán herself seems to acknowledge in recounting what it was like to be a 'foreign body' in the densely packed Hutongs of Beijing:

Nowadays, one can find different Hutongs areas: the ones located near of the touristic hotspots and temples, with wide streets and big residential spaces even with a private swimming pool inside, and the Hutongs with extremely narrow streets and modesty services, usually far from the center of the city. It is in these last ones where I found up the direct relation between poverty and physical proximity: families of 5 members living in 6 square meter spaces. With communal bathrooms there, the collective activities, such as cooking and eating, were carried out on

---

3   I coming from the very rural American state of Idaho with approximately 19 persons for every 2.5 km^2 i.e. each Idahoan has 1315789m^2 to themselves. Farfán also made the point that her Mexican cultural background sensitized her to proximity, especially physical touch, in a way that made her experience of Chinese ways of being together all the more alienating.

the streets of those neighborhoods. In my conception of a 'place to eat' I couldn't avoid the uncomfortable sensation of invasion by been walking through streets with people sitting on the floor eating off their plates placed directly on the floor too. Smells, noises, and such scenes made very difficult to establish a clear division between the private and the public space in those neighborhoods.

However, something definitely happened to us, to our bodies and to the conference from the moment Farfán bayed us stand up after her slide presentation. To explain, let me return to the rows of chairs. Chairs, especially the lightweight, stackable kind used for conferences, offer very clear affordances: sitting, not even slouching too much, and I wouldn't dare stand on them. They interlock to tighten and stabilize rows, forcing attentions forward. From in front of them, I found out as a moderator, they can seem threatening or cruel—especially with the first two rows empty—and have a mocking tendency to rattle and clack, as the audience shift from time to time (our of boredom one imagines). But we were asked to remove those chairs, to push them to the side, to liberate the space and to occupy it. Everyone got up and began wrangling with the interlocking links. The metal legs clanged and clattered as they got moved to the periphery, revealing a masking-tape grid of 20 one-meter squares on the floor.

Figure 1: Accidental dissidents: the feeling of one person per square meter.

Source: Markus Binner

The audience retook the center space and our bodies were close, very close as we balanced in our squares. I took the center square so as to encourage participants. There I began to sweat and instantly regret my choice. Surely, I feared, if the civilizing body-care products under my arms didn't hold, the olfactory affects invoked in others would destroy any credibility I'd gained by stepping into that middle square.

But all went well, and I began to exchange nervous glances and coy smiles with the others. Some giggled, some swayed to regain a feeling of personal bubble, the rest stood outside the grid, encircling us and taking mental notes.

We milled around in too-close-for-comfort-ness only a minute or so, but a spell had been broken. We didn't learn much of anything—I'd say—regarding it *is like* to be dweller of the most populace nation on Earth. What we experienced was much more the everyday situation of being on a crowded street, but that combined with the thought of unavoidable closeness and political punishment did give me pause. A knowledge transfer of sorts did take place, one that can only be expressed in conditional terms: What *would it be like* to be arrested for gathering just because one is crammed into a group of random onlookers? The injustice of such a situation was now more palpable for me. The complex idea of what Farfán had told us about the Chinese control of public space plus that brief moment of affect-filled artificial proximity somehow combined within my being. Vague disapproval turned into a very clear discomfort with such an idea. I identified myself all the more with my prior appreciation for freedom of movement and felt indignation against a regime that could punish people by such ambiguous means. I venture to guess that I am not alone—that others present felt the same.

And, for the rest of the conference, we as individual presentation-listeners did encounter each other quite differently. Whether or not the others also experienced the sort of epiphany Farfán was aiming for, again, I can only guess. But our identities as strangers to one another did begin to fade, from within and without. The chairs also became different. Suddenly, they were a place of refuge. We pulled them haphazardly into a willy-nilly seating arrangement. When I took my place—up front but now sort of out halfway into a crescent of onlookers—to thank Vanessa and introduce the next speaker, there was no glaringly empty first row anymore.

The workshop went on, with mostly frontal participations—and all the technical glitches that belong to projectors, USB keys and the various operating systems people must subscribe to, but all these issues that caused delays seemed less dramatic. Know-how was shared by those willing to jump up from that mess of seats to help, or hold the mic while I fiddled with this or that cable. It seemed that people had woken up somehow. And during the talks, it seemed that people were leaning in now—until lunchtime.

This idea and aim, for me, echoes how Hume might conceive of identity wrapped up in a bundle of sensory experiences and their secondary affects. But for Farfán an important lesson was to illustrate that in China seemingly random bodily proximity could itself be used against the whole population. Sure, the focus off the crowd's attention is at play. That attention is what coalesces the sensing collective, the affects amongst the members is what 'holds it together,' makes it one potentially dangerous thing. And the chilling aspect is that that very aesthetic experience could be misinterpreted by the authorities, who may designate groupings of people as dissenters simply by the inescapable fact that there's not enough room to keep one's distance!

3. SECOND ARTISTIC INTERVENTION: BITTER MASS COOKING

Figure 2: Bitter Mass Cooking.

Source: Markus Binner

Our lunch break was designed as an artistic experiment in its own right. "A group cooking session with the widely disliked taste," is how Markus Binner, artist-chef, describes his piece entitled "Bitter Mass Cooking." The participatory artwork is a complex 'game' that unfolded from a fairly simple set of 'rules' or 'suggestions.' Color-coded cards had been distributed during sign-in at the beginning of the day. These cards randomly assigned workshop-goers to a task in collectively cooking our lunch. The assignments were a division of labor of sorts that broke the tasks into either making one of three courses or setting up and serving the food or disrupting the rest—a point I will go into at length.

Bitter as the taste of resistance, collectively rejected, breed out by the food industry, needed by the body builds the basis of this work. In a collaborative cooking process we'll have time for the taste and the term.

The ingredients for the food served had in common some degree of bitterness, from radicchio to the "Chinese bitter melon"—a cucumber variety of which one bite will cause lips to pucker upon any subsequent sighting. I assume that it was quite a task of refinement to create edible dishes from these ingredients, but alas I cannot report on this. As I walked through the door that morning, I was handed a gray (the dullest color) card with "Conductor" written on it. Thus continued my identity as an organizer, and I was so busy 'conducting' I only had a chance to pop a piece of above-mentioned melon into my mouth and suffer the consequences. The consequences of being a conductor mostly meant dealing with the final group: the guerillas. This proved to be bitter indeed!

Once again, I was confronted with the conference space. How to rearrange the chairs (again!) and make room for all to sit and eat? What shape should the tables take? Restaurant-style four-tops? Banquet hall seating? What is the most conducive to a convivial atmosphere in which all could make the most of this shared experience?

None of these questions mattered. The guerillas made sure of that. After causing several conflicts and false starts amongst the cooks with various seasoning skirmishes, they turned their disruptive energy towards table rearrangement. According to the 'rules,' the guerilla-group was meant to

... develop ideas, suggestions, attempts to influence and change work processes and their results. They care, for maybe unliked transportation of ingredients, between groups, they create shortage and crises. They improve dishes, they develop innovations.

They innovated towering stacks of chairs on tables. They innovated napkins laid out to replace the table cloth, upon which an attempt was made fold it into a massive swan, like a fancy table decoration. Decorations were made of silverware; plates were hidden; in short, chaos. As an organizer, I had a special conductor's wand: my microphone. I used it as a bullhorn to put down the rebellion and eventually shamed the guerillas into innovating the table settings back into something recognizable—to give up the fight. (I wonder if they let themselves be influenced by being called "guerrillas" in the first place.) I was keenly aware I had to get us eating within the allotted timeslot, and when you want to make the 'trains run on time' there's but one place to go: I remember Anna Leander teasing me and finally coming to my aid when she saw how her techniques were exasperating me, especially when she remarked on my penchant for authority ("You like that microphone, don't you."), that I never in a million years would have admitted to myself ... and still bitterly look back on. The guerrillas, of course, weren't actually cowed into obedience, but I did have to raise my voice to convince them to switch sides. It was a careful negotiation of competing wills, the effort of which is akin to the philosopher Maine de Biran's confrontation between the active will and inert body, which I describe in detail below.

The whole Bitter Mass Cooking experience was a bit pressure-cooker for me, but I later learned it was a general feeling. All the participants were asked some time later to look back and give their impressions. Because the whole point of the experiment was to draw a collective response, here are a few others' points of view:

Figure 3: above: keynote speaker Hennion and Vanessa Farfán cooking with other participants; lower right: me looking rather worried at the chaos unfolding; middle: Landau-Donnelly improvising a means dish out; left: engaged eaters and talkers.

Source: Markus Binner

There are tensions between what both the six groups in their appointed roles or the individuals bringing their own norms and routines might consider 'good cooking' leading to clashes and compromises. There is no general definition for what is seen as 'good' in the process of food preparation nor one singular 'good menu' itself. What the experiment has shown, is that cooking is an inherently social practice and often equals a form of caring for each other.
—Julie Sascia Mewes

The participants were given three boxes of mixed up ingredients and an incomplete collection of recipes, and they were supposed to get together, define tasks, negotiate ideas and solve micro problems in order to prepare a three-course meal for everyone. The participants, aka cooks, enjoyed this process, because they were looking forward to the joint meals. This common experience really helped to form a cohesive group, which was capable of negotiating the challenges of collective forms of living.
—Torsten Klafft

A production machine set in motion—an initial division and ordering by task. Emergent, cooperative collaborations; breakaways renegotiating an assigned place to take on roles more fitting … Efficiencies and expertise emerging within some clusters; initiative and spontaneous redirection. A hum of productive, collaborative, inclusive activity. Anticipation—desiring the bitter? Desiring the disruptive; the unexpected. Sounds of chopping; sizzling. Pungency—nose-wrinkling, but with delicate back-flavors. The format (the feast) promising pleasure; the pleasure of shared experimentation, of a venture into the daring, the confronting–even the repulsive. The food is unexpectedly good—in small quantities.
—Susan Stewart

and even a poem:

Bitter mass cooking
if you cook rice for 30 people, it can be coarse or mushy
you get lots of free advice on how to do it
many cooks making lots of rice
what is an expert in this crumbling crunchy world
eating our wor(l)ds
granularity of rice
granularity of thought
food cracks open spaces of thought (and rice)
listening to people talking about practice
practicing listening
or not

hearing nothing while listening
doing nothing while practicing
what is practice worth if we're surrounded by walls
—Friederike Landau-Donnelly

In the end, we all ate and ate well. We all enjoyed the experiment and the buzz of excitement stayed with us for the rest of the conference. The next days' lunch was a prototype for the experiments carried out by my co-editors, Jan and Nora. The lunch experiments came up over and over over the next day and especially during our closing feedback session. Combined with Vanessa's ice-breaking intervention, they bodily, affective knowledge transfer that had occurred for "Sensing Collectives" really had created a collective identity of sorts. The workshop ended with us huddling in an extended circle, some sitting on the floors and table—those poor chairs, totally disoriented—and discussing intensely what exactly we had been 'getting into together' the last days.

4. A PHILOSOPHICAL INTERPRETATION

Now, there are many philosophical theories of the self, but only a handful offer us the tools we need to arrive at a self that is based on sensory experience and aligned volition—my two criteria for defining sensing collectives. I find though, that there are some fine examples in the works of the renowned Scotsman David Hume and an obscure Frenchman Maine de Biran. I will attempt a very short summary of the way that these trains of thought intersect to offer us a self whom the other authors of this volume and probably most readers may just take for granted—a self that is a *sensing self*, a self that at its core is a *will*. The reason such a self is important to sensing collectives is that its politics (will) are intertwined with the other part of its being: aesthetics.

The idea for sensing collectives, for me, follows a long and winding train of thought that I will try to summarize here as clearly possible. My aim is to arrive at a rough definition of self that can also serve as the basis of ideas about the kinds of collective identity treated in this volume.

So, what is identity, anyway? This is a central question of philosophy. What is the self? Where does it reside? How is it formed? What does it constitute? These are, in a roundabout way and in far simpler terms, the questions approached by the authors in this work and elsewhere, across the disciplines of not just sociology and politics but also to a(n ever greater) degree design, art, activism, among others. The key question to who figuring out the making and breaking of social orders seems again and again to be how do the selves of all those who make up a collective get influenced into forming their groups or leaving them as abandon causes.

Philosophy as forever been preoccupied with locating the self and through the centuries has looked in different realms. In ancient Greece, the obvious choice was in the realm of ideas. This world, it was thought, is merely a transitory and illusory: Plato's cave. But even here the idea of sense data influencing and forming those chained before the fire, marveling at the shadows—connecting them in a collective of unenlightened mortal misery—was central.

This is what struck me about the Sensing Collectives project. At the beginning we talked about a map or sorts, a typography of sensing-related ideas, practices, and actions that would help define, shape or destroy those very selves that make up the collectives. A strong methodological bent to much of the research presented in this volume is a focus on the first-person ethnographic perspective. Many of the researchers here are retrieving their fine-grained data from within themselves (and I too). Where philosophy and especially its sister discipline, phenomenology, struggle with the senses once inside our bodies and minds—wrangling between impressions, sensations, affections, and on and on to come to grips with the homunculus or lack thereof—, Sensing Collectives pragmatically takes for given that self can be acted upon via the senses and perception can be shaped to modify at least the self's adherence to some group or another. Nonetheless, I feel that it is important to deliver some*thing* to define what a sensing collective might be.

There is paradox at the heart of a sensing self. The philosopher who points this out most clearly to my mind is David Hume (1711–1776). He, for non-philosophers, is a founding father of skepticism and, weirdly, at the same time, epistemology itself. He held that we could know only through the senses and that anything that would require a leap of faith to believe in, just couldn't be called knowledge. Senses provided perceptions and "impressions"—think of a mind as matter and sensory input is pressed in, leaving an impression. These impressions could be cobbled together to give us "ideas": complex ideas and simple ideas. The who or what is being impressed upon isn't really Hume's concern, just that he has no experience of that thing. Now, this goes against the pragmatist philosophy of perception that underlies most of the thinking about sensing and sensation in this book—that it is an active and recursive constitution of sensory experience in that inputs are attended to according to a subject's notion of their relevance. But suffice to say that, here, I'm merely holding up as a frame Hume's bundle theory of the self, constituted of sense impressions and the simple idea that we in this volume are calling "affects." I am looking for a way of thinking about sensing collectives that gives some sense of the self that collectively feels the affect and where, potentially, a will emerges. Above, in my recount of Farfán's intervention I claimed that the affect of standing so close to one another transferred some knowledge; this requires some unpacking:

Hume was writing at a time when knowledge was mostly thought to be revealed by God to individual souls, or at least to priests who could disseminate authoritative knowledge. But he rejected this. For him, direct experience was paramount. Hume famously even doubted causation was knowable, because you cannot experience it. That knowledge must be founded upon some sort of data is of course something we take for granted in scientific discourse today, but here's the catch: we also take causation for granted. You only have succession. Event A happens and something B follows, but whether A is the cause and B the effect, it's essentially impossible to know. Why? Because we don't see anything occurring or transferring from A to B that we could call a cause. Immanuel Kant (1724–1804) would later solve this conundrum, placing the idea of causation within human reason. We don't need to see the cause transfer to occur, because we understand time and succession. Our understanding is geared to do so, so says Kant. But all this is merely an aside to illustrate Hume's view.

Now to Hume's self. He also thought there was no *thing* that is the self. In accordance with sense impressions delivering the basis for all that there is, he looks but proclaims that

> [e]ven when my perceptions are remov'd for any time, as by sound sleep; so long am I insensible of myself, and may truly be said not to exist. And were all my perceptions remov'd by death, and cou'd I neither think, nor feel, nor see, nor love, nor hate after the dissolution of my body, I shou'd be entirely annihilated, nor do I conceive what is farther requisite to make me a perfect non-entity. [Someone] may, perhaps, perceive something simple and continu'd, which he calls himself; tho' I am certain there is no such principle in me... I may venture to affirm of the rest of mankind, that they are nothing but a bundle or collection of different perceptions, which succeed each other with an inconceivable rapidity, and are in a perpetual flux and movement. (Hume 1763)

Herewith, Hume founds his "bundle theory of identity"; it comes down to 'when sensing ceases, there is nothing,' no will, no perceivable self, nothing to speak of except some feeling of continuity based on successive sense impressions and the very fact that they are successive. The rest of Hume's argument is more or less semantic in nature, delving into what we might mean when we say "force" or "necessary connection"—that which would underlie a will(power) and a self, the perceiver of the necessarily connected succession of sense inputs. Kant, again, offered an alternative, an antithesis even, but, again, that's not the scope here. I merely propose that we could think of our sensing collectives through analogy as some sort of collective bundled self or bundled collective of bundles selves, bundled by the aesthetics of which they are intertwined. Again, Farfán's experiment helps me to apply this thought: A sensing collective coalesces around nothing more than a shared sensory and affective experience, which is surely also bundled together with the existent ideas we had about the Chinese situation, but which did not have the same quality as after the experiment.

The other vital aspect of such beings that willingly join or unwittingly are corralled into such collectives is the will itself. While Hume questions its existence, volition as a foundation of selfhood also has a long tradition. One minor character in the philosophical pantheon and in this topic specifically is a lesser known but highly influential French philosopher by the name of Maine de Biran (1766–1824). He lived and wrote after Hume and partially in response to him. His is also a response to the most famous of French philosophers, René Descartes (1596–1650), whose writings from a century and a half prior to the other three thinkers presented here pretty much got us into this mess. Hume was also responding, with skepticism, to Descartes's "I think therefore I am" argument, the so-called "*cogito*"—which exists in the face of a doubt about every physical fact, every sensory input, literally positing a tiny demon intent on giving false sense impressions to offer only lies upon lies, a dire situation countered ultimately by the famous phrase.

Descartes line of thinking split the physical body from the mental self, creating the very problematic Dualism. If all we perceive is physical and falsifiable and only that thing that thinks is the true reality, the world is of two non-put-together-able places—a thought which Maine de Biran just couldn't stomach. Biran's self is inextricable from his body. Biran begins with a self that is part will, not a thought but an urge or desire to move. That will only finds fulfillment in the other part: the body. And how is he aware of his self? Hume might ask, where's your sensory evidence?

Biran has two feelings that support his claim. When he wills his body to move, he feels his body's muscles needing a push. The movement isn't like jumping out of a chair for him, but rather like getting out of bed; it takes effort. The two sensations Biran pairs together are "effort" and its necessary flipside "resistance"—since effortlessness lies the lack of any resistance. Biran's self is therefore *a willed effort meeting a bodily resistance*.

Now, there is plenty to say about the larger conversation revolving around these figures and their bundle theory of the self and effort/resistance theory of the self and intricacies, contradictions, alternatives, etc. For one, Biran's conception brings us much closer to the pragmatic view of senses championed by the social sciences: that sensing is a willed act, an act of attention focusing. Derrida held Biran's treatment of touch to be the perfect example of how sensing works (Thorsteinsson, 2022). Tactile sensation is the product of voluntary, willed movement—reaching out to touch—but we must stay on track and therefore turn back to the analogy that I'm grasping at.

My intention with this contribution has been to arrive at some fundamental understanding of the object of study for sensing collectives. When I read our own subtitle "politics and aesthetics intertwined" I see a potential nexus where that intertwining takes place: a bundle of sorts. Where I'm going should be obvious. The sensing collective is a bundle of similar or common sensations and affections that drives some group or class of people together in a collective identity. But in a pragmatic and, further, in a Biranian sense, this is also an active, willed sort of sensing that is entangled with a willpower, either springing from the affectation or driving the sensation. That identity would be a form of collective self, that is nothing but the intermingling of these sensations/affections which, at once, is the very thing wherefrom the thoughts, desires, and politics arise, i.e. a collective will expressed in the effort of doing, of performing, of carrying out one of the many practices that make up political action and identity expression. The other part of the coalescing of a sensing collective, besides bundling sensual experience, would thus be the willpower and associated resistance of the other bodies in that group and the effort of bringing them together.

5. INTERTWINING THE INTERVENTIONS

Finally, I would like to quickly link up each of our workshop interventions with the two theories I've summed up. Vanessa Farfán's proximity experiment is, for me, an excellent illustration of Hume's bundle theory of self. The similar experience of claustrophobia and discomfort of standing so close to a bunch of strangers gave each of those strangers something to shape who they were from there on out. And even Farfán's initial premise—that random bodily proximity had formed groups spontaneously, who, in the eyes of a Chinese authority, now belonged together in some sort of act of dissent—points to the double meaning of sensing collectives: The authorities ascribe group identity based on perhaps a common confusion as to why some Mexican woman is embossing the manhole covers. A collective self takes form or is given form whether judged from within or without. Regarding the self, Hume claimed there was 'no there there'—but only these constellations of sensory inputs or the combination thereof that correspond with the "simple ideas," or affects. In the social realm of multiple persons, this indeed has explanatory power, even we are talking about a very fluid or temporary collective, and 99% of the time it probably will dissipate.

And what is the glue that could hold it together? Here I reach back to Markus Binner's idea that the taste of bitter is the taste of resistance and link it up with Maine de Biran's notion of self as a trifecta of will, a resistant body and the effort to move it. In the lunch experiment, the various inputs and ideas of how to accomplish the task at hand was met with resistance on all sides—from within the collectives assigned to cook, from the conductors hurrying things along and from the guerillas monkeying things up. My guess, judging from the photos,[4] is that cooking together also broke down hierarchies to a degree—our keynote speaker, Antoine Hennion is pictured chopping veggies with master's students, for example. It was the interaction

---

[4] For photos and more on our workshop: www.sensing-collectives.org/workshop-gallery/

of the will to eat and the effort to get all those bodies to work together that created a collective and coherent self from multiple moving parts.

There is obviously a logical issue I face with combining Hume's bundle theory with Biran's trio of identity, and that is: Where Hume finds no evidence of a separate substance beyond the impressions and affects that moves or wills the body, Biran simply asserted there was (Schmaus, 2022). Hume's argument is that we are simply habituated to see a change of state and assume a will is responsible. Biran claims to *feel* the will. But philosophical paradox is not the focus of this volume, and thus I will take a pragmatic view and say that I merely see these theories as analogies to describe the phenomenon of sensing collectives. Hume and Biran's ideas are useful (to me) as a heuristic to conceive of how a collective will might coalesce around a certain issue through aesthetic means or, conversely, how a hegemonic regime might be face resistance or disruption through aesthetic interventions. In fact, it serves as a sort of criteria list for identification of a sensing collective: What is being sensed and how says something specific about the group doing the sensing. How the sensing individuals then act or think in concert and react to each other is an expression of the collective will. This enters the research-rich territory of contemporary philosophy of mind debates on extended mind (Clark and Chalmer 2010) or interesting theories on the relational theory of self (Gallagher 2008, Kyselo 2014), i.e. that we are not just *ourselves* but always definable in relation to our surroundings and others.

As far as I can remember, I've heard the phrase "likeminded individuals" used to signify political constituencies. If we are to believe Hume and others, there may be no 'mind' at all to account for an individual or even a will, but only a common sensing apparatus. Therefore, it may be more helpful to talk about 'like-sensing' collective, in which we can identify behavior that mimics a will based on common sensory and affective input. A sensing collective could thus be defined as a bundle of like-sensing bodies whose collective will is expressed in actions and behaviors that are born of the very act of coalescing around *the aesthetic*, i.e. that which is aesthetic, and being such a thing—a sensing collective—is itself political.

References

Binner. M. (2018) *Website for Markus Binner.* www.markusbinner.de. Last accessed: January 2022.

Clark A., Chalmers D.J. (2010). Chapter 2: The extended mind. In *The Extended Mind*. Richard Menary (Ed.) pp. 27–42. Cambridge, MA: MIT Press.; and available on line as: Andy Clark, David J Chalmers. "The extended mind." Cogprints. Last accessed: January 2022.

Descartes, R (1637). *Discourse on Method.* & (1641) *Meditations on First Philosophy.* Translated by Cress. D. A. (1998) 4th ed. Cambridge, MA: Hackett Publishing Company, Inc.

Farfán, V. (2018). *Website for Vanessa Farfán*. www.vanessafarfan.de. Last accessed: January 2022.

Gallagher (2008). Understanding others: Embodied social cognition. In *Handbook of Cognitive Science: An Embodied Approach*. Calvo, P., & Gomilla, A. (Eds.) pp. 429–452. Cambridge, MA: Elsevier Academic Press.

Hume, D. (1739). *A Treatise of Human Nature, Book I, Part IV, Of Personal Identity*. Available at: http://oll.libertyfund.org/titles/hume-a-treatise-of-human-nature. Last accessed: January 2022.

Hume. D. (1748). *An Enquiry Concerning Human Understanding*. The Project Gutenberg EBook. Available at: https://www.gutenberg.org/files/9662/9662-h/9662-h.htm . Last accessed: January 2022.

Kant, I. (1781). Zweite Analogie Grundsatz der Zeitfolge nach dem Gesetz der Kausalität. *Kritik der reinen Vernunft*. II. Buch II. Hauptstück Transzendentale Analytik. A 192.

Klanten, R., Hubner, M., Bieber, A., Alonzo, P., & Jansen, G. (2011). *Art & Agenda: Political Art and Activism*. Die Gestalten Verlag.

Kyselo, M. (2013), From Body to Self – Towards a Socially Enacted Autonomy, With Implications for Locked-in Syndrome and Schizophrenia. Osnabrück: University of Osnabrück.

Kyselo, M. (2014), The body social: an enactive approach to the self. Frontiers in Psychology. 12 September 2014. doi: 10.3389/fpsyg.2014.00986

Maine de Biran, P. (1802). Influence de l'habitude sur la faculté de penser. On the Bibliothèque National de France Gallica web archive, Paris: Henrichs.

Maine de Biran, P. (1834). *Nouvelles considérations sur les rapports du physique et du moral de L'Homme*. Posthumously published by Cousin, V. (Ed.), Paris: Ladrange.

Maine de Biran, P. (1859). *Œuvres de Maine de Biran*. Naville. E. (Ed.) Paris: Dezobry, E. Magdeleine.

Schmaus, W. (2022). Did Maine de Biran Refute Hume? In *Genesis and Posterities of Maine de Biran's Physio-spiritualism from 1800 to the 20th Century*. Milz M. (Ed.) Leiden, NL: Brill.

Sensing Collectives (2018). *Website for Sensing Collectives*. www.sensing-collectives.org. Last accessed: January 2022.

Thorsteinsson, B. (2022). Sensing Resistance? On Derrida's Reading of Maine de Biran. In *Genesis and Posterities of Maine de Biran's Physio-spiritualism from 1800 to the 20th Century*. Milz M. (Ed.) Leiden, NL: Brill.

Authors in Order of Chapters

Sophia Prinz (Prof. Dr.) is a professor of Design Theory and History at the Züricher Hochschule der Künste (ZHdK). She is currently working on a book project about the "migration of form" (together with Roger M. Buergel) and a research project exploring the relationship between social practices and design in global modernity.

Jonathan Luke Austin is an assistant professor of International Relations at the University of Copenhagen. His work explores the intersections of political violence, materiality, aesthetics, and technological design, with a focus on their global implications. His work can be explored at www.jonathanlukeaustin.com.

Anna Leander is a professor of International Relations at the Geneva Graduate Institute and at the Pontifical Catholic University, Rio de Janeiro.

Nona Schulte-Römer is a social scientist with an interest in public engagements with sociotechnical transitions, environmental exposure, and science communication. Her empirical focus is on the LED transition, light pollution, sustainable chemistry, 5G and the resurfacing of invisible infrastructures. After working at the Helmholtz Centers in Leipzig (UFZ) and Potsdam (GFZ), she has recently joined the ERC project "Wavematters" at the urban anthropology department of Humboldt Universität Berlin.

Susan Stewart is an adjunct research fellow with the Design Innovation Research Centre in the Design School, at the University of Technology Sydney. Susan has taught and researched across diverse design disciplines, from architecture to product and service design. Her focus is on the participation of designed things in shaping human actions, orientations, dispositions, and worlds. In particular, she seeks to understand the role of design in either consolidating or shifting practices.

Miguel Paredes Maldonado is a lecturer in Architectural Design at the University of Edinburgh, a chartered architect, and a partner in design research studio Cuartoymitad Architecture & Landscape (www.cuartoymitad.es). Interweaving writing with speculative design, his work investigates the intersections of digital computation, the urban public commons, and contemporary architectural discourse. His research has been published and exhibited internationally, most notably at the 11th and 16th editions of the Venice Architecture Biennale.

Hanna Husberg is a visual artist and researcher, who recently completed her PhD-in-practice project "Troubled Atmosphere – On Noticing Air" (Akademie der Bildenden Künste, Vienna), which through the lens of four different art projects looks at layered, inconsistent, muddled, unruly, contaminated gatherings of air, inquiring how air has been conceptualized and perceived, and how the construction of aerial imaginaries enables specific ways of engaging with the world and excludes others. Jointly with Agata Marzecová she is developing the interdisciplinary research project *Towards Atmospheric Care*.

Agata Marzecová has a dual background in environmental science and photography & new media. Her interdisciplinary practice is situated at the intersection of research, art, and ecology. Currently, she is working on *Towards Atmospheric Care*, a collaborative research project with Hanna Husberg, which explores the porous boundaries between aesthetics, science, and politics of air and the atmosphere. This collaboration has been supported by the Kone Foundation (2020–22)

Antoine Hennion is a professor at the CSI, Mines-Paris. He has extensively published in the sociology of culture, medias, design, services, and users. Drawing on music—an art relying on a range of heterogeneous mediations (instruments, bodies, scores, stages, medias, recordings…)—he developed a theory of mediation crossing cultural sociology and STS, and participated at the CSI in the growth of ANT. He then developed a pragmatist approach to attachments, from taste and practices as music, wine, or sport, to issues about care, aging, and disability, and presently migrants, he participates in several research groups or collectives (Attachments, a seminar on fragility; Pragmata, on pragmatist studies; Le PEROU, a group on migrants; and Origens Media Lab, on neo-ecologies), in order to discuss new pragmatist forms of inquiries in social sciences.

Michael Guggenheim is a reader at the Department of Sociology, Goldsmiths. He has researched and published widely on visual methods and experiments, researcher on food, disasters, and architecture and the relationship of lay people and experts.

Aline Haulsen studied Sociology at the TU Berlin and was a student assistant at the Department of Political and Governance Sociology. She is currently studying Urban

Geography at the HU Berlin. Meanwhile, she is also exploring the power of sensory perceptions in artistic projects. Exploring and learning about the manifold aspects of our world in the small and everyday sense is her concern in her everyday life as well as in science.

Nora Rigamonti is a research associate in the project "Taste! Qualitative-sensoric citizen science on the practice and aesthetics of eating" at the chair of Sociology of Politics and Governance at Berlin University of Technology. In her PhD, she focused on different entanglements of political and aesthetic practices and related in(ter)ventive democratic practices at the interdisciplinary DFG Graduate School "Innovation Society Today," where she was a research associate from 2015 to 2018 and is now an associate member.

Max Söding, (MA) Sociology and Technology Studies, works on topics ranging from digitalization to tasting or the city. Sensing, tasting, and trying things out are also important parts of his everyday life.

Jan-Peter Voß (Prof. Dr.) heads the chair of Sociology of Politics and Governance at Berlin University of Technology, since 2012. He did his doctorate at the department of Science, Technology and Policy Studies of the University of Twente. His research is located at the intersection of sociology, political science, and science and technology studies (STS), focusing on the intertwining of epistemic, political, and aesthetic practices in late modern processes of innovation and governance.

Friederike Landau-Donnelly (Dr.) is currently an assistant professor for Cultural Geography at Radboud Universiteit in Nijmegen, the Netherlands. Her research interests are situated at the intersection between political and spatial theory, with a focus on artist-led activisms in urban public space. Friederike's dissertation *Agonistic Articulations in the 'Creative' City – On New Actors and Activism in Berlin's Cultural Politics* has been published with Routledge in 2019, and she recently co-edited the volume *[Un]Grounding – Post-Foundational Geographies* with transcript Verlag, 2021.

Sebastian Sommer (MA) is a theater scholar who studies the performativity of social action. The focus of his interdisciplinary research is protest events from far right and authoritarian movements, such as PEGIDA. In addition to this, he is co-moderator of the working-group "Right(-wing) Protest Mobilizations" at the "Institute for the Study of Protest and Social Movements" (ipb) in Berlin.

Mirjana Mitrović is a PhD candidate and lecturer at Berlin University of the Arts with a focus on the *flâneuse* and the digitalization of the urban space. She holds a BA in Cultural Science and an MA in Latin American Studies. Working between Berlin and

Mexico City, she combines artistic practices and academic research, mainly about the influence of new technologies, especially the internet and smartphones, the everyday life of women and feminist activism as well as geographical, corporal, and mental borders and the crossing of these. www.mirjana-mitrovic.de

Marcela Suárez is a professor in Political Science at the Institute of Latin American Studies at Freie Universität Berlin (FU). She holds a PhD in Political Science also from the FU. Her areas of specialization are sociopolitical dynamics of new technologies, governance, knowledge asymmetries, techno-feminisms, and digital culture. Her current research project is entitled "Feminist Politics and the Fight Against Violence in the Era of Digitalization" and is financed by the Berlin Equal Opportunities Program.

Rose Beermann studied Cultural Studies at the European University Viadrina in Frankfurt (Oder) and completed the MA program in Choreography and Performance at the Institute for Applied Theater Studies in Giessen. Since 2013 she has been working as a freelance choreographer, director, and dramaturg in Berlin. She also works as a research assistant for Prof. Dr. Bojana Kunst at the Institute for Applied Theater Studies.

Markus Binner is an artist uses mostly food and language as material for his mostly collaborative work. His methods are experimental, the forms diverse like lectures, parties, buffets, books, menus, exhibits. His work is widely shown in museums, galleries, art clubs, public space, libraries, universities, restaurants.

Vanessa Farfán is a Mexican-born German artist based in Berlin. Currently, she is PhD candidate at the Bauhaus University, Weimar. Her work has been presented in: Ars Electronica (2019), Orpheus Institute (2019), Museum FLUXUS+ (2018), Galerie Weisse Elefant (2019) and the Beijing Cultural Exhibition Center (2014). 2018 was a fellow artist of the Schering Stiftung. She is currently fellow artist of the Stiftung Brandenburger Tor. www.vanessafarfan.de

Jacob Watson is a freelance translator and editor in Berlin. He studied philosophy and languages before obtaining his *Diplôme avancé d'etudes françaises & traduction* at the Université Marc Bloch, Strasbourg (2002). His fields are philosophy and law, sociology and history, art and film, most notably as house translator for the law journal *Ancilla Luris* of Zürcher Hochschule für Angewandte Wissenschaften. Recent book translations are *Work – the Last 1000 Years* (2018) by Andrea Komlosy and *Eros, Lust and Sin* by Franz X Eder (forthcoming). www.translabor.de

Social Sciences

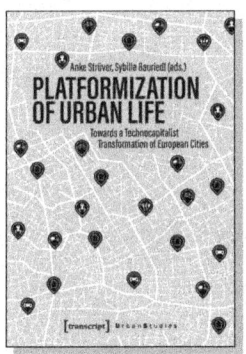

Anke Strüver, Sybille Bauriedl (eds.)
Platformization of Urban Life
Towards a Technocapitalist Transformation
of European Cities

September 2022, 304 p., pb.
29,50 € (DE), 978-3-8376-5964-1
E-Book: available as free open access publication
PDF: ISBN 978-3-8394-5964-5

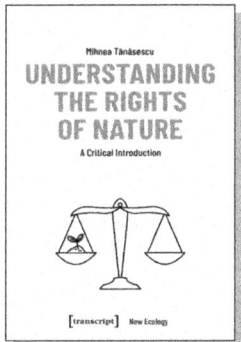

Mihnea Tanasescu
Understanding the Rights of Nature
A Critical Introduction

February 2022, 168 p., pb.
40,00 € (DE), 978-3-8376-5431-8
E-Book: available as free open access publication
PDF: ISBN 978-3-8394-5431-2

Oliver Krüger
**Virtual Immortality –
God, Evolution, and the Singularity
in Post- and Transhumanism**

2021, 356 p., pb., ill.
35,00 € (DE), 978-3-8376-5059-4
E-Book:
PDF: 34,99 € (DE), ISBN 978-3-8394-5059-8

**All print, e-book and open access versions of the titles in our list
are available in our online shop www.transcript-publishing.com**

Social Sciences

Dean Caivano, Sarah Naumes
The Sublime of the Political
Narrative and Autoethnography as Theory

2021, 162 p., hardcover
100,00 € (DE), 978-3-8376-4772-3
E-Book:
PDF: 99,99 € (DE), ISBN 978-3-8394-4772-7

Friederike Landau, Lucas Pohl, Nikolai Roskamm (eds.)
[Un]Grounding
Post-Foundational Geographies

2021, 348 p., pb., col. ill.
50,00 € (DE), 978-3-8376-5073-0
E-Book:
PDF: 49,99 € (DE), ISBN 978-3-8394-5073-4

Andreas de Bruin
Mindfulness and Meditation at University
10 Years of the Munich Model

2021, 216 p., pb.
25,00 € (DE), 978-3-8376-5696-1
E-Book: available as free open access publication
PDF: ISBN 978-3-8394-5696-5

All print, e-book and open access versions of the titles in our list are available in our online shop www.transcript-publishing.com